Apocalypse of the Alien God

DIVINATIONS: REREADING LATE ANCIENT RELIGION

SERIES EDITORS

Daniel Boyarin
Virginia Burrus
Derek Krueger

A complete list of books in the series is available from the publisher.

Apocalypse of the Alien God

PLATONISM AND THE EXILE
OF SETHIAN GNOSTICISM

Dylan M. Burns

PENN

UNIVERSITY OF PENNSYLVANIA PRESS   *Philadelphia*

THIS BOOK IS MADE POSSIBLE BY A COLLABORATIVE GRANT
FROM THE ANDREW W. MELLON FOUNDATION.

Published by
University of Pennsylvania Press
Philadelphia, Pennsylvania 19104-4112
www.upenn.edu/pennpress

Printed in the United States of America
on acid-free paper

10 9 8 7 6 5 4 3 2 1

Library of Congress Cataloging-in-Publication Data

Burns, Dylan M.
   Apocalypse of the alien god : Platonism and the exile
of Sethian gnosticism / Dylan M. Burns. — 1st ed.
      p. cm. — (Divinations : rereading late ancient
religion)
   Includes bibliographical references and index.
   ISBN 978-0-8122-4579-0 (hardcover : alk. paper)
   1. Apocalyptic literature—History and criticism.
2. Gnostic literature—History and criticism.
3. Gnosticism. 4. Neoplatonism. I. Title.
BL501.B87 2014
299'.932—dc23
                                 2013032143

Im Abstande erst erzeugt sich ja mein Leben.
—Gerschom Scholem, *Tägebücher* 2:245

CONTENTS

Following those given in the *SBL Handbook of Style* and *Oxford Classical Dictionary*. Sigla in quotations of ancient texts follow the Leiden Conventions, with the exception that "[. . .]" indicates a lacuna of unknown length, as well as longer stretches of multiple words or lines where the text is too fragmentary to render in any readable manner.

Acts Andr.	*Acts of Andrew*
Acts Just.	*Acts of Justin and Companions*
Ael. Arist.	Aelius Aristides
Or.	*Orationes*
Ael. Theon	Aelius Theon
Progymn.	Progymnasmata
Alc.	Alcinous
Epit.	*Epitome doctrinae platonicae (Didaskalikos)*
Alex. Lyc.	Alexander of Lycopolis
Allogenes	*Allogenes*
FS	Funk and Scopello (BCNH)
Turner	Turner (CGL)
(Allogenes) TC	*(Book of Allogenes), Tchacos Codex*
Anon. pro.	*Anonymous Prolegomena to Platonic Philosophy*
Ap. John	*Apocryphon of John*
Apoc. Ab.	*Apocalypse of Abraham*
Apoc. Adam	*Apocalypse of Adam*
Apoc. Elij.	*Apocalypse of Elijah*
Apoc. Enosh	*Apocalypse of Enosh*
1 Apoc. Jas.	*1 Apocalypse of James*
2 Apoc. Jas.	*2 Apocalypse of James*
Apoc. Paul	*Apocalypse of Paul*
Apoc. Peter	*(Coptic) Apocalypse of Peter*
Apoc. Peter (Eth.)	*(Ethiopic) Apocalypse of Peter*

Apoc. Zeph.	*Apocalypse of Zephaniah*
Apoc. Zeph. (Gk.)	*(Greek) Apocalypse of Zephaniah*
Ps.-Apollonius	Pseudo-Apollonius of Tyana
Ep.	*Epistulae*
Apul.	Apuleius of Madaura
Apol.	*Apologia (pro se de magia)*
Dogm. Plat.	*De dogma Platonis*
Flor.	*Florida*
Metam.	*Metamorphoses*
Arist.	Aristotle
Cael.	*De caelo*
Eth. Nic.	*Ethica nicomachea*
Gen. corr.	*De generatione et corruptione*
Metaph.	*Metaphysica*
Aristid. Ath.	Aristides of Athens
Apol.	*Apologia*
Arn.	Arnobius
Adv. nat.	*Adversus nations*
Asc. Is	*Ascent of Isaiah.*
Ascl.	*Asclepius*
Athenag.	Athenagoras
Leg.	*Legatio pro Christianis*
Att.	Atticus
Aug.	Augustine
Civ. dei	*Civitas dei*
Faust. Contra	*Faustum Manichaeum*
2 *Bar.*	2 *Baruch (Syriac Apocalypse)*
3 *Bar.*	3 *Baruch*
BCNH	Bibliothèque Copte de Nag Hammadi
BG	Papyrus Berolinensis 8502
Calc.	Calcidius
Comm. Tim.	*Commentarius in Timaeum*
Cav. Tr.	*Cave of Treasures*
CGL	Coptic Gnostic Library
Chald. Or.	*Chaldean Oracles*
Cic.	Cicero
Leg.	*De legibus*
Nat. d.	*De natura deorum*
CIG	Corpus Inscriptionum Graecarum
Clem. Al.	Clement of Alexandria
Exc.	*Excerpta ex Theodoto*
Paed.	*Paedagogus*
Protr.	*Protrepticus*
Strom.	*Stromateis*
Ps.-Clem.	Pseudo-Clementines
Hom.	*Homiliae*
Recogn.	*Recognitiones*

1 Clem.	*1 Clement*
2 Clem.	*2 Clement*
CMC	Cologne Mani Codex
Corp. herm.	*Corpus hermeticum*
Cyr. Al.	Cyril of Alexandria
Jul.	*Contra Julianum*
Dam.	Damascius
Comm. Phaedo	*In Platonis Phaedum commentarii*
Phil. hist.	*Philosophikē historia*
Vit. Is.	*Vita Isidori*
Democ.	Democritus
Dig.	*Digesta*
Dio Cass.	Cassius Dio
Dio Chrys.	Dio Chrysostom (of Prusa)
Borysth.	*Borysthenitica (Or. 36)*
Conc. Apam.	*De concordia cum Apamensibus (Or. 40)*
Consult.	*De consultatione (Or. 26)*
Cont.	*Contio (Or. 47)*
Dei cogn.	*De dei cognitione (Or. 12)*
De philos.	*De philosopho (Or. 71)*
Def.	*Defensio (Or. 45)*
Exil.	*De exilio (Or. 13)*
Grat.	*Gratitudo (Or. 44)*
Hom. Socr.	*De Homero et Socrate (Or. 55)*
Rec. Mag.	*Recusatio Magistratus (Or. 49)*
Rhod.	*Rhodiaca (Or. 31)*
Diog. Laer.	Diogenes Laertius
Diogn.	*Diognetus*
Disc. 8–9	*Discourse on the Eighth and the Ninth*
DK	Diels and Kranz, *Die Fragmente der Vorsokratiker*
Emp.	Empedocles
1 En.	*1 Enoch (Ethiopic Apocalypse)*
2 En.	*2 Enoch (Slavonic Apocalypse)*
3 En.	*3 Enoch (Hebrew Apocalypse)*
Ephr.	Ephrem Syrus
Comm. Gen. et Exod.	*In Genesim et in Exodum commentarii*
Epiph.	Epiphanius of Salamis
Pan.	*Panarion*
Eug.	*Eugnostos the Blessed*
Eunap.	Eunapius of Sardis
Hist. univ.	*Historia universalis*
VS	*Vitae sophistarum*
Euseb.	Eusebius of Caesarea
Dem. ev.	*Demonstratio evangelica*
Hist. eccl.	*Historia ecclesiastica*
Praep. ev.	*Praeparatio evangelica*

Ex. Soul	*Exegesis of the Soul*
Ezek. Trag.	Ezekiel the Tragedian
Ex.	*Exagōgē*
Gal.	Galen
Praen.	*De Praegnotione ad Epigenem*
Usu	*De usu partium corporis humani*
Gell.	Aulus Gellius
NA	*Noctes Atticae*
Gos. Eg.	*Egyptian Gospel*
Gos. Jud.	*Gospel of Judas*
Gos. Phil.	*Gospel of Philip*
Greg. Naz.	Gregory of Nazianzus
Or.	*Orationes*
Hekh. Rab.	*Hekhalot Rabbati*
Hekh. Zut.	*Hekhalot Zuṭarti*
Herm.	*Shepherd of Hermas*
Herodot.	Herodotus
Hist.	*Historia*
Hes.	Hesiod
Theog.	*Theogony*
Hipp.	Hippolytus of Rome
Haer.	*Refutatio omnium haeresium*
Hist. Rech.	*History of the Rechabites*
Hom.	Homer
Il.	*Iliad*
Od.	*Odyssea*
Hyp. Arch.	*Hypostasis of the Archons*
Hypsiph.	*Hypsiphrone*
Iamb.	Iamblichus
An.	*De anima*
Comm. Tim.	*In Timaeum Platonis commentarii*
Myst.	*De mysteriis*
Plat. Dial.	Dillon, *Iamblichi Chalcidensis*
Prot.	*Protrepticus*
Vit. Pyth.	*De vita Pythagorica*
Interp. Know.	*Interpretation of Knowledge*
Ir.	Irenaeus
Haer.	*Adversus haereses*
Jer.	Jerome
Comm. Gal.	*Commentariorum in Epistulam ad Galatas libri III*
Jov.	*Adversus Jovinianum libri II*
1, 2 Jeu	*The Books of Jeu*
Jos.	Josephus
Ant.	*Jewish Antiquities*
J.W.	*Jewish War*
Jos. Asen.	*Joseph and Aseneth*

Jub.	*Jubilees*
Jul.	Julian the Apostate
Ep.	*Epistulae*
Gal.	*Contra Galileos*
Or.	*Orationes*
Just. Mart.	Justin Martyr
1, 2 Apol.	*Apologia i, ii*
Dial.	*Dialogus cum Tryphone*
Lact.	Lactantius
Inst.	*Divinarum Institutionum libri VII*
Ir.	*De ira dei*
L.A.E.	*Life of Adam and Eve*
LSJ	Liddell, Scott, and Jones, *A Greek-English Lexicon*, 9th ed.
Luc.	Lucian of Samosata
Demon.	*Demonax*
Gall.	*Gallus*
Luct.	*De luctu*
Men.	*Menippus*
Nigr.	*Nigrinus*
[Philopatr.]	*Philopatris*
Sacr.	*De sacrificiis*
Somn.	*Somnium (Vita Luciani)*
Syr. d.	*De syria dea*
Vit. auct.	*Vitarum auctio*
Lyd.	John Lydus
Mens.	*De mensibus*
Mac. Mag.	Macarius Magnes
Apocrit.	*Apocriticus*
Macrob.	Macrobius
Comm. somn.	*Commentarii in somnium Scipionis*
Man. Hom.	*Manichaean Homilies*
Man. Keph.	*Manichaean Kephalaia*
Man. Ps.-Bk.	*Manichaean Psalm-Book*
Mar.	Marinus
Vit. Procl.	*Vita Procli*
Marc. Aur.	Marcus Aurelius
Mars.	*Marsanes*
FP	Funk and Poirier (BCNH)
Pearson	Pearson (CGL)
Mart. Pol.	*Martyrdom of Polycarp*
Max. Tyr.	Maximus of Tyre
Or.	*Orationes*
Melch.	*Melchizedek*
Mem. Marq.	MacDonald, *Memar Marqa*
Min. Fel.	Minucius Felix
Oct.	*Octavius*

NHC	Nag Hammadi Codices (codex number followed by treatise number)
Nic. Ger.	Nicomachus of Gerasa
Exc.	*Excerpta ap. Musici scriptores Graeci*
[Ps.-Iamb.] Theo. Arith.	*[Pseudo-Iamblichus] Theology of Arithmetic*
Norea	*Thought of Norea*
Num.	Numenius
Odes Sol.	*Odes of Solomon*
Olymp.	Olympiodorus
Comm. Alc.	*In Platonis Alcibiadem commentarii*
Comm. Gorg.	*In Platonis Gorgiam commentarii*
Comm. Phaedo	*In Platonis Phaedonem commentarii*
Orig.	Origen
Cels.	*Contra Celsum*
Comm. Jo.	*Commentarii in evangelium Joannis*
Comm. Rom.	*Commentarii in Romanos*
Hom. Jer.	*Homilae in Jeremiam*
Hom. Lev.	*Homilae in Leviticum*
Philoc.	*Philocalia*
Princ.	*De principiis (Peri Archōn)*
Orig. World	*On the Origin of the World*
OTP	*Old Testament Pseudepigrapha* (Charlesworth)
Paraph. Shem	*Paraphrase of Shem*
Parm.	Parmenides
Paus.	Pausanius
Descr.	*Graeciae descriptio*
PG	*Patrologia graeca* (Migne)
PGL	Lampe, *Patristic Greek Lexicon*
Phil.	Philo (of Alexandria)
Abr.	*De Abrahamo*
Agr.	*De agricultura*
Conf.	*De confusione linguarum*
Congr.	*De congressu eruditionis gratia*
Contempl.	*De vita contemplativa*
Her.	*Quis rerum divinarum heres sit*
Leg.	*Legum allegoriae*
Migr.	*De migratione Abrahami*
Opif.	*De opificio mundi*
Post.	*De posteriate Caini*
Prob.	*Quod omnis probus liber sit*
Prov.	*De providentia*
Somn.	*De somniis*
Spec.	*De specialibus legibus*
Virt.	*De virtutibus*
Philostr.	Philostratus
Vit. Apoll.	*Vita Apollonii*

Vit. soph.	*Vitae sophistarum*
Phot.	Photius
Bibl.	*Bibliotheca*
Pist. Soph.	*Pistis Sophia*
Plat.	Plato
Alcib.	*Alcibiades*
Apol.	*Apologia*
Crat.	*Cratylus*
Crit.	*Crito*
Euthyd.	*Euthydemus*
Gorg.	*Gorgias*
Leg.	*Laws*
Lys.	*Lysis*
Men.	*Meno*
Phaedr.	*Phaedrus*
Pol.	*Politicus*
Resp.	*Respublica*
Soph.	*Sophist*
Symp.	*Symposium*
Thaet.	*Theaetetus*
Tim.	*Timaeus*
Pliny the Elder	
Nat. hist.	*Naturalis historia*
Pliny the Younger	
Ep.	*Epistulae*
Plot.	Plotinus
Enn.	*Enneads*
Plut.	Plutarch of Chaeronea
Adol. poet. aud.	*Quomodo adolescens poetas audire debeat*
Amat.	*Amatorius*
Adv. Col.	*Adversus Colotem*
An. proc.	*De animae procreatione in Timaeo*
Cor.	*Marcius Coriolanus*
Def. orac.	*De defectu oraculorum*
E Delph.	*De E apud Delphos*
Fac.	*De facie in orbe lunae*
Fort. Rom.	*De fortuna Romanorum*
Glor. Ath.	*De gloria Atheniensium*
Gen. Socr.	*De genio Socratis*
Is. Os.	*De Iside et Osiride*
[Lib. ed.]	*De liberis educandis*
Pyth. orac.	*De pythiae oraculis*
Quaest. conv.	*Quaestiones convivalum libri IX*
Sera	*De sera numinis vindicta*
Stoic. Rep.	*De Stoicorum repugnantiis*
Superst.	*De superstitione*

Ps.-Plut.	Pseudo-Plutarch
De Vit. et Poes. Hom.	*De vita et poesi Homeri*
Fat.	*De fato*
Porph.	Porphyry
Abst.	*De abstinentia*
Agalm.	*Peri agalmatōn*
Aneb.	*Epistula ad Anebonem*
Antr. nymph.	*De antro nympharum*
Christ.	*Contra Christianos*
Isag.	*Isagoge sive quinque voces*
Marc.	*Ad Marcellam*
Philos. orac.	*De philosophia ex oraculis*
Sent.	*Sententiae*
Vit. Plot.	*Vita Plotini*
Vit. Pyth.	*Vita Pythagoricae*
Pre. Pet.	*Preaching of Peter*
Pr. Jac.	*Prayer of Jacob*
Pr. Jos.	*Prayer of Joseph*
Procl.	Proclus Diadochus
Comm. Remp.	*In Platonis rem publicam commentarii*
Comm. Tim.	*In Platonis Timaeum commentarii*
El. Theo.	*Institutio Theologica*
Plat. Theo.	*Theologica Platonica*
Ptol.	Ptolemy (the Gnostic)
Flor.	*Epistula ad Floram*
Quaest. Barth.	*Quaestiones Bartholomei*
Quint.	Quintilian
Inst.	*Institutio oratoria*
Sallust.	Sallustius
Deis	*De deis*
Senec.	Seneca
Ep.	*Epistulae*
Ot.	*De otio*
Prov.	*De providentia*
Tranq.	*De tranquilitate*
Seph. raz.	*Sepher ha-Razim*
Sext. Emp.	Sextus Empiricus
Adv. math.	*Adversus mathematicos*
ShirShabb	*Songs of the Sabbath Sacrifice*
Sib. Or.	*Sibylline Oracles*
Simpl.	Simplicius
Comm. cael.	*In Aristotelis de caelo commentaria*
Comm. Ench.	*Commentarius in Epicteti enchiridion*
Soph. Jes. Chr.	*The Sophia of Jesus Christ*
Steles Seth	*Three Steles of Seth*
Stob.	Johannes Stobaeus

Strab.	Strabo
Geogr.	*Geographica*
Suet.	Suetonius
Vesp.	*Vespasianus*
SVF	von Arnim, *Stoicorum Veterum Fragmenta*
Syncell.	George Syncellus
Ek. chron.	*Ecloga chronographica*
T. Ab.	*Testament of Abraham*
T. Job	*Testament of Job*
T. Levi	*Testament of Levi*
TC	Codex Tchacos
Ter.	Tertullian
An.	*De anima*
Carn. Chr.	*De carne Christi*
Cor.	*De corona militis*
Marc.	*Adversus Marcionem*
Nat.	*Ad nationes*
Scap.	*Ad Scapidam*
Scorp.	*Scorpiace*
Val.	*Adversus Valentinianos*
Ps.-Ter.	Pseudo-Tertullian
Haer.	*Adversus haereses*
Test. Truth	*The Testimony of Truth*
Theoph.	Theophilus of Antioch
Autol.	*Ad Autolycum*
Thund.	*Thunder: Perfect Mind*
Treat. Res.	*Treatise on the Resurrection*
Trim. Prot.	*Trimorphic Protennoia*
Tri. Trac.	*Tripartite Tractate*
Unt.	*Untitled Treatise* in Codex Brucianus
Xen.	Xenophon
Hell.	*Hellenica*
Mem.	*Memorabilia*
Zos. Pan.	Zosimus of Panopolis
Omega	*De lettera omega*
Zost.	*Zostrianos*
BFP	Barry, Funk, Poirier (BCNH)
LS	Layton and Sieber (CGL)

Apocalypse of the Alien God

Introduction

The terms "Christianity" and "Judaism" are difficult for students of
these ancient religions. Church historians remain unable to pinpoint
once and for all the emergence of "Christianity" from "Judaism";
scholars of Judaic studies debate when Judaism was "invented."[1]
"Christianity" and "Judaism" can feel like vacuous terms that house
a great diversity of groups, practices, and ideas whose differences
seem to outweigh their resemblances. Consequently, some scholars
feel more comfortable discussing Christiani*ties* and Judaism*s*, and
nobody is comfortable with the term used for groups that exist on the
borderlines between them: "Jewish-Christian"(!).[2] Even more problematic is the term "paganism," which is essentially a wastebasket
for the religious life of every ancient person who did not identify with
a cult of the God of Abraham. Yet we persist in using these terms,
despite our misgivings, and not just as a heuristic sleight-of-hand.
Sometimes there *are* significant differences between various groups
and their ideas, differences that *do* correspond somewhat to the way
that we moderns might use the terms "Jewish" or "Christian" or
"Hellenic" ("pagan" I renounce in this book).[3] These differences did
not fall from the sky. They were manufactured, in words, art, and ritual, by cultural warriors who believed that such differences mattered
and used them to legitimize their own interests.

This book is about some of those real differences and the development of the ideologies that crafted them—in this case, the competing
worldviews of "Christian" and "Hellenic" (i.e., Greek) philosophers.
It argues that one can identify when and where these worldviews

split for good: in the 260s CE, in Rome, in the reading group of the great Neoplatonic philosopher Plotinus. The master had a falling out with some of the Christian interlocutors of the group, sparked by the texts they read. After this controversy at the onset of late antiquity, it becomes very difficult to find academic, Hellenic philosophers with cordial relationships with their Christian counterparts. Instead, they regularly wrote polemical treatises denouncing each other's philosophy (even while still exchanging ideas). Here it becomes meaningful to talk of a Christian philosophy distinct from Hellenic philosophy—as a matter of cultural identity as well as intellectual enterprise—and a closed Platonic tradition, unfriendly to Jewish and Christian sources.

Unfortunately, this story gets (very) complicated when we try to learn about the Christian interlocutors of Plotinus and their controversial texts, and it is largely occupied—as is the bulk of this book, really—with what we know about them and, in turn, what these details tell us about the situation in Plotinus's circle. Fortunately, these details are not uninteresting: in fact, they furnish valuable evidence for deepening our understanding of an obscure Judeo-Christian literary tradition, Sethianism (so called due to its focus on the figure of Adam and Eve's third son, Seth, as savior and revealer). This book explains the contribution of Sethianism to Greek philosophy, and the reasons for its subsequent exile from the Hellenic schools; its relationship to Judaism, Christianity, and the "Jewish-Christian" groups that existed in the cracks between them; and the development of Jewish mystical traditions we know from the apocalypses and Qumran. This same tradition provides the most valuable evidence modern scholars possess for understanding the thought, background, and historical importance of any group of Gnostics—early Christians who were associated by their opponents with a myth of the creation of the world by a demiurge ("craftsman") of ambivalent ability and mores.[4] It appears that these sects referred to themselves as γνωστικοί ("knowers").

Plotinus's student Porphyry provides our only record of a personal encounter with ancient Gnostics that does not come from one of their bitter opponents among the church fathers:

> There were in his (Plotinus's) time many others, Christians, in particular heretics who had set out from the ancient philosophy, men belonging to the schools of Adelphius and Aculinus—who possessed many texts of Alexander the Libyan and Philocomus and Demostratus of Lydia, and who produced revelations of Zoroaster and

Zostrianos and Nicotheus and Allogenes and Messos and others of this sort who deceived many, just as they had been deceived, actually alleging that Plato really had not penetrated to the depth of intelligible substance. Wherefore, Plotinus often attacked their position in his seminars, and wrote the book which we have entitled "Against the Gnostics." He left it to us to judge what he had passed over. Amelius went up to forty volumes, writing against the book of Zostrianos, and I, Porphyry, wrote a considerable number of arguments against the book of Zoroaster, showing the book to be entirely spurious and contemporary, contrived by the founders of the heresy to fabricate the idea that the doctrines which they had chosen to honor were in fact those of the ancient Zoroaster.[5]

The translation of this passage will be discussed in detail below, but it is immediately clear that Porphyry gives us evidence more specific and reliable than what we have about any other Gnostics. First, he says that, in Plotinus's time, there were Christian heretics, Plotinus's refutation of whom he entitled *Against the Gnostics*; therefore, "Gnostics" were present in Rome and known to Plotinus and his group. Second, Plotinus discussed philosophical questions with these Gnostics, which means that they were sufficiently educated to participate in a sort of ancient postgraduate seminar. Third, these discussions led to disagreement, much of whose substance is extant in Plotinus's treatise *Against the Gnostics*. Finally, Porphyry mentions the books the Gnostics considered authoritative: "revelations" (ἀποκαλύψεις, i.e., "apocalypses").

Luckily for us, titles identical to several of the apocalypses mentioned by Porphyry were unearthed at Nag Hammadi (Upper Egypt) in 1945.[6] Thus the especial importance of Porphyry's evidence; when read in concert with Porphyry and Plotinus, these apocalypses, and other texts (mostly apocalypses as well) from Nag Hammadi that belong to the same literary tradition, enable us to pose and answer significant questions about the social background, literary preferences, theological proclivities, and ritual life of a particular group of Gnostics, who came into serious conflict with the great Platonic academics of their time.[7] One of these titles, *Allogenes*, means "foreigner," or "alien." As we will see, the concept of alienation figures strongly in the Sethian apocalypses, texts that describe a god so utterly transcendent and divorced from creation that he can only be revealed by an avatar who bridges a chasm between human and divine, descending from heaven to preach to the elect, who reside as "aliens" on this strange planet. Conversely, to Plotinus, everything about this message—from its vigorous use of Judeo-Christian language and literary traditions to its treatment of specific philosophical problems (such as divine providence or the afterlife of the soul)—seemed wrong, wrongheaded, and decidedly foreign: that is, alien. For both parties, albeit in entirely different senses, the Sethian literature offered a revelation (apocalypse) of the alien god to his alien worshippers.

One might then ask how it is that the Sethian literature and its Christian Gnostic readers wound up in Plotinus's circle in the first place. The Nag Hammadi discovery answers this question: some of the now extant Sethian literature—in particular, a group known as the "Platonizing" texts (*Zostrianos* [NHC VIII,1], *Allogenes* [NHC XI,3], *Marsanes* [NHC X,1] and the *Three Steles of Seth* [NHC VII,5])—appears to have been deeply conversant with advanced Platonic metaphysics and does not mention the figure of Jesus.[8] The question of dating the copies that were known to Plotinus and others, and thus the possibility of mutual philosophical influence between them, remains controversial; however, there is a scholarly consensus that some version of this literature was present at a crucial period in the development of Platonic metaphysics, and may have even contributed to the thought of Plotinus himself.[9]

Yet the importance of the Sethian literature is not limited to our understanding of the history of later Greek philosophy or even Gnosticism. Its indebtedness to the literary traditions and genre of Jewish and Christian apocalyptic literature merits its inclusion in the study of Jewish and Christian pseudepigrapha of the second and third centuries, a period for which our evidence is otherwise scarce. Some of these traditions deal with themes of self-transformation that we know not just from these apocalypses but from the Dead Sea Scrolls, again, furnishing valuable evidence for an obscure field of study—the development of Jewish mysticism between Qumran and the late antique ascent literature known as the "Hekhalot" ("palaces") corpus, a field the great scholar of Kabbalah, Gershom Scholem, termed "Jewish Gnosticism." Finally, these texts also occupy a liminal position along the notoriously permeable boundaries of Judaism and Christianity, and some of their doctrines are most recognizable in the context of the Syrian groups scholars label "Jewish-Christian," particularly the Elchasaites. The Sethian evidence from Nag Hammadi is thus indispensable for scholars trying to understand the negotiation and mutual permeation of the boundaries between emerging Christianity and Judaism.

The evidence for these conclusions is set out in the first six chapters of this book. Chapter 1 addresses an overlooked but significant implication of Porphyry's evidence: the physical presence of these Gnostics in the social context of a philosophical study group. The chapter thus explores the context of such groups in the Hellenic culture wars of the second and third centuries CE, where the Second Sophistic movement developed a Hellenophile ideology permeating educational life and was countered by a spike of interest in "Oriental" sages like those invoked by Plotinus's Christian Gnostic opponents.

Chapter 2 takes a close look at Plotinus's own writing about these opponents, who, he says, were once his "friends." He viciously attacks their cosmology, anthropology, and soteriology, accusing them of developing a kind of deviant Platonism. His criticisms apply not only to the apocalypses his Gnostics read but also to contemporary Christian Platonism in general, serving as evidence of the Christian background of the group and the more generally Judeo-Christian valence of their texts.

Chapters 3 through 6 introduce and discuss the Sethian Gnostic apocalypses themselves, alongside evidence from Plotinus that has been hitherto read in isolation from them. Chapter 3 examines the genre of the texts, grounding their rhetoric, motifs, and especially claims to authority in contemporary Jewish and Christian apocalyptic literature. Their approach to myth and revelation is sharply contrasted with contemporary Platonic models, which employed allegory to interpret myths; thus, to Plotinus, they appeared to be "another," alien "way of writing." Chapter 4 discusses the apocalypses' attitudes toward soteriology, focusing on the identity of the Sethian savior (a cosmic Seth who descends to earth throughout history to intervene on behalf of the elect), the ethnic valence of their soteriological language, and Plotinus's complaints about these conceptions with respect to his philosophy of divine providence. Chapter 5 looks at Sethian eschatology, both personal (handling the postmortem fate of the soul) and cosmic (handling the fate of the cosmos). In both of these chapters, it is clear that the apocalypses' stances, from a philosophical perspective, resemble Christian Platonism, not its Hellenic counterpart. Chapter 6 studies the strategies for divinization in these Gnostic texts. A review of these practices shows that they drew not from Platonic but from Jewish and Christian sources, particularly those associated with ancient Jewish mysticism, as preserved in the Dead Sea Scrolls, apocalypses, and Hekhalot literature. Moreover, recalling scholarly debate about vision and experience in Jewish literature helps us resolve obscurities in Sethian rituals themselves and theorize for what they could have been used in an ancient context.

Chapter 7 summarizes the aforementioned conclusions, offering a clearer picture of the function of the Sethian apocalypses, the lives of their authors, and their relationship to the Gnostics in Plotinus's circle. Moreover, the chapter discusses the texts' relationship with Judaism, Manichaeism, and Christianity (or "Jewish Christianity"), emphasizing the important role that Jewish literature plays in understanding Sethianism, the ways that Sethian literature helps elucidate the thorny problem of "Jewish Gnosticism," and the significance of the Sethian literature for the history of Jewish mysticism. Similarly, significant parallels to Manichaeism emerge that invite a reevaluation of exactly what kind of baptismal groups Sethianism grew out of, and where they might have been.

Finally, this book will defend a Judeo-Christian authorship of the Sethian treatises—even the "Platonizing" texts that do not mention Jesus Christ or Scripture!—thus rejecting the scholarly consensus that the texts represent a non-Christian or pagan development of Sethianism, or evidence of an outreach to paganism. Some have recognized already that "a lack of Christian features" does not necessarily indicate Jewish or pagan provenance.[10] Yet the boundary between Judaism and Christianity seems impossible to divine in much of the Sethian literature, particularly the Platonizing texts, which are laden with Neoplatonic jargon instead of biblical references. Perhaps this is no accident, because many of their Jewish and Christian features are associated specifically with groups that flourished precisely along these borderlines, groups (such as the Elchasaites, Ebionites, and author[s] of the Pseudo-Clementine literature) that have duly been named "Jewish-Christian" by modern scholars. As I will argue in the concluding chapter, it is likely that Sethian traditions developed in a Jewish-Christian environment like that which produced Mani, who also drew widely on Jewish apocryphal traditions in formulating a religion that honored Jesus of Nazareth as one of many descending savior-revealers—important, but not the object of every prayer or treatise.

The apocalypses brandished in Plotinus's seminar were thus the products of intellectuals from a community that, like Manichaeans or the Elchasaites, dwelt on the boundaries of Judaism and Christianity. Drawing from the literary traditions of the Jewish pseudepigrapha, they wrote their apocalypses as manuals for eliciting an experience of visionary ascent, using Platonic metaphysics as a meditative tool. While such practices are best understood in the context of contemporary Jewish mysticism, the Platonism that informs them also permeated the cosmological and soteriological thought of their authors, producing a Platonism that was at the forefront of Christian theology—hence their appeal to the Christian "heretics" mentioned by Porphyry. He and Plotinus recognized the Christian valence of this Platonism, and here drew a line in the sand between the Platonism of their Christian Gnostic interlocutors and their own thought. Hellenic Platonism thus began to be seen not just as a school interpreting Plato but a Hellenic philosophy distinct from and actively opposed to Jewish and Christian traditions, which the Platonists hoped to exile from their schools once and for all.

CHAPTER I

Culture Wars

Who were these followers of "Adelphius and Aculinus" in the time of Plotinus? Porphyry says that they were Christian heretics, but also trained Platonists. Nothing is known about Adelphius or the authors of other texts (now lost) the heretics brandished, "Alexander the Libyan and Philocomus and Demostratus of Lydia."[1] Aculinus appears to have enjoyed a reputation as a Platonist roughly contemporary with Plotinus.[2] Alexander the Libyan was known to Tertullian and Jerome as a Valentinian.[3] These figures all bore normal names (i.e., epigraphically attested as used by everyday people), not pseudepigraphic, authoritative titles.[4] They are Greco-Roman, showing that in this context, at least, the "heretics" identified themselves as Hellenes, who followed a Hellenic philosopher, Aculinus. Whence then the animosity of Porphyry and Plotinus? Porphyry's remarks about these Christian Platonists and the works they read tell us that cult, culture, and authority were at stake. The followers of Aculinus and the rest are accused of having sailed from the safe harbor of Hellenism, "deceiving many others and themselves being deceived, actually alleging that Plato really had not penetrated to the depth of intelligible substance."[5] These thinkers began their careers as students of the Hellenic "ancient philosophy," but came to betray it. He dubs them impostors, for they esteem the works of Oriental prophets over those of the Hellenes. Porphyry calls these works "apocalypses," or "revelations," a genre with which he was not unfamiliar, and lists the prophets who purportedly authored them—individuals with alien, foreign

names like "Zoroaster and Zostrianos and Nicotheus and Allogenes and Messos."[6]

What did it mean to challenge the authority of Plato with the
invocation of alien authorities? Was "Oriental" wisdom prized or
despised among ancient philosophers? What kind of people did one
meet in these circles anyway? Where did they come from, and how
did they feel about the ruling powers—the *non*-alien authorities of
Hellenism and Rome? Answering these questions requires us to step
back momentarily and ascertain the social environment in which the
appeals to these foreign authorities took place. As we will see, analysis of contemporary Christian and Hellenic philosophical circles
themselves sheds scarce light on the problem. Study groups in the second and third centuries were small, ad hoc affairs, about which it is
difficult to generalize—except that their participants all came out of
a deeply ideological rhetorical environment known today as the "Second Sophistic."[7] Modern research into this wider educational environment has blossomed, yielding important data for a "thick description" of members of a group like that of Plotinus—and the Christian
Gnostics who belonged to it as well,[8] thus providing the most extensive sociological information on the background of any known Gnostic group.[9]

PHILOSOPHY CLUBS

Gnostic literature itself says virtually nothing about the relationship
of Gnosticism to contemporary philosophical circles, much less the
culture informing them. References to philosophy in the Nag Hammadi corpus indicate that the Gnostics adopted stances about philosophical issues but excoriated contemporary philosophers, striv-
ing (like Tertullian), to distinguish themselves from contemporary
Greek education. Such anti-philosophical polemic is striking.[10] While
recorded Gnostic groups did not proclaim adherence to any particular philosophical sect, the high philosophical import of their texts
demonstrates that they must have spent quite a bit of time among the
philosophical sects, particularly the Platonists.[11] Irenaeus referred to
a school (διδασκαλεῖον) of Valentinus.[12]

Recalling the Judeo-Christian background of Gnosticism, one
can turn to Jewish and Christian texts in hopes of finding something
like a school in which Gnostics could learn philosophy. One looks in
vain. Rabbinic sources are silent about the interaction between Jews

and the Greek philosophical schools.[13] We are left with Philo, whose
account of the Therapeutae contrasts the sages' allegorizing of scripture with the oratorical display of the sophists.[14] Elsewhere, he refers
to his own education as propaedeutic.[15] Philo's status as a Jewish Platonist is obviously not comparable to that of the Sethian traditions
and thus provides no social context for them. His testimony indicates
nothing more than small schools of exegesis of the Septuagint. Here
he is very much in agreement with the greater movement in Hellenistic Judaism, as seen in the *Letter of Aristeas*, to defend the faith with
the idiom of Greek philosophy without becoming a partisan of it.[16]

Christian literature offers more information. There certainly was
a need for education in the instruction of catechumens, but anything
resembling formal schooling in theology seems unknown prior to
Pantanaeus's "catechetical school" in Alexandria in the mid-second
century CE.[17] The school's representatives, Clement and Origen, give
us examples of exegetical education in their day (like Philo), but not
of how or where they taught Platonism.[18] Origen's own homilies and
commentaries never refer to Greek philosophical sources, and explicitly discourage instruction in rhetoric.[19] Other sources give a different picture: Porphyry, not the most impartial of witnesses, says that
the textbooks used in Origen of Alexandria's school were essentially
the same as those in Plotinus's, which would mean Middle Platonic
commentaries, chiefly those of Numenius, and a good dose of Stoics
and Peripatetics.[20] Eusebius describes a wide curriculum ranging from
the basic to advanced study, where Origen was so overwhelmed by
classes that he assigned his student Heraclas to teach the "preliminar-
ies."[21] Yet there is no conclusive evidence that the "school" was formal, was officially affiliated with the (proto)-orthodox community,
or had a steady succession of teachers; rather, we see that a range of
instruction, including both elementary education and introduction to
philosophy, was available in a Christian context in the third century
CE.[22] However, this education was largely propaedeutic and in the
service of ethical, hermeneutical, and apologetic concerns.[23] It is hard
to imagine *Parmenides* commentaries or the *Chaldean Oracles* being
read or composed there. If Plotinus's opponents were educated in a
Jewish or Christian milieu like that of Philo or the Alexandrian "catechetical school," their texts do not show it. If we are to understand
the background and significance of Plotinus's Christian opponents
and their claims to foreign authorities, we must look at the culture of
the Greek schools themselves.[24]

It is no comfort that our knowledge of the social makeup of philosophical circles in the Roman Empire is also limited.[25] However, the modus operandi of philosophical discourse at least appears to be clear: Platonists of the first two centuries CE seem to have preferred a medium akin to the modern reading group or philosophy club. The character of each group seems to have been dependent on that of each particular teacher, as well as attendant circumstances.[26] For instance, Ammonius taught at what looked like his home.[27] (The same has been suggested of Philo, Justin Martyr, and Origen.)[28] Plutarch organized a group (σχολή) in which he lectured and texts were read and debated.[29] Like Apuleius of Madaura,[30] Aulus Gellius attended a formal but improvised classroom—his instructor, Calvenus Taurus Gellius, would have students over for dinner and even supervise outings.[31] Similarly, Iamblichus had his own school in Syria, where he set up a curriculum, lectured, and supervised journeys, in addition to taking his students to local festivals.[32] Very little is known of Porphyry's school, if he founded one at all.[33] If it existed, it could have been funded, like Plotinus's school, by a wealthy matron.[34]

Plotinus's career in Rome may give us a good idea of how philosophers set up shop—it was ad hoc.[35] When he arrived in Italy, he held his salons in the homes of his wealthy patrons.[36] Everybody there was considered to be comrades, from the serious students, like Amelius, to the wealthy patrons dropping in and out, like Marcellus Orontius or even the emperor himself.[37] In their seminars, they debated and conducted exegesis on difficult passages in his favorite treatises.[38] Fellow teachers engaged the group by epistle and the occasional visit.[39]

We see, then, that the philosophical reading groups were private, even if ostensibly open to anybody, which usually amounted to the philosophers' patron(s), advanced students, and young nobles getting their feet wet or completing their educations.[40] This distinction was fluid: a patron or noble could abandon politics for philosophy.[41] The bulk of serious students are said to have started their careers by studying in several groups before settling on a particular mentor within a particular school (αἵρεσις).[42] The most earnest students would formally declare their devotion to the study of philosophy.[43] Once ensconced within the school atmosphere, the students formed extremely close, even devotional, relationships with their masters.[44] While these groups were clearly small (perhaps up to a dozen people at a time, allowing for a revolving door of veterans and new arrivals) and ad hoc, they still followed the schedule of the ancient school year.[45] Relatively formal (if equally small) rival institutes of advanced study do not appear in Athens and Alexandria until the later fourth century CE.[46]

This brief survey of the evidence underscores how important Porphyry's evidence is among the ancient philosophical sources but tells us little about what the Gnostics known to Plotinus were like. As scholars like Arthur Darby Nock have suggested, sophistic literature offers us great evidence for fleshing out a picture of the social context of ancient philosophy.[47] The logic of the move is simple: philosophers (or at least Platonists) were, presumably, educated individuals; education in the Roman world began with grammar school and led to rhetoric; rhetoric was taught by sophists.[48] Philosophers, then, came from similar backgrounds to those of sophists and spent a good deal of their formative years, if not their entire lives, around them. Indeed, many philosophers began as professional rhetoricians before moving to philosophy.[49] An analysis of the culture motivating rhetorical education in the Roman Empire might answer our questions about Plotinus's Gnostic opponents and their interest in "foreign" authorities. Even Gnostics had to go to school, especially if they wanted to join the philosophy club.

GOING TO SCHOOL

Philostratus (early to mid-third century CE) understood himself to be part of a revival of the art of rhetoric traced back to the legacy of the classical sophist Aeschines, and distinguished from its more ancient counterpart today by the name "Second Sophistic."[50] The term describes the rhetorical culture spanning the years 50–250 CE, with roots in the mid-first century and ebbing away in the Rome of Plotinus and the rhetor Longinus.[51] This culture was no mere linguistic development in the history of rhetoric but a social movement that produced a concrete ideology.[52] This culture was shared with contemporary philosophers, through their common experience in basic schooling, rhetorical training, and religious life—and it strongly contrasts with Gnostic thought.

The close association of sophism and philosophy is indicated foremost by the terminology used by the ancients themselves.[53] Philostratus says he is writing about both sophists and philosophers, and that his circle, whose matron was "the philosophical Julia," included sophists, philosophers, and astrologers (γεωμετρίαι) in the 190s CE.[54]While

many intellectuals themselves sharply distinguished sophists and philosophers ("the lady doth protest too much"),[55] the professions were
also occasionally confused.[56] Such confusion is not surprising, given
that philosophical and sophistic texts often circulated in the same
schools. Philosophy was part of the sophistic education, if only as one
of many branches of study; the Platonic corpus itself loomed large in
rhetorical study.[57] Moreover, sophists were interested in all the various philosophical sects, at times eschewing adherence to any particular one.[58] Finally, sophists and philosophers were bound in the legal
sphere, occasionally sharing the privilege of exemption from taxa-
tion.[59] Such comparable civic status was to be expected, given the similarity of their civic roles.

These roles were deeply politicized. Some have emphasized that
Greek philosophers under the empire were quietists, bystanders to the
civic turmoil of their age. The "crises" of the imperial period, especially the third century,[60] have been repeatedly invoked in explaining
not only the origins of Gnostic "anti-cosmism"[61] but the pronounced
turn to mysticism that seems to occur with Plotinus.[62] This approach
is unsound for several reasons. The concept of a general political crisis is far too general as a singular, blanket explanation for particular anecdotes (such as Aristides' hypochondria). Gnosticism, suppos-
edly a symptom of decline, is traceable to that "happiest of reigns,"
Hadrian.[63] Finally, while the mid-third century CE did see a great deal
of political instability, it did not necessarily affect the empire's entire
population, for whom localized breakdowns of military power were
more tangible than political machinations in Rome.[64] Yet even without recourse to the clichés of dualism and anxiety, some persist in dis-
sociating the period's philosophy from social life and politics, and the
Gnostic literature is no exception.[65]

The concerns of contemporary politics were never far from the Platonists, for three reasons. First, basic training in rhetoric, a *sine qua
non* of philosophical education, necessarily entailed the discussion
and internalization of political topics. Second, the literature of the
Second Sophistic reveals a clear awareness of and engagement with
Roman politics; the classmates of the philosophers—and the Gnostics—were hardly quietists. Third, the socioeconomic background of
the sophists as well as the philosophers was one of wealth and, often,
political connections. As we will see, the deeply political background
of philosophy in the second and third centuries CE is the proper frame
for much of Plotinus's anti-Gnostic rhetoric.

In antiquity, the rhetorical arts—and the education system which rested on them—were developed for political purposes.[66] The study of basic rhetorical exercises (*progymnasmata*) involved various exercises designed to prepare the student for advanced work in mock-deliberative and legal speech and eventually the use of oratory in public life.[67] This training was steeped in the classical texts of Greek history and epic poetry. Stock themes rehearsed for use in oratory included invented narratives (πλάσματα) and Greek political history, but especially Homer, the unifying reference for exercises ranging from learning the alphabet to composing a prose declamation.[68] In other words, much like an undergraduate humanities course today, students would have probably read about Achilleus and Peleus before getting to Plato, much less *Parmenides* commentaries. The education shared by philosophers and sophists readied them for public life and enabled them to speak the universal language of Hellenism.

Deep involvement in the civic sphere did not necessarily entail fondness of the Romans. Generally, the sophistic texts do not reject Roman rule, which seems to be tolerated as a fact of life.[69] Plutarch writes approvingly of it, and disparagingly of Greece's infighting and decline.[70] The sophist Aelius Aristides, too, contrasts the Hellenic and Roman attempts at self-rule.[71] Philosopher and master rhetorician Dio Chrysostom insists that the present age is not evil and never speaks out against the greater regime.[72] The same is true of the historian Pausanias, and the famous doctor Galen.[73] Engagement with Roman politics was a marked improvement for the relationship between Greek thinkers and autocrats—the emperors Vespasian and Domitian appear to have despised philosophers, and "talking back" to a ruler is a cliché in Greek philosophy.[74] The Romans were hardly considered to be Hellenes themselves; rather, they are like barbarians who occasionally imbibe the draught of Hellenic education (παιδεία).[75] This is particularly evident in Plutarch's *Lives*, where his Roman subjects rarely behave like sophisticates, and *Political Advice*, where Roman rule is tolerated only on the grounds of Greece's own factionalism.[76] Yet even if the Romans themselves were considered uncultured, Rome was the best place to acquire—and demonstrate—one's education.[77]

The ambivalent attitude of Hellenophone intellectuals toward the government is in part explained by their privileged socioeconomic backgrounds and high standing in their communities. The sophists came from wealthy and often politically influential families.[78] They had friends in high places, commonly serving as intermediaries between their towns and the emperor himself.[79] Some sophists, like Polemo and Herodes, were personally beloved by the emperors.[80] Thanks to the crowds they could draw, crowds that included emperors, towns invited sophists to open shop in hope of stimulating the local economy.[81] There even was a tertiary pilgrimage effect whereby great sophists traveled to meet other great sophists, of course with their entourage in tow.[82] Aside from simply teaching and speaking,[83] sophists built monuments,[84] alleviated local factional politics,[85] officiated over civic cults and festivals,[86] served as administrators and military leaders,[87] and were general public benefactors.[88]

This evidence coheres well with what we know of the social environment of the Platonists from the first to third centuries CE, which was also elite, public, and male.[89] Our information about the lives of the Middle Platonists is admittedly scarce, but Dio Chrysostom, Plutarch, and Apuleius all assume that the philosopher has the ways and means to be active in public life, and expect him to do so.[90] Inscriptional evidence also testifies to the stature of philosophers in the public sphere.[91] The word "philosopher" (φιλόσοφος) is also used in honorary inscriptions to designate morality and wisdom in public life; philosophy was thus considered an appropriate reference for a public life well lived.[92]

The Neoplatonists mingled with politicians constantly and extolled political activity.[93] Plotinus's benefactrix has already been mentioned; his circle included senators and politicians.[94] Although he discouraged some of his students from pursuing politics further, he also intervened in political disputes, joined the entourage of Emperor Gordian, befriended Emperor Gallienus, and attempted to found a Platonic city-state ("Platonopolis").[95] Porphyry came from a wealthy, noble Syrian family—his name at Tyre was "Malkhus" (from the Phoenician/Punic for "king"), so Amelius nicknamed him "Basileus," while Longinus dubbed him "Porphyrios" ("royal purple").[96] While he, Plotinus, and Iamblichus certainly subordinated the political virtues to the contemplative, they nonetheless counted them as virtues, early but necessary steps for the embodied soul on the road to contemplation, not to be disparaged.[97] Similarly, Porphyry has only kind words for one of Plotinus's politically ambitious students, Castricius Firmus.[98] Iamblichus too came from a royal family in Syria (and was named accordingly), whither he returned after completing his study in the West.[99] His school's legacy was carried on by his patron, Sopater, who met an unfortunate end in court intrigue.[100]

The Athenian academy of Proclus was funded by wealthy benefactors whose families remained involved with the school across generations.[101] Proclus himself participated in local politics.[102] Even in the dark, final days of the school, Damascius too advocated the philosophers' political activism.[103]

One can also observe significant differences between the public lives of sophists and philosophers. For instance, in the confines of imperial quarters, it was the duty of the sophist to flatter, as distinct from philosophical frankness (παρρησία).[104] Although philosophers served in the public sphere, the bulk of their "performances"—lectures, debates, writing, philosophizing—was generally in-house, although public debates did happen.[105] Rivalry between sophists was normal, at times puerile, and occasionally applauded and enjoyed by high society, and even the participants.[106] Meanwhile, philosophers had rivalries, but this never bled over into humiliation or, significantly, authoritarianism. Such differences notwithstanding, most philosophers tended to be influential citizens, pundits, public intellectuals, or beneficiaries of wealth.[107] At the same time, in all of these spheres, sophists, philosophers, and their coteries saw themselves working not on behalf of the Romans but the Greeks.

GOING TO SACRIFICE

The noun Ἑλληνισμός—an "imitator of the Greeks, Greek-ifier"—is first used in 2 Maccabees 4:13, but in the Second Sophistic the term becomes associated with a kind of pan-Hellenism, articulated under the aegis of παιδεία ("education," or "culture").[108] Moreover, it came to indicate adherence to the civic cults associated with the Greek and Roman pantheon, as in the literature of the emperor Julian the Apostate (mid-fourth century CE).[109] Thus the term "Hellene" is preferable to "pagan" to describe the Hellenophone intellectuals of late antiquity.[110] These Hellenes we see portrayed in the literature of the Second Sophistic associated popular Greek religion and civic cult, a cultic conservatism that is also shared with the Neoplatonists. Like the political activism that philosophers took for granted, this cultic conservatism was also a crucial issue for Plotinus in his battle with the Gnostics.

The urban centers of the Second Sophistic were Athens, Smyrna, and Ephesus, yet for Philostratus, Hellas no longer had a strictly geographical sense but instead had a cultural one.[111] To the subject of his biography of Apollonius of Tyana (first century CE), he gives the line, "a wise man finds Hellas everywhere and a sage will not regard or consider any place to be a desert or barbarous."[112] His hometown is "a Greek city nestled among the Cappadocians," and Gadeira (modern Cadiz) is praised as a highly religious and "Hellenic" place.[113] According to Philostratus's *Lives of the Sophists*, Timocrates came "from the Pontus and his birthplace was Heraclea, whose citizens admire Greek culture."[114] Herodes addresses his students and admirers simply as "Hellenes."[115] Hadrian (the sophist) is "escorted by those who loved Hellenic culture, from all parts of the world."[116] The extrageographical and ethnic definition of Hellas is paralleled by Dio Chrysostom's account of the Borysthenians, who worship Achilles, wear beards, and are so "truly Greek in character" that a whole town turns out to meet the visiting sophist.[117]

Reflecting the period's turn toward Atticism, the Greek language itself takes on an almost magical quality in Philostratus's books.[118] Favorinus's Greek was so good that "even those in the audience who did not understand the Greek language shared in the pleasure of his voice; for he fascinated even them by the tones of his voice, his expressive glance and the rhythm of his speech."[119] Apollonius is portrayed as having spoken perfect Attic despite his Cappadocian rearing, speaking nothing else when traveling—which is easy, because everyone he meets who knows something of "philosophy" happens to speak Greek too.[120]

Thus Hellenism in the Antonine and Severan periods was defined by possession of the lore of Hellas, and, for those not born with Apollonius's supernatural mastery of the Pythagorean tradition, this was acquired through education. Yet the term παιδεία itself also came to mean "elite Greek culture" as much as simply "education."[121] In second-century legal texts, the educated (πεπαιδευμένοι) encompass grammarians, rhetors, and doctors, that is, the class of learned elites.[122] The literature of the period also associates elite, culturally Hellenic identity with the status provided by education: Dio Chrysostom often contrasts common education with philosophy, the true παιδεία, emphasizing its practical (i.e., political) side.[123] The uniquely Hellenic background of παιδεία is paramount for Plutarch even at the lowest stages of education, as it is for Lucian.[124] Galen, too, valorizes education when describing how he earned fame among the elite at Rome.[125]

The Hellenic valorization of παιδεία was publicly articulated not just in the sphere of rhetorical demonstration but in civic ritual as well, and the two often coincided, as at festivals.[126] The cultic sense of Hellenism is embodied in Philostratus's portrayal of Apollonius, who spends time making sure that local priests are running the local cults in a sufficiently Hellenic fashion,[127] rebuking the sacrifices of Babylon, discovering Indian sages who worship Greek gods, and correcting the Egyptian rites.[128] He is typical of the flowering of participation in traditional Greek religion and popular civic cult that forms the ritual background of the Second Sophistic. Plutarch served as a priest of Delphi, leading a public ritual life that should not be subsumed under his critiques of superstition.[129] The same Delphic Apollo exhorted Dio Chrysostom to launch his peregrinations and thus his career as a Cynic.[130] Like Plutarch, Lucian praised local civic cults, despite reservations about superstition.[131] Aelius Aristides devoted much of his life and writing to the service of Asclepius, as related in his *Sacred Tales*. The historian Cassius Dio practiced incubation and pilgrimage to temples across Asia and Greece, both in dreams and waking life.[132]

This background of Pan-Hellenic culture in the spheres of education and religion is crucial for the social context of the development of Platonism, including its Gnostic variety. The philosophers continued to enshrine παιδεία, but internalized it as cultivation of the soul. Possession of it defines the virtuous life, as in sophistic literature: Porphyry quips that "lack of education (ἀπαιδευσία) is the mother of all evils."[133] In the fourth century CE, Sallustius would assert that "in the educated (πεπαιδευμένος) all virtues may be seen, while among the uneducated (ἀπαίδευτος) one is brave and unjust."[134] At the same time, the Neoplatonists absorbed culture into the greater philosophical enterprise, despite remaining informed by it. Plutarch says that it is "necessary to make philosophy the center of education."[135] Two centuries later, in Plotinus's thought, παιδεία is much more: the positive development of the soul itself.[136] No wonder, then, that he chides the Gnostics for speaking in a way that does not befit the πεπαιδευμένος.[137] In his *Protrepticus*, Iamblichus likens the acquisition of παιδεία to the blind man finding eyes to see.[138]

Cultic conservatism was also shared by sophists and Platonists.[139] Adherence to the traditional cult is central to the proper (and legal) spiritual life as portrayed by Celsus (second century CE), writing an anti-Christian polemic.[140] Plotinus rejects the efficacy of astrology,

but not magic per se, and never discourages participation in civic religious life.[141] Porphyry's *On Abstinence*, meanwhile, esteems vegetarianism and so attacks sacrificial institutions, a position difficult to
harmonize with the rest of his corpus.[142] Yet even when he is dismis-
sive of a superstitious approach to cult,[143] he takes care to add that
he does not oppose civic law regarding sacrifice, and sometimes discusses ritual with enthusiasm:[144]

> For this is the principal fruit of piety: to honor the divine in the
> traditional (i.e. Hellenic) ways (τιμᾶν τὸ θεῖον κατὰ τὰ πάτρια), not
> because (God) needs it, but because He summons us by this vener-
> able and blessed dignity to worship him. God's altars, if they are
> consecrated, do not harm us; if they are neglected, they do not help
> us. . . . It is not by doing certain things or forming certain opinions
> about God that we worship Him properly. Tears and supplications
> do not move God; "sacrifices do not honor God; numerous votive
> offerings do not adorn God. Rather Intellect filled with God, firmly
> established, is united to God, for like must gravitate to like." . . . But
> as for yourself, as has already been said, "let the intellect within you
> be a temple of God."[145]

Iamblichus proclaimed ritual the crown jewel of the philosophical
life; one of his ancient admirers addressed him in a letter as "savior
of the whole Hellenic world," and Julian the Apostate based the theological content of his religious reforms on the philosopher's work.[146]
Iamblichus would probably not have minded, for he also supported
the contemporary Hellenic cult.[147] He is pictured by Eunapius as performing miracles for his disciples on the way home from a civic festi-
val, his participation in which would be consonant with his defense of
animal sacrifice in the cultic treatise *De mysteriis*.[148] In the early fifth
century, Macrobius insisted that the gods preferred to be worshipped
by means of traditional, civic cultic imagery, despite its disparity with
their transcendent essence.[149] As for Proclus, the title of his treatise on
theurgic practice says it all: *On the Hieratic Art of the Hellenes* (περὶ
τῆς καθ᾽Ἑλληνας ἱερατικῆς τέχνης).

Even in the second century, then, a social group of philosophers,
rhetoricians, and teachers began to identify themselves as "Hellenes,"
not by birth but by education, with παιδεία as their byword. To be
sure, more specific self-identifications were negotiated by more specific markers; moreover, alignment with Hellenism was compatible with the layering of other local and ethnic identities, and being
a Hellene meant different things in different parts of the empire.[150]
What all these accounts have in common, however, is a manufactured

heritage of Hellenic παιδεία with the shared ritual background of traditional Greek religion and civic cult. This is the heritage prized by
Plotinus and Porphyry, and which their Christian Gnostic interlocutors challenged. However, a more specific heritage was also prized in
the circles of philosophers—the pedigree of classical Greek philosophy. Plotinus's group went so far as to celebrate the birthdays of Plato
and Socrates.[151] Philosophers expressed their Hellenic heritage with
the tone and idiom of the Second Sophistic, but identified it foremost
with the Platonic "golden chain" reaching back to Plato and Pythagoras, and, through them, to the Orient of hoary antiquity.

BARBARIAN WISDOM, ALIEN WISDOM

The rise of pan-Hellenic nationalism in educated circles coincides—paradoxically, it seems at first—with a surge of interest in
the East as a source of primordial wisdom.[152] Thanks in part to
its nod to Judaism and its reception among the church fathers,[153]
Numenius's fragment from his dialogue *On the Good* remains the
most memorable example: "With respect to this, the one speaking
and providing an interpretation about something will go beyond
the Platonic tradition and fuse it (ἀναχωρήσασθαι καὶ συνδήσασθαι)
with the sayings of Pythagoras. Then, he must appeal to the jus-
tifiably famous nations, addressing their rituals, doctrines, and
accomplishments, insofar as Brahmins, Jews, Magi, and Egyptians
are in accord with one another, but only to the extent that they
agree with Plato (συντελουμένας Πλάτωνι ὁμολογουμένως ὁπόσας
Βραχμᾶνες καὶ Ἰουδαῖοι καὶ Μάγοι καὶ Αἰγύπτιοι διέθεντο)."[154] This
passage has often been invoked in the context of Gnosticism, a
movement that seems to meld some kind of Greek philosophical
learning with Oriental revelation (to say nothing of dualism). The
relevance of this problem for the social context of the Platonizing Sethian literature is obvious: the Sethian apocalypses bear the
names of ancient Eastern sages. They discuss Greek metaphysics,
but cite no Greeks, notably omitting Plato, to whom their debt
is clear. Modern interpreters have therefore explained the Gnostic reliance on extra-Platonic sources, as reported in Neoplatonic
testimonia, with recourse to the Antonine-Severan philosophical
appeal to alien wisdom made famous here by Numenius.[155] Conversely, some argue that Numenius himself was in the thrall of "*la
gnose orientale*."[156]

Alien wisdom *was* an issue, but *not* as formulated by Numenius. First, in much of the literature of the Second Sophistic and second-to-fourth-century Platonism, alien (or barbarian) wisdom is invoked in order to be subjugated by Hellenic παιδεία.[157] Second, the period also witnesses the rise of what I will refer to as "auto-Orientalizing" texts that contain Platonic teaching under the guise of an Eastern provenance. Together with a more general fetishization of Eastern wisdom that we find in Plato and Plutarch, we thus glimpse a diversity of "Platonic Orientalisms," which evoke, distance, and assimilate a manufactured image of Eastern learning in order to stake out a position on the Hellenic identity that was so important for the context of philosophizing in the Roman Empire.

This turn to the East as a source of wisdom in Greek philosophy is commonly chalked up by historians of Roman religion to the infusion of new Oriental cults (of Serapis, Isis, Attis, and Cybele, etc.) into Roman religion;[158] the result, a quasi-philosophical cultic "syncretism."[159] However, while these cults certainly were of great interest to those in educated circles and provided new points of reference in religious life, the Oriental cults are a red herring in the search for the significance of alien wisdom.[160] Rather, the reach to the Eastern civilizations as a source of wisdom is as old as Greek literature itself. By the first century CE, the idea of "the ancients" became bound to the idea that the Stoic λόγος (rational principle), and all the knowledge concomitant with it, is to some extent incarnate in all things.[161] Plutarch fully articulated this view (regarding divine providence): "Wherefore this very ancient opinion (παμπάλαιος) comes down from writers on religion and from lawgivers to poets and philosophers; it can be traced to no source, but it carried a strong and almost indelible conviction, and is in circulation in many places among barbarians and Greeks alike, not only in story and tradition, but also in rites and sacrifices."[162] Beyond the ethnographer's natural interest in the exotic, these texts display an appreciation for the pedigree of Eastern civilizations; by virtue of their age, they must know *something*.[163] Moreover, this single knowledge is consonant with that of the Greeks but expressed in variable myths and rites, humanity's understanding of which is fading.[164]

With the turn of the second century, however, one begins to glimpse the subordination of this discourse about alien wisdom to the primacy of Plato and Pythagoras.[165] At first glance, this subordination is masked by interest in discussing barbarian wisdom. The trope of scholarly pilgrimages to the Orient to obtain scientific and ritual knowledge is a fixture of the period's literature. Diogenes Laertius relates that Thales spent time in Egypt with the priests and measured the pyramids.[166] Pythagoras reportedly studied with "Zaratas" (Zoroaster),[167] explored Egypt,[168] and is assigned many travels by Apuleius.[169] Porphyry has him study with the Phoenicians and Hebrews.[170] Plato himself reportedly traveled to Egypt and wished to visit Persia and India.[171] In Philostratus, the Theban Dionysius travels to India, and Protagoras is said to have studied with the Persian magi during Xerxes' invasion of Greece.[172] A great deal of the *Life of Apollonius* is occupied with philosophical pilgrimages to Babylon, India, and Egypt.[173] Finally, Plotinus, too, tried to go to India—the only evidence of his interest in learning east of Egypt, hardly indicative of a debt to Indian thought.[174]

The study-sabbatical abroad was recommended by Hellenists in the early empire for two reasons.[175] One is the presumption, based on Posidonius's *logos* theology, that there exists a universal religion whose origin is prior to all contemporary civilization and whose evidence can be found among other, elder cultures.[176] For Dio Chrysostom, as for Plutarch, God's existence and benign rule is "a conception of him common to the whole human race, to the Greeks and to the barbarians alike, a conception that is inevitable and innate in every creature endowed with reason."[177] Lucian agrees that worship of the gods is universal, but adds that it originated among the Egyptians.[178] We see a somewhat different principle, however, in Pseudo-Apollonius and Philostratus. Hellenism is necessarily cosmopolitan and therefore often found outside the geographical confines of Hellas itself, sometimes in a purer state.[179] The question, then, is whether the universal religion is identified with Hellenism (as in Philostratus) or beyond it (with Plutarch et al.)

At the same time, second-century CE Greek philosophical literature remains deeply ambivalent about its relationship with Eastern teaching. In his *Borysthentica*, Dio Chrysostom details a myth composed by Zoroaster and preserved by the Magi both in song and "secret rites" (ἐν ἀπορρήτοις τελεταῖς), but also distances himself from the tale, on ethnic grounds;[180] presumably, he relates the story to tantalize the barbarian (yet Hellenophile) Borysthenians.[181] Meanwhile, Diogenes Laertius introduces his doxography by rejecting barbarian claims to archaic wisdom, even asserting that the first civilization was *Greek* civilization.[182] While the Chaldeans, druids, Indians, and

Persians were all innovators in astronomy, allegory, and ritual worship, he says, the first to actually worship the gods were primordial Greek ancestors, Musaeus and Linius. Philosophy began with Anaximander and Pythagoras; "thus it was from the Greeks that philosophy took its rise; its very name refused to be translated into barbarian speech."[183]

Similar ambivalence is found in second-century Platonists—even Numenius, who as quoted above (fragment 1a) asserts that the wisdom of the barbarian nations is consonant with that of the Greeks.[184] Some have asked if he particularly esteemed Judaism, or was even a Jew;[185] after all, Numenius knew some Hebrew scripture, and probably read Philo.[186] Yet only a superficial knowledge of Judaism is evident here. His supposed quotation of Ex 3:14—that God is ὁ μέν γε ὤν ("he who is")—has been widely taken as evidence of deep interest in Judaism, but is textually problematic.[187] However, Numenius elsewhere identifies Moses with "Musaeus," Orpheus's heir and founder of the Greek religion itself.[188] Fragment 1a (quoted at the beginning of this section), meanwhile, emphasizes that the nations should only be consulted *after* the Platonists and Pythagoreans, and then only insofar as they agree with Plato.[189] Most of Numenius's extant fragments explicitly cite Hellenic authorities: Homer, Hesiod, the Orphic texts, Pherecydes, Parmenides, and the Eleusinian mysteries, and it is by the standard of these authorities that he judges other sources of wisdom.[190]

Celsus, too, invokes "an ancient doctrine which has existed from the beginning" among the barbarians but not the Jews.[191] Yet Celsus does not explicitly set the philosophy of the Greeks *over* that of the alien nations, instead excluding Christianity and Judaism from "barbarian philosophy." It is worth noting, however, that Celsus compares Christian faith to the credulity of charlatans from the Orient, and that when he refers to "ancient traditions" (πάλαι δεδογμένα) as the foundation of his teaching, he provides a summary of Plato.[192]

A similar range of views are in third-century sophistic and Platonic texts. Philostratus leaves open the possibility that Greeks can learn from other peoples, but never is Greek wisdom upstaged or altered, while the scope of interests of comparison remains firmly in the realm of Hellenic thought.[193] Pythagoras and the Egyptians obtained the doctrine of the transmigration of souls from India;[194] Egypt, India, and Pythagoras are all in agreement in the polemic against blood sacrifice.[195] Notably, Palestine is mentioned only to be disparaged.[196] Philostratus also makes explicitly negative references to barbarian wise men, mentioning Egyptian and Chaldean frauds who took advantage of the need for religious comfort after earthquakes west of the Hellespont.[197] With his subject charged with being a sorcerer (μάγος) on account of the pilgrimages to Persian and Egyptian *magi* (μάγοι), Philostratus claims, as did Diogenes Laertius, that Empedocles, Pythagoras, and Plato all learned from the Orientals without becoming μάγοι themselves.[198]

Porphyry's position on the Greek tradition in the context of ancient wisdom (παλαιὰ σοφία) is complex and at times appears contradictory. Some scholars focus on his derogatory comments about the Greeks as a relatively young and ineffectual culture in the face of ancient wisdom.[199] In *On the Cave of the Nymphs*, he traces the use of caves as the first temples back to the consecration of Zoroaster, recalls Numenius's citation of Gen 1:2, and discusses Egyptian symbolism.[200] Just as Porphyry sometimes refers to Jesus positively as one of many representatives of the "ancient wisdom," he includes the Jews in the ranks of barbarian races that have tapped into universal truths.[201] Indeed, he appears to have sought a *via universalis*.[202] At other times, however, he suggests that the philosopher (assuming already the adoption of vegetarianism) ought to adhere to the cultic path of his or her native land,[203] thus emphasizing the distinctive character of his own background—Greek thought.[204] His *Life of Plotinus* provides a clue as to how to resolve these attitudes: the student Eustochius is said to have acquired "the character of a true philosopher by his exclusive adherence to the school of Plotinus."[205] Throughout his career, Porphyry is adamant about asserting the authority of the Platonic-Pythagorean tradition, particularly as manifest in the teaching of Plotinus. Like Numenius, he esteems barbarian wisdom but subjugates it, in the service of his own Greek tradition.

Iamblichus's attitude toward barbarian wisdom is even more ambivalent. In *On the Pythagorean Life*, he asserts that Pythagoras obtained knowledge of geometry and astrology from Egypt, numbers from Phoenicia, and astrology from Chaldea, yet the sage's trademark numerical theology is Orphic.[206] Iamblichus demarcates Greek and barbarian in the same breath as humans and animals, philosophers and the common rabble.[207] Disagreeing with Porphyry in his *Timaeus* commentary, he accuses his doctrines of being "alien to the spirit of Plato" or simply "barbarous."[208] On the other hand, in his commentary on Aristotle's *De anima*, he repeatedly sets the opinion of "all the ancients" (ἀρχαῖοι πάντες) against Pythagoras, Plato, and Aristotle, or simply "Platonists and Pythagoreans." Sometimes they agree, sometimes not, as when the "ancients" affirm that the souls of the pure are spared judgment, because they are pure already, while "the Platonists and Pythagoreans do not agree with the ancients on this matter, but subject all souls to judgment."[209] Writing in *De mysteriis* under the guise of an Egyptian priest, "Abammon," he prioritizes "Assyrian" and ancient Egyptian wisdom as the sources of Pythagoras and Plato.[210] In the same work, he invokes the *Dekadenztheorie* that we have already observed in Plutarch: primordial wisdom is being forgotten, and who better to remind the Hellenes of its contents than an Egyptian priest?[211] Yet one can also read this fetishization of Oriental wisdom as typical Hellenism, rather than a departure from Hellenism.[212]

The incongruency between these attitudes, noted but not resolved by commentators, is difficult to explain.[213] Iamblichus could have simply changed his mind over the course of his life, affirming Hellenism at some times more strongly than others. Unverifiable, this thesis also suffers from the impossibility of determining a chronology of his corpus.[214] Second, he may have chosen his rhetoric according to polemical context; if the *Vita* of Pythagoras is an anti-Christian work, as some have suggested, perhaps Iamblichus amplified the Hellenic tone accordingly.[215] With Porphyry, on the other hand, he would have required a different approach: to assume the pose of an Egyptian priest (*Mysteries*) or tar his opponent with the brush of barbarism (*Timaeus Commentary*). Third, like many innovators, Iamblichus commonly delights in "condemning his predecessors"; his identification with the "ancients" of the East may be less ideological than simply rhetorical convenience.[216]

After a review of this evidence, it seems clear that, under the early Roman Empire, classical clichés about universal learning and cultic practices of hoary, Eastern provenance underwent a dual change: intensification (hence increased frequency in the sources) but also reconsideration. With "ancient wisdom" universally present and accessible, the Greeks—identified with Plato, and especially his Pythagorean and Orphic sources—became, for some, first among equals. Dio Chrysostom's coy invocation of the "barbarous" Zoroastrian myth to communicate typical Stoic cosmology anticipates this development, and Diogenes defends the Greek origins of learning more zealously than any other pre-Julianic thinker. Yet the most consistent approach, mediating the doctrine of alien wisdom and the Greek tradition as the best manifestation of it, is somewhat later and mostly Platonic: Numenius, Philostratus, and Porphyry.

This shift away from the classical universalism of Plutarch (and Plato) coincides, not surprisingly, with the Second Sophistic and its celebration of Hellenic identity in παιδεία and civic cult. A second context, crucial for the more philosophically inclined sources discussed here, is the rapid growth of the Neopythagorean movement and the identification of Platonists with it.[217] "Plato pythagorizes" became a new cliché.[218] Numenius argues that Plato and Socrates were both actually Pythagoreans.[219] Pythagoras became a Hellenic culture hero by which the Greeks both engaged and subdued barbarian wisdom.[220] Third, the period witnesses the adoption of Orpheus, a barbarian by virtue of his Thracian heritage, as a Greek.[221] In earlier catalogues of sages, he is simply one of the ancient theologians of the barbarians;[222] but Diogenes claims Orpheus for the Greeks, Plotinus begins his anti-Gnostic work, the so-called *Großschrift*, with an allegorical reading of an Orphic cosmogony, Porphyry identifies Greek learning with Orphic hymns, and Iamblichus simply sets Pythagoras in the Orphic tradition.[223] By the time we arrive at Proclus, a Thracian is the Greek theologian par excellence.[224]

ALIEN PLATONISTS (AUTO-ORIENTALISM)

Other Platonists rallied instead to the Chaldeans and Egyptians: Julianus the Theurgist and Hermes Trismegistus. The Middle Platonic, Greek hexameters known as the *Chaldean Oracles* were reportedly produced by one "Julian the Chaldean" or his son, "Julian the theurgist," or both. Next to nothing else is known about them, and, despite, their association with the East, there is nothing in the *Oracles* that need be identified outside the realm of imperial Platonism.[225] Its doctrines of a transcendent first principle, a feminine World-Soul, ascetic ethic, and emphasis on soteriology and ritual are all at home in Middle Platonism, probably belonging to the second century CE.[226] Only Greco-Roman deities such as Zeus or Hecate are mentioned in the text, and the collection did not become known by its modern title—"Chaldaean Oracles *of Zoroaster*"—until the fourteenth century.[227] The "Chaldaean" origin of these verses is a facade used to layer an exotic veneer over

Greek philosophy in Greek verse, but its Oriental pose was precious to its readers—the Neoplatonists, beginning with Porphyry—and, clearly, its author(s).

The *Corpus Hermeticum*, a collection of Greek dialogues belonging to the larger body of philosophical dialogues ("Hermetica") starring the ancient demigod Hermes Trismegistus, presents a more complicated case, due to disputed provenance and the internal diversity (and thus dogmatic inconsistency) of its contents.[228] Accordingly, the Hermetica present dissonant views on Hellenism and alien philosophy, sometimes seeing learning and language as universal,[229] but also belittling the wisdom of the Hellenes and their puny attempts to render Egyptian wisdom in the Greek tongue.[230] As with the *Oracles*, however, the setting of the texts themselves—conversations between a decidedly Egyptian sage and other demigods—demonstrates that the texts seek to set themselves apart from contemporary Hellenophilia, even as they discuss Hellenic ideas. The pose was a success, and the Hermetica received a warm welcome among both Hellenic Platonists and Christian theologians.[231]

It is no surprise, then, that the "Orientomaniac" pseudepigraphy, as I shall call it, of the *Chaldean Oracles* and the *Corpus Hermeticum* has been contextualized in the Numenian milieu of Middle Platonism that reaches to the Orient for authority.[232] Yet, as discussed above, Numenius and others actually cite alien authorities in order to subordinate them to the Platonic and Pythagorean traditions. Still other thinkers, like Plutarch, instead saw ancient wisdom as manifest in the teaching and ritual of all nations.[233] The *Oracles* and Hermetic literature represent a third approach, which capitalizes on the prestige of ancient Oriental teaching to authorize a discourse composed in the Greek language about contemporary Greek metaphysics, by simply ignoring Hellas's claim to authority.[234] Some treatises among the Hermetica go further, and seem to actively rebel against Hellenic predominance by proclaiming the antiquity and superiority of alien speech and alien wisdom.

Each of these ways of negotiating the relationship between Greek philosophy and the traditions of older, Eastern cultures is a form of what James Walbridge calls "Platonic Orientalism," the respect of Platonists for the authority of the wisdom of the East.[235] The term retains much of the sense of Edward Said's concept of "Orientalism," as an idea that does the work of defining the self (i.e., "the West") through the creation of and reflection on an "other," here a distillation of the

manifold civilizations east of Greece and Rome (Numenius's "justi-
fiably famous nations") to a set of teachings and rites whose actual
relationship to any "Orient" is negligible.[236] As argued above, the
interest in the Orient as a primeval source of wisdom was nothing
new in the second to fourth centuries CE. "Platonic Orientalism" simply describes the popularity of this interest among the Platonic thinkers of the time in conducting what Chapter 4 terms "ethnic reasoning," the negotiation of their identities in decidedly ethnic terms, here
in the context of Greek higher education.

Weighing their knowledge of the Orient against this Platonic tradition, thinkers reached diverse conclusions about which authorities to
prize, and articulated their choice in the language of Hellenic identity
developed during the Second Sophistic. Plutarch, on the cusp of this
movement, eschews the language of παιδεία when talking about Egyptian mythology; Dio Chrysostom and Celsus engage the "barbarian
wisdom" of the Orient while distancing themselves from it; Numenius, Diogenes Laertius, Philostratus, and Porphyry, all deeply invested
in the language of Hellenism, take care to defend the priority of its
canon over the Orient. "Julianus" and "Hermes," finally, ignore the
Greeks altogether, attempting to validate themselves by auto-Orientalizing. A champion of both the *Oracles* and Hermetica, Iamblichus
auto-Orientalized within the context of discussing Greek philosophy,
identifying his views on psychology and the afterlife as those of "the
ancients" (as in *De anima*), or posing as an Egyptian ritual expert
(in *De mysteriis*) with the same authority as the masters of Plato and
Pythagoras. We might, then, ask which of this diversity of positions
on the relationship between Oriental and Hellenic wisdom we see
articulated by Plotinus—and which by his Gnostics.

CONCLUSION: A "THICK DESCRIPTION" OF PLOTINUS'S GNOSTICS AND THEIR TEXTS

The first of the "revelations" Porphyry mentions as read by the Christian Gnostics was purportedly authored by the famous Persian sage
Zoroaster. We cannot know the contents of his "apocalypse," but
the pseudepigraphic currency of the name "Zoroaster" was strong
indeed, even in Jewish and Christian circles.[237] The founder of the Persian cult was at times equated with Nimrod, apocalyptic seers such as
Baruch, Jeremias, and Balaam, and even Seth himself.[238] Porphyry's
remarks—this Zoroaster was "spurious and contemporary"—show

that the pseudepigraphic identification of authority with sources both remote and antique was, to Plotinus's group, offensive, deceptive, and futile.[239]

The other four figures are associated with extant Sethian apocalypses from Nag Hammadi, and with the world of intertestamental Judaism. "Zostrianos" was known to the Greeks as the grandfather of Zoroaster.[240] While the narrative pericope of the Nag Hammadi text *Zostrianos* (NHC VIII,1) seems to describe the eponymous sage as growing up in a community of Greeks and renouncing his paternity for another race—the "seed of Seth"—he must have been associated, by virtue of his famous grandson, with Armenia and Persia.[241] An *Apocalypse of Nicotheus* per se is not extant, but the name of the eponymous prophet is associated (in the *Untitled Treatise* found in the Bruce Codex) with the name Marsanes, which does adorn a Sethian apocalypse extant in Coptic (NHC X,1). Whether this treatise was present at Plotinus's circle is uncertain, although the copy we know from Nag Hammadi shows signs of thought from the fourth century CE.[242] The characters of both Nicotheus and Marsanes are present in the *Untitled Treatise*, exhibiting "powers" through which they achieve visions of the "only-begotten Son" of the Father that impress even the local angelic beings in heaven.[243] The figure of Nicotheus possessed considerable pedigree in the world of the Jewish apocalypses; according to Mani, he was in the same league as S(h)em, Enosh, and Enoch.[244] "Hidden" and "unable to be found," he was also associated by the fourth-century alchemist Zosimus of Panopolis with Zoroaster, Hermes, and others, as a mediator of knowledge about the celestial Adam.[245] "Marsanios" (certainly another form of the name "Marsanes") was known to Epiphanius as an Archontic (Gnostic) prophet who was "snatched up into heaven for three days."[246] Unlike that of Nicotheus, it is possible that his name is Semitic.[247] Both figures thus recall contemporary Jewish traditions of rapt antediluvian seers.[248]

A Jewish background is also indicated for the treatises assigned to Allogenes and Messos. "Allogenes" is a common Hellenistic Jewish word for a "stranger" or "alien or foreigner," for Seth, and apparently a common title for texts circulated by the fourth-century Gnostics known as the Archontics.[249] As Epiphanius writes, "(the Archontics) have also portrayed certain books, some written in the name of Seth and others written in the name of Seth and his seven sons, as having been given by him. For they say that he bore seven <sons>, called 'foreigners'—as we noted in the case of other schools of thought, viz. gnostics and Sethi-ans."[250] It is impossible to say whether the treatises he mentioned are related to the *Apocalypse of Allogenes* known to Porphyry.[251]

"Messos" is a name extant elsewhere only in the Sethian apoca-lypse from Nag Hammadi entitled *Allogenes* (NHC XI,3), appearing when the eponymous protagonist addresses the reader as "Messos, my son."[252] There is no extant work entitled "Messos," but the pos-sibility of an existence of one in Plotinus's circle cannot be ruled out.

For Porphyry, then, the source of the controversy between Plotinus and the local Christian "Gnostics" was the problem of how to weigh the authority of Plato against those of Jewish antediluvian sages and the apocalypses that bore their names. On the one hand, the adher-ents of Aculinus and others were educated interpreters of Plato. On the other hand, they thought that Plato was simply one of many teach-ers, some of whom were more ancient, geographically remote (i.e., Oriental), and hence more authoritative. Each of these teachers was associated with Judaism and Christianity, and, in several cases—Zos-trianos, Allogenes, and Nicotheus—with extant, Platonizing Sethian apocalypses from Nag Hammadi.[253]

What this data shows is that the invocation of foreign, alien revelations in a group like Plotinus's was sure to raise a few eye-brows, if not start a firestorm. Philosophers and sophists of the period, and it appears Gnostic thinkers as well, were male elites from wealthy backgrounds deeply invested in the prevailing socio-economic order. Public participation in political affairs and obser-vance of the civic cult were expected. Yet the framing, common to scholarship, of Gnostic mythos as inspired by (usually Jewish) revolt against the Romans clashes with the privileged social context that highly educated Gnostics moved in.[254] Rather, Gnostic myth recognizes and inverts the hierarchy that nurtured such privileged groups;[255] this inversion took place alongside the parallel develop-ment, within Sophistic and Platonic circles, of different ways of conceiving the Orient as a source of primordial wisdom—Platonic Orientalism. Many Orientalizing authors simultaneously fetishize and subordinate the status of Eastern sources to the authority of Plato and Pythagoras. Yet select groups, including Gnostics, pre-ferred to "auto-Orientalize," conjuring a visage of the East around their thought in order to differentiate themselves from, and even polemicize and rebel against, the Hellenophile environment of the Second Sophistic.[256] The Gnostics with their apocalypses voiced this

latter perspective, appearing hostile to Hellenism. Viewed against
the backdrop of skirmishes over the value of Oriental authorities in
the context of Greek thought, we see that Porphyry understood the
Christian Gnostics to be firing shots in what would become a culture war.

CHAPTER 2

Plotinus Against
His Gnostic Friends

The testimony of Porphyry about the heretics known to him and Plotinus is a fascinating and rich account of their encounter with living, breathing readers of Sethian apocalypses. He says that this literature circulated among Christian Platonists, who invoked alien, non-Hellenic authorities popular in Jewish lore (like "Allogenes"— "the stranger-foreigner") and challenged the authority of Plato and, by extension, the vigorous Hellenic cult(ure) of *paideia*. Both he and Amelius wrote treatises attacking these apocalypses. Plotinus wrote his own work responding to the heretics. Porphyry, editing his master's work following his death, entitled it *Against the Gnostics*; hence we consider these heretics to have been Gnostics themselves—certainly they were understood as such by Porphyry, and as will become clear, they subscribed to the myth of the fall of Sophia and her production of a faulty creator-god, to whom we can assign responsibility for the ills of the world we inhabit. He thus also assigned the work the alternative title, *Against Those Who Say That the Universe and Its Maker Are Evil.*[1] When we recall data culled from philosophical and sophistic sources about the sociopolitical environment of elite education, Porphyry's remarks thus allow the closest look we can get at a particular group of Gnostics, and the sort of cultural seas they must have navigated in order to arrive at a circle like that of Plotinus. Yet while Porphyry's testimony tells us a great deal about their background and the radical nature of their invocation of alien, oriental authorities in the context of Hellenism, it tells us little about the other doctrines to which these

Gnostics—and their apocalypses—subscribed. Indeed, Porphyry says nothing about the content of the Sethian works other than their pseudepigraphic claims to ancient, alien authority.

Here we must turn to Plotinus and the Sethian texts themselves. It is worth pausing to review Plotinus's polemic before proceeding to read it against the Sethian literature and other contemporary Platonic literature. The treatise—his thirty-third composition and the ninth tractate in the second partition of his collected works, arranged by Porphyry as six groups of nine (hence their title: the *Enneads*, Gk. "nines")—is famously technical and difficult, and comprehensive scholarly treatments of it are specialized and uncommon. Yet it is also difficult to read in isolation, being the last segment of the so-called *Großschrift*, a hypothetical "long treatise" cut into four pieces by Porphyry to fit his enneadic schema of Plotinus's corpus.[2] Even beyond the Großschrift, the entire Plotinian corpus could be seen as a witness to Plotinus's encounter with Gnosticism, and some have thus cast his thought in toto along the lines of their interpretation of this encounter.[3] In the interests of practicality, this chapter will focus only on *Ennead* 2.9 in particular as Plotinus's singular address to his Gnostic interlocutors, while referring when necessary to the rest of the *Enneads* and especially the Großschrift. Even this relatively restricted analysis, however, shows that he was not only concerned with his opponents' constructions of cultic identity and revelatory authority but also with very specific ideas they had about cosmology, soteriology, and eschatology. In each case, he holds, their philosophy breaks up the unity of the cosmos, introducing separation and alienation where he sees only continuity, a practice culminating, appropriately, in their own alienation from their fellow humanity and the (Hellenic) traditions that inspire them.

AGAINST THE GNOSTIC COSMOS

Unfortunately, Plotinus's discussion of Gnostic thought often seems to hide more than it reveals. He usually states a conclusion his opponents have reached and his (angry) response to it, without stating what arguments motivate both sides; the reader, hoping for a more full picture, must then sketch in various complex philosophical arguments between the lines. Nowhere is this more so than in the first ten chapters of *Ennead* 2.9, which plunge the reader into the middle of a series of polemics on seemingly unrelated topics: the number of divine intellects, the eternity of produced matter, the decline of the (World)-Soul, and the story of the Soul's creation of the cosmos.[4] However, each of these issues circulates around the problem of the creative activity of the undescended Soul—the entity mediating the divine Intellect and the physical cosmos, of which the individual soul, mediating a person's intellect and physical body, is a microcosm—with respect to time and narrative, the eternity of the world, and the character of its author.

This is not easy to see, because when Plotinus talks about the problem of creation, he phrases it in his own characteristic terms as the problem of the Soul's ability to create a good world, which for him is intrinsically bound with its character as an inhabitant of heaven along with divine Intellect. The Gnostics, he says, describe a "Soul" whose creation is bad because of a "descent" into matter, thus tainting its creative activity. Yet it is difficult to tell which characters in the Gnostic cosmogonic drama he is speaking about. Sometimes, he specifies arguments commonly made by Hellenistic thinkers to criticize the anthropomorphism of the demiurge's portrait in Plato's *Timaeus*, so he has none other in mind than the ambivalent, faulty demiurge of Gnostic myth, who crafts a deficient, even evil cosmos. Yet at other times he refers to the "decline" of the Gnostic "Soul," apparently meaning the story of the fall of Sophia, the mother of the demiurge. As we will see, he even (quite possibly in bad faith) accuses his opponents of conflating these characters in just this confusing way.

It is worth pausing here to briefly recount a classic variant of this story, presented in a particularly famous (and Sethianized) text known as the *Apocryphon of John*.[5] The story begins with a description of the transcendent first principle, the "Father," or "Invisible Spirit." Gazing into himself in the primordial water, his thought produces a divine Mother, the "Barbelo," the second, generative, principle from which the rest of reality is born.[6] With the "consent" of the Father, the Barbelo produces two quintets of aeons (Gk. "eternities"). (Here, as often in Gnostic literature, the divisions of salvation history into periods, or "aeons," is reflected in the atemporal celestial topography, where aeons seem to be beings or places that emanate from God as the eternal paradigm of the drama that plays out on earth as its reflection.)[7] Finally, the Father and Barbelo produce another principle, their Son, the Autogenes ("self-begotten"), an image of its parent. The Invisible Spirit anoints him and grants him authority. The Autogenes produces the Four Luminaries common to Sethian lore (Harmozel, Oroiael, Davithai, and Eleleth), who in turn produce twelve aeons, one of which is Sophia ("wisdom").

Sophia desires to imitate the beings from which she has sprung—she desires to produce—but, unlike the Barbelo, does so without the "consent" of the Father. Her creation is thus the misshapen, blind god Yaldabaoth, who with his angels creates the material universe and then mankind, beginning with Adam and Eve. Poor Sophia, meanwhile, repents. In order to recover the creative power that Yaldabaoth has stolen from her, she is able with the help of the superior powers to trick her son into passing this power into Adam. This spark of divinity is passed on to Adam and Eve's third son, Seth, from whom Gnostic humanity is descended—aliens to the world of Yaldabaoth, but akin to their Father, the Invisible Spirit, itself alien to the planet they inhabit. Yet the elect have forgotten their divine identity because of Yaldabaoth's minions, who torment them, exploiting the weakness and ignorance that accompany corporeal existence. Thankfully, a savior descends to humanity to preach the origins of man and the cosmos, expose Yaldabaoth and his powers as false gods, and thereby lend human beings knowledge of its source, the hitherto unknown, alien God. This knowledge is tantamount to salvation.

At first sight, it is then puzzling that Plotinus begins his response to this myth (and those who adhere to it) by ridiculing the doctrine of dual intellects (one unparticipatory, one participatory), one of Numenius's odder ideas, not extant in any Gnostic text.[8] His reason can only be that he wishes to emphasize the coherence of the three hypostases of his metaphysical system: One, Intellect, and Soul.[9] For Plotinus, the cosmic Soul, as a direct image of the Intellect, has direct access to it and dwells with it in the heavens; in turn, the various human, animal, and vegetative souls here on earth (which together compose the hypostasis of cosmic Soul) are in direct touch with their intellects (which together compose the hypostasis of celestial Intellect). He sees the possibility of there being two or more intellects in the metaphysical world as an unnecessary introduction of intermediaries between members of this triad of hypostases, which will lead to an infinite and absurd production of intelligible entities, or worse a decline of one of the hypostases.[10] Thus, the proliferation of a multitude of divine entities (familiar to even the casual reader of Gnostic texts) disturbs the hierarchy of intelligible beings and could even lead to the mistaken notion that the soul descends.

His same concern with the maintenance of the intelligible hierarchy and the undescended Soul motivates his next topic, the eternity of illuminated matter. In an especially dense passage, he argues that:

> If anyone says that it will be dissolved into matter, why should he not also say that matter will be dissolved? But if he is going to say that, what necessity was there, we shall reply, for it to come into being? But if they are going to assert that it was necessary for it to come into being as a consequence of the existence of higher principles, the necessity is there now as well. But if matter is going to remain alone, the divine principles will not be everywhere but in a particular limited place; they will be, so to speak, walled off from matter; but if this is impossible, matter will be illuminated by them.[11]

The context of this somewhat oblique argument is the proper order of derivation of the various strata of existence, and their eternity. The position that Plotinus defends at the end of the passage is the eternal generation, existence, and illumination (by Soul) of matter and its eternal, unchanging illumination by Soul.[12]

Like the discussion of dual intellect, the insertion of this difficult problem seems tangential but is in fact relevant, because it addresses the eternal creative activity of Soul and thus the production of a good, eternal world. For Plotinus, the nature of Soul is to create,[13] so it eternally generates and illuminates matter; yet matter is an absence of being and thus of goodness and reality.[14] Why would Soul (or, by extension, a demiurge), which is good, produce and illuminate something that is bad? The Gnostics argue, he says, that the badness of the created object must imply some lapse of judgment on the part of the creator. Plotinus proposes instead that the Soul's production of something unequivocally bad nonetheless must have been in this case a positive thing; because the Soul, undescended, eternally illuminates matter and thus bestows good on it without being part of it, Plotinus can assert the positive nature of the inhabited world and the eternal nature of this goodness while acknowledging the badness of matter, instead of ascribing badness to both its creator and what is created from it.[15]

Keeping in mind Plotinus's attention to preserving the undescended nature of the Soul in these opening chapters, his turn in chapter 4 to the topic of the Soul, its fall, and its demiurgic function is not so much jarring as it is tardy.[16] "If," he asks, "they (i.e., my Gnostic opponents) are going to say that it (the Soul) simply failed (σφαλεῖσαν), let

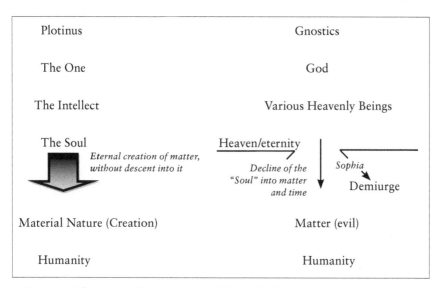

Figure 1. Plotinus on Neoplatonic and Gnostic Creation

them tell us the cause of the failure (σφάλματος . . . τὴν αἰτίαν)."[17] Plotinus is determined to show that the creation and its creator are good, not an error or "failure" or fall from heaven; or in his parlance that "Soul is not a declination (νεῦσιν), but rather a non-declination."[18] He thus sets up a series of *reductiones ad absurdum*: a decline took place either in time or outside time; neither is possible.[19] If Soul declined, it must have forgotten the intelligibles; but then it wouldn't be a demiurge anymore, since Plato says in his *Timaeus* the demiurge creates with reference to the intelligible forms.[20] If it does remember, then it does not decline. (See Figure 1 for a visual illustration of these ideas.)

Plotinus shifts gears, beginning to mock his opponents' anthropomorphic view of the creator, assserting that the demiurge did not create "in order to be honored" (ἵνα τιμῷτο).[21] More specifically, the demiurge did not create "through discursive (i.e., temporal, language-based) reasoning (διανοία)." He continues, asking, "when is he (the creator) going to destroy it (the cosmos)? For if he was sorry he had made it, what is he waiting for?"[22] As is well known, Plotinus here attacks his opponents along established lines of later Platonic defense of the *Timaeus* from Epicurean and Skeptic critics, who mocked the dialogue's account on the grounds of its crude anthropomorphism.[23] Middle Platonists responded by simply ceasing to read it literally.[24] Plotinus goes further in arguing that creative activity (ποίησις) occurs through the faculty of contemplation (θεωρία), not temporal, discursive reasoning (διανοία), which yields hesitation and, ultimately, all too human error.[25] Here, then, the Gnostic view of the demiurge closely coheres with the caricature of the *Timaeus* sketched by Hellenistic foes of Plato. However, just as with the problem of the generation of matter, Plotinus is perturbed by the problem of creation and destruction of the world in time and its implications for the character of the demiurge: why would he destroy the world unless he regretted making it, and what kind of creator is that?[26] Moreover, if the world was created in time, then it must have been planned with temporal, discursive reasoning, which, as we have already seen, Plotinus found unacceptable.[27]

The same criticisms of the Gnostic conception of the demiurge lie behind his ongoing polemic about the Soul's creative activity. He repeats many of the same points: the Gnostics do not understand (οὐ συνέντες) *Timaeus* 39b and thus falsify (καταψεύδονται) Plato's account of cosmogony.[28] The Gnostics, he continues, confuse the identity of the maker: sometimes it is the Soul, sometimes the discursive (διανοούμενον) Intellect, again perhaps exploiting the ambiguity between the characters of the demiurge and Sophia when they are conflated as the creative, Plotinian Soul.[29] Censuring the director of the world, he says, they identify it with the Soul, and so attribute to it the passions of incarnate souls.[30] Similar critiques are levied in chapter 8: by asking why the creation happened at all, the Gnostics misunderstand the essence of Soul itself, that is, creation via contemplation (θεωρία).[31] This misunderstanding, again, stems from the confused presupposition that the world is not eternal.[32]

Plotinus's objections—and his willingness to exploit the confusion between the characters in the Gnostic drama—are most clear in his summary of the Gnostic narrative of the "decline" of the Soul. He calls this doctrine "that one point which surpasses all the rest of their doctrine in absurdity (ἀτοπία)" (10.19–35): "For they say that Soul declined to what was below it, and with it some sort of 'Wisdom' (Gk. 'Sophia'), whether Soul started it or whether Wisdom was a cause of Soul being like this, or whether they mean both to be the same thing, and then they tell us that the other souls came down too, and as members of Wisdom put on bodies, human bodies for instance."[33] Next, Plotinus describes a different version of the Gnostic fall of Sophia, probably quoting from a version of *Zostrianos*:[34]

But again they say that very being for the sake of which these souls came down did not come down itself, did not decline, so to put it, but only illuminated the darkness, and so a reflection (εἴδωλον) from it came into existence in matter. Then they fabricate an image of the image (εἰδώλου εἴδωλον πλάσαντες) somewhere here below, through matter or materiality or whatever they like to call it—they use now one name and now another, and say many other names just to make their meaning obscure—and produce what they call the Maker, and make him revolt from his mother and drag the universe which proceeds from him down to the ultimate limit of reflections (ἐπ᾽ ἔσχατα εἰδώλων). The man who wrote this just meant to be blasphemous![35]

Plotinus counters both versions. With reference to the first, he simply disagrees that the Soul descended;[36] instead, it stays above.[37] *Without* a descent, then, Soul creates the world, and, with souls, enters it. This entrance is described variously in the *Enneads*; in one early treatise, it is a "self-willed gliding downward" that is freely made but also necessary, since the world's body must be inhabited by a soul (Plat. *Tim.* 34b8).[38] But, he emphasizes, this is not a "descent to the below and away from contemplation," although it does have a sense of "audacity" (τόλμα).[39]

The second version—that Soul did not decline but illuminated the darkness—is actually largely in agreement with Plotinus.[40] Consequently, he does not have much of an answer for it, instead (somewhat unfairly) conflating the two myths, and moving on to a critique of the demiurge himself: the craftsman of the Gnostic narrative is not much of a craftsman at all.[41] It works with reference to a mere "image of an image" of reality, hardly a fitting blueprint for the world.[42] Again, the temporality of the events in the myth is an issue: why would a demiurge wait to produce with images? How would it know an image by memory if it has only just been born, an ontological level below the image?[43]

Plotinus's disagreement with the Gnostics in these chapters clearly stems from a disagreement about the composition of the World-Soul, its relationship to time and to matter, and the logistics of its creative activity. Plotinus's position is unsatisfying to readers ancient and modern, but the issue strikes at the heart of his thought.[44] For Plotinus, as for Aristotle, philosophy begins with the individual soul's wonder about the origin of the world, leading to questions about its creation that blaze the path into Intellect and ascent to its ultimate source, the One.[45] Thus, the problem of the world's creation must be treated respectfully and produce an answer worthy of the dignity of the life of the mind.

Plotinus never explicitly attacks Gnostic aetiology and eschatology, but many of his jabs clearly show that he recognizes, and disapproves of, the idea that the world has a beginning and an end. Second, like Porphyry after him, Plotinus invokes the language of literary criticism to tar the Gnostic account of creation with the lowest possible philosophical categories used for production, imitation, and image. Philosophically speaking, the central debate of the first ten chapters of *Ennead* 2.9 concerns the Soul; however, the argument is consistently framed with reference to creation, temporality, and narrative imagery.

AGAINST THE GNOSTIC SAVIOR

The makeup of the Soul and its relationship to creative activity and time is inextricable from matters of physics and practical philosophy.[46] Most immediate is the issue of theodicy.[47] Plotinus accuses his opponents of wishing the world to be not just an image of the intelligible but the intelligible itself;[48] this is impossible, since the One *must* extend itself as far as possible, even, via the Soul, into an image of itself in the spatiotemporal realm.[49] Thus, we live in the best possible world, an "image (εἰκών)" of reality without an evil origin, despite the "many unpleasant things in it."[50] Such Panglossian indifference to inequality and human suffering, emphasized by his opponents, has surprised scholars by its "pitilessness."[51] But, for Plotinus, one must not "despise (καταφρονεῖν) the universe" but look to the whole order of beings, and, in this greater order, there is the greater good.[52] Later in the treatise, the same argument will be deployed to defend the traditional civic cult: despising the universe is tantamount to despising the gods in it, and that is just what makes someone bad (κακός).[53]

References to this "order in succession" (τάξις τῶν ἐφεξῆς),[54] contrasted with the break in the cosmos described in the classic Gnostic myth of the fall of Sophia, litter the *Enneads*.[55] As Plotinus notes in his discussion of matter, "of necessity, then, all things must exist forever in ordered dependence on one another," and this includes the "unpleasantries."[56] More contested and central to the administration of the cosmos than the banal injustices of daily life are the stars, whose goodness Plotinus expends considerable energy defending.

While his opponents esteem themselves superior to the planetary deities, he proclaims that the celestial bodies are good gods, have virtue, and are irrefutable evidence of a beautiful divine order that is not to be feared but imitated.[57] "They are essential to the completeness of the All and are important parts of the All," Plotinus argues.[58] What he means is that the stars order the cosmos; more specifically, while they do not determine our fates,[59] they transmit providential care to the subintelligible: "Every soul is a child of That Father. And there are souls in (the heavenly bodies) too, and intelligent and good ones, much more closely in touch with the beings of the higher world than our souls are. How could this universe exist if it was cut off from that other world? How could the gods be in it? But we spoke of this before, too: our point is now that because they despise (καταφρονοῦντες) the kindred of those higher realities, also, they do not know the higher beings either but only talk as if they did."[60] Several arguments are embedded in this transitional passage. First, the heavenly beings ontologically link the subintelligible to the supramundane.[61] Consequently, knowledge of the heavens is transmitted through them. Thus, by rejecting the stellar deities, the Gnostics have no knowledge of what lies beyond them.

Plotinus's opposition to Gnostic violation of the cosmic hierarchy, both with respect to theodicy and the administration of providence, is directly incumbent on the issue of soteriology, to which he immediately turns: "Then, another point, what piety is there in denying that providence extends to this world and to anything and everything? And how are they consistent with themselves in this denial? For they say that God does care providentially for them, and them alone."[62] For Plotinus, this view is philosophically unpalatable because it violates the modulated hierarchy of beings: the Gnostics do not know their place. They exalt themselves, set themselves separately above Intellect, claim to be "sons of God"[63]—but on the contrary, providence extends not to separate parts (individual, special humans) but unified wholes (all of humanity).[64] Second, this leads them to reject "the beings received from tradition (ἐκ πατέρων)."[65] For Plotinus, Hellenic tradition emphasizes the unity of the cosmos with all of humanity;[66] he wishes to defend the traditional, civic Greek cult, which is precluded by these exclusive claims to salvation.[67] Third, such claims presume an incoherent psychology, making an unsupportable distinction between "true," elect souls and false, "reflections" (εἴδωλα)" of souls, the non-elect.[68] In contrast, Plotinian salvation is universally accessible to all those who imbibe Hellenic learning (παιδεία).[69] As noted by Arthur Hilary Armstrong, Plotinus's criticism may have particular Gnostics in mind, but it extends to "all those who make the characteristic claim of Abrahamic religion to be the elect, the people of God, with a particular and exclusive revelation from him which causes them to reject the traditional pieties."[70]

Finally, Plotinus moves from physics to ethics. At first glance, it is tempting to differentiate the Gnostics of 2.9 [33] from (proto)-orthodox Christians on the basis of Plotinus's accusations of moral libertinism and general lack of interest in ethical philosophy.[71] However, his account of Gnostic libertinism is no more valid than the lurid descriptions, probably false, of a Clement or Epiphanius.[72] Rather, his opponents' rejection of the civic cult is tantamount in his mind to atheism. Together with the doctrine of elect soteriology (mutually exclusive with his view on providence), it thus merits a tarring with the brush of Epicureanism.[73] Moreover, he says that they do not compose treatises on virtue. This indifference to ethical matters puts them out of order with the hierarchy yet again, this time not with the hierarchy of the cosmos but with a philosophical approach to it: virtue precedes and even reveals God, not the other way around.[74]

Much as the debate over the composition of the World-Soul and its demiurgic activity presumed a rejection of Gnostic temporality and narrative imagery, these arguments over theodicy, soteriology, and ethics presume that the Gnostics failed to ascertain the proper location of divinity, its transmission, and how people show evidence of interaction with it. Multiplying needless intermediary entities, the Gnostics reject the entities that are actually necessary for the dissemination of providence (the stars), asserting that they have a special access to God via theophanies that exist outside the proper order of the universe. The ramifications of this axiom of divine theophany extend to a criminal soteriology, empty ethics, and, ultimately, pedagogy antithetical to the philosophical enterprise and its Hellenic heritage.

AGAINST THE GNOSTIC TRADITION

The beginning and end of *Ennead* 2.9. [33] 6 is worthy of special attention, because Plotinus embeds his discussion of the Gnostic World-Soul in various criticisms of the relationship between the Gnostics and Hellenic philosophical tradition. Scholars generally agree he is concerned with maintaining the integrity of Hellenic pedagogy against oriental "alien balderdash."[75] However unfairly, Plotinus here attempts to characterize the Gnostics as thinkers who initiate, not teach, and for him, this is not philosophy, but dangerous authoritarianism.

At the beginning of the chapter, he deplores the introduction of the subintelligible aeons of the Sojourn, Repentance, and Aeonic Copies (discussed in extant passages of *Zostrianos* and the *Untitled Treatise*).[76] These are "the terms of people inventing a new jargon to recommend their own school (εἰς σύστασιν τῆς ἰδίας αἱρέσεως). They contrive this meretricious language as if they had no connection with the ancient Hellenic school (τῆς ἀρχαίας Ἑλληνικῆς), though the Hellenes knew all this and knew it clearly, and spoke without delusive pomposity (ἀτύφως) of ascents (ἀναβάσεις) from the cave and advancing gradually closer and closer to a truer vision (τὴν θέαν ἀληθεστέραν)."[77] He continues: some of their ideas "have been taken from Plato but others, all the new ideas they have brought in to establish a philosophy of their own, are things they found outside the truth. For the judgments (δίκαι)[78] too, and the rivers in Hades and the reincarnations come from Plato. And the making a plurality in the intelligible world, Being, and Intellect, and the Maker different, and Soul, is taken from the words in the *Timaeus* (39e). . . . They themselves have received what is good in what they say (about) the immortality of the soul, the intelligible universe, the first god, the necessity for the soul to shun fellowship with the body, the separation from the body, the escape from becoming to being, for these doctrines are there in Plato."[79] The Platonic background of the Gnostics is not in question for Plotinus; nonetheless, they have founded their own school (αἵρεσις) by coining their own terminology to supplement the venerable teaching of Plato. What they add, however, sullies this teaching: useless subintelligible hypostases, and an incoherent doctrine of the World-Soul and the Demiurge. Moreover, much of what they take from Plato they misuse, especially with respect to the human soul's fallen nature and the worth of the body.[80] Finally, they justify the deviations from Plato by claiming that he and the "blessed philosophers" had no real knowledge of the intelligible nature (τὴν νοητὴν φύσιν), "ridiculing and insulting the Greeks . . . and saying that they are better than them," and "hunting fame by censuring men who have been judged good from ancient times by men of worth."[81]

Plotinus defends not only the philosophers' teaching on the composition of the intelligible world but also their mode of speech and pedagogy. The ancient Hellenes speak in a way "appropriate for the educated (πεπαιδευμένως)."[82] By contrast, the Gnostics need to learn to discourse courteously and philosophically (εὐμενῶς καὶ φιλοσόφως) and fairly (δικαίως), to learn with good will (εὐγνωμόνως).[83] Bestowing membership in the elect, they say their "gnosis" is "cultured (πεπεαιδυμένης) and harmonious," that they alone are capable of contemplation (while deviating from Plotinus's sense of the term) and "worthy of honor" on the basis of their souls.[84] Instead, they're stupid (ἀνόητοι), speaking provincially (ἀγροικιζόμενος).[85] With audacity (αὐθάδεια), they make "arrogant assertions" without proofs (ἀποδείξεις).[86] Twice, he says that since they do not argue like philosophers, "another way of writing" (ἄλλου ὄντος τρόπου) would be more appropriate to respond to them, and that he will quit describing their doctrines; and, twice he breaks his resolve by denigrating them anew.[87]

CONCLUSION: WITH "FRIENDS"
LIKE THAT . . . (A THICKER DESCRIPTION)

Aside from the two versions of the Sophia myth and his paraphrases of positions on cosmology, theodicy, and other philosophical topics, Plotinus tells the reader little about what his opponents actually think or believe. He does not give any references to their extra-Hellenic sources. He does not explain who his opponents say they are or where they came from. Nonetheless, the contours of *Ennead* 2.9 tell us a bit about his opponents, and this is firmly in agreement with Porphyry's evidence: they are steeped in Greek thought, and even identify with it, while deviating from it in significant ways. The most significant departure concerns the World-Soul and its demiurgic function, from which follow a number of un-Hellenic doctrines, including a cosmos created by an evil demiurge who wishes to destroy it, and which is engineered by malevolent stellar deities. Its illogical providential model transmits salvation to an elect few, who have a concept of salvation that is not earned as much as bestowed by an authority that rejects the cultic and intellectual traditions of Hellenism. It is a disordered universe, dreamt by disordered men who feel alien to it. Plotinus's critique is that of a conservative.

Reading Plotinus's works in conjunction with Porphyry's evidence, scholars have hypothesized numerous sectarian identities for the Gnostics of *Ennead* 2.9. Valentinians have been contenders for several reasons: the prominence of the school in Rome, the similarity of Plotinus's account of the fall of Sophia to that given by Valentinians, and perhaps most importantly the relative plenitude of evidence about Valentinians prior to the Nag Hammadi discovery.[88] The surfacing of Sethian rather than Valentinian texts with the titles of treatises mentioned by Porphyry has mitigated this hypothesis.[89] Other groups associated with Sethian tradition have also been suggested, such as the Barbelo-Gnostics known to Irenaeus or the Archontics.[90] Earlier scholarship suggested a pagan Gnostic group, reading Porphyry's evidence as referring to "Christians and others (belonging to non-Christian groups)."[91] Other contenders include the followers of one Alcibiades, who brought an "Apocalypse of Elchasai" from Syrian baptismal groups to Rome in the early third century CE, inspired by Pope Callistus I's support for second baptism for the remission of new sins—a thesis that is revisited in the conclusion.[92]

Based on the reading of evidence presented in this chapter, it is impossible to distinguish whether these Gnostics were Valentinians, Sethians, Barbelo-Gnostics, or Elchasaites, but it would be unlikely that they were Hellenes. An objection to this view is that if Plotinus's opponents were Christians, why did not he simply say so, as Celsus and Porphyry did in their polemical works? Yet it is not clear that Plotinus would have been able to recognize a Christian. As a long-time resident of Alexandria, he must have been familiar with Christian intellectuals like the Valentinians or the catechetical school of Clement and Origen.[93] As a longtime Platonist, he could have been familiar with Celsus's critique of Christianity or with Numenius's quip about the "Attic Moses."[94] Despite all this, there is no explicit evidence in his corpus of any knowledge of Christianity, and therefore such knowledge cannot be assured.[95]

Another factor is the question of how well Plotinus knew his opponents. In this context, it is worthwhile recalling the following passage from *Against the Gnostics*: "*We feel a certain regard for some of our friends* (φίλοι) [italics mine] who happened upon this way of thinking before they became our friends, and, though I do not know how they manage it, continue in it. . . . But we have addressed what we have said so far to our own intimate pupils, not to them (for we could make no further progress towards convincing them), so that they might not be troubled by these latter, who do not bring forward proofs—how could they?—but make arbitrary, arrogant assertions. Another way of writing would be appropriate to repel (them)."[96] Did Plotinus have Christian "friends"? Apparently so, and he considered them to be "votaries of Plato";[97] the problem is that they were also votaries of much else. If the evidence from Porphyry's *Vita Plotini* chapter 16 about Aculinus can be squared with Eunapius, Mark J. Edwards is most likely correct that Plotinus here attacks the Platonism of Gnostic colleagues from the circle of his old teacher in Alexandria, Ammonius Saccas. These colleagues were with him in Rome around the same time as Porphyry (ca. 263 CE), at a time when the group focused on discussing the makeup of the Soul and the intelligible world, just the topics that occupy the bulk of *Against the Gnostics*.[98] Therefore, the gulf between the Gnostic and Hellenic parties extended far beyond the single issue of authority, which then turned on the Christian invocation of Jewish seers against the speculations of the divine Plato.[99]

His polemic also allows us to "thicken" the description determined in Chapter 1 of his Christian "friends." Plotinus sharply criticizes them for "despising" the world instead of engaging it politically, which in turn leads them to reject the civic cult and festivities, worship of "the beings received from the tradition of our fathers."[100] Considering the close proximity of philosophers and sophists to political power (as discussed in Chapter 1), his claim that the Gnostics thumbed their noses at current events is striking. Moreover, despite their claim that their teaching is philosophical (πεπαιδευμένης), Plotinus says they are stupid (ἀνόητοι) and that they speak like bumpkins (ἀγροικιζόμενος), that is, not like Hellenes.[101] What Plotinus means is not that they are incapable of engaging technical metaphysics (the evidence from Nag Hammadi, as we will see, demonstrates otherwise); rather, they eschew the contemporary culture of philosophy, a way of life that goes back to ancients like Pythagoras and that encourages civic and popular cultic activity.

The situation was exacerbated by the pseudepigraphic appeal to the authority of Judeo-Christian antediluvian sages in their apocalypses. Plotinus's Gnostics seem to have adopted the auto-Orientalizing approach of the Hermetica and the *Chaldean Oracles*, entirely rejecting Hellenic claims to primeval wisdom. Like Porphyry, Plotinus recognizes that their effort to alienate themselves from Hellenic authorities is a direct attack on the culture of Hellenic education out of which they came. Moreover, the very way in which they present their wisdom is alien to the spirit of Hellenic investigative philosophy:[102] speaking "without proofs" (ἀποδείξεις), the Gnostics have, in his eyes, earned the appellation "rustic, bumpkin" (ἄγροικος); Celsus, Porphyry, and Julian all use the same term for Christians in their own polemics.[103] "Another way of writing" would be more appropriate to refute them.

To summarize our evidence about Plotinus's Christian friends, the Gnostic heretics also known to Porphyry, we can say that:

1. Unlike most sophists and philosophers in their day, they did not participate in public life.

2. They did not identify as "Hellenes," consciously eschewing the culture of contemporary Hellenophone intellectual life.

3. Their texts were revelatory—they did not present arguments so much as statements validated by their ancient, Oriental, authority.

4. *Despite all this*, they *did* claim a philosophical αἵρεσις, but, like other "auto-Orientalizers," they said it had priority over the Greek schools.

This last feature is striking, because, as we saw at the beginning of Chapter 1, Philo, Tertullian, and several Gnostic authors entirely reject the language of αἵρεσις. Instead, identification of Christianity as a αἵρεσις is a staple of Christian apologetics, exemplified in Justin Martyr.[104] This also explains why the Gnostics claimed their teaching was "cultured"—that is, consonant with παιδεία—and why Plotinus was eager to dispel this claim. What was at stake in the Plotinus-Gnostic controversy was the definition of philosophy itself: its relationship to public life, civic cult, Hellenic nationalism, and the provenance of the Greek intellectual tradition. Plotinus emphasizes consonance with each of these pockets of life; his opponents emphasize alienation from them. His old friends had become the most bitter of enemies, and as we turn to the Sethian literature that they read, it will not be difficult to see why.

Other Ways of Writing

Plotinus claims that the Gnostics do not write in a philosophical style, and so "another way of writing" would be necessary to refute them. Porphyry, meanwhile, denigrates the Sethian apocalypses as "forgeries" (πλάσματα), and it seems this formed the basis of his critique of the *Apocalypse of Zoroaster*.[1] Porphyry's use of the word "apocalypse" or "revelation" (ἀποκάλυψις) for these documents is tantalizing, and at first sight straightforward: These texts were apocalypses, "revelations" of some sort, stories dealing with whatever kinds of ideas that "revelations" traffic in. Yet the apocalyptic background of the texts has not been studied with respect to the Platonic tradition, much less Plotinus's criticism.[2] In fact, there are few studies of Gnostic apocalypses at all.[3] This chapter will therefore unpack the technical language of Plotinus and Porphyry's criticisms about "fiction," "forgery," and "myth," while introducing the Platonizing Sethian literature itself, which is deeply embedded in the literary culture of the apocalypses.

Indeed, three (of the four) Platonizing Sethian treatises—*Marsanes*, *Allogenes*, and *Zostrianos*—are apocalypses. Analysis of their genre and their pseudepigraphic appeal to authority reveals that numerous key motifs of the texts, particularly in their frame narratives, are common stock in contemporary Jewish and Christian apocalyptic storytelling. Their cultivation of authority using these motifs challenges the culture of παιδεία explored in Chapter 1, instead employing images and authoritative figures with currency in Judeo-Christian circles, alien to Hellenism. Finally, the Sethian texts do not reject Platonic terminology about imagery, but employ it to articulate contemplative technique and authorize the concept of revelation as a perfect "image" of reality transmitted by the unknown, alien God to the seer. Such revelations, other ways of writing, thus demand to be read literally, not allegorically—another way of reading than we find prized by the Neoplatonists, who did not write stories as much as allegorically interpret the ones they deemed to be good. All of this points to the need for a reevaluation of the provenance and target audience of the Platonizing Sethian literature and the evidence of Plotinus and Porphyry.

ANOTHER KIND OF STORY—THE SETHIAN APOCALYPSES

As noted earlier in this book, Coptic treatises bearing the titles of several of the apocalypses mentioned by Porphyry in *Vita Plotini* 16 were discovered among the Nag Hammadi hoard in Upper Egypt in 1945. These treatises appear to belong to a Gnostic literary tradition that spans a wider group of Nag Hammadi texts, first identified and dubbed "Sethian" by Hans-Martin Schenke.[4] The study of these Sethian treatises in the greater project of understanding the relationship between Plotinus and his Gnostic friends thus brings one to the study of Sethian tradition, and how it may have affected the particular issues that were contested by these thinkers. "Sethianism" describes a literary tradition defined by a family resemblance of various shared features, but chiefly the veneration of Seth, the third child of Adam and Eve, as revelator and even savior in the context of the "classic" Gnostic myth recounted at the beginning of Chapter One and criticized by Plotinus.[5] The tradition encompasses, if not a *system* of thought, a *school* of thought, which thus presupposes some kind of belief in the Gnostic myth.[6] Despite occasional criticism,[7] the category of "Sethianism" enjoys widespread scholarly acceptance, even from those who dub it instead "Classic Gnosticism"[8] or even eschew the term "Gnosticism" itself (thus speaking of "Sethian Christianity").[9] It is worth pausing to discuss this tradition here, since recent work brings into sharp relief the fact that nearly every Sethian treatise, even when they are Platonizing, is an apocalypse; therefore, the treatises criticized by Plotinus and Porphyry possess a very specific literary background that deserves to be explored in full.

One scholar of Gnosticism, John D. Turner, drew up a hypothetical but widely followed "literary history" of the movement that may have produced the Sethian literature.[10] This history is based on a perceived tension between three subgroups within the Sethian corpus identified by Schenke: midrashic texts concerned with exegesis of the Paradise narrative in Genesis, texts focusing on baptism and the incarnation of Christ in Jesus of Nazareth, and the Platonizing texts full of metaphysical terminology but no speculation about the story of the serpent in Paradise or Jesus of Nazareth. Turner thus speculated that the Sethian literature offers snapshots of three phases of the transformation of a single Gnostic group that arose out of speculation on Jewish themes, was Christianized in the second century CE with the incorporation of Barbelo-Gnosticism (speculation about the Barbelo, or divine mother known to Irenaeus) and separate traditions about the veneration of Seth, suffered persecution at the hands of the proto-orthodox, and attempted to find a home among contemporary Platonic thinkers, like Plotinus's group.[11] These later Sethians composed Platonizing but "pagan" apocalypses where Judeo-Christian motifs and ideas have been replaced with Platonic metaphysics, in an attempt to appeal to the philosophers.[12] As we know from Plotinus and Porphyry themselves, the rapprochement was unsuccessful, but these pagan apocalypses nonetheless deeply influenced the development of Neoplatonic thought. Thus, most scholars today refer to the Platonizing Sethian treatises as pagan apocalypses, written with the aim of appealing to the philosophical sensibility of Plotinus and other Hellenes.[13]

However, recent, groundbreaking research has forced us to reconsider the contours of Sethian tradition, by demonstrating that the Jewish midrashic texts first identified as "Sethian" are not Sethian at all. They possess few Sethian features (including the most important one—veneration of Seth himself), and instead belong to a separate Gnostic literary tradition dealing with Adam, Eve, and the serpent in the Garden of Eden. Hence, they should be termed "Ophite" texts (Gk. ὄφις = "serpent").[14] Much confusion, for instance, stems from the composite nature of one of the most famous treatises from this body of literature—the *Apocryphon of John*—which contains Sethian, Ophite, and Barbeloite themes.[15] In attempting to shoehorn the entirety of this composite text with a complex source history into the category of Sethianism, scholarship thus obscured the distinctive nature of the Ophite tradition underlying sections of it.

The distinctively apocalyptic nature of Sethian literary tradition was obscured, too. Once the Ophite material is set aside, Sethianism is left with apocalypses and treatises containing large apocalyptic sections.[16] The literary frame narrative governing the *Apocryphon of John* is both Sethian and an apocalypse.[17] The *Apocalypse of Adam*, a history of the descents of Seth to save his "seed" from its tormentors, the rulers of the cosmos, and three of the Platonizing treatises—*Zostrianos*, *Allogenes*, and *Marsanes*, featuring the ascent of a seer to discover the secrets of the intelligible cosmos—are all apocalypses. The fourth Platonizing treatise, the *Three Steles of Seth*, is an ecstatic liturgy, but its scribe dubbed it an apocalypse.[18] *Trimorphic Protennoia* is a revelation monologue complete with its own miniapocalypse featuring historical eschatology. Apocalyptic sections also litter the *Egyptian Gospel*, a text that begins with cosmogony and proceeds to a history of the seed of Seth and its rescue by its founder, who intervenes in various incarnations throughout history, before terminating in a liturgical section. The genre of the fragmentary *Melchizedek* is unclear, but this treatise seems deeply embedded in contemporary apocryphal traditions about the incarnation of the eponymous, celestial high priest (Gen 14:18–20; Heb 5:5–6) to battle the forces of darkness at the eschaton.[19] Another work distantly related to Sethianism—the bizarre cosmological speculations of the *Untitled Text* from Codex Brucianus—and recent discoveries, including the *Gospel of Judas* and the untitled treatise from Codex Tchacos provisionally titled the *Book of Allogenes*, are apocalypses as well.[20]

Are these works "apocalypses" in name only or could one describe their contents as "apocalyptic" as well? Certainly most of the Sethian literature uses the genre of apocalypse, which "carries that title (ἀποκάλυψις) for the first time in the very late first or early second century a.d. From then on, both title and form are fashionable, at least to the end of the classical period."[21] John J. Collins defines the apocalyptic genre as "a genre of revelatory literature with a narrative framework, in which a revelation is mediated by an otherworldly being to a human recipient, disclosing a transcendent reality which is both temporal, insofar as it envisages eschatological salvation, and spatial insofar as it involves another, supernatural world."[22] One of the chief virtues of this approach is its movement away from scholarship that privileged historical and political themes in apocalyptic, neglecting the many apocalypses that deal more with cosmology, the makeup and fate of the soul, and so on.[23] Other scholars have also emphasized the esotericism of the apoclaypses, that is, their focus on the revelation of hidden wisdom and cosmological secrets.[24] As we will see in later chapters, Sethian tradition offers both "historical" and "cosmological" apocalypses.

Even so, esotericism, eschatology, and historical change are merely subjects commonly discussed in ancient apocalypses, without defining the genre, whose content remains open. Rather, the genre of apocalypse is defined by function, or "what may be called the 'apocalyptic technique.' Whatever the underlying problem, it is viewed from a distinctive apocalyptic perspective. This perspective is framed spatially by the supernatural world and temporally by the eschatological judgment. . . . It provides a resolution in the imagination by instilling conviction in the revealed 'knowledge' that it imparts. The function of the apocalyptic literature is to shape one's imaginative perception of a situation and so lay the basis for whatever course of action it exhorts."[25] All apocalypses use elements such as frame narrative, stock motifs, and rhetoric to make extraordinary claims to authority that help address any sort of crisis experienced by the reader, which might result from political situations, but can be of an abstract or, as in the case of the Sethian apocalypses, even philosophical nature.[26]

Pseudepigraphy is perhaps the chief device used to bolster the authority of an apocalypse, authorizing the claims made by the text while creating a sense of self-definition.[27] The claim of "historical" apocalypses to stem from a figure of remote antiquity validates *ex eventu* prophecy and creates a sense of providential activity that consoles the reader.[28] In the "speculative" apocalypses, the device heightens the dynamic of concealment and revelation that lends a sense of gravitas.[29] Pseudepigraphy had an apologetic function, but this was necessarily audience-specific; not all antediluvian sages were created equal, at least in the Rome of the third century CE.[30] The decision to compose a treatise under the name of a "foreign" character like Zostrianos or Enoch, *as opposed to* Pythagoras, is significant, particularly among thinkers such as Numenius, Plotinus, or Porphyry for whom Platonic Orientalism was a live issue. Sethian literature thus employed a specific genre that used a body of specific literary motifs to make vigorous claims to authority in a scholarly environment where these specific claims would have been controversial. A close look at the Platonizing treatises' use of these motifs—literary traditions common to the Jewish and Christian apocalypses—will tell us a great deal about what kind of audience the Platonizing Sethian treatises must have been intended for, and what Plotinus meant when he said that another way of writing would be more appropriate for refuting their readers.

ANOTHER WAY OF WRITING

The frame narratives of *Marsanes*, *Allogenes*, and *Zostrianos* (I omit the *Three Steles of Seth*, because, as a liturgical work, it has almost no narrative to speak of) each employ stock motifs of Jewish and Christian apocalypses, chief among them being the pseudepigraphic appeal to the authority of Judeo-Christian seers. Other features are instantly recognizable within the context of Jewish and Christian apocalyptic tradition, including the disposition of the seer prior to enlightenment, the medium of the heavenly journey, and interaction with the revealer figure. Altogether, these traditions compose a distinctive way of writing of its own, which seeks to authorize its message by invoking themes and images, familiar to readers of the apocalypses, that its audience would have found convincing and respectable.

Marsanes is an apocalypse insofar as a revealer delivers cosmological secrets to the eponymous seer. The identity of the revealer is not clear, but two apocalyptic literary traditions are: the emphasis on the authority of the seer and the use of paraenesis. As discussed at the end of Chapter 1, the character "Marsanes/Marsianos" was the protagonist of other Gnostic apocalypses, known to Epiphanius and the author of the *Untitled Treatise* in the Bruce Codex.[31] Early on in *Marsanes*, a "third power of the Thrice-Powered One" describes to the seer the "silent" nature of the One beyond the One.[32] After what appears to be a visionary experience, it tells the seer, "it is necessary [for you to know] those that are higher than these and tell them to the powers. For you (*sg. masc.*) will become [elect] with the elect ones [in the last] times."[33] Marsanes himself repeatedly asserts his revelatory authority in the text, as when he addresses the reader at the beginning: "for I am he who has [understood] that which truly exists, [whether] partially or [wholly], according to difference [and sameness]."[34] Authorized to preach, Marsanes tells his readers to "[control] yourselves, receive [the] imperishable seed, bear fruit, and do not become attached to your possessions."[35] Each of the Platonizing apocalypses has paraenesis culminating in injunctions to missionary activity;[36] these are common in contemporary Jewish apocalyptic texts, such as 2 *Enoch*, 4 *Ezra*, or 2 *Baruch*.[37]

Allogenes also exhibits the traditions of pseudepigraphic authorization via identification with a seer, reinforcement of the seer's authority, and paraenesis, in addition to several other common apocalyptic themes: the protagonist's fear, periods of preparation between revelation, and the practice of inscribing and burying books. The treatise assumes the genre (closely related to apocalypse) of a testament, or will, to the seer's "son," Messos. If we acknowledge that the very name "Allogenes" refers to the author as a Sethian, that is, one of "another seed," as some scholars do, then we can "indirectly impute patriarchal status to Allogenes," who is probably of antediluvian origin.[38] Other scholars simply assign him the identity of an incarnation of Seth himself.[39] The *incipit* of the narrative is unpreserved; the reader is immediately thrust into a revelation dialogue between the seer and the angel Youel, describing the makeup of Barbelo and the first principle, a "Thrice-Powered Invisible Spirit." Allogenes grows upset:[40]

> "I was able (to conceive of transcendent things), although I was clothed in flesh. [I] heard about them through you, about the teaching which is in them (i.e., the revelations), since the thought that is in me distinguished those [which] are beyond measure and the unknowables. Because of this, I am afraid, lest my learning has produced[41] something beyond what is fitting." And then, O Messos, Youel, the one who belongs to all the glories, said these things to me. She [revealed (ϭⲱⲗⲡ)] these things, and said, "No one is allowed to hear these things, except for the great powers alone, O Allogenes, (for) a great power has been laid upon you, that which the father of the entirety, the eternal, laid upon you before you came to this place, so that you might distinguish those things which are difficult to distinguish, and so that you might understand those things which are unknown to the multitude, and so that you might be saved, in that one who belongs to you, that one who was first to save (others) and who does not himself need to be saved.[42]

What Collins terms the "disposition of the seer" is a stock element in apocalypses, particularly the disposition of fear, which is met by the soothing words of angelic mediators.[43] *Allogenes* skillfully applies the motif to the dilemma of the mystic—the problematic status of knowledge of what is necessarily unknowable—even while retaining its Jewish coloring. While the first principle of the Greek philosophers is unknowable, it is certainly nothing to be afraid of.[44] Sirach, on the other hand, discourages attempts to know too much, and in Hekhalot literature, knowledge of the Godhead is not only forbidden but dangerous.[45]

Youel's response fails to "steady" Allogenes, who once again expresses his fears and is reassured that he is both worthy of vision and responsible for communicating it to others.[46] The angel anoints and "strengthens" him. This "empowerment" of the seer by heavenly beings is common to the Platonizing Sethian texts. Paralleled only rarely in contemporary Platonic literature, the tradition is also clear in the heavenly journeys of 2 *Baruch* and the *Apocalypse of Abraham*, where the seer is occasionally "strengthened" by angels to ease the shock of the journey.[47]

The discussion continues along predictably metaphysical lines, and, finally, Allogenes, convinced of his worthiness, prepares himself for ascent through meditative techniques: "And when Youel, the one who belongs to all the glories, had said these things to me, she separated herself from me, leaving me. But I did not despair because of these words which I had heard; I contemplated myself for one hundred years. And I rejoiced by myself a great deal, since I was in a great light and a blessed path, since those, meanwhile, who I was worthy of seeing and then those who I was worthy of hearing about (are) those whom it is fitting for the great powers alone [. . .]."[48] "Breaks" in between revelatory discourses are another tradition in the apocalypses; Ezra and Baruch fast for seven days between visions.[49] The inordinate life span that enables Allogenes to meditate for a century is common to Jewish legends about the patriarchs.[50] Some kind of period of waiting between visions of "the Father" seems to be implied in a fragmentary passage of *Marsanes*.[51] It is not clear if such practices involved a withdrawal from contemporary urban life to the wilderness or understood retreat in a more metaphorical or limited fashion, or simply as apocalyptic literary cliché.[52]

Finally, upon his descent from the Barbelo, Allogenes is commissioned to write a book, presumably that bearing his name: "he (speaker unknown) said to me, write down [those things that I] will tell you, and I will remind you, for the sake of those who will be worthy after you. You must leave this book upon a mountain, and adjure a guardian: 'come, dreadful one.' And when he had said these things, he separated himself from me. As for me, I was full of joy, and I wrote down this book, which was set apart for me (to write), my son, Messos, so that I might reveal (ϭⲱⲗⲡ) to you those things which were preached before me, and that I received first in a great silence."[53] The ancient seer's composition of a revelatory manuscript for posterity is one of the most common traditions in apocalyptic literature, as in the *Ascension of Isaiah* or *2 Enoch*: "give them books in your handwriting, and they will read them and they will acknowledge me as the Creator of everything. And they will understand that there is no other God except myself."[54] The tradition showcases the esoteric nature of a revealed book, and explains how antediluvian texts could survive cataclysms or simply go unread for a long time.[55] Indeed, the device carries the eschatological implication that only the "last generation (the author's own)" could "break the seal of the mystery" of God's plan; or further, it is not the generation of the *author* that is being confronted with the revealed mystery but that of the *reader(s)*.[56]

A similar constellation of apocalyptic traditions is negotiated in the lengthy *Zostrianos*, which, thanks to its relatively well-preserved opening and closing, offers by far the most data. It begins with the eponymous seer reflecting on his circumstances prior to revelation: "I was in the cosmos for the sake of those of my generation and those who would come after me, the living elect. . . . I preached forcefully about the entirety to those who had alien parts. I tried their works for a little while; thus the necessity of generation brought me into the manifest (world). I was never pleased with them, but always I separated myself from them, since I had come into being through a holy birth.[57] And being mixed, I straightened my soul, empty of evil."[58] Frustrated with his community, he retreats and contemplates metaphysical questions alone, which eventually leads him to despair and a resolve to suicide, when an angel appears and intervenes.[59] The arrival of revelation to a seer in great emotional distress is common in the Jewish apocalypses.[60] Then Zostrianos "instantly and exuberantly ascended with the angel, into a great luminous cloud,[61] leaving my shell (πλάσμα) upon the earth, to be guarded by some glories. And [we] were rescued from the whole cosmos, and the thirteen aeons that exist in it, and their angelic beings. They did not spot us, and their ruler (ἄρχων) became disturbed before [our mode of] passage."[62] The tradition of the ascent to heaven via cloud is also widespread in Jewish apocalypses.[63]

The same is true of the stealthy passage through the clutches of the heavenly powers, which is replicated prior to Zostrianos's reembodiment at the end of the treatise, after his revelations: "Then, when I came down to the aeons of the [self-begotten] individuals, I received an [image (ειΝε)] that was pure, yet appropriate for sense-perception (αἴσθησις). I came down to the aeonic copies (ἀντίτυπος) and went to the aetherial earth. And I wrote three wooden tablets (πύξος), leaving them in knowledge (ⲉⲩⲅⲛⲱⲥⲓⲥ)[64] for all those who would follow me, the living elect. I came down to the perceptible world and I put on my image (ⲧⲱⲟⲩⲧ); since it was uneducated, I strengthened it, going around to preach the truth to everybody. Neither the angelic beings of the world nor the archons saw me, for I evaded a myriad of torments which nearly killed me."[65] This passage is obscure; it does not identify these steles with the text of *Zostrianos* itself, so they must be a separate work.[66] However, writing in heaven was commonly associated in Jewish pseudepigrapha with Enoch's role as a divine scribe, a role at the root of rabbinic traditions where, transformed into Metatron, he sits in heaven writing. [67] Zostrianos probably drew on this tradition, for, like the seer of 2 and 3 *Enoch*, Zostrianos has been transformed into an angel over the course of his heavenly journey and acquired supra-angelic knowledge.[68]

Meanwhile, Zostrianos's descent "invisible and unharmed" past a series of hostile archons is a leitmotiv of apocalyptic, Gnostic, and Manichaean ascent texts. In the *Ascension of Isaiah* the prophet witnesses the savior's descent to earth in a disguise, to avoid conflict with malevolent angels.[69] In a hymnic passage shared between the *Apocryphon of John* and *Trimorphic Protennoia*, the figure of Protennoia, a female savior, descends three times.[70] For Ophites, it is a preexistent Jesus himself who descends.[71] In *The Ascension of Isaiah*, the descent leads to his crucifixion.[72] In other texts, he assumes the role of Gnostic initiator, teaching disciples how to navigate the path to heaven by using "seals" or "passwords" to gain power over malevolent archons and angels.[73] The Manichaean Psalm-Book also features "wardens" (τελῶναι) whom the ascending soul must pass with the proper verbal offering, as obtained by the descending savior.[74] In each of these cases, the one who descends is a savior figure.[75] Zostrianos himself, then, appears to be not merely a seer but a savior, and perhaps even a Christ-figure.[76] Indeed, the treatise ends with an eschatologically oriented sermon calling its hearers to repent and abandon the body.[77]

Thus the opening and closing pericopes of *Zostrianos*, like *Allogenes* and what is extant of *Marsanes*, consistently and repeatedly employ stock literary traditions drawn from the apocalypses. It is a way of writing characterized by the acquisition of revelation from a heavenly mediator, a heavenly journey (by cloud), the composition of heavenly books, and paraenetic discourses, in this case concerned with Platonic metaphysics and a cognate ascetic practice. Perhaps most distinctively, it is a way of writing that uses pseudepigraphy to authorize itself, donning the garb of hoary characters of Jewish antiquity to narrate their fantastic heavenly journeys. Not merely the stories that are told but the Sethian storytellers themselves, it seems, presume an audience familiar with and receptive to the world of the Jewish and Christian apocrypha.

ANOTHER KIND OF STORYTELLER

Much of our evidence about Sethianism from outside the Nag Hammadi corpus underscores the debt of this literary tradition to the apocalypses, the distinctive kinds of stories they tell, and the distinctive storytellers they are ascribed to. Epiphanius of Salamis's evidence about the Sethians also shows that they routinely appealed to the authority of Judeo-Christian figures in apocalypses;[78] moreover, he employs the language of the Platonists to mock them. He claims that the Gnostics (or "Borborites") "forge (πλάττουσι) many books," with titles such as *Norea*, the *Gospel of Eve,* "books in the name of Seth," the *Apocalypse of Adam*, and the *Gospel of Philip.*[79] His Sethians relate a version of the tale of the Nephilim found in Genesis 6:1–4 and the *Book of the Watchers*. They also "have composed certain books, attributing them to great men (βίβλους δέ τινας συγγράφοντες ἐξ ὀνόματος μεγάλων ἀνδρῶν): they say there are seven books attributed to Seth; other different books they entitle *Foreigners* (Ἀλλογενεῖς); another they call an *Apocalypse Attributed to Abraham* (ἐξ ὀνόματος Ἀβραάμ . . . ἀποκάλυψιν); others attributed to Moses; and others attributed to other figures."[80] "The Archontics," continues Epiphanius, "have forged their own apocrypha (οὗτοι δὲ ὁμοίως βίβλους ἑαυτοῖς ἐπλαστογράφησάν τινας ἀποκρύφους)," including books of "the Foreigners" (τοῖς Ἀλλογενέσι καλουμένοις) and an *Ascension of Isaiah*, probably that known today.[81]

The Archontics also had a tradition about a certain "Marsanios" who was "snatched up" into heaven, as discussed in Chapter 1.[82] *Pistis Sophia* in the Askew Codex refers to a revelation dialogue between Jesus and Enoch in Paradise, resulting in the latter's composition of a book of mysteries, the *Books of Jeu* (probably those preserved in the Bruce Codex), which is protected by the archon "Kalapatauroth" so that it might survive the deluge.[83] In an unfortunately fragmentary passage, the Sethian text *Melchizedek* mentions Enoch along with Adam and Abel.[84] Finally, the Cologne Mani Codex[85] lists several apocalypses, with similar titles, circulating in the community of

Mani's childhood: an "Apocalypse of Adam," "Apocalypse of Sethel," "Apocalypse of Enosh," "Apocalypse of Shem," and "Apocalypse of Enoch."[86] Significantly, the entire catalogue is motivated by the need to recall past revelations, presumably accepted by the target audience, in order to validate the revelations of Mani himself.[87]

The Platonizing Sethian apocalypses of Nag Hammadi all make similar appeals to the authority of individuals within Jewish and Christian tradition.[88] Marsanes, Nicotheus, and Allogenes are all figures of Judeo-Christian provenance; only the name of "Zostrianos" is in itself ideologically neutral, since Hellenes, Jews, and Christians alike lay claim to the figure of his close relative Zoroaster.[89] Given the pedigree of their nomenclature and the total absence of Hellenizing features that would have appealed to readers steeped in the Second Sophistic and Neopythagoreanism, it is difficult to imagine that the pseudepigraphic device was used in Sethian apocalypses as an apologetic appeal *to* Hellenes.[90] The frame narratives of *Allogenes* and *Marsanes* are not entirely clear, but their apocalyptic personages and rhetoric both are very much in line with that of *Zostrianos*, and were recognized as such by Porphyry. Sethian pseudepigraphy associates the texts with figures populating Jewish and Christian apocrypha, who served in the worlds of Roman Judaism and Christianity as repositories of the ancient scribal culture of the Near East.

While there are messianic and prophetic elements to the personalities of our Platonizing seers, they are above all sages, scholars steeped in sapiential and philosophical lore.[91] As J. Z. Smith argues, "apocalypticism," featuring these sages, "is a learned rather than a popular religious phenomenon. It is widely distributed throughout the Mediterranean world and is best understood as part of the *inner history of the tradition* within which it occurs rather than as a syncretism."[92] Apocalyptic literature, whether historical or speculative, was produced by individuals within groups that had their own religious identities and attendant jargon and rhetorical motifs.

In the case of the Platonizing Sethian texts, such traditions are those of Jewish and Christian "scribal phenomena." Recipients of vision, such as Daniel, Ezra, Baruch, and especially Enoch are all described as scribes in their apocalypses.[93] The Sethian texts are thus invested with the worldview of Mesopotamian scribal culture, which saw an "interlocking totality" of phenomena that could be interpreted through cataloging them in lists and analyzing them as indicative of divine activity.[94] Yet these catalogues of natural phenomena are replaced, in the Sethian literature, by equally repetitive lists of heavenly beings and metaphysical jargon. Nonetheless, the Sethian sages are clearly designed to appear as scribal figures who possess, by unverifiable means (e.g., ascents, dreams, visions), superior wisdom and authority.[95]

What entitles the sage to this special knowledge is also largely contingent on cultural background. Ioan Couliano distinguishes between three types of heavenly journeys:[96]

1. "Call" or "elective" apocalypses (merit based): unknown in Greek literature but ubiquitous in Judeo-Christian literature.

2. "Accidental" experiences, where the heavenly journey follows some calamity that leads to a revelatory near-death experience. There is only one Jewish apocalypse in this type (3 Bar.), but it is the predominant form of Greek apocalypse (Myth of Er, etc.)

3. "Quest apocalypses," where the protagonist must employ special techniques in the pursuit of wisdom.

Judeo-Christian sages, such as those associated with Sethian traditions, are nearly always "elect" (type 1), invested by God himself with authority, at times resulting in quasi-worship of the seer.[97] A good example is Mani himself, in a letter to Edessa (italics mine): "The truth and the secrets which I speak about—and the laying on of hands which is in my possession—not from men have I received them nor from fleshly creatures, *not even from studies in the scriptures . . .* by His (the Father's) grace, He pulled me from the council of the many who do not recognize the truth and revealed (ἀπεκάλυψε) to me his secrets and those of the undefiled father and of all the cosmos. He disclosed to me how I was before the foundation of the world, and how the groundwork of all the deeds, both good and evil, was laid, and how everything of [this] aggregation was engendered [according to its] present boundaries and [times]."[98] Such extraordinary claims to authority are a hallmark of the apocalyptic genre, participating in the greater trend under the early Roman Empire to search for some kind of esoteric, "higher" knowledge.[99] There are a variety of traditions common to the genre that express these claims, and as discussed above, many of these are present in the Sethian apocalypses.[100] Together, they constitute a peculiar "register," a way of writing that strongly contrasts not just with sapiential literature but with the tone and idiom of Greek philosophy.[101]

Altogether, the remarkable claims to authority made in apocalyptic literature, advanced by means of narrative traditions and pseudepigraphic authorship, are designed to quell any doubts a potential reader may have about the topic at hand, whatever it might be.[102] Christopher Rowland remarks that this rhetoric tries to create a sense of "unmediated" or "direct" access to knowledge, but all apocalypses actually are transmitted (i.e., mediated) by an otherworldly figure.[103] What he seems to mean is that the "apocalyptic technique" is designed to assure the reader of the *complete veracity* of a worldview or set of propositions. While it is indeed mediated by narrative devices and characters, this worldview or conceptual set is assigned a truth value that is entirely positive, pure, and undistilled. In the context of *4 Ezra* and other apocalypses that deal with historical issues, this technique is consoling. In the context of Platonic epistemology, it is an extraordinary subversion of ordinary means of accessing knowledge.

WHAT IS A GOOD STORY?

Plotinus charges the Sethian apocalypses with being "fictions," πλάσματα; Porphyry uses the same word, with the sense of "forgery." In the context of Middle Platonism, the use of frame narrative, developed characters, and supernatural mythologoumena set the Sethian apocalypses in the realm of "fictions" (πλάσματα), together with "myths." The Platonizing treatises' use of the genre "apocalypse" is radical, because most Platonists of the period did not compose fiction or myths: they interpreted them, usually with allegory. This method was warranted by a Platonic epistemology that interpreted images as faulty, shadowy representations of heavenly realities. The philosophical contemporaries of the authors of the Sethian texts did think stories (myths) or fiction could "be good" (i.e., contain truths), but only if they were interpreted properly—that is, under the aegis of παιδεία, following training in philosophy and cult.

The association of storytelling, narrative, or "myth" (μῦθος) with fiction or "fabrication" (πλάσμα) goes back to the Presocratics. The words μῦθος and λόγος had startlingly different meanings in Epic Greek: μῦθος indicated effective, truthful, intimidating speech with masculine coloring; λόγος indicated similarly effective, but slippery and deceitful speech highlighted with feminine tones.[104] Empedocles and Parmenides associated the forceful claims of μῦθος with unverifiable explanations of mysterious phenomena: the postmortem fate of the soul, metaphysics, and cosmogony.[105] This complex of ideas surrounding storytelling first becomes associated with the term πλάσμα in Democritus: "some people, not knowing about the dissolution of mortal nature, having come to know all too well the evil-doing in everyday life, suffer throughout their lifetime from troubles and fears, fabricating falsehoods in the form of myths (ψεύδεα . . . μυθοπλαστέοντες) about the time that lies beyond death."[106]

Plato departs from his forebears (and followers) by eschewing the language of πλάσμα in the context of forged narratives, for two reasons.[107] First, to simply identify poetic myths as fabricated or made up does not suffice for his purposes; he wants to show exactly how representation of all sorts is removed from the real. Second, his chief target is Homer, who does not use the word πλάσμα to talk about such images but εἴδωλον and εἰκών.[108] Thus, when Plato talks about storytellers and poets, he refers not to μυθοπλασέοντες. Instead, he uses compounds involving μῦθος and λέγω ("speaking").[109] Fabrication is an issue for Plato, but he uses the verb ποιέω ("to make") and its compounds to associate it with μῦθος.[110]

There is no single discussion of imagery and fabrication in Plato, but a general picture of his views about them (followed in the later Platonic tradition, as we will see) can be drawn.[111] In the famous criticism of poetry as a form of second-order imitation (μίμησις) in *Republic* book X, Plato argues that any εἴδωλον ("reflection," "representation") is a mere imitation of a faulty likeness of reality, and thus is twice removed from it.[112] In the *Sophist*, it is distinguished from the εἰκών, which, bound with "likeness" is only once removed. As the Stranger says, "images" are "like" (εἰκός) but "other" (ἕτερον), as distinguished from mere "fantastic likenesses" (φαντάσματα), associated with "reflections" (εἴδωλα) that only appear to resemble reality but actually do not.[113]

However, εἴκονα are not simply valorized images as opposed to "bad" reflections; while they are less false, they are still removed from reality.[114] In the *Statesman*, for instance, they are unfavorably contrasted with παραδείγματα ("models"): "it is a hard thing," says the Stranger, "to demonstrate any of the more important subjects without using models. It looks as if each of us knows everything in a kind of dreamlike way, and then again is ignorant of everything when as it were awake."[115] Plato goes on to describe the use of models for the process of protracted comparison and sorting out real difference and similarity. Images (εἰκόνα) are formed by a similar process, but do not reveal any structural similarity between compared objects.[116] Indeed, they are only "like" their referents, shadows of real things.[117] Yet elsewhere, Plato acknowledges that it is necessary to use images or metaphors in a heuristic, albeit problematic, fashion.[118] When Plato employs didactic images, they do not stand on their own as accurate representations of reality but rather provide a foothold for one attempting to grasp it.[119] In the context of myth, this foothold is not cognitive: rather, poetry's utility lies in the response that it elicits in the cupidic faculty (ἐπιθυμία) of the hearers or readers that allows them to gloss over the disparity between the image and reality.[120]

Storytelling is thus useful for teaching individuals who cannot or will not accept philosophical methods and truths, such as children or the uneducated.[121] As recognized by the Presocratics, it is also useful for positing unverifiable theses about things like gods, demons, the afterlife, and figures of the distant past.[122] Yet Plato sometimes acts as if he is able to verify myths, saying that some are true, some false, as at the beginning of Socrates' eschatological speech in the *Gorgias*: "give ear then—as they put it—to a very fine account. You'll think that it is a mere tale (μῦθον), I believe, although I think it is a trustworthy account (λόγον), for what I'm about to say I will tell you is true."[123] He goes on to explain how Zeus decreed that souls would be judged by his dead sons, Minos, Rhadamanthus, and Aeacus "in the meadow, at the three-way crossing from which the two roads go on, the one to the Isles of the Blessed and the other to Tartarus. . . . This, Callicles, is what I've heard, and I believe that it is true." At the story's end, he adds, "maybe you think this account is told as an old wives' tale (μῦθος), and you feel contempt for it. And it certainly wouldn't be a surprising thing to feel contempt for it if we could look for and somehow find one better and truer than it."[124]

The principle here seems to be that a narrative cannot be verified on its own terms, but can be verified according to the degree to which it resembles a "true account" that is philosophically reached.[125] (Plato implies as much in the *Republic*, where the poets are accused of giving "a bad image of what the gods and heroes are like, the way a painter does whose picture is not at all like the things he's trying to paint."[126] In both cases, the informed hearer of poetry or viewer of paintings has access to the real thing.) It is thus that Plato's own eschatological myths come at the end of a dialogue to provide a paraenetic edge to the philosophical arguments that precede them.[127] They function on the level of images (εἰκόνα), since they are only likenesses of the true, that is, scientific, discourse.[128] (Indeed, the latter is a criterion, or model, of the former—not the other way around!) Similarly, Plato in the *Timaeus* refers to his cosmogonic story as a merely "likely (εἰκῶς) story" no less than seven times and can only justify assent to it, as in the *Gorgias*, on the basis of an ostensible lack of alternative accounts.[129] Other images used in his myths are treated with similar reserve or irony, justified by the need for paraenesis.[130]

For Plato, then, even the "best" kind of story—eschatological, paraenetic myths—are clearly not meant to be read as literal truths. Instead, they are, at best, distorted representations of truths; still less accurate (and so less "good") are the reflections that imitate these; finally, the stories of the epic poets merely imitate reflections, and so are thrice removed from the Forms. As with the Presocratics, the function of all myths, whether epic or philosophical, is twofold: to provide information about cosmogony and eschatology and to stir an emotional reaction in the audience to command assent to the doctrines therein. Thus, while storytelling occupies a central and necessary place in his philosophy, they are also subordinate to logical argumentation: the truth value of mythical reflections is determined by their agreement with philosophical doctrine, while that of the Platonic narratives themselves is incumbent on it. Since Plato's analysis of myth and poetry is dominated by his broader interest in the epistemology of representation (i.e., the relationship of imitation to the Forms), rather than the concrete truth-value of that which is represented (i.e., the historical value of a story), he generally eschews the language of fabrication (πλάσμα).[131] In this respect, he is, ironically, exceptional in the Platonic tradition, for later speculations would incorporate his terminology and critique of imagery into their discussions of mythoplasty.

HOW TO READ A STORY

Apart from Epicurean critique of Plato's myths,[132] interest in his brand of eschatological, paraenetic storytelling disappears from Greek philosophical literature until Plutarch.[133] However, Plutarch incorporates the growing trend of allegorization into his philosophy of myth as well.[134] He dryly observes that "some commentators forcibly distorted these stories through what used to be termed 'deeper meanings (ταῖς πάλαι μὲν ὑπονοίαις)', but are nowadays called 'allegorical interpretations (ἀλληγορίαις δὲ νῦν λεγομέναις).'"[135] He refers to the penchant of

Stoic thinkers to read classical Greek myths as scientific descriptions of natural phenomena encoded in "fabrications" (πλάσματα) consisting of poetry and etymological puns.[136] Plutarch clearly sees this as a good way to read a story, since he employs it himself, aiming to reveal metaphysical realities and defend the integrity of the traditional cult, as in his famous work *On Isis and Osiris*:[137]

> These stories (i.e., about Isis and Osiris) do not, in the least, resemble the sort of loose fictions and frivolous fabrications (μυθεύμασιν ἀραιοῖς καὶ διακένοις πλάσμασιν) which the poets and writers of prose generate. . . . Rather, these accounts contain narrations of certain puzzling events and experiences (τινὰς ἀπορίας καὶ παθῶν διηγήσεις). . . . Just as the rainbow, according to the account of the mathematicians, is a reflection of the sun, and owes its many hues to the withdrawal of our gaze from the sun and our fixing it on the cloud, so the somewhat fanciful accounts here set down are but reflections of some true tale which turns back our thoughts to other matters (οὕτως ὁ μῦθος ἐνταῦθα λόγου τινὸς ἔμφασίς ἐστιν ἀνακλῶντος ἐπ'ἄλλα τὴν διάνοιαν); their sacrifices plainly suggest this.[138]

While Plutarch distinguishes narrative from poetry, he describes it as a fabrication, as did the Stoics, yet goes further by incorporating Plato's language of imagery. Plutarch consistently uses the verb πλάσσειν to denote fabrication and forgery, throughout his corpus.[139] Plutarch's use of the term εἰκών is hardly uniform; his text gives many examples of its use in the aesthetic, poetic, metaphysical, and religious spheres.[140] One also observes the use of language about imagery to denote a problematic, but necessary, reflection of reality.[141] Myth, meanwhile, is usually assigned a relatively inferior truth value lower than discussion (διήγησις).[142] Plutarch would be followed by the Platonic tradition in stressing that while myth, and imagery in general, is defective and must be interpreted through the lens of philosophy, storytelling is also the first step in the path to reality:[143] "a myth aims at being a false tale, resembling a true one."[144] One must then read stories and interpret myths, but correctly, using allegory, as when defending the otherwise senseless rituals of idolatry.[145] Both his reasoning and terminology are paralleled by his contemporary, Philo, defending Genesis's account of creation.[146]

Plutarch was particularly interested in the myths of Plato, not merely as an interpreter but as an imitator.[147] He is unique among ancient writers in having followed Plato by composing his own eschatological tales.[148] As with so many of Plato's dialogues, the narrative is displaced; accounts that are secondhand are often third-rate, a device that mirrors the Platonic emphasis on images as displaced from reality, as emphasized in *On the Divine Vengeance*.[149] When Plutarch comes to relate the account of "Thespesius," he cautions his interlocutors (and readers) thus: "I fear you would take it for a mere story; I confine myself accordingly to what is likely (ὀκνῶ δὲ μὴ φανῇ μῦθος ὑμῖν. μόνον οὐ χρῶμαι τῷ εἰκότι)."[150] In *On the Daimon of Socrates*, Plutarch aligns the problematic but important status of myth with that of revelation: it must be acknowledged, but only becomes part of philosophical discourse once the discursive faculties are exhausted. For example, Galaxidorus claims that Socrates' philosophy had "more of the true philosophic stamp, choosing that simplicity and sincerity (τὸ ἀφελὲς τοῦτο καὶ ἄπλαστον) of his for its manliness and great affinity to truth. . . . (Socrates) took philosophy, left by Pythagoras and his company to a prey of phantoms, fables, and superstition (φασμάτων δὲ καὶ μύθων καὶ δεισιδαιμονίας), and by Empedocles in a wild state of exaltation, and trained her to face reality with steadfast understanding, as it were, and to rely on sober reason (λόγῳ νήφοντι) in the pursuit of the truth."[151] Later on, Simmias contrasts "myth and fiction" (μῦθος, πλάσμα) with "argument" (λόγος). Yet storytelling is not a bankrupt level of discourse: Theocritus replies, "myths, too, despite the loose (ἀκριβῶς) manner in which they do so, have a way of reaching the truth (ψαύει τῆς ἀληθείας)."[152] However, this problematic method of indexing the truth through faulty images is only a last resort, once philosophizing has reached a deadlock. Thus, after relating the Myth of Timarchus, Simmias says, you "have the story along with the argument (μετὰ τοῦ λόγου τὸν μῦθον)."[153]

What, then, is the point of composing myths for a philosophical dialogue? Plutarch, like Plato, wishes to have an effect on the readers that changes their behavior.[154] They also agree in evaluating the truth value of myth according to its agreement with tenets previously reached by philosophical methods and in only relating myths themselves following, not prior to, an argument. For Plutarch as for Plato, then, storytelling is an essential part of philosophical discourse;[155] yet while it does not simply adorn dialectic, myth is subordinate to it.

With Plotinus, meanwhile, it seems that we are distant from the literary approach of Plato and Plutarch.[156] Plotinus never refers to Homer by name, rarely invokes the deities of Olympus, and mostly ignores the myths of Plato, whose truth value does not seem to be distinct from poetry.[157] Most importantly, Plotinus tells no stories himself. Yet he had an idea of the right way to read a story, allegorizing a variety of tales and symbols, employing the same technical vocabulary as his predecessors.[158] He considered the ideas yielded by allegory to be reached in a somewhat arbitrary fashion, but argued that allegorical narration is useful for rendering atemporal truths comprehensible to temporally bound beings like ourselves.[159] Myths are, historically speaking, false and ultimately disposable; the image is abandoned by the seeker once united with the silent God.[160] However, they are a necessary step in the road to unification.

A salient example is the allegorization of Hesiod's myth of the castration of Kronos, a favorite target for critics and rallying point for traditionalists.[161] While he sometimes followed Plutarch and Numenius by referring myths to the fate of the soul, Plotinus here fixed the reference point to the intelligibles themselves, equating Ouranos with the One, Kronos with the Intellect, and Zeus with the Soul.[162] The violent imagery of the story describes the screeching halt that ontogenesis must reach if potentiality is to attain some kind of stability during actualization—only then is a vision of and return to the One possible.[163] While Plotinus did not employ these mythical figures often or even consistently, he vigorously defended the basis of their usefulness—the integrity of Nature, Soul, and Intellect—as, in turn, images of their immediate source, a chain of images that leads back to absolute unity:

> He (Zeus) says that it was not without purpose that he came forth
> from his father; for his other universe must exist, which has come
> into being beautiful, since it is an image of beauty; for it is utterly
> unlawful that there should be no beautiful image (θεμιτὸν εἰκόνα)
> of beauty and reality. This image imitates its archetype (μιμεῖται δὴ
> τὸ ἀρχέτυπον) in every way. . . . (It) is not the product of art (τέχνη),
> but every natural image (φύσει εἰκών) exists as long as its archetype
> is there. For this reason, those are not right who destroy the world
> of images while the intelligible abides, and bring it into being as if its
> maker never planned to make it. For they do not want to understand
> how this kind of making (ποιήσεως) works, that as long as that higher
> reality gives its light, the rest of things can never fail; they are there
> as long as it is there; but it always was and will be. We must use these
> (i.e., temporal) words because we are compelled to signify (σημαίνειν)
> our meaning.[164]

Hadot is probably right to see here an attack on Gnostic models of genesis (the passage occurs halfway into the anti-Gnostic Großschrift). Plotinus strikingly chooses to explain the origins of the world, an imperfect but necessary image of the perfect realities, not by rejecting a Gnostic myth of cosmic catastrophe but instead by allegorizing a Hesiodic one, the history of divine revolts.[165] Similar charges are leveled later in the Großschrift, in *Against the Gnostics*. In response to the Gnostic doctrine of Sophia creating in remembrance of the ἔννοια—a passage closely paralleled in *Zostrianos* (as discussed in Chapter 1)—Plotinus focuses on imagery. The Gnostics say that the soul illuminates matter, creating a "reflection" (εἴδωλον) in matter, and they "fabricate a reflection of the reflection" (εἰδώλου εἴδωλον πλάσαντες) identified with the demiurge.[166] He meets this with a barrage of questions: "Why did the demiurge not make the universe at the same time as it illuminated, instead of waiting for the production of reflection (τῶν εἰδώλων). . . . How did matter, when it was illuminated, make psychic, instead of corporeal, reflections (εἴδωλα ψυχικά)? . . . Is this reflection (εἴδωλον) a substance, or, as they say, a 'thought' (ἐννόημα)? . . . And why was there still any need to introduce into their system the maker of the universe derived from matter and reflection (ὕλης καὶ εἰδώλου)? . . . This is pure fiction (πλάσμα)."[167] Plotinus not only uses the term εἴδωλον to refer to a lower reflection of higher reality but associates the word closely with the Gnostic account, as opposed to his description of the Hesiodic myth displaying the three hypostases as higher-order "images" (εἰκόνα).[168] (Recall Plato's own subordination of reflection to image—see Figure 2.)

It is particularly striking given the association of reflection elsewhere in the *Enneads*, particularly with imagination (again, as in Plato) and the descent of the soul into matter, one of his central topics of disagreement with the Gnostics.[169] As with Plutarch, the universe is instead an image (εἰκών)—problematic, but necessary for obtaining knowledge of the intelligibles and, in Plotinus, for the procession of Being itself.[170] Moreover, Plotinus's aggressive use of the terminology of fabrication (πλάσμα) to disparage the Gnostic account of creation parallels the usage of Plutarch. While the term is used to describe the Pandora myth, which he believes indicates true things, it also has a disparaging sense elsewhere in the *Enneads*.[171] As Edwards argues, Plotinus considers that "this image the 'Gnostics' themselves bring into being . . . is the false child which the human demiurge is bound to conceive. As the makers of their own Demiurge, they are seen to be at three removes from the Real."[172]

By accusing the Gnostics of fabricating myths and forging their documents, Plotinus and Porphyry thus tried to undercut the apocalypses' claim to the authority of ancient Mesopotamian scribes and use

Plato	Plotinus
τὰ ὄντα = Reality	The One
εἰκών = image of reality (Plato's own myths)	εἰκών = image of the First Principle = the Intelligible Triad
εἴδωλον = reflection of reality (φαντάσματα)	εἴδωλον = earthly reflections of the intelligible; handiworks, etc.
μίμησις εἰδώλου = imitation of a reflection of reality (poetry, myth)	μίμησις εἰδώλου (poetry, myth) = εἰδώλου εἴδωλον (Gnostic myth) = πλάσμα

Figure 2. Synopsis of the Epistemological Status of Image and Fabrication in Plato and Plotinus

language that assigns a necessarily low truth value to the narratives, specifically, that of poetic imitation of reflection (three removes from the real) rather than images (one remove, like the myths of Plato and Plutarch). The heritage of this language is that of Greek literary criticism, which sought to identify stories and poetry as flawed, human fabrications that may resemble truths, but are not in themselves true. As the Presocratics and Plato realized, this did not entirely negate the usefulness of poetry and stories; rather, it required alternative reading strategies that privileged philosophical argumentation (λόγος) as a criterion for truth. Myths themselves, then, could not be read literally, but required interpretation under this criterion. Plutarch, Plotinus, and others were in agreement with Plato on this, but went beyond him in employing the strategy of allegory to reinterpret myths with currency in contemporary popular cult and literature. It is only with Iamblichus (ca. 300 CE), followed by Proclus, that literal and allegorical readings are simultaneously affirmed for the same narrative.

In the Platonic schools of the second and third centuries CE, then, philosophers did not read mythical narratives as depicting historical or literal truths, but decoded their scrambled images to reach superior, non-narratival representations of reality. Even when a philosopher such as Plutarch or Dio Chrysostom composed his own myths, these were couched in language exhorting the reader not to take them as depicting the reality themselves.[173] In other words, later Platonists usually did not write stories, but they had techniques for reading the best ones well. There are instances of metaphysical poetry, but they are rare.[174] More importantly, these cases are philosophical prose put to verse, distinct from narratives. They are not stories. More specifically, they are not apocalypses.

ANOTHER KIND OF READER

The narrative structure of the Platonizing treatises houses philosophical discourses in the literal terms of an ongoing process of revelation, complete with heavenly ascent and ecstatic visions. This narrative structure is not, as for the Neoplatonists, a scrambled reflection or image, expressed in temporal terms per the needs of temporally bounded language, which can be decoded to represent eternal truths. Instead, it is a bald assertion of the literal authority of the text and its contents, which have been expressed perfectly clearly at a particular moment in time, that is, the reception of revelation from a heavenly being. Since these heavenly beings are inhabitants of the Barbelo, they dwell among and thus have direct access to the Forms. Hence, they issue a discourse that is neither a reflection nor an image or likeness of real things but an accurate description of the realities in themselves, a description transcribed by the authorized seer and passed on to the reader. A glance at the use of the language associated with "imagery" in *Zostrianos* and *Allogenes* shows that that they employ the apocalyptic technique in a Platonic context to make an exceptionally strong truth claim as to the bare, literal truth of the metaphysical pronouncements contained in the text.[175] Not only are they the wrong kind of stories, related by alien storytellers, but they demand another kind of reader than the allegorizing Platonists.

Before making his heavenly journey, Allogenes receives a revelation describing the permutations of the aeon of the Barbelo, the first emanation of the transcendent first principle, known as the Invisible Spirit. This figure—known as the Mother in the myth related in Chapter 1—is roughly equivalent in the Platonizing treatises to the hypostasis of Intellect in Neoplatonic thought, while the Invisible Spirit essentially obtains the status of the transcendent One. The four Platonizing treatises refer to this Spirit's three "powers" in terms of the Neoplatonic triad of the principles Being, Life, and Intellect: Existence, Vitality, and Intellectuality.[176] Another feature distinctive to these texts is their subdivision of the Barbelo into three aeons— the Kalyptos (καλυπτός, "hidden"), Protophanes (πρωτοφανής, "initial manifestation"), and Autogenes (αὐτογενής, "self-begotten"). (For an illustration of the structure of the intelligible world in these treatises, see below, Chapter 5, Figure 3.) These subaeons also represent moments in the activity of the Intellect, snapshots of its identity as self-contemplated Intellect (akin to νοῦς νοητός in Plotinus), contemplating Intellect (νοῦς νοερός), and finally the demiurgic, discursive Intellect (νοῦς διανοούμενος).[177]

The metaphor of photographs is an apt one, because *Allogenes* describes these subaeons as perfectly accurate images: Barbelo "possesses the copies (τύπος) and forms (εἶδος) of those who truly (ὄντως) exist, the image (εἰκών) of Kalyptos." It "bears the noetic male Protophanes like an image (ΚΑΤΑ ΟΥϨΙΚⲰΝ)." It "has the divine Autogenes like an image."[178] The unfolding of the thrice powered as an actualized image of the Invisible Spirit that lends the Barbelo its activity is described in similar terms in *Zostrianos*: "and the whole, perfect, simple, and invisible Spirit was a Unity (ⲘⲚ̄ⲦⲞⲨⲰⲦ), Thrice-Powered, simple in Substance (ὕπαρξις) and Activity (ἐνέργεια), an Invisible [Spirit], an [image (εἰκών)] of that which truly (ὄντως) exists, the One!"[179] It is thus really an image of the invisible (Spirit, that is), since the One does not "receive form (μορφή)"; rather, it is a kind of metaform, a "form of a form (ⲈⲒⲆⲈⲀ Ⲛ̄ⲞⲨⲈⲒⲆⲈⲀ), a "form of the Activity that exists."[180]

The idea that the intelligible world is a mere image of the ineffable first principle is standard Platonism, particularly strongly articulated by Plotinus.[181] Yet the Sethian texts here describe the permutations of the Barbelo aeon not as images of descending quality but as perfect images. Moreover, they mythologize these permutations, assigning each a myriad of inhabitants, such as the "luminaries" of the Autogenes and Protophanes aeons. Even the Barbelo herself is said to "rejoice" before her source, the Invisible Spirit, and to "empower" someone before her, issuing an ecstatic doxology.[182] In Plotinus or his Greek contemporaries, such a statement would have to be read allegorically.

However, *Zostrianos* and *Allogenes* part ways with their philosophical contemporaries—and each other—on how one interacts with these images on a practical level. After Zostrianos is rebuked by the "angel of knowledge," as described above, he begins his heavenly ascent: "And then I knew the power that existed in me, that it was set over the darkness, because all light was in its possession. I was baptized there. And I received the likeness (ⲈⲒⲚⲈ) of the glories there, becoming like one of them,[183] passing out from the aetherial [earth] ([ⲔⲀϨ] Ⲛ̄ⲀⲎⲢ),[184] traversing the impressions (ἀντίτυπος) of the aeons, having washed there seven times with living water, once for each [of the] aeons."[185]

This reception of the "image of the glories" via heavenly baptism triggers his transformation into an angel.[186] The Platonic epistemology of imagery is assimilated to a Sethian practice: the seer's shedding of the false image of the body for progressively more primordial, true images in ascent. Thus, once Zostrianos finishes his revelation discourses, he receives "a [likeness (ⲉⲓⲛⲉ)] that was pure, yet appropriate for sense-perception (αἴσθησις)"—something that should be strictly impossible in a Platonic context. He then composes his heavenly books and descends past the aetherial sphere, whence "I put (back) on my visible form (ⲧⲟⲩⲱⲧ), which was unlearned, empowering it and walking around preaching the truth to everyone."[187]

Allogenes focuses instead on the practice of meditation. The angel Youel visits the seer, imparting on the earth revelation about the intelligible: "This is so because of the third silence of Intellectuality and the second undivided activity which appeared in the First Thought (ϯϣⲟⲣⲡ̄ ⲛ̄ⲉⲛⲛⲟⲓⲁ), that is, the Aeon of Barbelo, together with the indivisible by[188] the divisible likenesses (ⲓⲛⲉ ⲙ̄ⲡⲱϣ), and the Thrice-Powered One and the nonsubstantial Substance (ϯⲉⲩⲡⲁⲣⲝⲓⲥ ⲛ̄ⲁⲧⲟⲩⲥⲓⲁ)."[189] This knowledge is apparently conditioned by Intellectuality, the third activity of the Thrice-Powered as instantiated in Barbelo. The indivisible is manifested by means of divisible likenesses, or images. As mentioned above, Allogenes grows afraid that his knowledge extends beyond proper bounds. Nonetheless, he prepares himself for one hundred years, is taken out of the body, and receives a revelation from "luminaries of the virgin male, Barbelo," which deals, first, with these "divisible likenesses."

Allogenes is told not to be afraid, but to "withdraw" (ἀναχωρεῖν) to the Substance (ὕπαρξις), "and you shall find it standing and at rest, like a likeness of (ⲕⲁⲧⲁ ⲡⲓⲛⲉ)[190] the one who is truly (ὄντως) at rest and embraces everything silently and inactively (i.e., the Invisible Spirit)."[191] Then he will receive a "primary revelation of The Unknowable One, that one who, if you were to know him, be un-knowing of him!" They continue: "If you become afraid in that place, withdraw to the back, because of the activities (ἐνέργεια); and when you become perfect there, still yourself; according to the copy (τύπος) that is in you. Know thus that it exits in everything, according to this form (ⲥⲙⲟⲧ)."[192] Allogenes "listens to the Blessedness," and standing "not firmly but still," withdraws to the Vitality; there, "I saw an eternal, intellectual (νοερόν) undivided motion that belongs to all the formless (ⲁⲧⲉⲓⲇⲟⲥ) powers, unlimited by bestowing limit.[193] And when I wanted to stand firmly, I withdrew (ἀναχωρεῖν) to the Substance (ὕπαρξις) that I had found standing and at rest as an image and likeness (ⲕⲁⲧⲁ ⲟⲩⲣⲓⲕⲱⲛ ⲙⲛ̄ ⲟⲩⲉⲓⲛⲉ) of what I was cloaked in[194] by a revelation of the indivisible, and that one who is at rest."[195] The noetic movement experienced during meditation is here described in terms of adopting a stillness, an image of existence, which is in turn an image of divinity, preparing the seer for the "Primary Revelation"—the central apophatic discourse of the tractate.[196]

Zostrianos and *Allogenes* thus adapt the Platonic language of image to suit a rhetorical context familiar from the apocalypses—describing the transformation of the seer, resulting in angelification or assimilation to the Barbelo, respectively.[197] This adaption transgresses contemporary Platonism in several ways. First, like the Epistle to the Hebrews, the Sethian texts engage eternal, intelligible images to address temporal, "personal" eschatology: what is to come (salvation) is made present by divine intervention (in Hebrews, Christ's sacrifice of his body; in *Allogenes* and *Zostrianos*, the transmission of the revelatory account and text).[198] Revelatory intervention of this sort violates Platonic doctrines of God's eternity and immutability: any action of God in history implies a change in the divine nature.[199] For an "orthodox" Platonist, the eternal, celestial forms dwelling in νοῦς could never be communicated in the temporal, terrestrial world. Second, the Sethian texts' adherence to a nonallegorical, literal description of the revelation and ascent of a seer contrasts strongly with the allegories of contemporary Gnostic and Christian literature and also with Hellenic philosophical sources.[200] Plotinus and Porphyry thus charge not only that the Sethian texts are forgeries operating at a relatively low epistemological level (mythoplasty) but also that their readers do not interpret them in the fashion appropriate to this level (allegory).

It is instructive here to recall Alexander of Lycopolis's polemic against the Alexandrian Manichaeans, composed around the turn of the fourth century CE.[201] Alexander mentions local Manichaeans, converts from among his philosophically educated friends, who allegorically interpret the Greek Mysteries but not their own myths.[202] Like Plotinus, he struggles with responding to educated individuals who present their metaphysics with literal imagery whose mythoplastic absurdity is authorized by prophetic tradition, not allegorical interpretative apparatus:[203]

Using their old and new scriptures (which they believe to be divinely
inspired) as underpinnings, they express their private doctrines as a
conclusion drawn from these (οἳ τὰς παρ' αὐτοῖς γραφὰς παλαιάς τε
καὶ νέας ὑποστησάμενοι—θεοπνεύστους εἶναι ὑποτιθέμενοι—τὰς σφῶν
αὐτῶν δόξας ἐντεῦθεν περαίνουσιν), and they are of the opinion that
such conclusions admit of a refutation if, and only if, it happens that
something is said or done by them which does not follow from these
scriptures. The role attributed by the philosophers of the Greeks to
the postulates, namely the underived propositions upon which proofs
are based, is represented among these people by the voice of the
prophets. Their stories are undoubtedly of the same make (as those of
the mythographers who write about the crimes of Uranus or Kronos),
since they describe a regular war of matter against God, but they
do not even mean this allegorically (δι' ὑπονοίας), as did Homer, for
instance.[204]

Similar critiques of Christian myth as literal fictions (πλάσματα) were
leveled by Celsus, Porphyry, and anonymous Hellenic anti-Christian polemicists.[205] As far as Hellenic philosophers were concerned,
Christian revelatory narratives were stories that were bad (because
they extolled barbarian, alien authorities and literary traditions) and
that demanded to be read the wrong way (as literal representations
of truth). The terms and concerns are identical to those of Plotinus.

CONCLUSION: A HELLENIC CRITIQUE OF REVELATION

While their teaching concerns the workings of a Neoplatonic cosmos, the Sethian "teachers" Marsanes, Allogenes, and Zostrianos,
validated by their interpreting angels, make similar claims to authority as they recount the stories of their revelation and transformation,
tales couched in the literary traditions of the ascent narratives familiar from Enochic literature. In this context, the Sethian texts could
not possibly seek to appeal to contemporary philosophical schools.
Platonic teaching is here packaged for an audience that would have
been receptive to the apocalyptic technique and its claims to authority. The esoteric idiom of the apocalypses, employing repetition,
paraenesis, (occasionally) fantastic imagery, and an exhortation to
secrecy, is intended for an in-group.[206] Nor does the appeal to Oriental authority implicate them in some kind of Numenian, Oriental
Platonism. Rather, like the anti-Hellenic Hermetic texts discussed in
Chapter 1, the Platonizing Sethian treatises auto-Orientalize, authorizing their teaching with an appeal to alien, primeval sages. The
identification with non-Greek culture heroes indicates a desire to

break with, rather than assimilate to, contemporary Greek philosophical schools, suffused with the Hellenocentric ideology of the Second Sophistic. Yet the *Chaldaean Oracles* and Hermes won some kind of approval within these schools anyway. Why, then, did the auto-Orientalizing of the Sethian literature elicit the ire of Plotinus and Porphyry, rather than their fascination with the wisdom of the Orient? And why would the later Platonic tradition remain closed to the Gnostic Platonism of Seth?

Answering this question will occupy the rest of this book, but already we can begin to discern the outlines of an explanation by recalling the differences between the sort of good stories Platonists liked and the apocalypses the Sethians liked. Scholars have posed the question like this: if Plato, the ancient philosopher par excellence, wrote myths as a way of communicating truths about cosmology and eschatology, can we distinguish Gnostic philosophical myth from Platonic storytelling?[207] Yes we can. First of all, the revelatory authorities invoked in philosophical myths were significant; it *matters* whether one invokes Julianus the Theurgist, Er the Armenian, or Marsanios. Second, the eschatological myths of Plato and Plutarch are couched with warnings that they ought not be immediately assented to, and they are embedded in the same Platonic terminology used to discuss myths that require allegorical interpretation. The Sethian literature, meanwhile, uses apocalyptic literary traditions to demand the reader's assent to their contents. Third, the comparison of Sethian narratology to that of Plato and Plutarch is itself a stretch; most Middle Platonists did not compose myths, but allegorized them. Like Epiphanius, Plotinus and Porphyry condemned Gnostic apocalypses as mere forgeries. Like Alexander of Lycopolis, they could not accept an approach to myth mutually exclusive with allegorical interpretation. The apocalypses must have appeared to be another way of writing, alien in both style and content to the stories Platonists read. And indeed, as we saw in Chapter 2, Plotinus grows increasingly frustrated trying to respond to them using the language and idiom of Greek philosophy; another way of writing would be more appropriate, he says.

The authors of the Platonizing Sethian texts, while clearly aware of the philosophical tools underlying allegory, use those tools instead to stress the internal coherence of the Barbelo aeon, which in turn undergirds the authority of the message delivered by its emissaries. This "apocalyptic truth claim" compresses and inverts the Platonic order of the acquisition of knowledge. For Plato and the Neoplatonists, the vision of reality is attained over the course of a lifetime, beginning with observation of sensible images, moving along to contemplation of abstractions (i.e., intelligible images), and culminating in a vision of the things in themselves.[208] The Sethian texts, however, collapse this process into a single revelatory event in which a being from the top of the hierarchy descends to the bottom to impart an accurate description of reality, perhaps bringing the visionary straight to the top for a personal encounter with the beyond.[209] The identity of the seer is (pre)determined by divine selection. There is no procession, in order, of beautiful people, crafts, constitutions, virtues, and first principles. In the social context of Severan philosophy discussed in Chapter 1, no schools, masters, or performances of the civic cult are attended. Instead, by divine intervention, straight out of heaven,[210] these levels and media are skipped, and the privileged seer (and the reader) is immediately whisked away to a private vision of the first principles themselves. The sermon of *Zostrianos* is not the speech of Diotima.[211]

All of this indicates that we are dealing with specifically Judeo-Christian, in-house literature. No wonder Plotinus, Porphyry, and their readers found the Sethian apocalypses objectionable: they were clearly designed not for a pagan Neoplatonic but a Sethian audience, deeply indebted to Jewish and Christian traditions we know from the apocrypha. Their claims to authority would be valid in no other context. Their approach to a genre that stresses the authority of its own mythic account, rather than questioning it, was obviously unwelcome in contemporary Platonic schools. Viewing Sethianism as cultically and philosophically *un*-Hellenic—even in its most Platonic incarnation—renders intelligible many other narrative details of the texts that look strange in the context of Hellenic Platonism: the sage's fear of vision, heavenly journeys on clouds, frightening or angry angels who may need to be avoided during ascent, the acquisition of power or crowns from heavenly beings, the composition of revelatory testimony for posterity on steles or in (celestial!) books, and the pseudepigraphic appeal to sages with currency in biblically informed circles.[212] Each of these features concerns the idea of a sage who, having ascended into heaven, is transformed into a savior who descends to earth; it is to these Gnostic messiahs, the avatars of the celestial Seth, that we now turn.

CHAPTER 4

The Descent

While the entirety of Sethian literary tradition is cast in the shape of contemporary apocalypses, scholars have long distinguished between the texts that are also inundated with the language of contemporary Neoplatonic metaphysics—the Platonizing literature, *Zostrianos*, *Allogenes*, *Marsanes*, and the *Three Steles of Seth*—and those that are not. However, the more popular nomenclature to express this distinction in scholarship describes them as "ascent" (Platonizing, contemplative) and "descent" (apocalyptic, historical) treatises.[1] For Turner, the descent treatises develop Jewish traditions about the descent of Wisdom (Sophia) into the cosmos into a theology of the descent of Barbelo, the divine Mother;[2] the ascent treatises, meanwhile, reject the merciful descent of Barbelo, masculinizing her with epithets such as "thrice-male" and dividing her into the three sub-aeons of Kalyptos, Protophanes, and Autogenes.[3] Turner hypothesizes that, in the descent treatises, the Gnostic is passive and acquires revelation through the descent of Barbelo, while the ascent treatises describe active, meditative exercises wherein one thinks one's way to the primordial source using the techniques of contemporary Platonism, engaging the world of ideas—specifically, "authentic existents" (pure, eternal forms in Kalyptos), "unified individuals" (forms and souls existing prior to division, in Protophanes), and differentiated, "individual" forms and souls (in the Autogenes).[4]

Turner argues further that the distinction between descent to ascent treatises also reflects important changes in Sethian literary composition and temporality. While the descent scheme clearly derives from

Jewish sapiential and apocalyptic motifs and represents the "Jewish" and "Christian" stages of Sethian tradition, the Platonizing treatises are absent of Judeo-Christian themes, inspired instead by "Greek visionary literature," and represent the attempt to appeal to paganism.[5] Moreover, the descent works are centered on the "horizontal" history and eschaton of a sacred people (i.e., the seed of Seth), while the ascent works are focused on the "vertical teleology" of encountering intelligible reality.[6] They are uninterested in finite time and cognate salvation history, and so some scholars, as we will see in Chapter 5, have argued that the ascent treatises affirm the Hellenic dogma of the eternity of the world.

This chapter provides an overview of Sethian soteriology, focusing on the descents of the savior across Sethian tradition. It demonstrates that the distinction between ascent and descent treatises is an unhelpful one. Nearly all the Sethian treatises deal with some kind of descending savior, who is not the Barbelo but an avatar, an incarnation of Seth himself, coming down into the world to redeem the elect seed. Thus nearly all Sethian treatises—and each of the Platonizing apocalypses—are, properly, descent treatises, insofar as they focus on Seth's descent to earth to provide revelation and, ultimately, salvation. Those who choose to receive it are described with various ethnic terminology, for example, as the seed of Seth or an "alien race," which was a common self-designation in early Christian literature. The Platonizing treatises supplement this ethnic language of alienation to describe the chosen with language about the effects of divine providence on the souls of the elect, who are known as "perfect individuals." As we will see, Plotinus mocks this language in *Against the Gnostics*, as part of a polemic about the concept of divine election, which he views as deterministic and privileging a separate, alien race from the rest of humanity, thus violating the universal reach of God's providential care. All of this points to a fairly unified soteriology spanning the Platonizing texts and the rest of Sethian literature, one that is deeply indebted to Jewish and Christian ideas about salvation and the saved.

SETH AND HIS AVATARS

The deeply philosophical nature of the Platonizing treatises has led, at times, to their characterization as "non-mythological."[7] This should not, however, be taken to imply a marginalization of the centrality of the character of Seth to the identity of the elect, who are identified as his seed. In fact, there is great continuity throughout Sethian literature with respect to corporate religious identity, as expressed in terms of ethnicity. As George MacRae observes, "The most important feature of Gnostic speculation on Seth is the idea that Gnostics constitute a special 'race' of Seth," the unspoiled perfect image of Adam, who was created in the image of God himself.[8] Some Christians even likened Seth to Christ, and Manichaeans knew him as both apostle and savior.[9] The comparison is acute for our understanding of Sethian religious identity: in both Sethian and Manichaean literature, Jesus of Nazareth is occasionally mentioned as one of many revelatory figures from biblical tradition who is an incarnation of a salvific heavenly being. Sethian literature is distinct in focusing on this being, Seth, both in his celestial, atemporal existence and his various incarnations throughout history.

"Proto-orthodox" Christianity, Manichaeism, and Sethianism all drew from a common biblical heritage in which Seth was understood to be a revealer, as in the so-called apocryphal Adam literature, where he records the premortem testament of his father, the first man.[10] Syncellus reports that Seth experienced, at the hands of angels, rapture and revelation about the imminent rebellion of the Watchers.[11] He was often invested with Enochic features, whether as the inventor of astronomy or as a scribe preserving predeluge history on tablets made of stone and clay, to survive a flood and a conflagration, respectively.[12] Seth was also known as the father of the elect, which "birthed" language about the "seed" or "race" (σπορά, γενεά) of Seth.[13] The roots of this tradition are probably Jewish, but largely preserved in Syriac Christian literature.[14] Stroumsa hypothesizes that such traditions were at the root of later Sethian language about the seed of Seth.[15] Regardless, Sethian tradition was not alone among the Abrahamic faiths in viewing Seth as the primal ancestor not just of humanity but particularly of the elect.[16]

Sethian Gnosticism develops these traditions about Seth in myriad ways, but consistently points to him as a celestial being who descends to earth throughout history in the service of humanity's salvation. The *Apocalypse of Adam* is a testament in the style of ancient Adam apocrypha, where Seth transcribes his father's last words (in which is embedded a further revelation from three men, another Jewish tradition) and leaves it on steles for future readers to discover.[17] However, Seth is also the father and even savior of the elect. The text identifies

"knowledge" (γνῶσις) as part of the "seed of the great aeons"; Seth
himself is named for the "seed of the great generation (γενεά)," presumably the race that possesses knowledge.[18] Later, when the revelation to Adam (as recounted to Seth) begins, the three men tell him
that he will hear "about the aeon and the seed of that man to whom
life has come, who came from you and from Eve, your wife."[19] These
elect are "strangers" known as the "seed of men," and who receive
the "life of knowledge."[20] While the *Apocalypse of Adam* does not
spell it out in explicit terms, the constellation of the themes of knowledge, foreignness, and descent around the character of Seth points to
a soteriological model in which the literal descendants of the primeval ancestor are those who will be saved, in part thanks to his direct
intervention in history.[21] Indeed, the salvific "Illuminator," whose
appearance catalyzes the end of the world, is probably to be identified
with Seth (notably descending "[out of] a foreign air").[22]

The *Egyptian Gospel*, too, elaborates on "the great Seth," who
is not just a savior but a heavenly being.[23] The beginning of the text
describes the emanation of divine beings from God prior to the cosmogenesis, elaborating on the birth of Seth and the hymns he utters in
praise of God, along with the four luminaries of the Autogenes aeon.[24]
He is also closely related to a mysterious Sethian mythologoumenon,
the character of the "Thrice-Male Child," a fellow denizen of the
Autogenes aeon.[25] However, as in the *Apocalypse of Adam,* Seth is
also an earthly revelator; in fact, he appears to be the author of the
text itself, having left it "in the mountain that is called Kharaxio," so
that, "by the will of the divine Autogenes," it might "reveal this incorruptible, holy race (γενεά) of the great savior (σωτήρ)."[26] The "great
savior" is almost certainly the "great Seth" himself, who intervenes in
history several times to protect his offspring through various human
incarnations.[27] When the devil sends various disasters to test them,
Seth requests from the higher aeons guardians for his seed.[28] Eventually, he personally descends in three cataclysms (the flood, the fire,
and the final judgment) to save the race; in his third descent, he incarnates as Jesus Christ.[29]

Seth's role as savior follows naturally from his having obtained
and guarded his own seed. Prior to the creation of the world, Seth
praises various deities, and "asks for his seed." The divine *genetrix*
Pleistheia appears, "the mother of the lights, the glorious mother,
the virgin with the four breasts, bringing the fruit from Gomorrah
as spring and Sodom, which is the fruit of the spring of Gomorrah

which is in her. She came forth through the great Seth. Then, the
great Seth rejoiced about the gift which was granted him by the
incorruptible child. He took his seed from her, she with the four
breasts, the virgin, and he placed it with him in the fourth aeon, in
the third great Luminary, Davithe."[30] The seed of Seth is, like him,
hypostasized in the Autogenes aeon in the third luminary. It appears
to be "sown" only after the character Repentance (μετάνοια) prays
for the salvation of the two seeds. "The great angel Hormos" prepares the seed of Seth through "corruptible (i.e., mortal) virgins,"
"in a discursively-begotten holy vessel (λογογενὴς σκεῦος)."[31] The
passage seems to mean that, until Christ, there were multiple virgin births, producing the "race of Seth"; but after Christ, one can
be inaugurated into the line of the saved. Eventually, the seed is
described as "the race that came into existence through Edokla,"
who also gives birth to Truth and Justice, "the origin of the seed of
the eternal life which is with those who will persevere because of the
knowledge of their eternal life. . . . This is the great, incorruptible
[race] which [has] appeared in three [worlds]."[32]

Thus, the *Egyptian Gospel* features a tripartite soteriological
model, consisting of the elect seed, the damned, and undecided contemporaries who can become saved through baptism and the acquisition of knowledge (γνῶσις), that is, Seth's seed. This mechanism
for salvation preexists (since it was born before the creation of the
world) and is accessible to any who will receive it (since Seth reveals
it).[33] These individuals are almost certainly "those who are worthy
of the baptisms [of] the renunciation and the ineffable seals of [their]
baptism, these have known [their] receivers (παραλήμπτωρ) as they
[have learned] about them, having known [through] them, and they
shall not taste death."[34] While the seed of Seth was once a biological inheritance, through the intervention of Seth-Christ, the seed has
become figurative. Seth himself, meanwhile, fulfills dual roles as both
heavenly hypostasis, dwelling with the luminaries of the Autogenes
and the Thrice-Male Child, and earthly savior, thanks to his multiple incarnations. One of these incarnations is Jesus Christ, or "Yesseus Mazareus Yessedekeus," "the living water" and "Child of the
Child."[35]

Although Seth and his descents are not the primary topic of the
Platonizing Sethian treatises, this basic soteriological template seems
to underlie them, and at times is necessary to make sense of them.
Zostrianos depicts Seth as a heavenly being; one of the luminaries

of the Protophanes, Setheus, even seems to be named after him.[36] Elsewhere, the text consistently partners Seth with his "alien" father, (Ger)adamas, Adam's mother, Meirotheia, and the "Perfect Child," a constellation recalling the *Egyptian Gospel*: "Since Adam, the [perfect] man, is an eye of [Autogenes], it is his knowledge that comprehends that the divine Autogenes is a discourse of [the] perfect Intellect of truth. And the son of Adam, Seth, comes to each one of the souls; verily, he is knowledge (γνῶσις), sufficient for them. For this reason, the living seed (σπορά) came into existence. As for Meirotheia [. . .]."[37] As the Perfect Child, Seth is probably to be identified further with a manifestation of the Thrice-Male Child, "Yesseus Mazareus Yessedekeus, the commander, [. . .] who is the Child, [the] Savior, the Child."[38] The same Yesseus or Child of the Child also headlines the baptismal hymn concluding the *Egyptian Gospel*, as noted above. The possession of "sufficient knowledge" is what characterizes the souls that inhabit the aeon of Repentance. In *Zostrianos*, then, Seth seems to play a role in the transition of certain souls from the Sojourn to the Repentance, retaining his role as patron of the elect as he begins his scribal activity and ministry. The ascended Zostrianos is a descending savior, having been transformed into an incarnation of Seth.[39]

Like Seth himself, his elect progeny exists in the heavens. The "sons of Seth" can be found in the third luminary of the Autogenes aeon, Davithe (again recalling the *Egyptian Gospel*).[40] Yet Zostrianos says, at the beginning of the treatise, "I was in the cosmos for the sake of those of my generation (ϭⲟⲧ) and those who would come after me, the living elect (ⲥⲟⲧⲛ̄ ⲉⲧⲟⲛϩ̄)."[41] Immediately after his suicide attempt (described in Chapter 3), an angel tells him to "return, another time, to preach to the living race, to save those who are worthy, and to strengthen the elect (ⲛⲓⲥⲱⲧ[ⲛ̄])."[42] He embarks on his long heavenly journey, and, finally, having returned to earth, begins his sermon with the words, "Ye living, the Seed of the holy Seth, pay heed (ⲉⲓⲙⲉ) (to me)!"[43] The heavenly seed of Seth is, as in the *Egyptian Gospel*, a preexisting salvific state acquired by some on earth, Seth's "living elect," who are the recipients of Zostrianos's revelations. Its transmission is not biological but noetic, open to all but rejected by many, the "dead" souls.[44] The influence of the *Egyptian Gospel* on *Zostrianos* extends beyond doxology to a shared soteriological model, featuring multiple descents of a heavenly Seth to save his seed, which participates in its heavenly counterpart.[45]

Allogenes is concerned with contemplative practice, not soteriology, and neither Seth nor Adam is mentioned in the text. Yet scattered references in the text to eschatology and the saving activity of its eponymous seer seem difficult to explain without presuming some kind of soteriological template like that of *Zostrianos* or the *Egyptian Gospel*. The text refers to people who will *not* be saved: before his ascent, Allogenes is told by Youel that it is not fitting to speak about the Invisible Spirit to "an uninstructed generation."[46] In the middle of a technical negative theological discourse later on, the "luminaries" declare that someone who mistakenly identifies God with his attributes "has not known God" and is "liable to judgement."[47] Salvation seems to be available to whoever is receptive to the message of the seer, although here it is identified not with the seed of Seth but with the first emanation of reality itself, the Thrice-Powered: "if it is conceived of (νοεῖν) as the ferry-man of the boundlessness of the Invisible Spirit [that] subsists in him, it (the boundlessness) turns him to it[self],[48] so that it might know what is [within] him and how it exists, and of (how) it became[49] salvation for all, being a cause of those who truly exist."[50]

"Salvation for all" must have been made available through a figure mentioned by the angel Youel, "that you might be saved in that one who belongs to you, that one who was the first to save and who does not need to be saved."[51] This figure is probably the Thrice-Male Child: " Verily, it (the Barbelo) acts separately (κατὰ μέρος) and individually, continuing to rectify the sins, things (that) come from Nature (φύσις). He has the divine Thrice-Male, being salvation for them all, along with the Invisible Spirit."[52] We can also probably identify the savior with Seth, given the text's repeated mention of the savior Thrice-Male Child (closely associated with the cosmic Seth of the *Egyptian Gospel*), the name of the seer Allogenes (a name recalling Seth), and the similarity of his ministry to that of Zostrianos.[53] The identities of the savior's earthly incarnations are unspecified because the seer encounters him on the most primal and noetic of levels.[54]

Meanwhile, the Neoplatonic doxologies of the *Three Steles of Seth* are principally concerned with the salvific power of Seth and his seed. As in *Zostrianos*, Seth, "the father of the living and immovable race," is associated with his father, Geradamas (whose name, as we will see, means "alien Adam"): "because of you I am with that very one (i.e., God). You are light, since you behold light. You have revealed light."[55] The elect is identified as Geradamas's offspring, as when Seth declares, "You are from another race (γένος), and its place is over another race. Now, {you are from another race, and its place is over another race.} You are from another race, since you are different. You are merciful, because you are eternal; your place is upon a race, since you made them all increase, on account of my seed; for it is you who knows it, since its place is upon begetting (ϫπο). And some come from other races, since they are different; and their place is over other races, since their place is in life."[56] By being an alien and begetting an alien race, Geradamas manifests the alien divinity in the mundane.[57] He is a thrice-male savior, like the Thrice-Male Child of *Allogenes*: "(You are) the one who has caused the thrice-males that truly exist to become male three times. The one who was divided from the pentad, the one who was given to us by a thrice-power, the one who was sent without begetting, the one who came from the superior for the sake of the inferior, going out into the midst . . . We bless you, thrice-male, for you have united the all through them all, for you have empowered us. You came about through One; from One you came forth; you have come to One; You have saved, you have saved, you have saved us, crown-bearer, crown-giver!"[58] Just as the Thrice-Male Child in *Allogenes* is an instrument of the Barbelo that reveals the Invisible Spirit, Geradamas and Barbelo in the *Three Steles of Seth* are also tools used by the transcendent to reveal unity by unifying the elect; they mediate differentiated salvation to the differentiated particulars.[59]

Although Seth's descent itself is not described, it is clear that he in turn transmits knowledge of the divine (the "steles" themselves) and begets the race of Adam. In fact, the pseudepigraphic pose of the text ("Dositheus" claims to have made a copy of Seth's steles for the elect to read, "just as they were inscribed there") could assume that Seth has descended to write them; how else could they have been left for Dositheus to read?[60] It is clear that the *Three Steles* are a liturgical text, meant to be read aloud; thus the reader is meant to identify with Seth, and so Adam, the perfect human.[61]

The *Three Steles* also offer pause for methodological reflection; this analysis of them focuses on the first stele, which is addressed to Barbelo.[62] The second stele repeats similar themes, but the third is, like *Allogenes*, almost entirely concerned with the One and epithets for the unknowable God. Nothing is said there of Adam or Seth. The *Steles* are a good example of how even the Platonizing texts emphasized different parts of their soteriology with respect to different aspects of practice—that is, contemplation (*Allogenes*) versus doxology (*Three Steles*)—and how these emphases yielded diverse thematic emphases. Yet it is clear that the third stele should not be read apart from the first two; similarly, *Allogenes*, though focused on the unknowable God, has evidence of Sethian soteriological themes in the foreground, and so should not be divorced from them.

It is difficult to see soteriological themes in the remaining Sethian texts, but in the *Apocalypse of Adam*, the *Egyptian Gospel*, *Zostrianos*, *Allogenes*, and the *Three Steles of Seth*—an undisputable "core" of Sethian literature, including most of the Platonizing stream of the tradition—Seth is featured as father of the primordial race, mediator between humanity and Adam (and thus God), the revealer of salvation history and cosmological secrets, and the savior of mankind.[63] He descends to earth for the sake of the salvation of the elect, whether as bringer of the eschaton or Platonizing prophet, and is associated with the Autogenes aeon and, particularly, the salvific figure called the Thrice-Male (Child). The elect are ethnically circumscribed by virtue of their heritage in the lineage of Seth, another seed who has begotten an alien race—language we will revisit in Chapter 5. Only the *Apocalypse of Adam* deviates (albeit slightly) from this model, by eschewing the Barbeloite appellation "Thrice-Male" and the Neoplatonic jargon.[64]

However, and most importantly, each text presents a descending revealer-savior who incarnates several times throughout history—usually once as Seth, perhaps also as Jesus Christ. This particular model of the multiple incarnations of a heavenly savior is particular to the Jewish-Christian Christology heresiologists ascribed to the groups known as the Ebionites, and especially the Elchasaites: "Some others . . . procured a foreign volume, named for a certain Elchasai. . . . They do not confess that there is but one Christ, but that there is one above and that he is infused into many bodies frequently, and now into Jesus. Similarly, they confess that he was begotten of God at one time and at another time he became a Spirit and at another time was born of a virgin and at another time not so."[65] The Pseudo-Clementine literature, too, describes a "True Prophet" who incarnates in various ancient patriarchs and prophets, before manifesting as Jesus. Drawing from this heritage of Mesopotamian traditions about salvific revelators incarnating in history, Mani proclaimed himself to be the Paraclete, possessed by the same spirit who was present among the patriarchs and other religious authorities.[66] (Indeed, the scholarly

consensus is that Mani was raised in an Elchasaite community.)[67] This
pattern of descents of the incarnating savior is recalled not only by the
Sethian texts themselves but also by Porphyry's evidence about them,
which presented us with the rapt antediluvian seers "Nicotheus" and
"Marsanios." Scholars have long described the Platonizing texts as
pagan in part thanks to Jesus's absence from them, but the criterion
of his presence is a straw man. The avatars of Seth we know from
Nag Hammadi and Porphyry are products of Mesopotamian revelatory literature informing Jewish-Christian groups and Manichaeism,
which conceived of the savior as descending to earth in a variety of
historical personages. The description of Seth's elect in ethnic terms,
too, is grounded in contemporary Judeo-Christian rhetoric.

SETH AND HIS RACE

Only *Allogenes* minimizes ethnic language (because of its focus on
contemplative practice rather than soteriology), yet the Sethian use of
such language to describe the body of the elect remains little understood.[68] While modern theories of ethnicity commonly distinguish
between ethnicity (a cultural attitude) and race (a biological fact), we
cannot export this distinction to antiquity, where words spanning the
reaches between ἔθνος and γένος seem to have been interchangeable.[69]
Sethian references to "race," the "seed" of Seth, and the "resident
alien topos" indicate not simply biological speculation but markers
of cultural and cultic identity. It is worth choosing the term "ethnicity" to govern the range of ethnoracial discourse in order to emphasize collective identity as a social rather than biological group since,
excepting the *Apocalypse of Adam*, membership in the elect seed of
Seth is not biological but spiritual.[70] As Denise Kimber Buell emphasizes, while ethnicity in early Christian contexts is always pegged
to a conception of descent or primordial origins ("fixed"), it is also
"fluid," shifting to "exclude and include groups," a dynamic she calls
"ethnic reasoning."[71] Two ancient discourses of ethnic reasoning illuminate the Sethian apocalypses and their Christian readers in Plotinus's Roman seminar: Christian language about a "new" or "third"
race and the Hellenocentrism popularized in higher education during
the Second Sophistic.

Early Christian sources are replete with racial self-designations, such
as the "new race" of the *Epistle to Diognetus*.[72] In other texts, Christians contrast themselves with Greeks and Jews, calling themselves a

"third race";[73] Tertullian reports that the designation was well known enough to have become a pejorative among their persecutors, while the *Martyrdom of Polycarp* employs it to contrast the "god-loving and God-fearing race" of Christians with their Hellenic and Jewish tormentors.[74] Aristides even claims that Christians trace their descent to Jesus.[75] Clement, probably inspired by Justin, holds that the race of the elect (i.e., Christians) actually existed before the creation of mankind, and so other races.[76] The Valentinian *Tripartite Tractate* distinguishes the elect from the Greeks and the Jews.[77] The background of this language lies in Jewish texts that identify the Jewish people as a race (γένος), often in distinction from their rivals or opponents.[78] This point is important: the presence of language about race alone does not amount to "ethnic reasoning" but rather is a product of the use of language about race to distinguish groups and identities.[79]

Christian language about a "new race" that preexists and is foreign to the cosmos, is mutable (i.e., accessible to would-be converts), and defines the elect group is probably behind the development of Sethian ethnic reasoning. The models are functionally similar: in the Sethian texts, the cosmic Seth and his seed exist in the intelligible realm prior to the material world but are manifested in humanity through the revelations and preaching of seers, who seem to be incarnations of Seth himself. Moreover, they rely on a shared set of biblically informed symbols and motifs (Adam, Seth, occasionally Jesus Christ) to explore myths of primordial origins. At the same time, the Hellenic contemporaries of the authors of the Sethian texts, and especially their philosophical sparring partners in the Greek schools, also engaged in ethnic reasoning, negotiating a constructed Hellenic identity that was defined by participation in public life, civic rites, and the culture of παιδεία, as argued in Chapter 1.[80] Platonic Orientalism thus constitutes a type of ethnic reasoning that was particularly common in philosophical circles of the period, as is evident by a glance at texts like the *Corpus Hermeticum* or *Chaldaean Oracles*.

It is precisely in this environment, with reference to both the new race of the Christians and Platonic Orientalism, that Sethian language about race in the Platonizing Sethian texts took on the character of ethnic reasoning. While their salvific models and, to a lesser extent, biblical characters coincide, Sethian language about race differs from that of their proto-orthodox contemporaries as well; it may even be directed against them. As noted in the previous section, Sethian portrayals of Seth are not paralleled by proto-orthodox Christian sources. Moreover, Sethian tradition clearly prefers the idiom of a "seed" rather than a "new," or "third," race. While it is obvious that the Sethian γένος is to be contrasted with the "ways of others" and the non-elect (in the language of *Zostrianos*), there are no explicit references to Greeks or Jews in the texts.

Sethian ethnic reasoning may then tell us more about its audience than its theological underpinnings: the primacy of Christian ethnic reasoning in apologetic and martyrological circles may provide a clue as to its appeal to the Christians in Plotinus's seminar in Rome in the 260s CE, with two persecutions (the Decian [250 CE] and Valerianic [257–60 CE]) in recent memory.[81] Moreover, Sethian ethnic reasoning helps us understand the function of its particular brand of Platonic Orientalism. Like the authors of Hermetic literature or the *Chaldean Oracles*, the Platonizing Sethian apocalypses discuss Greek metaphysics but affirm a distinctly non-Hellenic identity. Buell has argued that, "ethnic reasoning allowed Christians not only to describe themselves as a people, but also to depict the process of becoming a Christian as one of crossing a boundary from membership in one race to another."[82] When we recall that for the Neoplatonists, ethnicity was chiefly defined by mastery of the Greek classics, Sethian ethnic language, culled from the traditions of Jewish apocrypha, must have signaled a rejection of Hellenic heritage. More strikingly, the Sethian texts describe their in-group and its teaching not simply as superior to other races or nations but as "elect," "saved," in contrast to souls that will be destroyed. Surely members of the Sethian elect were educated in the Hellenic schools, but there is no sign in the texts that they continued to identify as Hellenes, and many signs that they regarded themselves as something much more—"the living, the Seed of the holy Seth!"

How exactly did one become one of the seed of Seth, and how fixed was this membership? Some scholarship has followed the heresiologists in charging Gnostic soteriology with determinism, granting elect status only to those lucky enough to be born with knowledge of the divine.[83] Plotinus himself disparages his Gnostic opponents' ideas about divine providence, as follows:

1.   By claiming that their souls are superior to the movement of the heavenly spheres (fate)[84] and thus not subject to their authority, the Gnostics disrupt the proper order or hierarchy of the cosmos; access to knowledge and, ultimately, wellbeing is thus barred to them.[85]

2. The Gnostics contradict themselves by simultaneously denying providence's extension to the universe and claiming that it
   extends to them alone.[86] Yet providence extends less to parts
   than to wholes.[87]

3. Gnostic claims to be superior to the stars and sole beneficiaries of providence led them to reject the traditional cult in
   favor of their identity as "sons of God."[88]

Charge (3) has already received some attention above, in Chapters
1 and 2; removing oneself from the contemporary civic cult was not
a welcome idea to Plotinus or other contemporary Platonists. With
respect to (1), Plotinus is silent as to how exactly his Gnostics opponents claim they can acquire knowledge without the stars and the
supervision of fate. He could mean that, for the Gnostics, the seam-
less transmission of being and knowledge via the hierarchy of the
cosmic order is rejected in favor of an earthly theophany and revelation.[89] As argued in Chapter 3, revelation possesses a truth value that,
in Platonic terms, is beyond the proper station of everyday, much less
mythopoetic, language.

Some scholars have followed Plotinus in arguing that the concept of revelation itself implies a deterministic view that salvation is
bestowed from without, not chosen from within.[90] Yet as we have
seen in this chapter, membership in the Sethian elect was not biologi-
cally determined. Moreover, the paraenetic discourses and sermons
strewn about *Zostrianos*, *Allogenes*, and *Marsanes* make it clear that
the author(s) of the texts intended their revelations to be intelligible
to others. Sethian literature thus used ethnic terminology to express a
universalist soteriology wherein ethnicity was mutable, and thus the
race of the saved was open to all, although many rejected the offer to
their detriment.[91]

SETH AND HIS CHOSEN

Plotinus's charge that the Gnostics simultaneously deny the extension of providence (Gk. πρόνοια, "forethought") to the world, while
affirming that it belongs to them alone, remains to be explained. The
first half is intelligible enough in light of Gnostic ideas of the creation
of the cosmos: responsibility for making the world belongs not to
the providential activity of God but to a flawed, even evil, demiurge,
who is mentioned in a passage of *Zostrianos* that Plotinus appears

to have known.[92] In the Barbeloite theogony of the *Apocryphon of John*, for instance, the Barbelo aeon is equated with providence, the "first thought" of the Invisible Spirit, long before the creation of the cosmos, which transpires as a grand accident rather than as a result of any divine plan.[93] The Gnostic friends thus are unique among their philosophical contemporaries in divorcing providential care for material creation from providential care for humanity, and then denying the former while affirming the latter. The Platonizing Sethian treatises *Zostrianos* and *Allogenes*, meanwhile, known in some form to Plotinus, appear to present a more complex, technical version of this view, in which the divinity's "foreknowing" of itself seems to produce a "primordial manifestation" of Being and the ensuing rush of intelligible reality.[94] Yet this "first thought" of the Invisible Spirit—the Barbelo and its subaeons, the Kalyptos, Protophanes, and Autogenes—is also active in the salvation of souls, the souls of the elect. A look at these passages shows that Plotinus was familiar with Sethian nomenclature for the elect and mocked it in the context of his polemic about Gnostic providence.

As we will see in Chapter 5, *Zostrianos* identifies the Sethian elect who have escaped from the cycle of reincarnation as "individuals" (ката оүа, probably translating τὰ κατὰ μέρος, or τὰ καθ' ἕκαστα from the original Greek text) or "perfect individuals" who inhabit the Autogenes aeon. The text emphasizes that while all souls have "types" of heavenly realities (i.e., the eternal, unified Platonic forms), their "resemblances" differ from one another and thus are multiple and divided.[95] However, the elect in the Autogenes are more unified, and obtain additional celestial baptisms: "but whoever did not commit any sin, because knowledge (γνῶσις) was enough for him, he certainly is not concerned about anything, since he has repented. And there are baptisms arranged in addition. With respect to the path up to the self-begotten ones, that thing in which you have (just) now been baptized each time, (a path) that is worthy of seeing the perfect (τέλειος) individuals (ката оүа)—it is knowledge (γνῶσις) of the entirety, since it has come into being through the powers (of) the self-begotten ones."[96] These perfect individuals are "a mixture of ideas of individual things and souls that are aware of themselves and things other than themselves as individual, non-integrated particulars," contrasted with two logical categories that govern wholes, species (εἶδος) and genus (γένος).[97] These logical *differentiae* ultimately derive from Plato's *Sophist*, but were used widely in second- and third-century literary sources, philosophical and otherwise, among Hellenes and Christians alike.[98] As Porphyry writes, "what is most generic is said of all the genera, species and individuals under it, while the genus prior to the most specific species is said of all the most specific species and the individuals, the mere species is said of all the individuals, and the individual (ἄτομον) is said of only one of the particulars (τὰ κατὰ μέρος)."[99] Presumably, those on the path in the Autogenes are the individuals, who, still being partial (μερικός), might become perfect: "and a partial (μερικός), primordial form exists among each and every one, so that they become perfect in this way: for the four self-begotten aeons are perfect (τέλειος) individuals (ⲕⲁⲧⲁ ⲟⲩⲁ) belonging to the wholly-perfect (παντέλειος) (individuals) [that exist prior to][100] them, the [perfect] individuals."[101] Thus there is a third grade of individuals, the wholly perfect beings.

While "wholly perfect" is a common appellation for the Barbelo and beings within it superior to the Autogenes, the wholly perfect individuals seem to be associated with the subaeon of the Protophanes and its baptisms, presumably on account of its power to "join" individuals so that they are in "fellowship."[102] The elect soul's apprehension of the unity of the source of the various particulars (individuals) that are categorized by species and genera is tantamount to further celestial baptism in the higher realms of the Barbelo: "And when one has understood the source (ἀρχή) of these things (coming) into being, how everything appears from a single authority, and how everything being joined comes to be divided, and how everything that has been divided comes to be joined once more, and how the parts (μέρος) join with the wholes and the species (εἶδος) and the genera (γένος)—if one ever understands these things, he is baptized in the baptism of the Kalyptos."[103] Ultimately, absolute unity of the intelligibles—the eternal Platonic forms themselves, things "that truly exist"—are only in the Kalyptos, the "hidden" aeon.[104] Thus the luminaries of the Barbelo praise Kalyptos: "The individuals are alive, and (so are) the four (luminaries), who are seven-fold! ηοοοοηαηω! It is you who is before them, it is you who is (with)in them all, and they are in the Protophanes, perfect male Harmedon, the Activity of all those who exist together (ⲉⲓⲟⲩⲙⲁ)! Since the perfect individuals existed, the Activity of all the individuals manifested: the divine Autogenes."[105] Doxologies addressed to the Barbelo in the *Three Steles of Seth* also identify (in the first person!) elect souls as perfect individuals existing "together": "we bless you (*masc. sg.*) eternally. We bless you, we who have been saved, we, the perfect individuals (ⲛⲓ ⲕⲁⲧⲁ ⲟⲩⲁ ⲛ̄ⲧⲉⲗⲓⲟⲥ). We are perfect on account of you, those who became perfect with you."[106]

Allogenes offers a similar account; Barbelo "empowers" the "individuals (ⲕⲁⲧⲁ ⲟⲩⲁ)," and they receive apprehension (ἔννοια)—presumably of the source of the genera, that is, the Invisible Spirit—by means of a "First Thought (ϣⲟⲣⲡ̄ ⲛ̄ⲉⲛⲛⲟⲓⲁ)."[107] Allogenes praises "the [perfect] individuals, and the all-perfect (παντέλειος), [those who are] together, and the [. . .] [who][108] are before the perfect ones."[109] Barbelo "acts separately (κατὰ μέρος) and individually (ⲕⲁⲧⲁ ⲟⲩⲁ), continuing to rectify the sins, things (that) come from Nature (φύσις). He has the divine Thrice Male, being salvation for them all, along with the Invisible Spirit."[110] The Thrice Male is the chief salvific figure in *Allogenes*, perhaps a paradigm of Seth himself. As in *Zostrianos*, he seems to occupy a place between the Autogenes (the one "in whom the [self-begotten ones exist]") and Protophanes subaeons (as "the thought of those who exist together [ⲉⲓⲟⲩⲙⲁ]"), the "measure and unique knowledge" of the individuals.[111] It is clear that Barbelo (identified with πρόνοια) here extends salvation, referred to elsewhere in the treatise as "first thought," to individuals through its agent, the Thrice-Male Child.

The structure and activity of the Barbelo closely resembles that of Intellect (νοῦς) in contemporary Platonism: the Kalyptos corresponds roughly to Plotinus's creative, contemplating Intellect, the Protophanes to its "demiurgical capacity," and the Autogenes to the universal Soul that encompasses all souls, or in the jargon of Numenius and the *Chaldaean Oracles*, a discursive "Second Intellect."[112] As the first deity posterior to the Thrice-Powered Invisible Spirit in *Zostrianos*, Kalyptos is precisely the locus where parts, even in a unified, "partless" sense, come into being. Its creative (but nondiscursive) activity is thus tantamount to a unification of parts, extended to individuals, but only in the noetic sphere.[113] At the same time, the way in which *Zostrianos* and *Allogenes* treat "individuals" is alien to contemporary Platonism in several ways. First, Barbelo's unifying activity has a clearly soteriological tone, unlike Plotinus's Intellect. Second, the particular individuals unified by the Protophanes and Kalyptos aeons are not just ideas but "immortal souls" that have been transformed into ideas. Plotinus actually mocks this language in a passage of *Against the Gnostics*.[114] Third, the revelatory framework of the Sethian treatises presupposes an irruption of providential activity into the sphere of fate.[115] Arguably, the bestowal of saving revelation by descending agents of the Barbelo (identified as "providence," πρόνοια) in *Zostrianos* and *Allogenes*, the incarnations of Seth, would qualify as a direct intervention in worldly affairs by providence.[116] This "interventionist" approach implies a view affirmed by Stoics and many early Christian writers, namely that providence directs all worldly affairs and individuals.[117] Indeed, it was particularly common for early Christians to claim that providence, via Christ, had freed them from the shackles of fate.[118] Certainly this theme informed the Christian heretics reading the *Book of Elchasai* in Rome in the mid-third century CE, who called themselves προγνωστικοί (Gk. "foreknowers"), but it is quite possible that they were also informed by versions of the Platonizing Sethian treatises, inundated with language about the saving power offered by the First Thought of the Invisible Spirit, and, like the rest of Sethian tradition, indebted to the baptismal circles in Syria and Mesopotamia that produced Elchasai and Mani.[119]

CONCLUSION: A HELLENIC CRITIQUE OF GNOSTIC PROVIDENCE AND SALVATION

Plotinus makes the puzzling argument that the Gnostics simultaneously deny providence while claiming it only applies to them; instead, he says, providence cares for wholes (i.e., universals like "humanity"), but not parts (i.e., particulars like "individual human beings"). The latter statement is a Platonic dictum used to banish charges that present evils are evidence for a lack of God's providential care.[120] The former statement is a condemnation, common among Hellenic critics of Christianity, of the idea that providence extends strictly to the souls of the elect, rather than the entire universe.[121] While Plotinus's charge that Gnostic salvation is deterministic does not tally well with our reading of the Sethian literature itself, here he points to a real difference between himself and his Gnostic friends—and the books they read. Both Sethian Gnostic literature and contemporary Platonists seem to reject determinism in that they both hold saving truth to be open to any who are willing to listen to it. Yet Sethian literature goes further in stating that those who do listen and assent to it are special, different, alien from others—perfect individuals whose souls will be under the special care of providence in the Barbelo aeon after death, just as the emissaries of the Barbelo, the avatars of Seth, descended to earth in bestowing saving revelation in the first place. These descents

of Seth are the central soteriological events throughout Sethian tradition, even in the Platonizing treatises.

Armstrong remarks that while Plotinus may have his old friends in
mind, his criticism extends to "all those who make the characteristic
claim of Abrahamic religion to be the elect, the people of God, with
a particular and exclusive revelation from him which causes them
to reject the traditional pieties."[122] While Sethian ethnic reasoning
recalls proto-orthodox language about belonging to a third race, and
Sethian ideas about providence are in line with Christian and Stoic
thought, the general complex of soteriological ideas explored in this
chapter does not belong specifically to Christianity but to what Armstrong terms "Abrahamic religion." It is hard to read about the seed of
Seth without recalling Jewish notions of Israel's election, and, indeed,
the Sethians seem to have agreed with the Apostle Paul in persisting in
the language of elect soteriology—distinguishing between those who
will be ultimately saved and those who will not—while opening salvation up to "the nations."[123] Similarly, the reincarnations of Seth are
not indebted to exclusively Christian traditions but also to the Jewish
Christianities that appeared in ancient Mesopotamia and described
the savior as returning to earth on many occasions, sometimes as
Jesus of Nazareth. Plotinus criticizes Judeo-Christian notions of soteriology in general, but Sethian soteriology is particularly indebted to
Jewish Christianity.

Turning now to the journey of the Sethian elect to heaven and the
fate of those who do not ascend but would be "left behind," we will
find the same is true of Sethian eschatology. While Platonists distinguished between better and worse souls throughout their reincarnations over an infinite span of time, they would eventually become
better (and worse) again. Like their Jewish and Christian contemporaries, however, the Sethians believed that the world was not eternal, and therefore repentance in this life was an immediate and grave
concern.

CHAPTER 5

The Ascent

While we have found Plotinus's complaints about the Gnostic approach to writing and divine providence to reflect the contents of the Sethian literature that informed his friends, many of his arguments deal with cosmological concerns—the preexistence of matter, its relationship to the fall of Soul, and the eternity of the world. The Platonizing Sethian apocalypses, however, focus on supracosmological matters—the world of the intelligibles. This does not mean that Sethian literature avoids cosmological questions; rather, they come up in passing, in allusions to knowledge presupposed of the reader, as we saw in passages about the Sethian elect. Moreover, they tend to address "unverifiable" speculations common to apocalypses about cosmology and the postmortem fate of the soul. In Greek philosophy, these problems fit the rubric of myth (μῦθος) and "theoretical philosophy," or physics.[1] Today, biblical scholarship tends to lump them together under the term "eschatology," a term central to debate over defining the genre of apocalypse: do apocalypses generally tend to handle historical, political topics pertaining to the end of the world, or speculative, cosmological topics pertaining to the fate of the human soul?[2] Observing that only a handful of apocalypses deal strictly with history while many address the soul's existence after death, scholars recognize that apocalypses deal with eschatology both "cosmic" and "personal," handling the fate of the world and individual souls, respectively.[3]

Gnostic texts, too, present a diversity of eschatologies, reflected in Sethianism: we find "historical-cosmic" apocalypses in the

Apocalypse of Adam, *Egyptian Gospel*, and *Trimorphic Protennoia*, while the Platonizing treatises clearly focus on "personal" and "realized" eschatology.[4] Thus, while a Sethian position on matter's preexistence and the fall of Soul remains unclear, a careful reading of the texts, guided by Plotinus's evidence, allows one to discern clear positions on other matters, such as ethnically phrased soteriology and providence (discussed in the previous chapter) and personal and cosmic eschatology (discussed here). Sethian literature envisions not just the elect using ethnic reasoning common among contemporary Christians but also another motif, the sense of being "resident aliens" in an age creeping closer to its own destruction—and the destruction of non-elect souls. These positions about cosmological and personal eschatology are, like language about the elect as a different race alienated from contemporary society, deeply at odds with those of contemporary Platonists, closer to those of contemporary Christian philosophers, and central to the polemics between Hellenic and Christian thinkers of the second to fourth centuries CE.

THE STRANGE AND THE DEAD: DEATH AND REINCARNATION IN *ZOSTRIANOS*

The only detailed discussion of personal eschatology in a Sethian treatise can be found in *Zostrianos*, but these sections of the manuscript are badly damaged. Any interpretation of them must be provisional, yet together with hints and asides in other sections of the text, one can reconstruct a teaching that describes the various categories of souls, the destruction of one type, the reincarnation of others, and the release from the cycle of rebirth for a precious few. This reconstruction is a worthwhile endeavor, because it reveals the nomenclature used for the elect across Sethian tradition, providing valuable shading and color to the outline of the seed of Seth sketched in Chapter 4. Furthermore, as discussed at the end of the chapter, a teaching that accommodates the reincarnation of some souls and the destruction of others is at odds with contemporary Hellenic Platonism but paralleled in a select few Christian groups, and Jewish Christians in particular.

The teaching of *Zostrianos* on the postmortem fate of the soul employs specific terminology also found in the *Egyptian Gospel*, *Marsanes*, and the *Untitled Treatise* in the Bruce Codex.[5] It is hinted at by complaints of Plotinus, who remarks that his Gnostic opponents introduce unnecessary strata of Being into the intelligible world, including hypostases of the "exiles, aeonic copies, and repentances."[6] As scholars have long recognized, these hypostases are also mentioned in the *Untitled* treatise: God "created the aetherial earth (ⲡⲕⲁϩ ⲛ̄ⲁⲏⲣ), a dwelling-place for those who had come forth, that they should remain there until the establishment of those below them. After that, the true-dwelling place; within this, the place of The Repentance (μετάνοια); within this, the Impressions (ἀντίτυπος) of Aerodios. After that, the Sojourn (παροίκησις), the Repentance inside this, the self-begotten reflections. In that place, they were baptized in the name of the Autogenes, the one who is divine over them."[7] However, the function of these aeons was not clear until the discovery of *Zostrianos*. In this text, the eponymous seer begins his ascent to heaven, by passing the "aetherial earth," the aeons of the Impressions (ἀντίτυποι), Sojourn, and Repentance. He is baptized and made an angel before meeting one "Authronios, the ruler on high," to whom he poses questions about the various kinds of souls and their relationship to the Impressions.[8] The heavenly interlocutor describes the creation of the world and the "education" (probably punishment) of souls and the dual nature of the aeons: "And [the souls][9] [that] are pure are trained (γυμνάζειν) by the impressions (ἀντίτυπος), which receive a model (τύπος) of their souls while they still exist in the material world. They came into existence after the emanation of each of the aeons, and they are taken, one after another, from the copy (ἀντίτυπον) of the Sojourn (παροίκησις) to the Sojourn that truly exists, (and) from the copy of Repentance (μετάνοια) to the Repentance that truly exists, and [from the] (aeonic) copy of the Autogenes to the [Autogenes] that truly exists."[10] This passage seems obscure, but it contains valuable information on the makeup of the heavenly world. Zostrianos encounters the Impressions, Sojourn, and Repentance after traveling past the "aetherial earth," which Macrobius says is a common Platonic term for the moon.[11] The "Impressions" seem to be copies of the Sojourn and Repentance "that truly exist," as well as of the Autogenes aeon. (See Figure 3 for a diagram of this scheme.)

Thus, between the moon and the Autogenes (the lowest level of the Barbelo), there exist the "real" Sojourn and Repentance aeons, and inferior "impressions" or reflections of them below. The text specifies that it is in these lower Impressions of the metempsychotic aeons that souls are "trained." There are "eternal glories" and "places of judgment" there.[12]

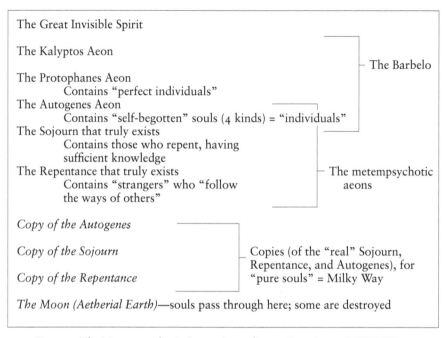

The Great Invisible Spirit

The Kalyptos Aeon

The Protophanes Aeon
    Contains "perfect individuals"
The Autogenes Aeon
    Contains "self-begotten" souls (4 kinds) = "individuals"
The Sojourn that truly exists
    Contains those who repent, having
    sufficient knowledge
The Repentance that truly exists
    Contains "strangers" who "follow
    the ways of others"

The Barbelo

The metempsychotic aeons

Copy of the Autogenes

Copy of the Sojourn

Copy of the Repentance

Copies (of the "real" Sojourn,
Repentance, and Autogenes), for
"pure souls" = Milky Way

The Moon (Aetherial Earth)—souls pass through here; some are destroyed

Figure 3. The Metempsychotic Aeons According to *Zostrianos*, NHC VIII,1.5–6, 12.

In the *editio princeps* of *Zostrianos*, John Sieber notes the presence of the aeon of the "Sojourn," and identified it as a "temporary residence" for the soul, probably since the Liddell and Scott *Greek-English Lexicon* translates the word παροίκησις as "the transmigration of souls."[13] However, as Luise Abramowski observes, the only reference given by the *Lexicon* for this translation is to Plotinus's mention of the aeon in his anti-Gnostic polemic, where the context in no way indicates the function of the aeon, transmigatory or otherwise.[14] She sees that the term παροίκησις had a specific and important coinage in ancient Christian circles and dismissed Sieber's claim that by παροίκησις, *Zostrianos* refers to the transmigration of souls.

    While Abramowski is correct about the Christian provenance of the term, the aeon of the "Sojourn" in *Zostrianos* does seem to be the locus of metempsychosis, for it lies below the intelligibles, above the moon, and souls are trained there, as it contains places of judgment. The moon and its whereabouts was a common site in contemporary Platonic thought for the process of reincarnation; Numenius and a Hermetic writer suggested instead the Milky Way.[15] *Zostrianos* describes the training and judgment of souls taking place in the Impressions of the Sojourn, Repentance, and Autogenes aeons, which appear to be farther away from the earth than the moon. It would appear that these "Impressions" constitute our galaxy, or as Turner suggests, the fixed stars in general, and that the training of souls is their punishment between lives, which makes them "pure."[16]

Other souls appear to come to rest in the "true" Sojourn, Repentance, and Autogenes aeons, as explained by the character Ephesech: "And while those (μέν) who are worthy are guarded, others (δέ) who are not from this race (γένος) [are] [. . .][17] But if one strips off the world and lays aside [nature],[18] and while (μέν) that one who [has] no dwelling-place and power, and because he is following the ways of others (ⲉⲃⲏⲩⲉ ⲛ̄ⲧⲉⲅⲉⲛⲕⲟⲟⲩⲉ), he is a stranger (ϭⲁⲗⲏⲩⲧ); but (δέ) whoever did not commit any sin, because knowledge (γνῶσις) was enough for him, he certainly is not concerned about anything, since he has repented."[19] Those who "follow the ways of others" and become "strangers" are those in the Sojourn: "for there are three forms of immortal souls: first (μέν), those who have rooted themselves upon the Sojourn do not have reproductive power, being those who follow the ways of others."[20] They are contrasted with those in the Repentance aeon, who are characterized by their asceticism and acts of repentance after sinning.[21] The third group, meanwhile, are the "self-begotten" souls in the Autogenes, who also have four kinds.[22] These three types of immortal souls are contrasted with "utterly perished" souls, who have four "species (εἶδος)" in turn spread out over nine kinds during earthly existence, each with its own "species" and "custom."[23]

However, the following passages offer an alternative division, this time of five types of humanity (ⲣⲱⲙⲉ), three of which are immortal souls. The first type appears to be destroyed by fire:[24] "And the one who [. . .] the [stranger (ϭⲁⲗⲏⲟⲩⲧ)] [. . .] in the perceptible (αἰσθητόν), living [world], and the dead one [. . .] all of the [. . .] [obtain salvation] [. . .] dead one. [. . .] And all those did not need salvation (from the) first, but rather they are [truly] saved, because they exist in humility.[25] And as for the dead (type of) humanity, its soul, mind, and body [are] all [dead]. Sufferings [. . .] material (ὑλικόν). Some [. . .] The fire [. . .]."[26] Meanwhile, "the second (kind of) humanity is the immortal soul that exists among the mortals, worrying for itself, for it [seeks] whatever is to its advantage in every situation, [and it] experiences corporeal suffering. [. . .] [it has] [an] eternal god. It

associates with daimones (δαίμων)."[27] This first type should be
identified with the souls that "pass away" with the world, probably at the end of time. The second type seems to be ensconced
in the cycle of reincarnation. Both of these types would probably
ascend to the moon or Milky Way after death, where they are
either destroyed in fire or sent back to earth, respectively.

The third type is "the kind of humanity that exists in the
Sojourn (παροίκησις):[28] when it comes to discover the truth that
exists inside of itself, it is distant from the deeds of others who
exist wrongly (κακῶς), being obstacles."[29] The fourth, then, is
the type that repents: "as for the kind of humanity that repents
(μετανοεῖν), if it leaves the dead things, (and) desires the things
that actually exist, the immortal mind and immortal soul [. . .]
hurrying, for their own sakes, first making an inquiry about it,
not (about) conduct (πρᾶξις) but (about) works."[30] The fifth type
is the elect: "As for the elect type of humanity, it is the (type)
that seeks it(self) and its mind, finding both of them. And how
many powers it has! The type of humanity that has been saved
is the (type) that has not known these things,[31] [. . .] exactly as
they actually exist, but rather it (is) itself[32] through the Word, as
it exists [. . .] it took their [. . .][33] everywhere, having become
[simple] and one. For this type of race was saved, because it is able
to pass through (χωρεῖν) everything. It becomes [. . .][34] everything. If it wants, then it separates itself again from everything,
and it withdraws (ἀναχωρεῖν) itself, for it becomes divine, having
withdrawn to God."[35] The reason for providing an alternative
division of the kinds of souls and their fates in the metempsychotic aeons is not clear—in fact, the ever-inquisitive seer then
asks for another set of distinctions![36]

Nonetheless, one can harmonize the two descriptions in *Zostrianos*.[37] Noting that the three kinds of "immortal souls" dwell
with the "utterly perishable souls" (who have four species and
nine kinds of bodily existence) because of the fall of Sophia, the
second type of humanity (mortal souls who dwell with the first,
dead type of humanity) would encompass all immortal souls during earthly existence. Thus, according to *Zostrianos*, souls after
death seem to be transmitted throughout the Sojourn, Repentance, Autogenes, and their corresponding Impressions or copies, where there is judgment or punishment. Some immortal souls
are judged to be sinners caught in the ways of others and are sent

First schema: four kinds of souls, three immortal (24.21–28.22)

1. Autogenes: contains immortal, self-begotten souls (4 subtypes)

2. Repentance: contains immortal souls for whom knowledge was enough, sinned, repented, and practiced asceticism (6 subtypes)

3. Sojourn: contains immortal souls who are strangers, because they follow ways of others

4. Mortal souls: These "utterly perishable souls" have four species and nine kinds of existence; Immortal souls dwell with them "because of Sophia."

Second schema: five kinds of humanity, four of them being immortal souls (42.10–44.22)

1. Autogenes Aeon: elect, contemplative souls

2. Repentance Aeon: repenting, ascetic individuals drawn to immortal things

3. Sojourn Aeon: associated with deeds of others, but draws away from them when it gains self-knowledge

4. Immortal souls that exist amongst the mortals, undergoing reincarnation in the "Impressions" of the metempsychotic aeons

5. Mortal type of humanity: perishes in fire, probably at the end of time

Figure 4. The Kinds of Souls in Zostrianos (Listed in Descending Order of Ontological Priority)

back to mortal existence. Immortal (but apparently wayward) souls wind up in the Sojourn and Repentance. However, *the only group referred to as elect* are those in the Autogenes who "withdraw to themselves," that is, practice contemplation.[38] (See Figure 4 for schemas of the two divisions.)

Because of the fragmentary nature of the manuscript and the likely corrupt quality of its translation from Greek, these passages seem to offer more questions than answers. Do they describe the universal salvation of humanity?[39] Probably not; the first, "mortal" type of soul is destroyed, most likely by fire. Other stray passages in the Sethian treatises corroborate this reading.[40] Thus, humanity is divided into the elect, the damned, and souls that are immortal but are not as yet fully saved. Second, are immortal souls associated with the Sojourn and Repentance aeons then reincarnated, or have they transcended the cycle of death and rebirth? And if they are still being reincarnated, can they fall from immortality and eventually be destroyed? Put otherwise: are they "elect"?

RESIDENT ALIENS FOR AN ALIEN GOD

The background of the terms "sojourner," "repenter," and "self-begotten" reveals the soteriological rank they indicate in *Zostrianos*. The term "self-begotten" clearly refers to the elect, and they are, naturally, located by the text in the aeon of the Autogenes. As argued in Chapter 4, they are also identified as individuals, that is, particular ideas; they are unified in the Protophanes aeon into perfect individuals who exist "as one" or simply "together." The Repentance is probably a hypostatization of the repentant act of Sophia following her descent into matter and the production of the world.[41] Yet what exactly souls in this aeon are "repenting" of is not immediately clear, nor is its relationship to the Sojourn. A look at the concept of exile in Jewish and early Christian literature shows that the Sethian use of it derives from contemporary Christian use of what Benjamin Dunning dubs the "resident alien topos," the valorization of estrangement from the world.[42] Thus, the term "sojourners" designates the elect; "repenters" could indicate proselytes, converts to Sethian thought.

The word παροίκησις ("sojourn," "exile") and its cognates are very rare, although not completely unknown, to Hellenic writers.[43] Greeks generally demonized the theme of exile, which represented an alienation from public life, especially the civic (political) and cultic (ritual) spheres.[44] Philo, Plotinus, and Porphyry sometimes describe the soul as a wandering foreigner to be freed from the body at death, but the metaphor serves ascetic, rather than cultural, ends and represents an extreme within Greek philosophical tradition.[45] The specific term παροίκησις and a theological understanding of the theme of exile is more common in ancient Judaism, but understood with ambivalence: at best, strangers are to be pitied, patriarchs endure their sojourns through faith, and many writers downplay the idea that Israelites were anything other than citizens in their own land.[46] While the term is almost absent in the apocalypses, the Hebrew Bible most commonly indicates cosmic alienation with גר ("stranger"), translated in the LXX as πάροικος.[47] It refers to sojourning individuals such as Abraham (paralleled by Israel's own exile),[48] as well as minorities of foreigners living in and dependent on Israel for their well-being (again paralleled by Israel's dependence on God).[49] The πάροικος is also associated with the gentile "foreigner" or "stranger" (ἀλλογενής, which also translates גר), usually idolatrous Hellenes negatively juxtaposed with the Jews.[50]

Philo's concept of the embodied but wise soul as a stranger on earth is atypical for a Jew of the first century CE, but very much "at home" in early Christian literature, where negative valuations of exile are very rare.[51] Hebrews recalls Septuagintal language about Abraham's exile to paint him as a successful πάροικος because of his faith.[52] 1 Peter is directed "to the elect, strangers in the world," who are encouraged, "as sojourners and strangers, to abstain from sinful desires."[53] 2 *Clement* assures readers that their sojourn in the flesh will be short.[54] It also expresses political withdrawal, as in Philippians 3:20, which declares that "our citizenship is in heaven," a theme famously echoed by 1 *Clement*, the *Epistle to Diognetus*, and Tertullian.[55] Clement of Alexandria says that "no one is a stranger to the world by nature, their essence being one, and God one. But the elect man dwells as a sojourner (ὁ ἐκλεκτὸς ὡς ξένος πολιτεύεται), knowing all things to be possessed and disposed of."[56] In the *Odes of Solomon*, Jesus identifies himself as a foreigner.[57] Origen declares that "we are now in an alien land. . . . For the ruler of this age rules here, and God is alien to his sons."[58]

The resident alien topos is also a positive self-designation in much Gnostic literature.[59] The term seems to have acquired a general sense of "elect" to some Gnostics,[60] although in rare cases it was also used in a derogatory sense as well.[61] Basilides, describing the soul incarnated in matter, said, "I am an exile in the land, and a sojourner (πάροικος . . . καὶ παρεπίδημος) among you."[62] In the Cologne Mani Codex, once Mani has obtained revelation, he describes himself as a "stranger" in his community.[63] The resident alien motif survived as a positive self-designation in Mandaeanism.[64] In the salvation history of the Sethian *Apocalypse of Adam*, "strangers" (ϣⲙⲙⲟ) receive gnosis, enter another land, and "sojourn" (ϭⲟⲓⲗⲉ).[65] While the purpose of this activity is not immediately clear, it is obvious that these strangers are to be identified with the elect, persecuted by the demiurge Saklas because they do not obey his commandments.[66] The text's savior figure, "the Illuminator" (probably Seth himself), descends to earth from "foreign air" (ⲟⲩⲁⲏⲣ ⲛ̄ϣⲙ̄ⲙⲟ).[67]

The particular term "foreigner" (or "stranger," ἀλλογενής) seems to have been especially important in Sethian tradition, where it refers to Seth himself. After describing the sad fate of the first children of Adam and Eve, Cain and Abel, LXX 4:25 dubs Seth "another seed" (σπέρμα ἕτερον). Some traditions contrasted this new, superior seed with the sinful seed of Cain (and at times Abel), or simply pronounced Seth the father of all humanity.[68] Sethian Gnostics, meanwhile, often replaced the title "another seed" with "another race" (ἀλλογενής), as did the Sethians (as reported by Epiphanius), who claimed that Seth, once born to Adam and Eve, was taken away to heaven to be protected and taught by the angels before being returned, pneumatic, invisible, and safe from the demiurge.[69] The Archontic "Books of the Foreigners" were associated with "seven books in the name of Seth"; in fact, this group simply called Seth ἀλλογενής.[70] One of their "Books of the Foreigner" is probably a version of the Platonizing Sethian text *Allogenes* (NHC XI,3), which also seems to identify Allogenes with Seth. Codex Tchacos contains a fragmentary treatise, whose title is unrestored as of yet, which is probably another *(Book of) Allogenes*. Its eponymous protagonist argues with Satan, even explaining to him that "I am called 'Allogenes,' because I am from another race—I am not from your race."[71] In the *Egyptian Gospel*, the "self-begotten" aeon is "alien" (ἀλλογένιος, ἀλλογενής); in *Zostrianos*, the fourth epithet for the fourth light of the Autogenes aeon, Eleleth, is "Allogenios."[72]

Another instance of a Sethian resident alien is the character Pigeradamas, a primal, heavenly Adam. As Howard Jackson suggests, the name is probably a combination of the Coptic definite article ⲡⲓ and the Semitic גר, "stranger."[73] Ontologically speaking, Pigeradamas seems to occupy the lower reaches of the Autogenes aeon.[74] In the *Three Steles of Seth*, Geradamas has a revelatory function and is described in ethnic terms: "the perceptible world knows thee because of thee and thy seed. . . . Thou art from another race (ⲡⲕⲉⲅⲉⲛⲟⲥ), and its place is over another race."[75]

The widespread Sethian use of the resident alien topos as a positive self-designation is the proper background for interpreting the meaning and function of the aeon of the Sojourn in *Zostrianos*, *Ennead* 2.9, and the *Untitled Treatise* in the Bruce Codex. Cognates of παροίκησις to discuss themes of exile and sojourning are almost nonexistent in Hellenic texts, but quite common in Jewish and Christian literature. (Indeed, Plotinus is puzzled and angered by the inclusion of the παροίκησις aeon into Sethian cosmology; he *does not recognize* what it is.) However, Jewish literature almost always uses the theme in a negative sense; only Christians (and Christian Gnostics) reconfigure the theme to communicate a positive meaning. Thus, as recognized by Abramowski, the aeon of the Sojourn in Sethian texts probably had a Christian valence, and it was certainly informed by the much wider Sethian discourse about being an "alien" (ἀλλογενής) in the world.[76] *Zostrianos* envisions, like the Valentinians or Manichaeans, a multitiered body of elect; the sojourners seem to occupy the bottom rung.

How exactly they differ from the repentant and self-begotten souls, however, is still obscure. Jackson has observed that the term רג could denote a proselyte (convert) in Hellenistic Judaism, so perhaps the same is true of the complex of related "alien" terminology in Sethianism.[77] Now a sojourner becomes repentant when she or he attains inner truth, "distant from the deeds of others"; the phrase "deeds of others" recalls exactly the wayward practices of Zostrianos's community that he despises.[78] By this reasoning, individuals who have abandoned the ritual practices of other cultures have become participants in Sethian ritual life, which seems to be chiefly characterized by baptism and especially asceticism.[79] If this reading is correct, the Sethian terminology for conversion inverts the Jewish sense of "sojourner"; the Septuagint specifically translates גר as πάροικος only when it *cannot* mean "convert" (προσήλυτος).[80]

In any case, *Zostrianos* affirms the doctrine of reincarnation, distinguishing between four kinds of souls: the perishable and three elect types, sojourners, repentant, and self-begotten. The background of the language about the aeon of the Sojourn is biblical and, in the Sethian context, probably Christian, since ancient Jewish literature usually employs the motif in a negative sense. One can speculate that sojourners are distinguished from other immortal souls by virtue of being proselytes, strangers, in the Sethian community; repenters have advanced to a higher level without being completely saved.[81] It is clear that the only true elect are the self-begotten souls. It is possible that this means that while the sojourning and repenting souls still reincarnate (accounting for the immortal souls who inhabit earth on account of Sophia's fall), the self-begotten souls have left the cycle of reincarnation entirely. If so, *Zostrianos* would be an early witness to the idea, which does not appear in explicit form in extant Neoplatonic sources until Porphyry.[82]

It is reasonable to export this reconstruction of Sethian personal eschatology from *Zostrianos* to the rest of Sethian literature. Its distinctive terminology is widespread in Sethian texts: the metempsychotic aeons also appear in *Ennead* 2.9, *Marsanes*, and the *Untitled Treatise* in the Bruce Codex; the aeon of Repentance is in the

Egyptian Gospel; the resident alien topos that informs the Sojourn aeon is in the *Apocryphon of John*, the *Three Steles of Seth*, *Zostrianos*, and *Allogenes*. Some model like that proposed here (as in Figures 3 and 4) appears to undergird the entire tradition; certainly all the texts are compatible with it.

LEFT BEHIND

The key difference between Sethian and Platonic conceptions of providence, then, is soteriological: while it extends to all individuals, it does not necessarily *save* all individuals.[83] Plato himself would agree that some people will simply be punished in the afterlife on account of their poor choices; yet he and his readers in the late Platonic schools also assumed that such souls would eventually reincarnate into an infinitude of other lives, some of which would be better, some of them worse. However, two of the Platonizing Sethian treatises, *Marsanes* and *Zostrianos*, affirm that the world will be destroyed; other passages about the "dissolution" of souls assume that its inhabitants will perish as well. If the cycle of reincarnation ends for *all* beings, then some (presumably most) of them will not be among the elect perfect individuals at the end of time, and "pass away" with the world. Such a view is mocked and deeply criticized in *Against the Gnostics*.

In other words, cosmic eschatology has ramifications for personal eschatology. Yet in an effort to harmonize the Sethian treatises with contemporary Platonism, modern scholars have read these passages as presuming just the opposite. For instance, *Marsanes* asserts that "the entire defilement (ⲭⲱⲣⲙ̄) [was saved (ⲧⲏⲡ[ϥ̄ ⲟⲩⲭⲉ]ⲉⲓ)] ... <I> have come to know it, the intelligible (νοητός) world; <I have come to know>,[84] as I was deliberating that in every way is the sensible (αἰσθητός) world worthy of being saved entirely (ⲁⲧⲣⲉϥⲟⲩⲭⲉⲉⲓ [ⲧⲏ]ⲣϥ̄). [For] I have not ceased speaking [of the] Autogenes."[85] In *Marsanes*, the Autogenes aeon preserves the world through its demiurgical activity, as did the Thrice-Male Child in other Sethian treatises.[86] Scholars have used this passage as justification for making heavy restorations to a lacunose passage of *Zostrianos* that envisions the Autogenes as the savior of the world, through ensuring its eternal preservation.[87] These restorations are themselves questionable, but more importantly, they produce the untenable scenario that Plotinus's Gnostic friends produced Sethian apocalypses in support of their thought that nonetheless conflicted *with their own views* about cosmic eschatology, while agreeing with those of Plotinus.

Rather, *Zostrianos* envisions a world with an end. At the end of his sermon, the seer invites his hearer or reader to

> look at the dissolution (oγωτ̄ϧ) of this place, and follow the indissoluble unbegottenness (†μ̄ντατμιcε) . . . Dissolve (ϧaλ eϧoλ) yourselves, and that which has bound you will be dissolved. Save yourselves so that it (i.e., the soul) will be saved! The loving Father has sent you the Savior (σωτήρ) and he has strengthened you. Why do you hesitate? Seek, when you are sought. Listen, when you are invited. For time (χρόνος) is short. Do not be deceived; great is the aeon of the aeon of the living, (and great are) the punishments of those who remain unpersuaded. Many are the bondages and the torturers that seek you. Flee quickly, before destruction reaches you. Look to the light, and flee from the darkness. Do not be led astray to your destruction![88]

We need not then read *Marsanes* as breaking from Sethian tradition in affirming the eternity of the cosmos, but as entailing a sense of monism whose contours are not clear. It could be an oblique allusion to the common Judeo-Christian idea, known to Plotinus's Christian friends and the *Untitled Treatise* in the Bruce Codex, of a "new earth," an eternal "heavenly" realm that will replace the material cosmos upon its destruction at the eschaton.[89] Another option is that the Autogenes "saves" the cosmos from its own dissoluble character in an act of divine providence, an idea common to philosophers across sectarian and confessional boundaries.[90] The close association we saw in Chapter 4 of the Autogenes aeon with salvific activity and the Barbelo, the first thought of the Invisible Spirit, supports the hypothesis that its maintenance of the cosmos is a providential activity.

However, Christians such as Athenagoras and Origen held that God could also allow the world to eventually pass away.[91] *Marsanes'* references to the "end times" and the fate of sinners appear to agree: " . . . It is necessary [for you, (Marsanes), to know] those that are higher than these and tell them to the powers. For you (*masc. sg.*) will become [elect] with the elect ones (neτcaτ̄ι) [in the last] times ([aн̄ϧ] ἀϧeγ ᷒ηϧeoγaeιω)."[92] Salvific revelation appears to be open to all, but is rejected by the "sinners," who will be destroyed. *Zostrianos* says (probably of the dead kind of humanity) that "because they did not know god, they shall pass away (ϧωλ eϧoλ)."[93] The luminaries of *Allogenes* claim that someone who mistakenly identifies God with his attributes "has not known God" and is "liable to judgement."[94] Both treatises refer to "judges" and "judging" of souls.[95] It does not appear that any Sethian text is universalist.[96]

There is therefore continuity between the various "cosmic" eschatologies of the Sethian treatises, for the non-Platonizing treatises also assert that this world will end. The *Trimorphic Protennoia* describes the "coming end of the aeon (ⲑⲁ[ⲉ]ⲏ ⲙ̄ⲡⲁⲓⲱⲛ ⲉⲧⲛⲁϣⲱⲡⲉ)," which is followed by the harrowing of hell and the arrival of an aeon that is "without change" (ⲡⲁⲓ̈ ⲉⲧⲉ ⲙⲛ̄ⲧⲁϥ ⲙ̄ⲙⲁⲩ ⲛ̄ⲟⲩϭⲓⲃⲉ).[97] The *Apocalypse of Adam* refers to three cataclysms: flood, fire, and the arrival of the messianic Illuminator, after which "the whole creation that came from the dead earth will be under the authority of death."[98] The *Egyptian Gospel* also refers to the cataclysms of flood, fire, and the consummation (συντέλεια) of the aeon.[99] Seth exists to found the immovable race, because of which "[the] silence [and the] voice might appear, so that the [dead] aeon [may raise itself,] [and] (finally) dissolve (καταλύειν)."[100]

As far as Plotinus was concerned, the "dissolution of the present aeon" was tantamount to a rejection of the Platonic (and Aristotelian) doctrine of the material world's eternal existence: "When is it (the demiurge) going to destroy it (the world)? For if it was sorry it had made it, what is it waiting for? If it is not sorry now for creating the world, then why will it be sorry later? Or, if it is waiting for the souls of the 'Individuals' (τὰς καθ' ἕκαστον ψυχάς), then why haven't they all come yet?"[101] Notably, he jeers at the Platonizing treatises' references to the elect as "individuals." He adds that "they introduce all sorts of comings into being and passings away (γενέσεις καὶ φθοράς)," reflecting their fundamental misunderstanding of Plato's account of creation in the *Timaeus*, which is not a literal description of an anthropomorphic demiurge discursively reasoning his way through forming the cosmos but a "likely story" representing eternal, divine contemplative activity.[102] The Gnostics are "people who assume a beginning for what is eternal; then, they think that the cause of the creating was a being who turned from one thing to the next and thus changed."[103]

Plotinus is in the mainstream of Platonists in asserting the incorruptibility of the created cosmos, a thesis often leveled against Jewish and Christian eschatology.[104] A common strategy was to concede visible, physical change while affirming the world's fundamental eternity, a view held by both Plato and Aristotle.[105] Celsus and others mocked the dramatic language associated with eschatology in scripture, drawing from the greater wellspring of philosophical critique of myth.[106] Sallustius and Macarius Magnes' Hellenic interlocutor, like Plotinus, emphasize how Christian cosmogony and eschatology compromised God's eternal creative activity, arguing that "the universe itself must be imperishable . . . because if it perishes, God must necessarily make either a better or a worse or the same or disorder."[107]

Most of the Sethian treatises do not say what the future aeon might look like—the *Egyptian Gospel* and *Trimorphic Protennoia* do not say whether there will be a new world at all, while Plotinus's Gnostics and the *Untitled* treatise appear to be familiar with a new earth—but each of the three attacks levied by Hellenes against Christian eschatology certainly could be levied against the Sethian literature surveyed here.[108] Indeed, early Christian literature is replete with descriptions of a final judgment of souls, the end of the world, and the reconstitution of the world as an eternal, perfect kingdom.[109] While some of the church fathers may have attempted to reconcile biblical accounts of the destruction of the cosmos with Greek philosophy, no such attempt appears to be made in the Sethian texts, whose foreboding, paraenetic tone is more in agreement with contemporary apocalypses as well as non-Sethian Gnostic texts.[110] Absent from the Sethian texts is the language of hope about the "new creation" or nondestructive transformation that one occasionally finds in Jewish and Christian eschatological passages.[111] Even when the eventual reconstitution of the world is emphasized, its prior cosmic dissolution is presumed.

At the same time, Sethian eschatology remains distinctive in the landscape of early Christianity, since it appears to eschew the doctrine of the cosmic destruction by fire (ἐκπύρωσις) that was popular among Christian Platonists, such as the Valentinians or Justin Martyr. Moreover, the soteriology of *Zostrianos* affirms both the doctrines of reincarnation and the end of the world, a view shared by only a few Christian writers, associated with Gnosticism: Basilides, Elchasai, Mani, and the author(s) of *Pistis Sophia*.[112] Notably, two of these—Elchasai and Mani—are also associated with Jewish Christianity, affirming multiple descents of the same revealer and drawing liberally on Jewish apocalyptic traditions. Finally, it is worth emphasizing the internal diversity of Sethian cosmic eschatology:[113] much as with the authors of the apocalypses and the New Testament, some Sethian texts appealed to traditions, going back to Isaiah, of the world's need for postcatastrophic reconstitution as a new earth, an idea that, it seems, Plotinus singled out for ridicule. Others, including

Zostrianos, *Marsanes*, and probably *Allogenes*, were content to focus on the dissolution of this aeon.

CONCLUSION: A HELLENIC CRITIQUE
OF GNOSTIC ESCHATOLOGY

Zostrianos holds that the postmortem fate of the soul is to ascend to heaven and experience reincarnation. While it is clear that some souls are not elect, there are also grades of the elect, including sojourners (or strangers), repenters, and the self-begotten. Only the latter appear to have entirely escaped the cycle of reincarnation. However, all these souls are characterized by membership in the seed of Seth, which appears to be open to all beings who hear the Gnostic "call" of Seth himself, having manifested in history in the guise of saviors and seers; this latter tradition is probably related to contemporary Jewish-Christian soteriology as reflected in the Pseudo-Clementines or accounts about the Elchasaites and Ebionites. Persistent use of the resident alien motif and ethnic reasoning is strongly reminiscent of contemporary Christian and Gnostic descriptions of the elect as a race of sojourners, divine beings temporarily locked out of heaven. Moreover, it is central to the controversy between Plotinus and the Christian Gnostic readers of the Platonizing Sethian apocalypses, reflecting the latter's rejection of the Hellenic public sphere in its political and cultic permutations.[114]

However, ethnic reasoning was not problematic on account of supposed determinism but because of its relationship to providence. The Sethian identification of the self-begotten elect as (perfect) individuals unified by providence (the Barbelo) assigns them a position where only individuals who have chosen to join the ethnically circumscribed elect, rather than *all* individuals, are saved. This position was viciously attacked by Hellenic critics of Christianity. According to *Zostrianos*, *Marsanes*, and (probably) *Allogenes*, non-elect souls will be destroyed along with the rest of the material world at the end of time. This, too, resembles a position held by contemporary Christians and Gnostics that was central to their polemical encounters with Hellenic intellectuals. While it is clear that the treatises are deeply involved in contemporary Platonism, when it comes to personal eschatology, Sethian texts appear to have preferred an approach that was certainly unique, but overall much more compatible with contemporary Judeo-Christian thought than Hellenic philosophy.[115]

Moreover, the emphasis on personal eschatology in the Platoniz-ing Sethian texts ought not to be confused with a lack of eschatology in general or a movement away from apocalyptic themes or use of the apocalyptic genre.[116] Indeed, what Turner terms the "horizontal" Sethian treatises do emphasize cosmic eschatology while the "ver-tical" treatises emphasize personal eschatology, but the dichotomy should not be drawn too sharply, and does not extend to a corre-sponding dichotomy between eschatologies historical and realized.[117] "Horizontal" and "vertical," with corresponding eschatologies "cos-mic" and "personal," are not the most helpful terms to distinguish the Platonizing apocalypses from the rest of the Sethian tradition. The same is true of the "ascent and descent" distinction. Certainly the Platonizing texts are imbued with Neoplatonic thought and focus on contemplative ascent rather than soteriology, but, as argued in Chap-ter 4, they also presume a soteriological schema featuring the avatars of Seth as *descending* saviors.

Scholarship has long overemphasized the personal and realized character of Gnostic eschatology, especially in contrast to apocalyp-tic eschatology, which shares its "dualism," "pessimism," or interior-ization or negation of history.[118] Scholarship has interrogated these clichés and found them wanting, but there *does* seem to be a peculiar affinity between texts usually described as "Gnostic" and the apoca-lyptic genre. Thus MacRae argues: "Both apocalyptic and Gnosticism center on the acquisition (by revelation) and the communication of a knowledge that exercises saving power in the present by its future-ori-ented content. . . . The latter is one manifestation of the former, albeit in extreme form."[119] It is the distinctive apocalyptic truth claim—the acquisition of undistilled, saving knowledge from beyond, thanks to a supernatural mediator—that lends apocalyptic and Gnostic texts a common character.

Often, this claim is made about the unverifiable realm of personal eschatology. An essentially doxographical approach has been levied here in hopes of diagnosing how the authors of the Sethian literature thought about the postmortem fate of the soul with respect to con-temporary Hellenic and Christian thought. Yet such speculations—and the accounts about them contained in the ancient apocalypses—mirror the ecstatic experiences of real people anticipating death.[120] These experiences, these practices of the authors and readers of the Sethian literature, remain to be examined.

CHAPTER 6

The Crown

The ritual practices described in *Marsanes* (NHC X,1) are distinctive among the Platonizing Sethian literature, encompassing such diverse activities as alphabet mysticism and the use of arcane ritual instruments.[1] Scholars have thus referred to these practices and the greater range of rituals in Sethian literature (such as baptism) as "Sethian theurgy."[2] For philosophers like Iamblichus and Proclus, "theurgy" (θεουργία)—"god-work" (θέος + ἔργον)—included purification, hymns, prayers, the animation of statues, possession, the conjuration of spirits, and mystical contemplation, derived mainly from the second-century *Chaldean Oracles*.[3] Use of the term "theurgy" to describe the rituals of the Sethian Gnostic literature thus implies that Sethian engagement with the Neoplatonic tradition went beyond metaphysics and entered the realm of ritual practice. After all, recent scholarship has emphasized Gnosticism's persistent engagement with Neoplatonism, as discussed in the Introduction.

A close look at the provenance and mechanics of Sethian ritual offers a different perspective. *Zostrianos* deals with celestial baptism and ecstatic speech;[4] the *Three Steles of Seth* and *Allogenes* employ ecstatic speech and prayer, but no baptism; *Marsanes*, meanwhile, refers to magical objects and contains a protracted discussion of the properties of the letters of the alphabet. It is less well known that the same texts also describe the transformation of the seer into an angel, or beings even greater than angels. In each of these cases, it is clear that Sethian ritual and mysticism is at odds with contemporary Hellenic intellectual conversation about theurgy and best contextualized with reference to ancient Christian and Jewish mystical literature. Sethian literature, rather, extols the use of "barbarian speech" in "alien hymns" to elicit transformation into supra-angelic beings, violating the Neoplatonic hierarchy of beings where human souls are inferior to divine powers. Just as Sethian concepts of revelation, providence, and salvation are incumbent on a rupture in the cosmos that annuls a prior rupture in heaven—the unfortunate creation of the cosmos and the trapping of human souls within it—Sethian divinization turns the Platonic cosmos on its head, identifying certain human souls as superior to all but the Invisible Spirit itself. Viewing Sethian practices against this backdrop also helps sort out difficult hermeneutic questions about the language used to describe these practices, and permits hypothesis about how and for what the texts were used.

ALIEN HYMNS

Sethian literature is distinct among Gnostic traditions in its fondness for strings of letters peppering the manuscripts—so-called alphabet mysticism or vowel spells—but some aspects of their function, particularly their relationship to angelic beings, remain little understood. In *Marsanes*, this technique appears to be harmonized with contemporary Platonic psychology. After a discussion of the makeup of the intelligible realm, the treatise's discourse shifts to the subject of the manipulation of the soul through meditation on the zodiac and the alphabet. These pages of the manuscript are highly mutilated but appear to identify five "configurations" of the soul evoked by use of four kinds of letters, corresponding to the cosmic Soul, its composition, and its various kinds of movement (described in Plato's *Timaeus* 35a–36d).[5] Next, the text describes powers of syllabic combinations, and, eventually, words.[6] The author of the text employed this alphabet mysticism as one of a variety of anagogic techniques, which together formed a part of a greater "lecture series" of mystical exercises.[7] This series appears to have been focused on showing individuals how to change the "configuration" of their soul. The "why" of *Marsanes*' alphabetic mysticism is thus clear, but the "how" remains mysterious.[8]

Although the state of the manuscript leaves much to the imagination, *Marsanes*' alphabet mysticism appears to invoke and in some way compel the aid of angels in order to effect its rectification of the fallen soul's condition. As Birger Pearson notes, the transition to the section of the treatise dealing with the zodiac and the alphabet is intro-duced with an imperative: "Name them!" (ϵριονοмαzϵ).[9] "'Naming,' or 'calling upon' the gods and the angels," he continues, "involves not only knowing their names but being able to pronounce their names correctly in chants or incantations. The purpose of this exercise is to effect the ascension of the soul past the astral barriers inhabited by these 'gods' and 'angels.'"[10] Thus, the manipulation of the shape of the soul is achieved through a heavenly journey that in turn requires the naming of angels.

Are the letters of the Greek alphabet the angelic names themselves? Probably not, but they do seem to have power over the relationship between humans and angels. *Marsanes* holds that angels are difficult beings who must be placated or coerced in order for the ascent to pro-ceed apace. A description of some of the syllables contrasts the seer with angels: "but the rest are different: αβϵβηβιβοβ, in order that you [*masc. sg.*] might [gather] them, be separated from the angels, and produce some effects."[11] Another passage, whose subject is unfortu-nately lost, asserts that "they did not stop without being revealed, nor did they stop without naming the angels. . . . For these reasons, we have acquired sufficiency; for it is fitting that each one acquire power for himself to bear fruit, and that we never cast aspersions [on] the mysteries."[12] Part of *Marsanes*' teaching about the power of the alphabet thus involves the separation of the seer from angelic beings during the heavenly journey through being able to name them; pre-sumably, further celestial advancement elicits "psychic reconfigura-tion." An important clue from the Bruce Codex (discussed later in this chapter) indicates that the seer Marsanes was reckoned in Sethian tradition to possess a status superior to that of the angels, perhaps earned, in part, through knowing the proper names, that is, psychic properties of the alphabet.[13]

Other Sethian texts also feature alphabet mysticism but focus on ecstatic speech within doxologies, particularly as associated with the "Doxomedon-aeon" ("aeon of the Lord of Glory"). The *Egyptian Gospel*, for instance, offers a brief vowel spell where the letters are each written twenty-two times—the number of letters in the Hebrew alphabet:[14]

> Domedon Doxomedon came forth, the aeon of the aeons, and
> the [throne (θρόνος)] which is in him, and the powers [that] sur-
> round him, the glories and the [incorruptible beings]. [The] Father
> of the great [light] that came forth from the silence is [the great

Doxomedon]-aeon in whom [the Thrice-Male] Child rests. And
the throne of his [glory] was established [in it], [this one] which
is unrevealable name [is written], on the tablet (πύξος) [. . .] one
is the Word, the [Father] [of the light] of the entirety, the one
[who came] forth from the silence, while he rests in the silence, he
whose name [is] an [invisible] symbol. [A] hidden, [invisible] mystery proceeded from ιιιιιιιιιιιιιι[ιιι] ηηηηηηηηηηηηηηηηηηηηηη[ηη ο]
οοοοοοοοοοοοοοοοοοο υυ[υυυ]υυυυυυυυυυυυυυυυυ εεεεε[. . .]
εεεεεεεεεεεεεεε ααααααα[αααα]ααααααααααα ω ω ω ω ω ω ω
ω[ωωω] ω ω ω ω ω ω ω ω ω ω ω And [thus] did the three powers
bless the [Great], Invisible, unnamable, virginal, uncallable Spirit
and [its] male virgin.[15]

Also known in the text as the "great aeon" and the Domedon-
Doxomedon ("Lord of the House–Lord of Glory"),[16] this aeon seems
to designate not a single entity but a place, evidently the divine
throne room in which the soteriological entity, the Thrice-Male
Child, resides.[17] The title "Lord of Glory" is a common designation
for God as the judge on his throne in various doxologies in *1 Enoch*.[18]
The appellation enjoyed an afterlife not only in Sethian but also in
Manichaean literature.[19]

In the Platonizing Sethian text *Zostrianos*, this same Doxomedon
aeon is mentioned briefly in the context of a discussion of the aeons
of the Protophanes subaeon of Barbelo.[20] Significantly, the discourse
immediately moves on to an ecstatic doxology of the Supreme Being,
the source of the living individuals (i.e., the elect) joined together in
the Protophanes: "φοη ζοη ζηοη ζηοη ζωσι ζωσι ζαω ζηοοο ζησεν ζησεν!
The individuals are alive, and (so are) the four, who are seven-fold!
ηοοοοηαηω! It is you who is before them, it is you who is (with)in
them all, and they are in the Protophanes, perfect male Harmedon,
the Activity of all those who exist together!"[21] Another vowel doxology is directed by the Barbelo herself toward the One: "I live in
[. . .] you live, One. [. . .] The one] who is three lives;[22] it is you
who are three, which is three multiplied, [. . .] E E E, the first of
seven, [. . .] the third [. . .] the second [. . .] εεεε αααααα."[23] *Allogenes* features no extant vowel spells, but a noteworthy passage mentions a celestial feminine entity (probably Barbelo, although a lacuna
hides the subject) who "manifested by means of an Activity that is
at rest and silent, having made a sound (ϩροου) like this: 'ZZA ZZA
ZZA!' And when she heard the power and was filled. . ."[24] Another
lacuna interrupts the description, but four lines later the reader is
immersed in another doxology, probably uttered by Allogenes'

angelic interlocutor, Youel, directed toward Armedon, probably related to the "Protophanes, perfect male Harmedon" mentioned by *Zostrianos*: "Thou art great, Armedon! Thou art perfect, Epiphaneus! But according to the Activity that is thine, the second power and Understanding, that which derives from Blessedness: Autoer, Beritheus, Erigenaor, Orimenaios, Aramen, Alphages, Elelioupheus, Lalameus, Yetheus, Noetheus! Thou (*masc. sg.*) art great; whosoever knows [you],[25] knows the entirety. You are one, You are one, the one that is good, Aphredon! You are the aeon of the aeons, the one that exists for eternity."[26] Here, Aphredon is also called "aeon of the aeons," a title associated with the Doxomedon aeon–Autogenes in the *Egyptian Gospel* and, as we will see, the Son in the *Trimorphic Protennoia*.[27]

At times, the Sethian doxologies employ extensive abbreviation or codes that only superficially resemble ecstatic speech. A good example is from the *Trimorphic Protennoia*: "they blessed the perfect son, the Christ, the only-begotten God. And they gave glory, saying, 'he exists! He exists! The Son of God, the Son of God, it is he [who] exists, Aeon of aeons, beholding the aeons that he begot. For you begot them by your will alone—for this reason, we glorify you: ⲙⲁ ⲙⲱ ⲱ ⲱ ⲱ ⲉⲓⲁ ⲉⲓ ⲟⲛ ⲉⲓ the Aeon of [aeons], the aeon which he gave.'"[28] The Greek letters at the end of the doxology are not an ecstatic utterance at all, but say in Coptic, "Meirotheia! Meirotheo! Thrice-great," and then in Greek, "thou art first, thou art (the one who) exists! Thou art the Aeon of the aeons!"[29] One can produce other examples in the *Egyptian Gospel* and *Zostrianos*, when Ephesech utters praise of the Thrice-Male Child, "Akron [. . .] The thrice-male, [five]fold first and last, twice times 10,000 times three (in) [one] (ⲁⲁ[ⲁⲁⲁ] ⲱⲱⲱⲱ ⲃⲓ ⲧⲣⲉⲓⲥ ⲉ[ⲓⲥ]).[30] You are a spirit from spirit; you are light [from] light, you are [silence] from silence, you [are] Comprehension (ἔννοια) from Comprehension, the son [. . .],[31] seven . . . ??[. . .] ???"[32] The passage concludes with a mysterious sigil in the manuscript; like the quadrangles interrupting a speech in the manuscript of *Trimorphic Protennoia*,[33] the purpose of these cryptograms and their proximity to Sethian tradition (as opposed to the transmission of the texts in Coptic) remain unknown.

At first glance, it does not appear that these diverse sorts of alphabet mysticism have much in common: in *Marsanes*, an author knowledgeable of scholarship on the Greek alphabet has applied that learning to contemporary Platonic psychology, yet in the context of obtaining the aid of or mastery over angels. In the *Egyptian Gospel,* vowel spells seem to be associated with the praise of the supreme deity having manifested himself on the Merkabah, which has been hypostatized into a second god itself, Doxomedon, "aeon of the aeons," also associated with the Autogenes. In *Zostrianos,* this deity seems to be associated instead with the Protophanes aeon, or (H)armedon, who also appears in a doxology in *Allogenes* following on some kind of "buzzing" sound produced by a feminine entity, probably the Barbelo. Yet in each case, alphabet mysticism is part of praise of the supreme being at a particularly high level of heavenly ascent, and the encounter with the second permutation of Barbelo (Domedon-Doxomedon or Protophanes). Most importantly, these doxologies are associated with angels: in *Marsanes,* with naming and separating oneself from them; in the *Egyptian Gospel,* with joining the angelic "glories" inhabiting the divine throne room; in *Zostrianos* similarly, except with the "glories" here described in the Platonic jargon of elect "unified individuals"; and in *Allogenes,* with the angel Youel, who utters the ecstatic praise to show the doxologies to the seer, who in turn presumably passes them on to his readers. The seers—and their readers—appear to participate in the praise of the first principle taking place in heaven, among the angels. As we will see, *Marsanes* does not ignore or dispense with this aspect of Sethian tradition, but rather presumes it and articulates what is implicit in the other Platonizing Sethian texts: that the seer himself has been transmogrified, divinized, made superior to the angels, and thus possesses power over them.

Turner proposes a different philosophical context for Sethian use of "syllables of power"—the esoteric Platonism of Hermetic literature and Iamblichus.[34] In *Corpus Hermeticum* tractate 16, the author claims that the discourse of Hermes he is about to report

> will be entirely unclear when the Greeks eventually desire to translate our (Egyptian) language to their own and thus produce in writing the greatest distortion and unclarity. But this discourse, expressed in our nation's language, keeps clear the meaning of its words. The very quality of the speech and the <sound> of Egyptian words have in themselves the energy of the objects they speak of. Therefore . . . keep this discourse uninterpreted, lest mysteries of such greatness come to the Greeks, lest the extravagant, flaccid, and (as it were) dandified Greek idiom extinguish something stately and concise, the energetic idiom of (Egyptian) usage. . . . This is the philosophy of the Greeks, an inane foolosophy of speeches (ἐστὶν Ἑλλήνων φιλοσοφία λόγων ψόφος).[35]

Under the guise of the Egyptian priest "Abamon," Iamblichus replies to the critique of invocation leveled by his teacher, Porphyry, which he quotes:

> "but invocations (κλήσεις)," the objection goes, "are addressed to the gods as if they were subject to external influence (ἐμπαθεῖς), so that it is not only daemons that are thus subject, but also the gods." In fact, however, your assumption, (dear Porphyry), is not correct. For the illumination that comes about as a result of invocations that reveal and will themselves, and is far removed from being drawn down by force, but rather proceeds to manifestation by reason of its own divine energy and perfection, is as far superior to (human) voluntary motion as the divine will of the Good is to the life of ordinary deliberation and choice. It is by virtue of such will, then, that the gods in their benevolence and graciousness unstintingly shed their light upon theurgists, summoning up their souls to themselves and orchestrating their union with them, accustoming them, even while still in the body, to detach themselves from their bodies, and to turn themselves towards their eternal and intelligible first principle.[36]

Both passages are relevant to Sethian alphabet mysticism, since they deal with two major topics of debate among Platonists about language: the cultural politics of using foreign words (ὀνόματα βάρβαρα) in a Greek environment and the (im)possibility of humans wielding power over the divine, their superiors, with mere words.

The harmonization of ecstatic speech with alphabetic speculation is attested relatively early in Middle Platonism by the Neopythagorean Nicomachus of Gerasa (second century CE).[37] But in the third century CE, the use of "foreign sounds" in a Greek philosophical environment was challenged by Plotinus and especially Porphyry, in the context of the Gnostic controversy. In *Ennead* 2.9, Plotinus denigrates his Gnostic friends' use of the practice, for "when they write magic chants (ἐπαοιδάς), intending to address them to these powers, not only to Soul but to those above it as well, what are they doing except making the powers obey the word and follow the lead of people who say spells and charms and conjurations, any one of us who is well skilled in the art of saying precisely the right things in the right way, songs and cries and aspirated and hissing sounds (μέλη καὶ ἤχους καὶ προσπνεύσεις καὶ σιγμοὺς τῆς φωνῆς) and everything else which their writings say has magic power in the higher world? But even if they do not want to say this, how are the incorporeal beings affected by sounds (πῶς φωναῖς τὰ ἀσώματα)?"[38] While Plotinus mocks the kind of sounds made by the Gnostics during their invocations, he is more concerned with the philosophical implications of the practice, that is, that human souls could have power over divine beings, and more specifically that corporeal utterances could affect *any* incorporeal entity. Plutarch had earlier speculated that the language of spirits is superior to and more rarefied than human language,[39] but Plotinus questions the efficacy of physical speech itself in the context of dealing with the intelligible world.

Porphyry addresses each of these themes in his attack on theurgic practices, the *Letter to Anebo*. While Plotinus is content to mock the meaningless utterances of the theurgists, Porphyry explicitly attacks them for sounding like barbarian nonsense: "And what is the point of meaningless words (ἄσημα ὀνόματα)? Why, out of all the meaningless words, are the barbaric preferred to our own? For if whoever hears them looks to their signification, it is sufficient that the conception (ἔννοια) remains the same, whatever the words may be that are used. For (the God) who is invoked is not Egyptian by race; nor, if he were Egyptian, would he use the Egyptian, or, in short, any human language. For either all these are the artificial fabrications of sorcerers (γοήτων . . . τεχνάσματα), and veils originating from our passions through offering devotions to the God, or we naively hold conceptions about divinity contrary to reality."[40]

Porphyry here echoes a similar criticism, leveled by Celsus, of the Orientalizing fashion of using barbaric, exotic names for the deity instead of one's native Greek.[41] (Rhetorically, the move is subtle: while the argument is that God has no preference with respect to language, for Celsus and Porphyry both, the default one resorts to is, of course, Greek.) He also recalls Plotinus's discomfort with a hierarchy in which a theurgist has power over celestial, incorporeal beings: "It confounds me endlessly, (the idea) that those who invoke superior beings command them as though they were actually their inferiors."[42]

In *De mysteriis*, Iamblichus responds to all these charges under the auto-Orientalizing pose of the priest "Abammon." He defends ecstatic use of meaningless words, arguing that the words only appear meaningless because their divine nature is ineffable, which makes the words even more divine. Their intellectual symbolic relationship to divine things is also present in the human soul.[43] As for barbarian names, the gods granted the "meaningless" incantations to the Egyptians and Assyrians specifically for religious ceremonies; therefore, their Oriental provenance is sanctioned by heaven. Moreover, the Oriental tongues are more ancient, and thus superior, so their traditional names for the gods should be preserved, remaining untranslated.[44]

Iamblichus agrees with Plotinus and Porphyry that no human could have authority or power over the gods. Rather, as the sole active agents in the theophany, divine beings elevate the theurgist who uses incantations.[45] His defense of the divine hierarchy—where humans are at the bottom—is most clearly articulated in his defense of animal sacrifice. Porphyry charges theurgists with claiming to "feed" the gods in sacrifice, which would ostensibly make them superior to the gods; Iamblichus recognizes the problem, but denies that theurgists are doing any such thing: "Why, then, do the advocates of this view (of Porphyry's) not go on to overturn the whole order of nature, so as to place us in a higher rank, and make us more powerful (than the daemons)? For if they make us the nourishers and fulfillers of the needs of the daemons, we will be causally superior to the daemons; for it is a general rule that each thing derives its nurture and fulfillment from that to which it owes its generation. . . . For Soul is brought to completion by Intellect, and Nature by Soul, and all other things similarly are nourished by their causes. If, then, it is impossible that we are the originating causes of daemons, by the same reasoning we are not responsible for their nourishment."[46] Similarly, in responding to Porphyry's more general charge that theurgists' attempts to draw demons and divine powers down into the corporeal sphere disregards the stature befitting incorporeal beings, "Abammon" simply rejects the idea that theurgists operate on the worldly level at all.[47] Rather, they interact with the transcendent realm using rites that are powered by the gods; thus the theurgists "imitate the order of the gods."[48]

While the fusion of ecstatic speech and speculation about the psychic properties of the alphabet thus appears to go back to the earliest Platonic theurgists, discussion of the practice in the schools of the third and fourth centuries CE focused on its implications for two ongoing debates: the worth of Oriental wisdom, and how to respect divine agency in ritual. The authors of the Platonizing Sethian treatises must have been aware of these questions, but they were not interested in articulating their own theoretical position, as Origen did.[49] Rather, their texts simply employ ecstatic speech and alphabet mysticism. While clearly educated in the highest tiers of Hellenic learning, they reject the Hellenocentric criticism of barbarian ecstatic speech proffered by Plotinus and Porphyry. Instead, like the *Chaldean Oracles*, the *Corpus Hermeticum*, and Iamblichus, they auto-Orientalize, intentionally blending their Greek metaphysics with exotic hymns and ululations. No sign of actual knowledge of Oriental languages is evident; for instance, the author of the *Egyptian Gospel* mentions Semitic letters on a wooden plank adorning the Merkabah, but shows no sign of being able to actually read them.[50]

However, *Marsanes* departs from Iamblichus in assuming that its "syllables of power" do indeed carry force in the heavenly realms; presumably, "naming" the angels gives one power over them and even "separates" one from them. For Iamblichus, such an irruption of power from below is impossible. At best, such attempts to gain power over divine beings—base magic—simply fail, as opposed to the attempts of theurgists. Human beings, with their fallen, descended souls, owe the efficacy of theurgy to the downward flow of divine power through a hierarchy of gods, daimones, and divine souls.

The ecstatic speech in the rest of Sethian literature also recalls magical, not theurgic, texts. Strings of vowels commonly adorn magical papyri, such as P.London Or. MS 6796: "Yea yea, for I adjure you [by the] dew of heaven and the fat of the land. I adjure you by [the] cup of blessing that [is placed before me . . .] until [. . . holy]. I [adjure] you [today by] your own very [head] and your [holy tabernacle] and the power of the [holy] vowels, [which] are these: AAA OOO MMM. [. . .] holy god, I invoke [you—I], Severus, son of Joanna—so that [you might send] the power of the holy [. . .] to me, and it might come."[51] In later Christian magic, the seven vowels were equated with the archangels, and could be used to invoke them.[52] Within the apocalyptic frame narratives of the Sethian texts, vowel spells are clearly doxological ecstatic speech uttered by the mystic overcome by an encounter with divinity. But as fixed textual artifacts (preserved at Nag Hammadi), they could have had two uses for their readers. First, they could have been employed to adjure and control the supernatural beings encountered during heavenly journeys.[53] In this sense, they also recall *historiolae*, spells whose incantation sums up or embodies a particular popular myth recited in order to activate the spell's potency.[54] Alternatively they could be read, like the *voces magicae* of the Hekhalot literature, as performances of the divine name, whose nonsensical nature expresses the utter identity of action and meaning in divine speech.[55] The vowel spells of Sethian literature are not only evidence that Sethian tradition drew on elements of contemporary magical practice in formulating its myth and ritual; the seer employing the vowel spells is in the possession of power and potent language that, from the perspective of Iamblichus's theorization of ritual practice, are not claimed by theurgists, but by mere sorcerers.[56]

ANGELS ALIEN TO HUMANITY

The authors of the Sethian treatises were not exactly sorcerers (γόητες), for they did not hold that, as *humans*, they were superior to heavenly beings. Instead, several of their texts describe how seers would, in the course of the ascent to heaven, be transformed into angels and even acquire supra-angelic authority. Such transformations appear to have been associated with celestial baptism, as discussed in the *Trimorphic Protennoia* and *Zostrianos*, which constitute the primary evidence for the practice in Sethianism. *Zostrianos*, the *Untitled Treatise*, and *Marsanes* describe the superiority of the divinized seer to his angelic peers, also assumed in *Allogenes* and perhaps the *Three Steles*. Close parallels in Jewish and Christian apocalypses and even the Dead Sea Scrolls indicate a background in Second Temple Judaism.

There are two sets of baptisms described in *Trimorphic Protennoia*. The feminine savior—here known as "Voice"—describes herself:

> I cast a voice of the sound unto the ears of those who do not know me, and I call you (*pl.*) to the exalted, perfect light; when you (*pl.*) enter it, you (*pl.*) will receive glory from those who give glory, and those that enthrone will enthrone you (*pl.*). You (*pl.*) will receive a robe (στολή) from those that give robes, and the baptizers will baptize (ⲣ̄ⲃⲁⲡⲧⲓⲍⲉ) you (*pl.*). You (*pl.*) will become a glory, among glories,[57] that which you originally dwelled in, (back) when you were luminous.[58]

Later, the same Voice describes her deliverance of the baptismal initiate in the rite of the Five Seals:

> As for me, I put all of them on—but then I stripped them off that person, donning radiating light, that is, the knowledge of the thought of paternity.[59]
>
> I delivered him unto those who give robes—Ammōn, Elassō, (and) Amēnai, and they enrobed him with a robe of light.
>
> (Next), I delivered him unto the baptizers, Mikheus, Mickhar, and Mnēsimous, (and) they baptized him. Then they purified him in the fountain of the water of life.[60]
>
> Next, I delivered him unto those who enthrone, Bariēl, Nouthan, (and) Sabenai, (and) they enthroned him by means of a throne of glory.[61]

Then, I delivered him unto those that glorify, Ēriōm, Ēlien, (and) Phariēl, (and) they glorified him with the glory of paternity.

And those who snatch away,[62] Kamaliēl, [.]anēn, (and) Samblō, great holy assistants of the luminaries,[63] snatched (him) away, taking him to a luminous place of his paternity.

And he (received) the Five Seals through the light of the mother, Protennoia . . . "[64]

Both passages describe a baptismal process involving stripping off the corporeal body and donning a celestial one (i.e., a robe) along-side a (presumably hymnic) practice of giving, receiving, and being assimilated to "glory."[65] This transformation probably takes place in heaven, although whether it mirrors a physical rite is not clear.[66]

In *Zostrianos*, the eponymous seer is taken to heaven on a cloud. He "becomes like the glories" as he passes through the "aetherial [earth]."[67] Next, he is baptized as he goes through the copies of the aeons and the realms of the Exile and Repentance, finally arriving at the Autogenes aeon, the lowest sector of the aeon of Barbelo: "I stood there, staring into the light of the truth that truly exists from [a] self-begotten root [with some] great angels and glories [. . .][68] in number. I was baptized in the [name of] the self-begotten deity by the powers that exist [upon the] living water: Michar and Mi[chael], and I was purified by the great Barpharanges. And they [glorified][69] me and wrote me (ⲥⲁⲣⲧ̄) into glory. [I was] sealed (σφραγίζειν) by them, those who exist upon these powers, [Michar], Michael, Seldao, Ele[nos], and Zogenethlos. And I [became] an angel able to see [god][70] and I stood up on the first aeon, which is the fourth, with the souls."[71] He praises various incarnations of Seth, before encountering Pleistheia, "the [mother of the angels].[72] And I was [baptized] for the second time, in the name of the divine Autogenes, by the same powers. I became an angel (ἄγγελος) of the male race (γένος). And I stood upon the second aeon, which is the third (i.e., Davithe), with the sons of Seth. I blessed each of them, and I was baptized for the third time in the name of the divine Autogenes by each of the powers. I became a holy angel, stand-ing upon the third, that is, the second [aeon] (i.e., Oroiael). For the second time I [blessed] each one of them. And I was baptized [for the fourth] time by [each of the] powers, becoming a perfect [angel]. And [I stood upon] the fourth, [which is the first], aeon (i.e., Harmozel), and I [blessed each one of them.]."[73] *Zostrianos*'s baptismal liturgy explicitly results in the seer's becoming an angel, again in concord with a hymnic practice of giving and receiving glory.

Glorification in *Zostrianos* appears to be hypostasized into deities that are referred to simply as glories. During his ascent, glories protect Zostrianos's body, and he receives an "image" of glories before leaving the aetherial earth.[74] They are crucial to the salvific mechanism envisioned by the text: "For the sake of [this (i.e., the descent of the soul)], these powers have been appointed for their salvation, and they exist in this world. In the self-begotten ones, corresponding to each of the aeons, glories stand so that someone who is down here in the world might be saved alongside them. The glories are perfect living thoughts (νόημα). It is impossible for them to perish, because they [are] models (τύπος) of salvation, something that each one of them receives when he becomes saved. And (each one) has a model (of salvation), receiving power from each one of them, and (each one) has glory as an aide (βοηθός) just as he passes out from the world."[75] The glories are associated with angels; at the beginning of his transformation, Zostrianos stands with "angels and glories." In the intelligible world, angels exist "in great glory."[76] The extended title of the revelator-angel Youel in the Platonizing treatises is "she who belongs to the glories, the male, virgin glory."[77] Like Youel, they participate in Zostrianos's divinization, anointing him.[78] They are at times associated both with the Protophanes aeon and the luminaries of Barbelo, and, notably, with the τύπος of the divine that exists in the seer, as in the passage quoted here.[79] Thus a Greek philosophical term is superimposed on recognizably Jewish, angelic language to describe *Zostrianos*'s key soteriological intermediaries.[80]

Investiture is not described, but *Zostrianos* implies that a physical transformation of the seer has taken place. Once he has ascended to the aetherial earth, he has already forsaken the body, the "dead creation inside," and left it behind.[81] The process culminates in his assimilation to the grade of "completely perfect" elect and the acquisition of a crown: "They set me down, and left. And Apophantes, with Aphropais the virgin-light, came to me, and he brought me to the great perfect male Intellect, Protophanes. And I saw all of them there, in the form in which they exist, as one; and I united with them all, blessing the Kalyptos aeon and the virgin Barbelo, and the Invisible Spirit. I become completely perfect, having received power, with them having written me into glory and having sealed me. And I received a perfect crown there, coming to the perfect individuals, and they asked me (about) everything. They listened to the enormities of knowledge (I had to offer), rejoicing all the while and [receiving] power (from me)."[82] Having become first an angel and here crowned and "completely perfect," Zostrianos is now a revelator himself, teaching individuals in the Autogenes aeon. He is superior to the angels and glories that inhabit the aeons below the Protophanes,[83] which is what enables him to slip past the demiurge and his archons unnoticed on his way back to earth.[84]

Although they do not explicitly describe angelification, a similar process of celestial liturgy involving glorifying, self-glorification, and physical transformation occurs in other Sethian texts. They may be related to accounts of hypostatized cosmic entities (such as the Barbelo and her constituents) that "stand" and utter praise in heaven, as are found in the Barbeloite cosmogony of the *Apocryphon of John*. The *Egyptian Gospel* features a deeply complex angelology and series of celestial baptisms and doxologies, which is the context for the text's vowel mysticism discussed earlier in this chapter: "Pronoia passed through all the aeons which I mentioned before. And she established thrones of glory and [myriads] of angels [without] number [who] surrounded them, [powers and incorruptible] glories, who [sing] and glorify, all giving praise with [a single voice], with one image, [with one] never silent [voice . . .] the Father, and the [Mother, and the] Son [. . .] [the] pleromas [that I] mentioned [before], who is [the great] Christ, who is from [. . .] [who is the] child, Telmaēl Telmakhaēl [Ēli Ēli] Makhar Makhar [Seth, the] power which truly lives, and the [male virgin] who is with him, Youel."[85] The speaker of the baptismal liturgy concluding the text is also transformed when he assumes an "armor of light."[86]

Allogenes is, much like Zostrianos, "taken by the eternal Light out of the garment" before the appearance of the luminaries and the "primary revelation of the Unknowable One."[87] His guide up to this point has been the angel Youel, who appears to be himself a divine name or glory with affinities to Metatron and the angelic interlocutor Ioel in the *Apocalypse of Abraham*.[88] The patriarch's introduction to the divine being features a long description of his fantastic garb, which recalls the divine glory.[89] At the same time, "Jaoel" is a combination of the three root letters of the Tetragrammaton with the usual "el" ending; thus the angel tells Abraham that "a power in virtue of the Ineffable name is dwelling with me."[90] Like the character Doxomedon, the feminine Youel appears in Manichaean thought, known as "the Maiden of Light" Ioel.[91] Allogenes' chief interlocutor before meeting glories in heaven is an angel whose background in contemporary Jewish apocalyptic literature recalls glorification and the Divine Name itself. The seer's conversation with this entity results in his rapture and the acquisition of "power" that allows him to receive information that is beyond the ken of all but the greatest powers.[92]

The *Three Steles of Seth* also explores a dynamic of glorification and self-transformation; again and again, the congregation declares its praise of the highest beings, who are themselves described as "glory."[93] The practice of glorification is what defines the elect body: "you (sing. masc.) have commanded us, as one who is elect, to glorify you to the extent that we are able. We bless you because we have been saved. We glorify you at all times; because of this, we glorify you: that we might be saved to eternal salvation."[94] Seth is changed by this activity: "many times I joined in giving glory with the powers, and I became worthy of the immeasurable majesties."[95] One who remembers these things and gives glory "always shall become perfect among those who are perfect and impassable beyond all things."[96] It is unclear whether the speakers are in heaven or on earth, or if the text implies angelification, since angels are nowhere mentioned; however, it is clear that the elect is circumscribed here by the activity that characterizes the celestial activity of angels in other Sethian texts.

Finally, a particularly thorny passage in the *Untitled Treatise* of the Bruce Codex is best understood in light of Sethian evidence about angelification. The text concerns the prophet Marsanes and his relationship to another prophet, Nicotheus (whose apocalypse appears to have been read in Plotinus's circle),[97] as well as the heavenly powers:

> Indeed, to speak of him (i.e., the Invisible Spirit)—specifically, of the manner in which he exists—with a tongue of flesh—this is an impossibility. For they are great ones, those who pass beyond powers so that they might hear through Comprehension (ἔννοια) and follow him; (for this is impossible), unless they (i.e., the heavenly powers) find a kinsman of theirs in (some)one that is able to hear about the places from which he originally came. For everything follows from its root, since man is a kinsman of the mysteries. For this reason, mankind has heard a mystery. The powers of all the great aeons have worshipped (ογωϣτ) the power that is in Marsanes. They said, "who is that one who has seen these things before his very own eyes?" For his (Marsanes') sake, he (the Only-Begotten) manifested in this way (ϫⲉ ⲉⲧⲃⲏⲏⲧϥ̄ ⲁϥⲟⲩⲟⲛϩ̄ ⲉⲃⲟⲗ ⲛ̄ⲧⲉⲓϩⲉ) Nicotheus spoke about him (the Only-Begotten). He (Nicotheus) has seen him (the Only-Begotten); for he (Nicotheus) is that one (ϫⲉ ⲛ̄ⲧⲟϥ ⲡⲉ ⲡⲉⲧⲙ̄ⲙⲁⲩ). He said, "the father exists, surpassing every perfection." He has revealed the invisible, thrice-powered, perfect one. Each of the perfect men saw him; they spoke of him, glorifying him, each in his own way.[98]

"Nicotheus" saw the Only Begotten, for he has also become an incarnation of him by virtue of his vision. This recalls the way in which Zostrianos and Allogenes are transformed into reincarnations of Seth following their visions, transformations that in turn authorize their revelations. Like the *Three Steles*, angels per se are nowhere mentioned here; yet as with *Zostrianos* and *Allogenes*, the seer(s) has been transformed into a being superior to angels (or, in this case, the powers), capable of edifying them and eliciting worship from them in the heavens.

Such supra-angelic knowledge and authority following transformation appears to belong to the eponymous prophet of *Marsanes*: "For it is I who have [understood] that which truly exists, whether partially or [wholly], according to difference, [I apprehended][99] that they exist from the [beginning in the] entire eternal place, namely, everything that has come into being, whether without Substance or whether by means of Substance, those who are unbegotten, and the divine aeons, together with the angels and the souls which are without guile and the psychic [garments], likenesses [of the] simple things."[100] As in *Trimorphic Protennoia* and *Zostrianos*, the acquisition of "garments" of light elicits transformation. Elsewhere, Marsanes seems to speak as though *he* were the Barbelo, and says that he dwells in the Barbelo.[101] It is unclear if Marsanes enjoyed the company of angels, but he certainly has surpassed them. This status explains why he has the authority to say, as discussed earlier in this chapter, that alphabet mysticism and astrological speculation controls and "separates" one from the angels as it shapes the human soul into a divine being.[102]

To be sure, the various descriptions of celestial liturgy, glorification, and angelification described here differ from one another in many details. Yet a pattern nonetheless emerges from the data: almost every Sethian text presumes that in some way, the material body can be abandoned, the divine can be glorified, and the seer can be transformed into a more luminous state, among or transcending the angels. The only text that does not discuss this practice, the *Apocalypse of Adam*, describes the mythology that underlies it: Adam and Eve "resembled the great eternal angels," after having learned "a word of knowledge of the eternal God," that is, what the text teaches. Moreover, the elect "will be like those angels, for they are not strangers to them."[103] The theme of Adam having been made superior to powers and angels, a tradition treated widely within the Syrian and Armenian Adam literature, is also found in the apocalypses known to Mani.[104]

Like the superiority of the human essence to even that of the angels, the greater complex of elect individuals transforming, glorifying angels, and ultimately becoming supra-angelic is a peculiar feature of Jewish and Christian literature, particularly the apocalypses. Greco-Roman sources certainly describe interactions with and worship of angels, but not in similar contexts of celestial glorification and self-transformation.[105] Some later Platonic sources mention angels, but not fellowship with them, much less transformation into them.[106] Yet Jewish and Christian apocalyptic literature abounds with descriptions of the elect becoming angels or superior to angels. Scholars have often recalled 2 *Enoch* with reference to the celestial baptism of the *Trimorphic Protennoia*: "And the LORD said to Michael, 'Go, and extract Enoch from [his] earthly clothing. And anoint him with my delightful oil, and put him into the clothes of my glory.' And so Michael did, just as the Lord had said to him. He anointed me and clothed me. And the appearance of that oil is greater than the greatest light, and its ointment is like sweet dew, and its fragrance myrrh; and it is like the rays of the glittering sun. And I looked at myself, and I had become like one of his glorious ones, and there was no observable difference."[107] *1* and *3 Enoch* also provide parallels.[112] The Enochic celestial angelification does not focus on baptism, but the acquisition of angelic, priestly vestments, a common motif in Jewish mystical literature.[109]

This comparison of Sethian celestial baptism and angelification to liturgical transformation in the apocalypses is worth revising and expanding. A stronger parallel is the importance of glorification and doxology in both Sethian and Judeo-Christian apocalyptic literature. It is important to distinguish the activity of glorification from speculation about God's glory as a manifestation of divine presence, creative power, or the angelic Angel of the Lord, evidence for which is slim in Sethian literature.[110] Meanwhile, visionaries in the apocalypses, like the Sethian seers, not only witness but come to participate in the heavenly liturgy.[111] If these visionaries come to attain angelic status in doing so, it is possible that, as in the *Apocalypse of Zephaniah*, they have come to learn an angelic language and employ it in their hymns.[112] In other texts, the seer joins in the *kedushah*, having been granted a heavenly crown, another motif common to Jewish, Christian, and Sethian ascent literature.[113] This dynamic of glorification and transformation via participation in the celestial doxology among the angels recalls the Sethian material reviewed in the previous section.

As in *Zostrianos* and *Allogenes*, transformation in Jewish literature often takes place in heaven. The idea that the souls of the elect
become angels in heaven is an old one. In *1 Enoch* and especially
Daniel transformation to a heavenly state is the reward of the righteous, who probably endured persecution under and after Antiochus
IV Epiphanes.[114] In the Dead Sea Scrolls, the Synoptic gospels, and
Christian monastic traditions, righteous or pure souls live like angels
after death.[115] Together with investiture, the Hellenistic emphasis on
martyrology in celestial angelification is preserved in later, including Christian, apocalyptic literature. The *Apocalypse of Zephaniah*
features the seer's transformation into an angel through glorification
and an enrobing on a boat in heaven.[116] *2 Baruch* and the *Ascension of Isaiah* say the righteous, having become angels via the acquisition of the heavenly garment, will later become greater than the
angels.[117] Angelified patriarchs also include Adam, Enoch, Abraham,
Jacob, Melchizedek, and Moses.[118] Jesus Christ was also compared to
an angel.[119]

While the liturgical transformation of the self in Sethian literature seems to stem from first-century baptismal traditions, it seems to
have also picked up on Hellenistic Jewish traditions about angelified,
divine intermediaries. Moreover, it agrees with Jewish and Christian
apocalypses of the first to third centuries CE in describing the process
of angelification as one of the righteous acquiring a new robe or coat
while glorifying the deity and joining the heavenly liturgy, perhaps
while using angelic speech, a process culminating in the acquisition
of supra-angelic knowledge and authority. Descriptions of angels as
heavenly priests in robes of light in the Qumran *Songs of the Sabbath
Sacrifice* may indicate that such traditions stemmed from the Levite
priesthood and spread to Gnostic and Jewish groups from there. In
contemporary Platonic doctrine, such authority is outside the provenance of human souls, who are relatively low in the hierarchy of
divine beings and so need divine power to flow on down to them.
Angelified or divinized seers in Jewish and Sethian literature, meanwhile, are at least on a par with heavenly beings. Sethian celestial
liturgies were thus most likely derived from Jewish apocalyptic traditions and adapted into a Christian Sethian context, much as some of
the church fathers absorbed Jewish traditions about angelification.[120]

One can be more specific by addressing what kind of presumptions
the various texts have about the body and practice. The Sethian treatises are in line with ascent apocalypses and the Hekhalot literature

in dealing with bodily transformation, as opposed to Qumran, which does not address physical transformation at all.[121] Similarly, like the apocalypses and Enochic tradition, but unlike the Dead Sea Scrolls, the seer takes on angelic characteristics through ascent to heaven, instead of cultivating a divine presence on earth.[122] As at Qumran, such transformations were accomplished in communal liturgies (exemplified in the *Three Steles of Seth*), as opposed to the individualistic practices of the Hekhalot literature, although all three sets of texts culminate in descriptions of *unio liturgica*.[123] Yet the Sethian traditions differ from apocalyptic and Hekhalot literature alike in stressing the celibate background of the practice, as indicated by their disparaging remarks about femininity and the flesh.[124] Sethian self-transformation was therefore probably related to contemporary Christian ascetic practice that allowed one to "live like an angel" and so gain revelation through visions, and it reveals a dimension of hitherto unnoticed ascetic activity within the Nag Hammadi texts.[125]

WHO WEARS THE CROWN

If Zostrianos, Allogenes, and other Sethian seers are archetypes of the elect, then the texts bearing their names indicate an achieved level of realized eschatology.[126] Did their readers then consider themselves angels? Does Zostrianos's donning of a crown at the summit of his ascent reflect the possibility of a similar angelification and crowning for the reader of his apocalypse? It is helpful here to recall scholarly debate about how the members of the community that produced the Dead Sea Scrolls articulated their elect identity with respect to angelology.[127] Some have argued that the Qumran texts presume an "angelomorphic" elect body, and that this is clear from a smattering of references in addition to rereadings of several of the corpus's most well-known treatises.[128] Many of these readings are spurious.[129] The *Community Rule* and *War Scroll* do not refer necessarily to angelified human members of the community in a "realized eschatological" sense but to the presence of angels accompanying the pure of body and spirit—in the community and the future war, respectively.[130] The *Songs of the Sage* claims that the pure "shall be priests, his just people, his army and his servants, the angels of his glory," but it is not clear whether the passage refers to transformation on earth or a postmortem angelic investiture.[131] Other passages are more salient; the "egomaniac" author of the *Self-Glorification Hymn* sees himself as on par with the angels and probably superior to them.[132] In the *Hodayot*, the psalmist describes himself (presumably) as "the depraved spirit you have purified from great offence so that he can take a place with the host of the holy ones, and can enter in communion with the congregation of the sons of heaven."[133]

The collection of twelve hymns known as the *Songs of the Sabbath Sacrifice* appears itself to be an angelic liturgy, performed in heaven. Since the text's only reference to human beings is not to celestial hymnists but the yawning gulf that exists between human and divine beings,[134] most readers distinguish the humans from the angels in the text, although one may still see it as a "vehicle" for "communal mysticism," the "virtual" experience of communion with angels.[135] At the same time, one can still recognize that the earthly recitation of the hymns was meant to evoke some kind of identification with angels.[136] A similarly balanced approach suits the Sethian texts. While only *Zostrianos* and the *Trimorphic Protennoia* explicitly describe the transformation of the elect into angels, the complex of practice associated with angelification in both texts—doxology, transformation, superiority to the angels—*is* undoubtedly widespread in the rest of Sethian literature, particularly the *Egyptian Gospel* and the *Three Steles of Seth*. It is hard to imagine that texts so interested in angelic liturgical themes were written and read by individuals who in *no* way likened themselves to angels.

The communal context of the *Songs of the Sabbath Sacrifice* probably can be extended to the Sethian texts as well. This same reference of the Qumran text to human worshippers is in the first-person plural ("our priesthood"; "the offering of our mortal tongue"; etc.), indicating that the recitation of the hymns was a communal exercise, meant to produce mass ecstasy.[137] One is reminded of similar language in the baptism concluding the *Trimorphic Protennoia* and the hymns of the *Three Steles of Seth*, which also probably indicates a communal, ecstatic ritual milieu.[138]

The more interesting question is: how can humans (earthly beings) claim to be angels (heavenly beings) while still on earth? Why would one make a seemingly nonsensical claim, such as "I am a red parrot," or, in Zostrianos's case, "I turned into a male angel"? A critical reader is forced to conclude either that ancient writers who claimed to become angels "mean it and they are wrong, or (that) they mean it, but we can never understand what they mean."[139] Some scholars avoid this quandary by simply asserting that the Qumran community had not in fact experienced "realized" eschatology, experienced it "partially," or obtained a proleptic experience of the postmortem fate of the soul.[140] More generally, many historians neglect the experiential reality that lies beyond the production of religious texts, preferring to locate testimony of remarkable experiences in the realm of genre cliché.[141]

Such approaches are also misreadings of the texts, which discuss a range of figures (like Adam, Moses, Zostrianos, or Marsanes) that are simultaneously human, angelic, and supra-angelic, at times meriting worship.[142] There is no reason to assume that the readers of the Platonizing Sethian treatises, philosophically acute though they must have been, found such figures—or themselves—problematic either. This is not to say that they did not *make* problems: indeed, early Christian communities struggled with how to deal with individuals who claimed to have become angelic beings. Like the Qumran community, the Sethian elect probably saw itself as angelified and saved in this lifetime, albeit as a proleptic experience of the salvation that would come with death and the escape from the cycle of reincarnation.[143] Christian readers of the Sethian texts—like Plotinus's Gnostic friends in Rome—maybe have considered martyrdom an opportunity to gain a crown while departing this life.[144] This quality of being saved was tantamount to transformation into an angelic being. From a practical perspective, angelic status most likely manifested in ascetic practices and participation in earthly liturgies that involved ecstatic speech and vision, as seen in the *Three Steles of Seth*.

WHO DESCENDS TO THE WATER

The hermeneutic questions about angelification engaged here can also help us rethink difficulties in theorizing two more well-known Sethian rites, baptism and the "Five Seals." The central issue in the study of Sethian baptism is the diversity of its character and even presence in Sethian scripture.[145] The *Egyptian Gospel* describes how the preexistent, celestial Seth incarnated on earth to save his seed, the elect, by appearing as Jesus Christ and instituting baptism.[146] *Trimorphic Protennoia* concludes with a baptismal rite involving the stripping off of the physical body and the acquisition of a new body of light. *Melchizedek* also includes a long baptismal prayer.[147] The myths of *Apocryphon of John* and *Trimorphic Protennoia* share a complex of baptismal theology in which the revealer is accompanied by the descent of the spirit into the water of life.[148] During his ascent to heaven to receive revelations of Platonic metaphysics, Zostrianos receives no fewer than twenty-two baptisms, some resulting in his angelification.[149]

Yet other Sethian texts seem to *reject* baptism: once Zostrianos finishes his ascent to heaven, he comes back to earth and preaches, "do not baptize yourselves with death."[150] In the *Apocalypse of Adam*, some kind of "defilement" of the "water of life" takes place.[151] The Archontics, familiar with Sethian tradition, are reported by Epiphanius of Salamis to have rejected baptism.[152] Ophite texts such as *On the Origin of the World* associate water baptism with Yaldabaoth.[153] In each of these cases, it is not clear whether these passages indicate Sethian rejection of the validity of baptisms carried out by other Christians (including Gnostics) or a rejection of water baptism altogether in favor of the truly "living" water of the spirit, such as we find in Mani.[154] Finally, there are no references to baptism at all in the *Three Steles of Seth*, *Allogenes*, and *Marsanes*.

We run into a similar problem with the "Five Seals," mentioned in the *Egyptian Gospel* as well as two texts related to Sethianism, but also sharing their own separate redaction history—*Trimorphic Protennoia* and the "Pronoia Hymn" of the long recension of *Apocryphon of John* (which also has Ophite features).[155] The Five Seals is a rite that is given to humanity in the third descent of the savior to earth, in the guise of Jesus Christ.[156] In the *Gospel*, the seals appear once in a baptismal context, but they are usually celestial hypostases dwelling in heaven.[157] Each of the texts describing the Five Seals is quite otherworldly, and it is not clear whether the rite took place on earth or in heaven.[158] The function and origins of the Five Seals are not immediately clear, and no one claims to have definitively identified their contents.[159] Scholars once argued that the Five Seals simply must have been a form of water baptism.[160] Others have suggested a baptism without water (i.e., baptism by visionary experience) or a postbaptismal fivefold chrism dependent on the fivefold structure of the Autogenes with the Four Luminaries.[161] A problem with this reading is that accounts of anointing are very rare in Gnostic texts, but it must be admitted that early Christian language about liturgical seals referred both to baptism and chrism.[162]

The foregoing analysis in this chapter helps us make sense of this tangle of evidence. Scholars have already recognized that the Five Seals' focus on "living water" is indebted to Johannine and Barbeloite theology, that is, the concept of Jesus Christ as the true water and the Father's production of the Barbelo through his gazing into the primordial waters, described in the Barbeloite theogony of the *Apocryphon of John*.[163] Language about baptism and water associated with the Five Seals in the Sethian texts reflects these themes. It is not clear whether these seals are an anointment, but it is clear that they do not necessarily describe baptism with water, for Barbeloite language about water is metaphorical, dealing with celestial water made of light. Thus several Sethian treatises reject earthly water baptism in favor of heavenly "water."

How, then, could this language used to discuss a physical rite (Five Seals qua baptism, as in the *Egyptian Gospel*) reflect a *nonphysical* understanding of what defines the rite (water)? This question is related to another problem—did the rite take place in heaven or on earth? Just as in the cases of angelomorphism at Qumran or Sethian angelification, testimonia about the reception of baptism and the Five Seals must have come from a live, physical ritual setting that was understood as a participation in the celestial liturgy, with its own baptism in the "water" of light. One cannot exclude the possibility that physical water was used as a *typos* of celestial water, but the immaterial water of light was undoubtedly the focus of the rite. Read this way, the absence of the Five Seals from the Platonizing texts does probably indicate a focus on self-performable ritual whose primary tool is the text itself but not necessarily a general shift away from communal ritual life, which one would then use as the basis for hypothesizing a change to the Sethian community in general.[164] Rather, the Five Seals was one of several rituals that the authors and readers of the Sethian texts employed in the divinization of the self, alongside the models of self-transformation into divine light and participation in the heavenly doxology explored in the rest of this chapter. A lack of baptismal references in some texts, meanwhile, reflects not a movement away from Judaism or Christianity but rather a focus on celestial baptism or even a transbaptismal transformative practice analogous to what we find in certain Jewish-Christian circles.

HOW TO USE A SETHIAN APOCALYPSE

Having examined piecemeal the passages describing the practices that informed the authors of the Sethian texts, we can turn to the question of how the texts themselves may have been used. Obviously the *Apocalypse of Adam* and *Egyptian Gospel* focus on cosmogony and

salvation history, and would have been interesting to readers pursuing ancient lore among the various apocalypses; yet the purpose of
the Platonizing treatises, which combine the genre of apocalypse with
lectures on Neoplatonic metaphysics, hymns to heavenly beings, and
accounts of self-transformation, is much more opaque. Scholars' sug-
gestions that they are manuals of some kind used to elicit visionary
experiences or meditative states cannot be far off, but remain impre-
cise.[165] Did readers of these texts, like those who used the Hekhalot
literature, regard simply reading them as a practice in itself?[166] The
copy of *Allogenes* from Nag Hammadi, a *Lesemysterium* where the
act of reading the text's negative theology functions as a conjuration
of sorts of the transcendent Invisible Spirit, says "yes."[167] Might be
same be true of all the Platonizing Sethian texts?[168]

Plotinus's evidence gives us an example of Christian Gnostics who
read these texts and probably did obtain some kind of visionary experience, which might explain their haughty claim to be superior to the
stellar gods (just as Enoch or Marsanes became superior to the angels)
and their disinterest in Platonic authority, favoring instead their
own revelatory truth claims.[169] The apocalyptic genre of the manuals, as argued in Chapter 3, serves to validate the authority of the
manual and the practices contained within it; rather than reflecting
a movement away from Sethian myth and history, revelations involving Sethian mythologoumena are used to justify the texts' contemplative content. This content remains focused on Greek metaphysics,
but the genre has replaced philosophical argumentation characteristic of more traditional Greek thinkers like Plotinus. Certainly highly
educated individuals (like Plotinus) would have been interested in the
texts anyway, but they also could have been addressed to lay meditators who possessed a minimum of Greek philosophical expertise
but neither the inclination nor ability to spend years exegeting difficult passages in Plato and Aristotle, preferring contemplative practice to scholasticism. Nothing in the Platonizing Sethian apocalypses
requires the reader to follow an argument. Rather, they present a
metaphysical system, with which the reader is presumed to be already
familiar, mapped out for navigation through mental cognition. It is
helpful here to recall the Hekhalot literature, where contrived frame
narratives feature rabbinic heroes who attain visions of the heavenly
palaces (the Hekhalot) and throne (the Merkavah). It is obvious that
they are meant to serve as models for aspiring seers and are complex enough to presume some level of familiarity on the part of the

reader.[170] Meanwhile, the Platonizing treatises, while beholden to the Jewish lore that also informs the Hekhalot texts, have replaced palaces and the heavenly temple with categories of Greek philosophy.

It is unlikely that the aspiring seers reading the Platonizing treatises operated alone. Other ancient visionary ascent manuals, like the Hekhalot texts, the *Mithras Liturgy*, and the Hermetica, appear to speak one-on-one, but obviously reflect a communal environment or shared cultic milieu in which these visions were obtained.[171] The same is true of the various practices surveyed above—the Five Seals, ecstatic speech, and angelification are all practices that, in the Jewish and Christian parallels, reflect a communal environment. Language in the first-person plural peppers important ritual passages in the Sethian texts, such as the celestial baptism of the *Trimorphic Protennoia* and the ecstatic hymns of the *Three Steles of Seth*. The paraenesis of the speaker in *Marsanes*, discussed in Chapter 3, seems to presume an audience that is more like a congregation than an individual seer. Moreover, the Platonizing treatises do not contain exclusively contemplative instruction; each of the treatises also features paraenesis, particularly focused on asceticism. Here again, the *Corpus Hermeticum* and the Gedullah hymns of *Hekhalot Rabbati* serve as useful parallels, pointing to a community as intended readership.[172] However, unlike the "technical" Hermetica and the Hekhalot texts, the Sethian tractates are impregnable to beginners. In both form and content, they are utterly insider-specific. While they are certainly products of ritual life, they presume knowledge of it and thus are bereft of the detailed instruction of the Hekhalot literature or magical papyri that we might expect in a grimoire.

The Platonizing Sethian treatises thus appear to be manuals intended to teach individuals how to elicit visionary experience culminating in contact with the Godhead. While they appear to have been written by individuals with advanced philosophical training, they are directed toward contemplative thinkers who are comfortable with (in this case, thoroughly Sethianized) Platonic metaphysics but are not interested in philosophical argumentation or Platonic proof texts as valid authorities.[173] Thus the incorporation of metaphysical jargon indicates neither an attempt to parley with a different (Hellenic) social group nor to win the approval of particular philosophers (like Plotinus). Rather, some educated readers of Sethian literature believed that Neoplatonic metaphysics offered a useful metaphysical blueprint that could be mapped onto Sethian mythologoumena and used in the service of contemplating the deity. The treatises also mention various ritual practices in an offhand way, apparently assuming the reader's knowledge of them. All of these practices have parallels as being performed in a communal setting. Thus, while they could be used in private, the Platonizing Sethian apocalypses appear to have originated in a community interested in Sethian literature and to be intended for members of that community who already had obtained both some philosophical and ritual training.[174]

Aside from the practices of meditation and hymning, the Platonizing treatises do contain hints of other techniques used to induce ecstasy. The codes and cryptograms littering the texts could have served the purpose of seals, passwords employed by visionaries to navigate the heavenly plane, a trope common to Gnostic and Hekhalot ascent literature.[175] Asceticism was probably another productive agent in obtaining visions. While no particular rules for ascetic life are described in the Sethian texts, one can guess that their readers were informed by regimens of fasting and celibacy.[176] The latter is all but certain given the disparaging remarks about femininity in the treatises, and is surely related to their ubiquitous language extolling the "maleness" of Sethian mythological figures.[177]

These practices could have deeply informed the ritual life of the readers of the Platonizing texts. The Hekhalot literature contains valuable accounts of how a combination of fasting, purification, and prayer could elicit visionary experience.[178] Like ascetics at Qumran or in early Christian communities, the authors and readers of the Sethian literature must have thought that asceticism amounted to "living like the angels." These ascetic practices would have been combined with doxology (proleptic to the aforementioned ecstatic speech) and, in the case of the Platonizing texts, meditation undertaken with a Neoplatonic metaphysical framework culminating in negative theology. The centrality of doxology to vision, especially cogent in the *Egyptian Gospel* and *Zostrianos* but found in each of the Sethian texts, is functionally identical to the *unio liturgica* that seems to have been the object of the Jewish authors of the Qumran and Hekhalot texts. Such a visionary practice probably undergirded the rite of the Five Seals, which is best understood in the context of Jewish liturgies that took place in a similarly altered, liminal state of consciousness, where water is understood as light and earth as heaven.

If the reconstruction proposed here is correct, a vibrant, communal ritual life emerges behind even the Platonizing Sethian texts.

Membership in communities reading Sethian texts centered on rejection of water baptism. As the *Three Steles of Seth* attests, individuals in these communities would together praise traditional Sethian mythologoumena, sometimes producing ecstatic visions in the process. These doxologies were buttressed by a rigorous ascetic lifestyle involving celibacy and fasting. Some individuals who obtained visions of the beyond and participated in the heavenly liturgy appear to have called themselves angels; it is possible that, like the Qumran community, the purveyors of Sethian tradition saw themselves at least in fellowship with the angels. Particularly well-educated members of this community composed visionary manuals reflecting this ritual life, but organizing the cosmos according to Neoplatonic metaphysics for lay meditators. Hence their appeal to friends of Plotinus, who were interested in contemplative technique, Greek metaphysics, and the alien authorities of Judeo-Christian sages.

CONCLUSION: THEURGY WITHOUT DIVINE WORK?

Having reviewed the spectrum of Sethian ritual practices—alphabet mysticism, doxology, angelification, and baptism—we can once again ask if they merit the term "theurgy." They do not. While Iamblichus defended ecstatic speech from Plotinus and Porphyry on Platonic Orientalist grounds, he denied that such practices exerted any power over the gods; rather, they served as channels for divine manipulation of the human realm, through the theurgic intermediary. Thus, the varieties of Sethian alphabet mysticism (particularly in *Marsanes*) that appear to presume superiority to angels would be declared base sorcery by *both* sides (i.e., Porphyry *and* Iamblichus) in the Neoplatonic debate over theurgy.

The practices associated with self-transformation are more complex in a theurgic context. The acquisition of a luminous body does recall, at first blush, the Chaldean subtle body, the famous "vehicle of the soul" (ὄχημα) of the theurgists.[179] In the *Chaldean Oracles*, the vehicle is found mainly in contexts dealing with the entrapment of the soul in matter.[180] It is a husk or shell encasing the soul, to be abandoned during postmortem ascent following performance of theurgic rites in the present life.[181] Sethian metamorphosis, meanwhile, is anagogic; once out of heaven, the seer ascends and changes into a divine being, while the luminous vehicle of the theurgists is katagogic, acquired when one *leaves* heaven. The *Three Steles of Seth* notwithstanding, the way of

ascent is *not* always the way of descent. These themes are not paralleled in Hellenic theurgic sources. The evidence about theurgic practice in the Sethian texts (including the Platonizing tractates), like the
evidence about literary genre and eschatology, inclines toward Judeo-
Christian tradition and away from contemporary Hellenic thought.

The term "Sethian theurgy," then, implies a continuity in ritual
technique and effect between Hellenic Neoplatonism and Sethian
Gnosticism that does not actually exist. To be sure, both Sethian
seers and Chaldean theurgists practiced autodeification, but they
employed different ritual technologies. They also had different conceptions of what it means to become divine. Sethian self-transformation and angelification belongs to the trajectory of Jewish and Christian apocalyptic conceptions of the reward of the righteous in heaven
and the transformation of Jewish patriarchs and sages into angelic
intermediaries invested with divine glory. The kinship of the human
with the divine at the expense of the present creation is a leitmotiv of
Gnostic thought, expressed in Sethian tradition through emphasizing
the alien nature of elect humanity, who are foreigners on this planet
but fundamentally at home when approaching the unknown, alien
God, the Invisible Spirit.[182] Thus the cheerful (if baroque) tone in the
Sethian descriptions of the celestial realms: as we saw in Chapter 3,
Zostrianos and Allogenes lament their studies prior to ascent, but feel
rather at home once they have been transformed in the Barbelo. As
the rapt, elect congregation of the *Three Steles* exclaims: "We rejoice!
We rejoice! We rejoice!"[183]

CHAPTER 7

Between Judaism, Christianity, and Neoplatonism

Having examined the culture wars taking place among second- and third-century intellectuals, Plotinus's polemic against his friends in Rome, the literary heritage of the apocalypses they circulated, and the views these texts espoused about soteriology, eschatology, and divinization, we can now step back and outline a more broad and comprehensive picture of what was at stake in the Plotinus-Gnostic controversy and the significance of the Sethian literature beyond its philosophical import. Indeed, the reading of the Sethian texts proposed in this book also tells us a great deal about ancient religious identity among Christians, Jews, Gnostics, and Hellenes. On the one hand, it is clear that Sethianism, even in its Platonizing incarnation, is closely related to traditions that are obviously embedded within contemporary Judaism and Christianity, yet not easily classifiable as belonging to one movement or the other. It is thus a strong witness to the artificial nature of the terms used to describe ancient religious discourse and the great indebtedness of one branch of Gnostic thought to Jewish lore. On the other hand, the present reading also lays bare very real differences in how second- and third-century philosophers came to see the world, and thus serves as a marker of the departure of a distinctly Judeo-Christian philosophical worldview from its Hellenic forebears, a way of thinking that was in many ways alien to the classical tradition.

JEWISH MYSTICISM, MANICHAEISM, AND JEWISH CHRISTIANITY

The strong parallels between the Hekhalot literature, Dead Sea Scrolls, and Sethian visionary practice raise the question of Sethianism's relationship with ancient Judaism, once limited to speculation about the old red herring of "pre-Christian Gnosticism."[1] The same is true of the importance of the apocalyptic genre and apocalyptic literary traditions in Sethianism. Despite several fine short studies, there is little scholarly discussion of these parallels.[2] This lacuna in scholarship can be explained as follows: study of the Jewish-Gnostic question has focused on the vexed problem of Gnostic origins, to little avail, and so frustrated other efforts to put Jewish and Gnostic texts in conversation with one another.

However, the unsolvability of the problem of Gnostic origins should not deter students of Gnosticism from raising the issue, mostly sounded by scholars of Judaism, of the relationship between Gnosticism and early Jewish mysticism.[3] Scholem is primarily responsible for having initially delineated the latter topic as a field of study, focusing on rabbinic and early-medieval Hekhalot texts in his survey of ancient literature.[4] He neglected the apocalypses and was surprisingly uninterested in the new find at Qumran, but Gnosticism played an important role in his reconstruction of the emergence of Jewish mystical tradition. For Scholem, Gnostic texts are evidence of a Hellenized "Jewish Gnosticism" that could be reconstructed from Gnostic, rabbinic, and Hekhalot literature.[5] Although his argument has been met with considerable criticism, his line of reasoning is still followed today, leading some to assert a Jewish source for Christian Gnostic traditions that can be inferred from the Hekhalot texts, the pseudo-Clementines, and Samaritan sources.[6] This approach suffers from a "parallelomania" that relies on presumed early dating for texts that could be far too late to read as evidence pertinent to the emergence of Gnosticism, or, in this case, Sethianism.[7]

Others have pointed out that the Gnostic authors of Merkavah scenes in the Ophite *Hypostasis of the Archons* and *On the Origin of the World* must have been aware of and interested in Jewish Merkavah traditions.[8] The Valentinian thinker Theodotus and a doxological passage in the *Egyptian Gospel* also devote attention to the heavenly throne.[9] Thus Ophite, Sethian, and Valentinian traditions each speculated on a characteristically Jewish mystical theme, explored particularly in the Hekhalot literature. Another interesting parallel is the strangely persistent association of heaven, angels, and "knowledge" in the Dead Sea Scrolls.[10] This language need not be related to Gnosticism, and probably derives from the idea that angels are privy to heavenly mysteries, which makes them good agents for revelation.[11]

This book adduces further meaningful parallels between Sethian Gnostic and Jewish mystical literature. In addition to the common well of Jewish mythologoumena (beginning with Seth himself!) and the literary (apocalyptic) traditions surveyed in Chapter 3, one might add persistent language about "power" and "empowerment" to characterize interactions between heavenly and earthly beings, descriptions of "crowns" in heaven, the culmination of visionary ascent in the joining of the heavenly liturgy, and the angelification of the seer.[12] These parallels indicate some kind of relationship between Sethian Gnosticism and Jewish mystical literature. Sorting out what kind of relationship this could be requires caution. A good example is the problem of *Zostrianos* and Enochic literature. Madeline Scopello has argued, probably correctly, that *Zostrianos* is textually dependent on *2 Enoch*, while Turner considers the angelification of Zostrianos to be genetically antecedent to the account of *3 Enoch*.[13] The comparison is acute, but difficult to work with; *3 Enoch* is almost certainly much later than *Zostrianos*, and there are no direct textual parallels such as those adduced by Scopello with *2 Enoch*.[14] It is hard to explain how the Gnostic texts could have left no marks of unmistakably Gnostic influence on their supposed descendents in the Hekhalot texts. It is more likely that *Zostrianos* and *3 Enoch* both draw on *2 Enoch* in particular and presume a wide familiarity with Jewish apocalyptic traditions.[15]

A similar line of reasoning might be used to explain the wider complex of parallels between Sethianism and Jewish mystical texts. Angelification, ascents to heaven, and other practices were probably common scribal lore in Hellenistic Judaism. Different groups drew on this stratum of wisdom in different ways as they splintered and evolved in late antiquity, which explains the broad but significant parallels between groups indebted to Jewish traditions that are definitely not extant in contemporary Hellenic or proto-orthodox Christian thought.[16] A primary interpreter of this stratum, contemporary with the redaction of apocalyptic and rabbinic traditions, Sethian Gnostic literature merits a sizable place in histories of the apocalypses and of Jewish mysticism.

This reasoning also has important ramifications for the evaluation of the history of Sethian thought. Distinctively Jewish themes and ideas about storytelling, the currency of various authorities, elect soteriology, eschatology, and self-transformation are widespread and central to even the Platonizing Sethian treatises. These themes must have entered Sethian tradition at a very early stage, and they are what differentiate it so strongly in tone and idiom from contemporary Greek thought. What is not immediately clear is whether they entered in a Christianized form.

The question of the relationship between Sethianism and Christianity is best tackled while keeping in mind the persistent parallels to Manichaeism that have been observed throughout this book. Indeed, much that Sethian and Jewish apocalyptic traditions share with one another is also to be found among the Manichaeans. As the Cologne Mani Codex attests, Mani himself was familiar with Jewish apocalypses (including an *Apocalypse of Sethel*) and appears to have obtained his own visions in a Mesopotamian Elchasaite community, the Mugtasilah ("cleansers"), whose practice was centered on repeated baptism and an ascetic lifestyle predicated on vegetarianism, farming, and probably encratism.[17] Like those of the Jewish-Christian Elchasaites and the Manichaeans, the Sethian tradition appears to have drawn from a common well of Jewish priestly lore glimpsed in the Dead Sea Scrolls and Hekhalot literature. It was inspired by Jewish, apocalyptic texts and built a salvation history around multiple descents of the primeval ancestor Seth. Yet it also offered an encratic regime that is rather unlike the asceticism of the Essene community or Merkavah mystics, to say nothing of its occasional interest in the figure of Jesus Christ as an incarnation of Seth. All this—baptismal community, encratism, deep interest in Jewish lore, belief in reincarnation, and a veneration of Jesus as one of many incarnations of the savior—points to a community like the one in which Mani was born and raised.

Scholars have long wondered about the relationship between Manichaeaism and Sethianism, noting that Sethian anti-baptismal polemic, particularly in the *Apocalypse of Adam* and *Zostrianos*, could derive from a milieu that produced Mani.[18] Manichaeism typically divides the world into fourteen aeons, while the *Apocalypse of Adam* segments cosmic history into thirteen plus one kingdoms.[19] The four hundred thousand descendents of Ham and Japheth in the *Apocalypse of Adam* also appear in the Manichaean *Homilies*, the saved number four hundred thousand in the *Book of the Giants*.[20] This book adduces further parallels: Chapter 3 showed that the seers of Sethian texts closely resemble those of the apocalypses mentioned in the *Cologne Mani Codex*. Platonists criticized the revelatory epistemology of Sethianism and Manichaeism in the same way. Manichaean eschatology posits a transmigration of souls periodically visited by a descending redeemer who adopts a variety of historical personages preaching salvation and establishing an elect who will be saved at the end of the world, a peculiar model that is precisely paralleled by the Sethian texts.[21] Further, as in Manichaeism, the Sethian Jesus is one of many important figures in salvation history who, while certainly a part of the soteriological system, is not always the focus of attention or even mentioned. Finally, several important Sethian mythologoumena, such as Youel and the Doxomedon Aeon, are also present in the Manichaean pantheon. One could add that, as in Sethianism, the Manichaeans saw Seth as a salvific foreigner.[22]

In light of these parallels, old and new, some kind of genetic relationship between Sethianism and Manichaeism is all but certain; the question is where it originates, if any such point can be divined at all. Böhlig posited the influence of Manichaean missionaries in the later third century on Sethians in Egypt, but most of the parallels indicated in the above belong to Sethian traditions that are at least contemporary with, if not prior, to the Platonizing apocalypses read in Plotinus's circle in Rome in the 260s.[23] Besides the mission of Mani's disciple Adda, there is no evidence for Manichaeans in Egypt until the very end of the century, so, even if the Christian Gnostics in Plotinus's circle were fellow Egyptians or reading Egyptian Sethian texts, they or their literature could not have been influenced by a Manichaean mission.[24]

Just as Sethian parallels with Jewish mystical texts more likely indicate a common wellspring than a direct genetic relationship between Sethianism and Merkavah literature, parallels with Manichaean texts more likely indicate a common background in ascetic, visionary baptismal cult than Sethian Gnostic contact with Manichaean missionaries. If the relationship between Sethianism and Manichaeism is best explained by a common background in Syro-Mesopotamian Jewish baptismal groups, then Sethian literature itself is probably a product of such a group, perhaps one like the community of Mani, either belonging to or resembling the Elchasaites. Some scholars have argued that Plotinus's Gnostic friends were themselves in possession of revelatory

Elchasaite literature taken from Mesopotamia to Rome by the Elchasaite missionary Alcibiades, who was known to Hippolytus.[25] This view has not commanded much assent, but the approach taken in this book validates its insight, namely, that the Sethian apocalypses read by these Gnostics were themselves products of a milieu similar to that of Elchasai and his missionary, Alcibiades—a hypothesis discussed further below. They therefore merit closer attention from specialists in the religion of Mani, which too emerged from such a milieu.

Once we see Sethian traditions not as simply oscillating between Jewish, Christian, or pagan influences but rather as broadly indebted to the very particular mixture of Jewish apocalyptic and Christian baptismal traditions we find in the Mesopotamia of Mani, we can slice the Gordian knot of perhaps the most difficult problem in Sethian literature—how to read the presence of the figure of Jesus of Nazareth, with respect to understanding the relationship between Sethianism and Christianity. Indeed, it is Jesus's absence from the Platonizing treatises (excepting perhaps *Zostrianos*) that, for most scholars, indicate their pagan provenance and provides a telos for Turner's literary history of Sethianism, culminating in the supposed expulsion of Jewish, Christian, and apocalyptic themes in favor of Greek metaphysics in an attempt to Hellenize a Gnostic sect.[26] Comparing Sethianism and Manichaeism helps us see that the criterion of Jesus's presence and references to scripture in a treatise to mark a nonpagan provenance simply points to a straw man. Despite the insistence of our modern sense of Judaism and Christianity, the ancient world birthed movements that do not fit scholars' categories of these terms but rather fall between and beyond them, without necessarily belonging to contemporary Greco-Roman culture either.

Indeed, Chapters 3 to 6 show that the Platonizing Sethian treatises are hardly representative of Hellenic Platonism, even though they do not identify Jesus Christ as the Messiah. Instead, they assume a revelatory epistemology that was decisively rejected by Hellenic philosophers (who preferred allegory for interpreting myth) but was tolerated, if not embraced, in Jewish and Christian thought. Sethian providence appears to directly affect the lives of particular individuals who are characterized as the elect, a position assaulted by Platonic critics of Christianity. Their eschatology decidedly affirms the end of the world and ultimate destruction of non-elect souls, a view faithful to Judeo-Christian scripture and apocrypha, vigorously defended by the Fathers, and attacked by their Hellenic interlocutors. Finally, the background of the texts' rituals in Syro-Mesopotamian ascetic baptismal circles that placed a priority on glossolalia, angelification, and visionary experience culminating in unio liturgica is consonant with not just Jewish literature but Christian texts like the *Ascension of Isaiah*.

The relative paucity of philosophically inclined Jewish literature from the Roman Empire means that our evidence for Hellenized Judeo-Christian counterparts to the Sethian texts' epistemology and eschatology is, accidentally, largely Christian. The evidence presented here, on its own, could be products of a particularly Platonized Judaism. Other aspects of the treatises do, however, lean toward themes we associate with Christianity: their persistent descriptions of the Sethian elect as a race associated with the resident alien motif are decidedly at home in the world of early Christianity, not Hellenism or Judaism. Their ascetic practice in the service of mysticism was probably centered on encratism, which does not fit the Jewish evidence from Qumran or the Hekhalot literature. Together with the strong correlations between their positions on eschatology, providence, soteriology, and revelatory epistemology and those adopted by the church fathers, it is easy to see why the Platonizing Sethian treatises would have appealed to Christian intellectuals like Plotinus's friends, and a few scholars hypothesize that it is likely that they were written by Christians employing Sethian traditions.[27]

Ought one refer to these intellectuals instead as Jewish-Christian in light of the similarity of many of their ideas to Elchasaeism? On the one hand, Sethian soteriology, eschatology, baptismal practice, and dependence on Jewish apocalyptic traditions is most strongly paralleled not just among the Elchasaites but among other Jewish-Christian groups like the Ebionites and the authors of the Pseudo-Clementines. By this reasoning, it would be safe to simply say that Sethianism emerged from a generally Jewish-Christian milieu. On the other hand, if there is any defining characteristic of Jewish Christianity, it is adherence to the Law while recognizing Jesus of Nazareth as Messiah—an issue absent from the Sethian treatises. We therefore cannot say that Sethianism emerged out of Jewish Christianity, but that it emerged from the borderlines between Judaism and Christianity, drawing on Christological and eschatological traditions associated with groups scholars today call Jewish-Christian, together with a wealth of Jewish apocryphal lore. The liminal position Sethianism occupies between Judaism and Christianity does not merit dismissal of its Judeo-Christian characteristics and relegation of it to a vague sense of paganism but rather calls for further study in the context of other ancient Jewish and Christian sects that also passed back and forth along the developing borderlines of these faiths.

Nonetheless, from a philosophical perspective, the authors of the Platonizing Sethian treatises should be heralded as representatives of advanced Christian Platonism, and in terms of theological capability should be classed with contemporary third-century theological giants like Clement of Alexandria or Origen. They part ways with their orthodox Christian contemporaries on the creation of the world (assigned to a demiurge separate from the high God), use of the apocalyptic genre (Clement and the other Fathers wrote allegories, not apocalypses), encratism, and perhaps rejection of water baptism; in comparison with the emerging rabbinic movement and Jewish Christians, meanwhile, they appear to have been uninterested in writing about the law of the Torah.

THE "ACUTE HELLENIZATION" OF PLATONISM AND THE EXILE OF SETHIAN GNOSTICISM

As discussed in the Introduction, recent scholarship has emphasized the strong ties between Sethian Gnosticism and Neoplatonism and even suggested that key aspects of Neoplatonic thought ultimately derive from pre-Plotinian Gnostic sources. The thesis defended here— that the Platonizing treatises were written by and for an audience familiar with and receptive to Judeo-Christian ideas and themes, and could hardly have served in an attempt to appeal to Hellenes—does not demonstrate a lack of engagement between Sethian Gnosticism and Platonism or minimize the importance of Sethian Gnosticism for the history of philosophy. Rather, it is clear that this Judeo-Christian, Gnostic philosophical literature was at the forefront of contemporary Platonic metaphysics, produced by highly educated individuals deeply inundated in the culture wars of Greco-Roman education. It is likely that Plotinus had acquaintance with Gnostic ideas before the 263 controversy, but it appears that cross-fertilization between him and the Gnostics did not extend beyond metaphysics and mysticism: those committed to the ideas contained in the Sethian apocalypses bitterly disagreed with him about issues of authority, storytelling, cosmology, eschatology, soteriology, and practice, and were consequently exiled from the Platonic tradition.

In any case, ostensible Sethian influence on Plotinus and other Neoplatonists is a red herring. The crucial import of the Plotinus-Gnostic controversy is not any hitherto-unnoticed Gnostic thinking in Plotinus's school but the way in which it catalyzed the "acute Hellenization" of Platonism itself.[28] After the controversy, Platonists enshrined the conservative Hellenocentrism of the Second Sophistic that colored Greek education in the second and third centuries CE. We can glimpse this turn in three pockets of evidence. The first two are associated with Iamblichus—the closing of the Platonic "canon" and the codification of Platonic philosophy as a cultically Hellenic practice—while the third concerns how Porphyry, himself a player in the conflict with Gnosticism, wrote about another of the foremost Christian Platonists of his day, Origen of Alexandria. Together with Origen's *floruit*, then, the development of the Platonizing Sethian literature and its circulation by Christian intellectuals in Rome in the mid-third century CE marks the transition of Christian philosophy to an enterprise independent from the traditional Greek philosophical schools.

As discussed in Chapter 1, second- and third-century CE Greek philosophers were interested in the wisdom of the East, including Jewish and Christian thinking, but usually considered the Greeks to be the first among equals of the known nations. Even so, as the presence of the Christian Gnostics reading Sethian literature in Plotinus's school indicates, Christians and Hellenes of the period still participated in interconfessional reading groups. The Platonic Orientalism that fetishized Eastern thought almost certainly contributed to the desire of Hellenic philosophers to engage with Judeo-Christian ones. However, even a brief look at the interaction of these same Platonic Orientalists with their Christian contemporaries in late antiquity shows that the situation changed when the Christian Gnostics left Plotinus's circle. Hellenic and Christian philosophers continued to be educated in the same schools, but their cohabitation produced strained relationships at best, as between Prohaeresis and Eunapius of Sardis (in the later fourth century CE) and bitter enemies at worst, as between Gregory Nazianzus and Julian the Apostate (in the mid-fourth century CE).[29]

The closest Hellenes and Christians would come to another interconfessional Platonic circle was Hypatia's group in Alexandria, which included both Hellenic philosophers and mathematicians as well as Christians interested in Hellenic education, such as the future bishop Synesius of Cyrene. Tellingly, this circle ended in violence, due to

Hypatia's involvement in civic life (typical, as we have seen, among Platonists and Pythagoreans), which challenged the authority of the zealous patriarch Cyril.[30] Future Platonist teachers there, such as Ammonius or Olympiodorus, feared the Christian authorities and so actively avoided association with Hellenic cult or theological polemics.[31] Later, in Athens, Damascius would condemn their approach as cowardice.[32] Indeed, their stature did not match that of the Athenian Platonists, who after Hypatia's death succeeded in poaching Alexandria's students, further radicalizing the split between Hellenic and Christian philosophers.[33]

Conversely, our Hellenic sources from the fourth century onward—conciliatory or not—appear to depict a quiet but clear banishment of Jewish, Christian, and particularly Gnostic literature from authoritative philosophical discourse. After the Plotinus-Gnostic controversy, Platonists only mentioned such materials to excoriate or dismiss them because of their ideas about authority, medium of expressing truth, soteriology, eschatology, and ritual life. Of the entire extant post-Plotinian Platonic tradition, only Porphyry and Julian demonstrate intimate familiarity with scripture, and conscript it into the service of verbal assault.[34] In his extant corpus, Iamblichus never mentions Jews or Christians. Gnostics come up once (a passage we will review below). Eunapius occasionally bemoans the decay of the Hellenic cult he saw around him, but shows no intimacy with Judaism or Christianity.[35] This condemnation of silence was followed in the Athenian school: Proclus and Damascius occasionally remarked on an unhappy state of political affairs, complaining of the "ignorance" about cosmological matters among unnamed contemporaries—the Christians.[36] While the Platonic teachers in Alexandria were more cautious than their Athenian contemporaries, they did not deign to engage (much less approbate) Judeo-Christian scripture or philosophy—even when teaching Christians.[37]

In the spirit of Platonic Orientalism, Iamblichus fused the *Chaldaean Oracles* with a structured curriculum of the Platonic dialogues and its tradition of interpretation stretching back to the Middle Platonists. This educational program persisted to the crackdown on Athenian Neoplatonism in 529 CE, with no sign whatsoever that Jewish, Christian, or Gnostic literature was circulated. While Platonists before the Plotinus-Gnostic controversy championed Plato and Pythagoras as the bedrock of philosophical inquiry, they also exhibited interest in sources outside the Hellenic tradition that they hoped to harmonize with it. After the controversy, the canon of Platonism became limited to Plato, his commentators, and a healthy dose of Aristotle, alongside alien authorities already comfortably subdued by Orientalizing Hellenism.

Platonic approaches to civic cult and ritual practice also changed immediately following the Plotinus-Gnostic controversy. As argued in Chapter 1, Greek philosophical schools in the second and third centuries CE were cultically conservative. Plotinus was offended by the lack of respect Christians had for "the traditions of our fathers" and the obvious incongruency between the ritual life depicted in their treatises and that which he expected a Greek philosopher to lead. Iamblichus's incorporation and theorization of theurgic rituals into Neoplatonism, however, went far beyond Plotinus and Porphyry; while philosophers were already considered ritual specialists in the public sphere of the civic cult, they had become mystagogues in the private sphere of the philosophical circle. By virtue of their status as theurgists, the post-Iamblichaean Platonists saw themselves as custodians of the (rapidly shrinking) Hellenic ritual life.[38] While Iamblichus theorized how theurgy actually worked, the social background of theurgy—the cult and color of later Neoplatonism—was set by the position Plotinus took against the Gnostics, and exported by Porphyry to Hellenism's greater conflict with Christianity.

It is worth pausing to speculate as to how the Gnostic controversy may have contributed to Iamblichus's initial turn to theurgic ritual. He was a younger contemporary of Porphyry and probably in touch with Amelius upon the latter's return to Syria after the death of Plotinus. It is difficult to imagine that he had not heard of the master's Christian Gnostic friends, the Platonizing apocalypses they circulated in the seminar, and the refutations that Porphyry and Amelius wrote of them. He knew the *Enneads*, and thus *Against the Gnostics* and Plotinus's critiques of the Gnostics' cultic improprieties and disrespect for Hellenic authority. Yet he also sternly objected to Plotinus's thesis that Soul had not entirely descended into the body, and so remained separate from it, always connected to the intelligible world.[39] Iamblichus countered that Soul had in fact descended, and needed purification and rectification in the present life through ritual practice in order to regain communion with God. By focusing on ritual, ecstasy, and nonrational interaction with the Godhead, Iamblichus countered an excess of philosophical "god-talk" (theology) with a way of life, "god-action" (theurgy).[40]

In the one explicit reference to Gnostics in the Platonic tradition after the *Life of Plotinus*, Iamblichus says that Gnostics also affirm the descent of Soul into the world "because of derangement and deviation."[41] His lack of invective against them in this context is striking, and perhaps can be accounted for by the hypothesis that he *agreed* with them on the Soul's descent into matter.[42] After all, both Iamblichus and the authors of the Sethian texts trafficked in rites that purify the individual and permit a vision of the Godhead in this life. It is important to remember, however, that while this general foundation for theurgic practice seems to have been agreed on by Iamblichus and the Gnostics, he shows no sign of having adopted their specific practices of celestial baptism or angelification. More importantly, the Sethian goal of obtaining a supra-angelic status with power outstretching that of heavenly beings directly contradicts his own concept of divinization, in which divine energy, of its own accord, trickles down to the theurgist, who uses rites to become receptive to it, as argued in Chapter 6. The avatars of Seth annul their alienation from the Invisible Spirit once they have attained divinization; the Neoplatonic theurgist becomes, in this life, the temporary beneficiary of divine powers. The Hellenes were much more cautious about claiming kinship with their own alien God, the One.

Iamblichus also eschews Sethian mythologoumena, instead settling for a fetishized caricature of Egyptian and Chaldaean wisdom traditions—a Platonic Orientalism that was culturally safe for Hellenes to brandish. This explains the puzzling fact that the Hermetica and the *Chaldean Oracles* obtained authority in later Platonic circles, while other mythologizing, Orientalizing sources (like the Sethian apocalypses) did not. Even if their auto-Orientalizing was intended to distinguish their Platonism from Hellenic ideology, it was possible for anti-Christian Platonic Orientalists, like Proclus, to absorb them as consonant with traditional Greek cult. Unlike the Platonizing Sethian treatises, the Hermetica and the *Oracles* did not invoke Judeo-Christian authorities or support positions about providence, eschatology, and divinization that were objectionable to Hellenic Platonists.[43] Despite their auto-Orientalism, the Hermetica and the *Oracles* were mostly consistent with Hellenic Platonism, and they were therefore accepted.

At the same time, we have no evidence of Iamblichus actively rejecting Gnosticism either. Instead, he lists Gnostics alongside other philosophers (like Empedocles), as if they were a school (αἵρεσις).

And why not? Plotinus too says that they considered themselves a "school," complaining that they claim to belong to a different school and set themselves apart (perhaps as a new race, like other Christians), even though the substance of their learning is to be found in Plato, a Hellene. His charge—and indeed much of the evidence about the conflict with his Gnostic friends and their apocalypses—is echoed in some of Porphyry's famous remarks in *Against the Christians* about another Christian school Platonist, Origen of Alexandria.[44] Having complained about Christian attempts to use Hellenic techniques of allegory to "find an explanation of the wickedness of the Jewish writings rather than give them up (τῆς δὴ μοχθηρίας τῶν Ἰουδαϊκῶν γραφῶν οὐκ ἀπόστασιν)," he says that

> This kind of absurdity must be traced to a man whom I met when I was still quite young, who had a great reputation, and still holds it, because of the writings he has left behind him. I mean Origen, whose fame has been widespread among the teachers of this kind of learning. For this man was a hearer of Ammonius, who had the greatest proficiency in philosophy in our day; and so far as a grasp of knowledge was concerned he owed much to his master, but as regards the right choice in life he took the opposite road to him. For Ammonius was a Christian, brought up in Christian doctrine by his parents, yet, when he began to think and study philosophy, he immediately changed his way of life conformably to the laws (πρὸς τὴν κατὰ νόμους πολιτείαν); but Origen, a Hellene educated in Hellenic learning, drove headlong towards barbarian recklessness (τὸ βάρβαρον τόλμημα); and making straight for this he hawked himself and his literary skill about; and while his manner of life was Christian and contrary to the law (παρανόμως), in his opinions about material things and the Deity he played the Greek, and introduced Greek ideas into alien fables (τὰ Ἑλλήνων τοῖς ὀθνείοις ὑποβαλλόμενος μύθοις). For he was always consorting with Plato (et al.) . . . and he used also the books of Chaeremon the Stoic and Cornutus, from whom he learnt figurative interpretation, as employed in the Hellenic mysteries, and applied it to Jewish writings.[45]

Porphyry here unfavorably contrasts Hellenic and barbarian, Judeo-Christian learning, reckoned as "contrary to the law." Scholars have debated whether Porphyry refers here to legally sanctioned persecution of Christianity or to the "divine law" of the order of the cosmos, but as we have seen in Plotinus's polemic about Gnosticism in Chapter 2, these readings are by no means mutually exclusive.[46] The created and eternal orders are images of one another, belonging on a single spectrum of Being emanating from the One; ideas contrary to natural law (i.e., the resurrection of the Body or the eventual destruction of the cosmos) could only, to Plotinus and Porphyry, have been mirrored by behavior contrary to earthly law.[47] Moreover, just as Plotinus relegates the epistemological status of Judeo-Christian, Gnostic myth to the grade Plato assigns to bad poetry—a "reflection of a reflection," as discussed in Chapter 3—Porphyry regards the Jewish stories allegorically interpreted by Origen as "alien fables" (τοῖς ὀθνείοις μύθοις), as a bad, foreign kind of story.[48] Finally, Porphyry juxtaposes Origen's lawless, barbarian Christian life with his Hellenic origins. It is not necessary to read him as asserting a pagan upbringing for Origen.[49] Like Plotinus on his Gnostic friends, Porphyry is frustrated that Origen, despite his years of immersion in Greek culture , claimed "to possess a universal philosophy based on a set of barbarian texts from the very edges of the Greco-Roman world."[50]

Against the Christians was probably written around 300 CE.[51] We see then that a real transformation has taken place between the formation of Plotinus's school in Rome and the dawn of the fourth century, by which time Porphyry is likely to have completed his polemical work on Christianity and Iamblichus reached his floruit. Half a century before, Christians reading Gnostic apocalypses replete with Neoplatonic contemplative and metaphysical terminology could spend time in a circle of Hellenic philosophers, and Jewish and Christian sources were reckoned as alien but safe barbarian wisdom, mentioned by Hellenes in the same breath as the teaching of Egypt, India, or Persia. Plotinus's friends and the Sethian literature thus occupied, with Origen, what was then a liminal state in which Hellenic and Christian philosophers frequented the same philosophical circles.[52] Yet on the eve of the Great Persecution, Porphyry seems to regard Judeo-Christian teaching as incompatible with Hellenic tradition. In the wake of the Gnostic controversy, he and Plotinus determined that the stories prized by Judeo-Christian tradition were full of values alien to the way of life esteemed by the Platonists and cosmological ideas incompatible with Platonism, and thus sought to abolish the more liminal, free zone in which Christian and Hellenic Platonists had previously comingled.

Iamblichus must have thought Porphyry's views legitimate, and proceeded to reconceptualize Hellenic religion as a theurgic tradition with its own brand of Platonic Orientalism; his silence on Judaism and Christianity speaks volumes, and became the standard for Platonic philosophical literature through the end of the school. Thus the Sethian deity—the Great Invisible Spirit—even when described with the jargon of technical Greek thought, became a truly alien God to the Platonists, who did their best to exile Him, consigning him to forgotten obscurity. Meanwhile, the readers of the Sethian apocalypses had used the theme of alienation to describe their experience of the cosmos with respect to this deity.[53] It is precisely these worldly matters—public life, authority of tradition, medium of communicating learning, soteriology, eschatology, and ritual—that alienated the Neoplatonists from the Sethian texts and their Christian readers, and incited them to identify their school with the cause of Hellenism as both philosophy and religious confession.

RETHINKING SETHIAN TRADITION

The dual theses of this book—the location of Sethian tradition, including the Platonizing treatises, within the spectrum of Jewish Christianities and its catalyzing effect on the fixing and closing of the Platonic tradition—are best integrated and recapitulated through a brief presentation of a hypothetical history of Sethian Gnostic traditions and their interaction with Neoplatonism.

Most scholarship has argued that the absence of baptism and Jesus Christ from several of the Sethian treatises could be accounted for by origins in a Palestinian community, either a pre-Christian group related to Johannine tradition, followed by a secondary "Christianization" taking place in later recensions of Sethian literature, or a pre-Christian Barbeloite group influenced by new baptismal ideas (Johannine or Pauline).[54] This perspective overstates the importance of Johannine themes to the wider Sethian tradition, since they are mostly found in the *Apocryphon of John* and *Trimorphic Protennoia*. These texts certainly contain both Johannine and Sethian traditions, but are also dependent on Ophite sources. Their most distinctive feature, the incarnation and tripartite descent of Barbelo-Providence featured in the "Pronoia Hymn," seems to be extraneous and even mutually exclusive with Sethian salvation history, which instead deals with the multiple incarnations of Seth (*not* Providence-Barbelo) in history as savior. Like the *Gospel of Judas*, they are composite texts that incorporate Sethian traditions or underwent Sethian redaction, but probably belong at the later end of its development, around the turn of the third century CE.[55]

One can therefore dispense with the idea of pre-Christian Jewish Sethianism, thus giving a later date for Sethian ideas and texts and compact their composition to the late second and early third centuries CE, with the Platonizing texts probably coming somewhat later.[56] Aside from the Platonizing treatises, we are then left with the *Egyptian Gospel*, the *Apocalypse of Adam*, and *Melchizedek*. Dating these texts on internal grounds is hopeless, but there is no reason not to assign the *Egyptian Gospel* and *Apocalypse of Adam* to the later second century CE, since the Platonizing treatises appear to be dependent on traditions contained in them, while interest in Seth as a savior figure seems to arise in contemporary Christian literature only around the end of the second century CE.[57] *Melchizedek* probably is from a similar period.[58] The anti-baptismal polemic in *Apocalypse of Adam* is a criticism of water baptism in the vein of Mani and the Sethians known to Epiphanius.[59] Like Mani, the originators of Sethian tradition must have rejected the baptismal practices of proto-orthodox Christians or the Elchasaites; instead, they favored the rite of the Five Seals, a practice (unction?) symbolizing the five senses, which was based in first-century transformative baptismal traditions but rejected physical water as polluted in favor of the induction of ecstasy, which put one in contact with celestial "living water." This is certainly the tradition that was incorporated into the celestial baptisms of the *Trimorphic Protennoia* and *Egyptian Gospel*, which also mention the Five Seals.

As Turner recognized, the doxologies of *Zostrianos* are dependent on the *Egyptian Gospel*.[60] Its negative theology resembles the Platonism of the anonymous *"Parmenides" Commentary* and Plotinus. Its Greek original was probably, then, written in the first half of the third century CE, and read in Plotinus's seminar.[61] The same is probably also true of the *Three Steles of Seth*. *Allogenes* and *Marsanes* are trickier. *Allogenes'* negative theology, meanwhile, strongly resembles post-Plotinian thought, which is best explained by assigning the text's Nag Hammadi redaction to the fourth century CE (at the earliest).[62] This emphasis on continued engagement of Neoplatonism by the Gnostics (or perhaps vice versa) is strengthened by Turner's dating of *Marsanes* to the fourth century, on the grounds of its similarity on points of Neoplatonic theology to the thought of Iamblichus's student Theodore of Asine.[63] The other Sethian treatises as preserved at Nag Hammadi could also bear the marks of redaction and rewriting in the fourth century and beyond.[64]

The focus of these various texts on matters of salvation history, cosmology, and contemplative metaphysics gives us virtually no information about their geographical provenance, but once we recognize that Sethianism is not necessarily an offshoot of a Johannine baptismal group, there is no reason to privilege Palestine as its hypothetical place of origin.[65] Other options for the development of Sethianism present themselves. Assuming that the tradition developed in proximity to the Jewish-Christian Elchasaites, for instance, one can point to several potential host groups in different locations—the trans-Jordanian Sampsaeans-Elchesaeans (known to Epiphanius), the Palestinian Elchasaites reading an *Apocalypse of Elchasai* later brought to Rome by Alcibiades of Apamea (known to Hippolytus and Origen), and the Babylonian Mugtasilah, who raised Mani.[66] However, an attractive hypothesis is the composition of Sethian texts in Apamea around the turn of the third century CE; we know Elchasaite traditions and literature circulated there, and the city apparently was a desirable place for Platonists, since it produced Numenius and Iamblichus. Amelius retired there. One scholar has recently opined that the *Chaldaean Oracles* were written there.[67] It is the only city other than Rome where Elchasaite and Platonic works are known to have coexisted among Gnostic traditions in the second and third centuries CE. It would have been a fine place for such diverse trajectories to begin to coalesce into hybrid and highly redacted Sethian texts like the Platonizing treatises—at least as likely as Alexandria and certainly in closer proximity to the Syrian baptismal traditions related to Elchasaeism and Manichaeism. This much being said, the treatises could also have been composed in a diversity of environments: *Melchizedek*, for instance, is probably from Egypt and shows little interest in either Platonism or the baptismal polemic that brings Apamea to our attention.[68]

A provisional narrative that fits this reading of the textual evidence goes as follows: Sethian speculation, drawing from Barbeloite, Sethite, and Jewish mystical ideas, developed in contact with Syrian (Jewish)-Christian circles related to the Elchasaites or a baptismal group very much like them, in the early or mid-second century CE. Sethian books were included with the literature brought by the Elchasaite missionary Alcibiades from Apamea to Rome in the 220s, where it found an audience among local Christian heretics.[69] A piece of evidence supporting the hypothesis of circulation of our Platonizing Sethian works in the community that received Alcibiades is Hippolytus's remark that the readers of the book of Elchasai called themselves "foreknowers" (προγνωστικοί).[70] Nothing we know about the Elchasaites and their book indicates that they were interested in providence or the first thought of the deity, but the Sethian texts are replete with this language used in a soteriological (albeit contemplative) context, and the heresiologist refers these foreknowers not to the immediate followers of Elchasai himself but to his later, Roman readers.[71] Hippolytus implies that the "foreknowledge" of which they spoke came from the *Apocalypse of Elchasai*, but it is more likely that they were referring to versions of *Zostrianos*, *Allogenes*, and the like.

It is impossible to demonstrate whether the Platonizing Sethian treatises were written in Rome then or had already been composed before Alcibiades' mission, but it is clear that they were written by advanced Jewish-Christian metaphysicians as in-house visionary and ritual manuals to be used by somewhat educated lay meditators already familiar with Sethian asceticism and ritual practice. Their readers believed themselves to be elect individuals under the care of the Barbelo, whom some had encountered in their visions, and referred to themselves as "individuals" or possibly "foreknowers" (per Plotinus and Hippolytus, respectively). The appeal of the Sethian texts to these Roman Christians would have included the apologetic theme of Sethian ethnic reasoning, popular in Christian apologetic and martyrological texts. The crowns that litter the Sethian texts may have also been read in a martyrological context, not insignificant considering that the controversy with Plotinus follows immediately upon the Decian and Valerianic persecutions (250, 257–60 CE). Plotinus's Christian friends, members of one of many Christian communities in Rome, were evidently advanced enough thinkers to merit discussion in his seminar, which could make them eligible candidates for having authored the treatises themselves.

Regardless, Nag Hammadi's *Zostrianos*, earlier redactions of *Allogenes* and *Marsanes* (or the closely related *Apocalypse of Nicotheus*), and perhaps also the *Three Steles of Seth* were read in Plotinus's seminar and critiqued. The catalyst in the explosion of the conflict between Plotinus and the Gnostics was likely Porphyry.[72] Regardless of the degree of the master's prior affinity with Gnostics, after Porphyry's arrival in 263 CE, he fell out with them on grounds cosmological, eschatological, ideological, and cultic, drawing the lines much as Porphyry and later Hellenes would draw the line between Hellenic and Christian Platonists. Plotinus probably was interested in the mystical practices the Sethian texts had to offer and willing to ignore their objectionable cosmological and soteriological content. Porphyry, who would later in life become a champion of Hellenic conservatism and a severe critic of Christianity, must have advised his teacher that there is more to the study of Platonic philosophy than mysticism, and that the Sethian treatises were replete with philosophical stances that demanded refutation, as would the errant doctrines of the Stoics or Epicureans. A proper Hellenist himself, Plotinus was won over, set his best students against the Sethian literature, and composed *Ennead* 2.9 for students loyal to his more traditional Platonism, thus exiling the local Christian Gnostics from his school.

However, Gnostic thinkers—probably related to Plotinus's friends, although of this we cannot be sure—continued to engage Neoplatonism even after Plotinus's death. *Allogenes* and *Marsanes* both show signs of interest in Iamblichaean thought. *Marsanes*' alphabet mysticism probably is based on the speculation of Iamblichus's student, Theodore of Asine. Iamblichus himself likely had access to Gnostic texts and thought they were worthy of at least mention in doxography, although best ignored most of the time. Plotinus and Porphyry's push against Gnostic Platonism was not, then, entirely successful; it took the polarization of Hellenic and Christian thinkers along cultic lines in post-Constantinian Rome for the engagement between Gnosticism and Neoplatonism to cease completely.

This does not mean, however, that Sethian literature stopped being read and reconfigured; the Egyptian Archontics and Borborites known to Epiphanius were reading apocalypses containing Sethian traditions, and the *Untitled* treatise in the Bruce Codex presents isolated, broken characters and principles of Sethian tradition, probably from the fourth century.[73] It is entirely possible that the Roman Gnostics known to Porphyry stayed in Rome, assimilated to the local churches, and continued to circulate Sethian literature.[74] The origin of the Nag Hammadi texts themselves, of course, remains mysterious as well; but whether one considers them to be products of monks or urban occultists, buried in the fourth century CE or centuries later, the appeal of the Platonizing treatises' apocalypticism, contemplative practice, angelology, and encratic asceticism to their Coptic translators and scribes would have been undeniable.[75]

It is precisely this potpourri of apocalyptic myth, Neoplatonic thought, and Jewish divinization that makes Platonizing Sethian texts so obscure yet fascinating today. They set off a battle royale amongst some of the greatest thinkers of the third century CE, brandished by Gnostic Christians deeply involved in the ancient equivalent of a high-octane graduate seminar. Together with the accounts written about this conflict by their opponents, these texts provide us our most sure and vivid knowledge about a group of ancient Gnostics. Moreover, this group emerged into the philosophical spotlight out of a sociocultural zone where Jewish and Christian ideas about cosmology, anthropology, salvation, and authority are omnipresent, but Judaism and Christianity themselves remain slippery categories. In spite of their philosophical prolixity, the Platonizing Sethian apocalypses furnish an invaluable glimpse into the cultural traditions and dynamics out of which Judaism, Christianity, and Manichaeism were formed. Under the aegis of Plato, the last Hellenes defined themselves against these same traditions and thus against the God of Abraham, soon also to be the God of Muhammad.

APPENDIX: READING PORPHYRY ON THE GNOSTIC HERETICS AND THEIR APOCALYPSES

Γεγόνασι δὲ κατ᾽ αὐτὸν τῶν Χριστιανῶν πολλοὶ μὲν καὶ ἄλλοι,
αἱρετικοὶ δὲ ἐκ τῆς παλαιᾶς φιλοσοφίας ἀνηγμένοι
οἱ περὶ Ἀδέλφιον καὶ Ἀκυλῖνον
 . . . ἀποκαλύψεις τε προφέροντες Ζωροάστρου καὶ Ζωστριανοῦ
καὶ Νικοθέου καὶ Ἀλλογενοῦς καὶ Μέσσου.

There were in his (Plotinus's) time many others,
Christians, in particular heretics
who had set out from the ancient philosophy,
men belonging to the schools of Adelphius and Aculinus
 . . . who produced revelations of Zoroaster and Zostrianos
and Nicotheus and Allogenes and Messos.

The opening sentence of *Vita Plotini* chapter 16 contains a number of philological difficulties. How one chooses to approach them deeply affects consideration of the identity of the Gnostics in Plotinus's circle and their controversial apocalypses. The language of the crucial first clause is tricky. First, there is the question of how to translate αἱρετικοί, here rendered "heretics." Considering the common, non-pejorative use of the term in Greek philosophy,[1] most translators prefer to render it with "sectarians" or "school" and so on.[2] Yet Porphyry was an active opponent of Christianity, familiar both with biblical texts and contemporary philosophical debate about them. It is probable that he was familiar with the pejorative Christian sense of αἱρετικοί, "not orthodox," that is, "heretics," and, like Julian the Apostate, chose to use it when talking about certain Christian groups.[3] The choice between these two options is a false one. Like Plotinus, Porphyry clearly regarded these Christians as wayward Platonists intent on founding their own school, but he was also surely capable of recognizing that they were different from the proto-orthodox and nastily derogating them as such.[4]

More difficult is the construction πολλοὶ μὲν καὶ ἄλλοι αἱρετικοὶ δὲ . . . : is ἄλλοι apposite to αἱρετικοί, marked by δέ and opposed to the πολλοί, marked by μέν? In this case, the passage would read "there were many Christians, and then there were others, heretics. The heretics" would belong to a group of "others," who are opposed to the "many Christians," and thus were non-Christian adherents to pagan gnosis.[5] I prefer the reading by which ἄλλοι is apposite to πολλοί by καί, minimizing the contrast between the subjects marked by μέν and δέ, in which case the text means "there were many others, Christians, in particular heretics."[6] Thus, the heretics (δέ) belong to a larger group of "other Christians" (μέν).[7]

Next, does ἀνηγμένοι οἱ περὶ Ἀδέλφιον καὶ Ἀκυλῖνον refer to Christian heretics specified as individuals who belonged to the school of Adelphius and Aculinus who simply rejected "the ancient philosophy"?[8] Or did they instead *start out* from the Greeks, presumably ending somewhere else, meriting Plotinus's ire? As Howard Jackson argues, ἀνάγεσθαι does not simply mean "abandon" (*pace* Armstrong) as much as "set out on a voyage."[9] The latter option is thus to be preferred: Porphyry specifies that the heretics were Platonists who had gone astray.

Finally, in English translation it is unclear whether "revelations of Zoroaster and Zostrianos" signals a single work of revelations ascribed to them both or two separate apocalypses. Indeed, the former could be indicated by the evidence from NHC VIII,1, whose scribal colophon (a cryptogram) reads, following the title *Zostrianos*, "words of truth of Zostrianos, god of truth; words of Zoroaster." However, the καί between the two names in Porphyry does signal not just two individuals but also two apocalypses: an *Apocalypse of Zoroaster*, refuted by Porphyry, and *The Apocalypse of Zostrianos*, refuted by Amelius, as Porphyry says. The colophon in NHC VIII,1 appears to be not a title, but the embellishment of a scribe familiar with Zostrianos's association with the figure of Zoroaster to a work entitled *Zostrianos*. The relationship of the *Allogenes* mentioned by Porphyry to a hypothetical *Apocalypse of Messos* is ambiguous. Henri-Charles Puech notes that the titles mentioned by Porphyry are separated by a καί, probably indicating different books (i.e., an *Apocalypse of Allogenes* and *Apocalypse of Messos*).[10] The titular subscript concluding NHC XI,3 ("Allogenes") probably indicates a single, independent work familiar with the figure of Messos, to whom another apocalypse was ascribed, although it is possible that Porphyry was confused, and sundered in his reading a single treatise in two.[11]

Altogether, then, Porphyry says the opponents were Christian heretics who had trained as Platonists. Among the writings they brought to the seminar were at least four apocalypses, assigned individually to Zoroaster, Zostrianos, Allogenes, and Nicotheus, and perhaps another to Messos.

INTRODUCTION

1. E.g., Cohen, *The Beginnings of Jewishness.*

2. This rhetorical strategy is widely employed in pedagogical and popular writing—e.g., Holland Lee Hendrix on "Early 'Christianities' of the 2nd and 3rd Centuries," in the PBS television special (later adapted for the web) *From Jesus to Christ* (http://www.pbs.org/wgbh/pages/frontline/shows/religion/first/diversity.html, accessed July 18, 2012).

On "Jewish-Christianity," see Jackson-McCabe, "What's in a Name?" For a succinct exemplar of the classical approach, followed here—which is to designate the groups in question "Jewish-Christian" because of their adherence to Torah Law alongside recognition of Jesus of Nazareth as the Messiah—see Paget, "Jewish Christianity." For further references and a survey of the problem with respect to Sethianism, see Burns, "Jesus' Reincarnations Revisited."

3. For a fine criticism of the term "pagan," see O'Donnell, "Late Antiquity: Before and After." I use the term "Hellenic" instead not because I believe that it successfully covers all the same territory as "pagan" might (as if that were a laudable goal) but because the bulk of the non-Abrahamic traditions engaged in this book are Greek, and "Greek-ness," or "Hellenicity," was a primary term of self-identification for adherents to these traditions. Cameron makes a fine argument in defense of the use of "pagan," but this argument can be applied only to the second half of the fourth century CE (*Last Pagans*, 17).

4. Accepting laudable criticisms of the category "Gnosticism" and its discursive baggage (M. A. Williams, *Rethinking "Gnosticism"*, esp. 51–53, 265; King, *What Is Gnosticism?* esp. 168–69), this study nonetheless follows the approach of Layton, "Prolegomena." Others basically following Layton include Marjanen, "What Is Gnosticism?" 2ff; Pearson, "Gnosticism as a Religion," 94ff; Logan, *The Gnostics*, 9; Pleše, "Gnostic Literature," 164; esp. Brakke, *The Gnostics*, 29–51. Some have objected that this term does not appear as a term of self-designation in the Nag Hammadi hoard, which has bequeathed to us so many of these "Biblical Demiurgical" myths (the term is Williams's, from *Rethinking "Gnosticism"*); rather, the

term is an invention of the heresiologists, who used it sarcastically to denigrate their opponents (M. A. Williams, *Rethinking "Gnosticism"*, 42; King, *What Is Gnosticism?* 167). One might reply that the mythological valence of Gnostic literature leaves no room for an academic, self-designating term like "Gnostic" (Layton, "Prolegomena," 344, followed by Brakke, *The Gnostics*, 47–48; cf. M. A. Williams, "Was There a Gnostic Religion?" 74). A problem with this reply is that if we accept that "Gnostics" constituted a discrete social group who transmitted to us only aetiological myths and metaphysical tractates, we are shut off from any secure knowledge about the group beyond these myths—including questions of their social makeup, interactions with contemporaries, etc. This is why Porphyry's evidence (see next paragraph in text) is doubly important, because it gives us a firm social and temporal context for fixing the use and interpretation of a body of extant Gnostic texts—the "Platonizing" Sethian apocalypses, as I call them below.

5. Porph. *Vit. Plot.* ch. 16, text and tr. Armstrong (LCL), significantly modified. See the Appendix for discussion of this rendering of the opening lines.

6. Robinson, "Nag Hammadi: The First Fifty Years." The origin of the codices is unknown; see recently Logan, *The Gnostics*, 12ff.

7. Recognized decades ago by Schenke (ap. Klijn, "A Seminar on Sethian Gnosticism") and Layton, "Prolegomena," 348.

8. Tardieu has identified a source shared by *Zost.* and Marius Victorinus's treatise *Adversus Arium* that deals with negative theology and describes God in terms that recall the anonymous Turin commentary on Plato's *Parmenides* (Tardieu, "Recherches sur la Formation"; Hadot, "Porphyre et Victorinus: Questions et hypothèses"; Turner, "Introduction: *Zostrianos*," 76–77; idem, "Commentary: *Zostrianos*," 579–608; idem, "Introduction: *Allogenes*," 141–54; idem, "Gnostic Sethians," 42–51; idem, "Victorinus," 72–79). The implications of this body of evidence for rewriting the Gnostic role in the development of these ancient metaphysicians continues to be debated; see recently Turner, "Platonizing Sethian Treatises"; Chase, "Porphyre Commentateur."

9. Thus Mazur, "Platonizing Sethian Gnostic Background," esp. 14, an argument followed by Brakke, *The Gnostics*, 83, 137; see also Narbonne, *Plotinus in Dialogue.* It remains unclear, however, whether it is possible to prove that key innovations in Platonic metaphysics originated with Gnostic thinkers. An early dating of the Greek *Vorlagen* of the Coptic versions of *Zostrianos* and *Allogenes* necessarily implies that "Platonists of Plotinus' own school met the (Being-Life-Mind) triad first in the works of their (Gnostic) adversaries; that, declining to borrow openly, they adopted it under camouflage" (Edwards, "Christians and the *Parmenides*," 2:196; see also Attridge, "Gnostic Platonism," 25). Yet this dating is under debate. Rasimus, meanwhile, dates the Turin commentary prior to Plotinus, assigning authorship to the Sethian authors of the "Platonizing" Gnostic apocalypses themselves ("Porphyry and the Gnostics," followed by Mazur, "Platonizing Sethian Gnostic Background," 30–31; Burns, "Review," 299–300). Although this question is not the focus of this book, I will return to it in Chapter 7.

10. With respect to Judaism, see Layton, *Gnostic Scriptures*, 21; King, *What Is Gnosticism?* 188; Luttikhuizen, "Sethianer?" 85. More generally, see Brakke, *The Gnostics*, 85. Abramowski also observes Christian features in *Zostrianos* ("Nag Hammadi 8,1 'Zostrianos', das Anonymum Brucianum, Plotin Enn. 2,9 (33)"). This study agrees with most of her arguments and seeks to offer many more in support of Judeo-Christian authorship for the other "Platonizing" treatises as well .

CHAPTER 1

1. There was, however, a fourth-century sect of Christians known as the Adelphians—Puech, "Plotin et les gnostiques," 164. Cf. Elsas, *Neuplatonische und gnostische Weltablehnung*, 49–52.

2. The fourth-century historian of philosophy Eunapius of Sardis says he was a co-disciple of Porphyry, Amelius (another pupil of Plotinus), and Origen (on whom, see Chapter 7—Eunap. *VS* 4.2.1[Giangrande]). He composed both "treatises in prose (συγγράμματα) and discourses (λόγοι)" (ibid.). λόγος has too wide a lexical range to signify a specific genre of text, but the meaning of συγγράμματα is clear, and since λόγος is clearly opposed to it, Eunapius probably means a narrative (dialogue) or a collection of pithy sayings or oracles. In any case, he adds, the writings were "without charm" (ἀκύθηρον). Eunapius's reliability here is questionable, since Origen was a co-disciple of Plotinus, not Porphyry (C. Schmidt, *Plotins Stellung*, 15; Puech, "Plotin et les gnostiques," 164). John Lydus mentions an Aculinus who wrote a book on the ὑπομνήματι τῶν ἀριθμῶν (Lydus, *Mens.* 4.76); we are probably here dealing with different figures (thus C. Schmidt, *Plotins Stellung*, 18–19; Tardieu, "Les gnostiques," 519; pace Puech, "Plotin et les gnostiques," 164, followed by H. Jackson, "Seer Nikotheos," 255–56). Edwards supposes that the Aculinus mentioned by Porphyry and Eunapius is the second of Plotinus's respected colleagues from Ammonius Saccas's school in Alexandria, who had lapsed into Gnostic thought ("*Aidōs*," 231; "Gnostic Aculinus," 377). Cf. Brisson, "Amélius," 815.

3. Ter. *Carn. chr.* chs. 16–17; Jer. *Comm. Gal.* (PL 26:33). See also C. Schmidt, *Plotins Stellung*, 20–21; idem, *Koptisch-Gnostische Schriften*, 613; Puech, "Plotin et les gnostiques," 164–65; Elsas, *Neuplatonische und gnostische Weltablehnung*, 26.

4. Tardieu, "Les gnostiques," 517.

5. ἐξηπάτων καὶ αὐτοὶ ἠπατημένοι, ὡς δὴ τοῦ Πλάτωνος εἰς τὸ βάθος τῆς νοητῆς οὐσίας οὐ πελάσαντος. Here he alludes to Ps.-Paul: γόητες . . . πλανῶντες καὶ πλανώμενοι (2 Tim 3:13), citing Tardieu, "Les gnostiques," 520.

6. A literary giant, he surely could distinguish between ἐξηπάτων συγγράμματα ("treatises," i.e., a scholarly work by a real author—what Eunapius, for instance, assigned to Aculinus) and ἀποκαλύψεις (pseudepigraphic revelations—C. Schmidt, *Plotins Stellung*, 19).

7. With the first "golden age" of rhetoric having taken place in the Greece of the fifth century BCE.

8. Geertz, "Thick Description," esp. 9–10. Only on rare occasions have scholars of Gnosticism even raised the possibility of looking at the subject with respect to contemporary rhetorical culture (Böhlig, "Grieschiche Schule," esp. 15, 30, 33–34, 44; Säve-Söderbergh, "Pagan Elements," 78–79; P. Perkins, "Christian Books and Sethian Revelations," 698–701).

9. Attempts at providing sociological descriptions of Gnostic groups and their backgrounds have been frustrating. See Green, "Gnosis and Gnosticism," 97 n. 11 for earlier scholarship, which did little more than indicate the relevance of sectarian identity; more recently, see M. A. Williams, *Rethinking "Gnosticism"*, 96–101; Dunderberg, *Beyond Gnosticism*, 162. For an example of the limitations of the "Grant hypothesis" of origins following the failure of the Jewish revolts, see Green, *Economic and Social Origins*.

10. Doxographies about providence can be found at *Eug.* NHC III,3.70.1–71.13; *Soph. Jes. Chr.* NHC III,4.3.92.7–93.24; *Tri. Trac.* NHC I,5.108.13–109.24; see also Parrott, *"Eugnostos* and 'All the Philosophers'"; Dunderberg, *Beyond Gnosticism*, 178–81.

11. Whittaker, "Platonic Philosophy," 121. It is worth recalling that the heresiologists unhesitatingly associated Valentinians with Plato (Ter. *An.* 23.5; Hipp. *Haer.* 6.29.1).

12. Ir. *Haer.* 1.11.1; Dunderberg, "School of Valentinus," 72.

13. Geiger, "Sophists and Rabbis."

14. Philo *Contempl.* chs. 29, 31, 75–78.

15. Philo *Congr.* 11, 74–6, 146–50. On these passages, see Grant, "Theological Education," 180; Sterling, "School of Sacred Laws," 156; Dunderberg, *Beyond Gnosticism*, 183.

16. A milieu amply discussed in Hengel, *Judaism and Hellenism*.

17. Regarding the education of catechumens, Grant, "Theological Education," 181, recalls Heb 5:11–12 and 6:1–2 and several Valentinian texts (*Treat. Res.* NHC I,4; Ptol. *Flor.*); see also Festugière, *Révélation*, 2:44–45. On the "catechetical school," see Euseb. *Hist. eccl.* 5.10; van den Broek, "Christian 'School,'" 39 n. 2; van den Hoek, "Catechetical School," 59–60 n. 1.

18. Grant, "Theological Education," esp. 180; Wilken, "Alexandria"; Dawson, *Allegorical Readers,* 219ff. For Clement and παιδεία, see Buell, *Making Christians*, 119.

19. Grant, "Theological Education," 185; cf. Watts, *City and School*, 162–63. This probably precludes the kind of basic education he received (τῇ τῶν ἐγκυκλίων παιδείᾳ [Euseb. *Hist. eccl.* 6.2.7]).

20. Porph. *Christ.* frg. 20 (Berchman) = frg. 39 (Harnack) = Euseb. *Hist. eccl.* 6.19.8; for Plotinus's "syllabus," see Porph. *Vit. Plot.* 14. If Porphyry is correct, we see a different advanced Platonic reading group in Alexandria than that of Ammonius Saccas, unless the Christian Origen was a member of this group along with Plotinus and Aculinus (see further below, p. 244n49).

21. *Hist. eccl.* 6.15, 6.18.2–3.

22. See van den Broek, "Christian 'School,'" 41, on Euseb. *Hist. eccl.* 6.3.6.

23. See esp. Wilken, "Alexandria."

24. Surprisingly, little work as been conducted on Greek education in the context of Gnosticism. See Dunderberg (*Beyond Gnosticism*, 23, 190), regarding Valentinianism; the direction is intimated without follow-up by Emmel, "Gnostic Tradition in Relation to Greek Philosophy," 128–29.

25. Surveys of the evidence about the social and cultural background (and indeed physical location of) philosophical circles in the Roman Empire include Fowden, "Pagan Holy Man"; idem, *Egyptian Hermes*, 177–86, on late antique Alexandria; Dillon, "Academy"; idem, "Self-Definition"; Grant, "Theological Education," 182; Hahn, *Philosoph*, esp. 56–85; Sterling, "School of Sacred Laws"; D. O'Meara, *Platonopolis*, 13–26; Edwards, *Culture and Philosophy*.

26. Snyder, *Readers and Texts in the Ancient World*, 119.

27. Dillon, "Self-Definition," 67. On Ammonius, see C. Jones, "The Teacher of Plutarch"; idem, *Plutarch and Rome*, 9, 13, 16, 67; Dillon, *Middle Platonists*, 189–92.

28. Sterling, "School of Sacred Laws" (Philo); Broek, "Christian 'School,'" 44 on *Acts Just.* 3 (Musurillo); Euseb. *Hist. eccl.* 6.3.8 (Origen).

29. Plut. *E Delph.* 385a; *Adv. Col.* 1107e, cit. Dillon, "Self-Definition," 67.

30. Apul. *Apol.* 23.1 (Harrison); idem, *Metam.* 11.27.

31. On Calvernus Taurus, see Dillon, *Middle Platonists*, 237–47; Anderson, "Aulus Gellius," 1853–54; Tarrant, "Platonist Educators," 456; Snyder, *Readers and Texts in the Ancient World*, 111. For life as his student, see Gell. *NA* 7.13, 17.20, 18.10, 19.6.

32. On the school in general, see Fowden, "Pagan Holy Man," 40; on the problem of its location (Daphne or Antioch?), see Dillon, "Iamblichus," 869–70; on the syllabus, see Dillon, "Iamblichus," 871–73; on field trips, see Eunap. *VS* 5.2 and Dillon, "Philosophy as a Profession," 409; on festivals, see Eunap. *VS* 5.1.12–15.

33. For Porphyry's chronology, see A. Smith, "Porphyrian Studies," 720–21; for his skepticism about the school's existence, ibid., 765, esp. n. 298; see also Marrou, "Synesius of Cyrene," 133. Cf. Dillon, "Philosophy as a Profession," 406; idem, "Iamblichus," 868.

34. In this case, his wife, Marcella, as suggested by Dillon, "Philosophy as a Profession," 406.

35. Dillon, "Self–Definition," 71; idem, "Philosophy as a Profession," 402–3. See also Snyder, *Readers and Texts in the Ancient World*, 111 (on Taurus), and Cribiore, *Gymnastics*, 34 (on Libanius).

36. Porph. *Vit. Plot.* 9 (for Plotinus's base in Rome, the house of a widow; Origen, too, was funded by a matron [Euseb. *Hist. eccl.* 6.1.13]), 2 (on the rural estate in Campania to which he retired in illness).

37. Porph. *Vit. Plot.* 7, 12.

38. Porph. *Vit. Plot.* 17–18; see also Edwards's notes ad loc.; Dillon and Hershbell, "Introduction: *De vita Pythagorica*," 22.

39. Dillon, "Philosophy as a Profession," 409–10. For surprise visits from "visiting scholars," see Porph. *Vit. Plot.* 14; Eunap. *VS* 5.3.4.

40. Porph. *Vit. Plot.* 1.3. Gell. *NA* 2.2 demarcates between *sectatores* and *assistentes*; Porphyry (*Vit. Plot.* 7) mentions the ζηλωταί, following

the Pythagorean distinction between ζηλωταί ("youngsters") and ἀκροαταί ("hearers"), for which see Porph. *Vit. Pyth.* 37 (des Places); Iambl. *Vit. Pyth.* 29 (Dillon and Hershbell). For commentary, see Fowden, "Pagan Holy Man," 39; Hahn, *Philosoph*, 76–77; Watts, *City and School*, 31–32.

41. Thus Rogatianus (Porph. *Vit. Plot.* 7).

42. A stock cliché in imperial philosophical biography: see Just. Mart. *Dial.* 2–9; Luc. *Men.* 3; Clem. Al. *Strom.* 1.1.11 (Stählin); Porph. *Vit. Plot.* 3; Eunap. *VS* 4.1.2 (Porphyry), 7.1.11 (Julian); Jer. *Jov.* 2.14 (on Antisthenes); Mar. *Vit. Procl.* 9–11.

43. See, for example, Plut. *E Delph.* 387f, on which see Dillon, "Academy," 66.

44. Fowden, "Pagan Holy Man," 38–39; idem, *Egyptian Hermes*, 190–91; Burns, "Proclus and the Theurgic Liturgy," 128–31.

45. Porphyry arrived during summer vacation (*Vit. Plot.* 5), on which see Marrou, *History of Education*, 268.

46. Marrou, "Synesius of Cyrene," 132–34.

47. Nock, "Prolegomena." Similarly Anderson, "*Pepaideumenos* in Action," 154: "it is worthwhile to notice that the social study pioneered for sophists (and doctors) by Bowersock can easily be extended to philosophers."

48. Marrou, *History of Education*, esp. 212; see also Bonner, *Education*, esp. 34–75, 163, and the essays collected in Johann, *Erziehung und Bildung*.

49. On Porphyry, see Eunap. *VS* 4.1.2; Heath, *Menander*, 67–69. On Proclus, see Mar. *Vit. Procl.* 8. On Gregory Thaumatourgos, see *Or. pan. Orig.* 5.26.

50. Philostr. *Vit. soph.* 481. In this chapter, I employ Philostratus liberally (with Bowersock, *Greek Sophists*; Anderson, "Second Sophistic: Some Problems," 104; idem, "Aulus Gellius," 1854–55), but next to outside sources, in this case philosophical literature. On defining the Second Sophistic, see Bowersock, *Greek Sophists*, 9ff; Swain, *Hellenism and Empire*, 1–13, analyses to which I am indebted in the following. Cf. the criticisms of Brunt, "Bubble"; Gordon, "Review of Swain, *Hellenism and Empire*"). See also the oeuvre of Bowie, but esp. "Greeks"; Kennedy, *Classical Rhetoric*, 47; Reardon, *Courants* ; Anderson, "*Pepaideumenos* in Action," 80–89; idem, "Second Sophistic: Some Problems," 92–96; Swain, "Sophists and Emperors," 362–63; Staden, "Galen and the Second Sophistic," 33 n. 1.

51. Anderson, *Second Sophistic*; Swain, *Hellenism and Empire*; Kennedy, *Classical Rhetoric*, 50. For Paul and Philo as witnesses to the "roots" of the Second Sophistic in the first century CE, see Winter, *Philo and Paul Among the Sophists*.

52. Swain, *Hellenism and Empire*, 2, 88–89.

53. Nock, "Prolegomena," xvii–xix; Stanton, "Rhetors and Philosophers"; Anderson, "*Pepaideumenos* in Action," 118–23, 130–31, 155; idem, *Second Sophistic*, 133–43.

54. On grouping sophists and philosophers, see Philostr. *Vit. soph.* 479; idem, *Vit. Apoll.* 8.7.8; similarly Eunap. *VS* 2.2.2. For the circle of Julia, see Philostr. *Vit. soph.* 622; idem, *Vit. Apoll.* 1.3; Dio Cass., 75.15; Bowersock, *Greek Sophists*, 102ff; Swain, *Hellenism and Empire*, 386–87.

55. Ael. Arist. *Or.* 3.688–89 (Behr); Philostr. *Vit. soph.* 556; Quint. *Inst.* 10.1.35 (cit. André, "Écoles philosophiques," 36–37); Apul. *Flor.* 18.18, 20.4 (Harrison et al.); idem, *Apol.* 3, 5–6, 12, 39 (see Hijmans, "Apuleius," 396–97, 416–30); Dio Cass. 71.35.1–2, 77.19.1–2; Gell. *NA* 2.5, 3.13, 17; Max. Tyr. *Or.* 1.8. Galen simply uses the term "Sophist" for any educated person he disagrees with (Staden, "Galen and the Second Sophistic," 34–36).

56. For the inscriptional evidence, see Bowersock, *Greek Sophists*, 11–12. Literary evidence includes Plut. *Quaest. conv.* 710b; Dio Cass. 76.15.7. Philostr. *Vit. soph.* 484 seems to consider glib philosophers effectively sophists—thus Anderson, "Second Sophistic: Some Problems," 96–97; cf. Kennedy, *Classical Rhetoric*, 47.

57. Philostr. *Vit. soph.* 564, 567; Quint. *Inst.* 12.2.8; Eunap. *VS* 4.1.2–7; Nock, "Prolegomena," xviii–xix; Heath, *Menander*, 73–78; Trapp, "Philosophy," 477–78. Sextus Empiricus provides a counterexample as a philosopher who disparages schools of rhetoric. For sophists on the Platonic corpus, see Fowler, "Second Sophistic," 106–11.

58. See Nock, "Prolegomena," xxv–xxvii, for sources and discussion. Further, see Philostr. *Vit. Apoll.* 1.7; Porph. *Vit. Plot.* 20.

59. *Dig.* 27.1.6.1–8. For a survey of the other evidence, see A. Jones, *Greek City*, 220–26, 277–304; Bowersock, *Greek Sophists*, 31ff; Griffin, "Philosophy," 21; Swain, *Hellenism and Empire*, 236 n. 184; Trapp, "Philosophy," 471–74. Cf. Clark, "Translate into Greek," 116.

60. While the history of later Rome as a series of "crises" has achieved the status of cliché, the term remains useful to describe the political difficulties of the third century CE (roughly 235–70: from the death of Alexander Severus to Aurelian's success [Potter, *Prophecy*, iix, 18; going up to the Tetrarchy is Carrié and Rousselle, *L'Empire romain en mutation*, 90–111]).

61. Cumont, *Oriental Religions*, 42–43; Puech, "La gnose et le temps"; Dodds, *Pagan and Christian*, 17–30, 35; Elsas, *Neuplatonische und gnostische Weltablehnung*, 246; Rudolph, *Gnosis*, 287; Alexander, "Jewish Elements in Gnosticism," 1066. For responses, see Lane Fox, *Pagans and Christians*, 64–66; M. A. Williams, *Rethinking Gnosticism*, 101–15, 225–29; King, *What Is Gnosticism?* 175–89.

62. *Pace* Cumont, *Oriental Religions*, 19–24; Festugière, *Révélation*, 1:5, 12; idem, "Cadre de la mystique hellénistique," 84; idem, *Hermétisme et mystique païenne*, 13, 69–72; but esp. Dodds, *Pagan and Christian*, 1–3, 30, 36, 80, 92, 100, 135; Rudolph, *Gnosis*, 291. See also Andresen, *Logos und Nomos*, 273–74; Dragona-Monachou, "Divine Providence," 4454. For the ostensible role of the influx of Oriental cults, see n. 203 in this chapter.

63. MacMullen, *Roman Government's Response*, esp. 15–16. See also Swain, introduction, 2 (regarding Duncan-Jones, "Economic Change," 50–52); Edwards, *Culture and Philosophy*, 26–27. In the context of Gnosticism, see Nock, "Milieu of Gnosticism," 444; Alexander, "Comparing Merkavah Mysticism and Gnosticism," 13.

64. Potter, *Prophecy*, 18; cf. Brown, *World of Late Antiquity*, 22; Carrié and Rousselle, *L'Empire romain en mutation*, 105.

65. Edwards, *Culture and Philosophy*, 26; cf. D. A. Russell in Dio Chrysostom, *Orations*, 2–3. Turner, for instance, argues that the Platonizing treatises abandon the sociohistorical concerns of apocalyptic literature for a purely individualistic focus on eschatology ("Introduction: *Zostrianos*," 50, 223–24. On Gnosticism as a retreat from worldly politics, see, for example, Gianotto, "Pourvoir et salut."

66. Swain, *Hellenism and Empire*, 90; see also Kennedy, *Classical Rhetoric*, 50–53; *pace* Bowie, "Importance of Sophists," esp. 54 (cf. idem, "Greeks," 5–6).

67. On rhetorical curricula, see for instance Quint. *Inst.* 1; Lact. *Inst.* 10; Bonner, *Education*, 250–76; Kennedy, *Classical Rhetoric*, 49; D. A. Russell and Wilson in Menander, *Rhetor*, xi–xxix; Cribiore, *Gymnastics*, 56–59, 220; Swain, *Hellenism and Empire*, 90, esp. nn. 63–64; Heath, *Menander*, esp. 4–51, 217–54; Trapp, "Philosophy," 478–83; Watts, *City and School*, 4.

68. On stock themes in rhetorical education, see Bonner, *Education*, 277–87; Bowie, "Greeks," 7; idem, "Geography," 71; Cribiore, *Gymnastics*, 232–38; Swain, *Hellenism and Empire*, 95. For the use of Homer, see Cameron, "Poetry and Literary Culture," 345; Bonner, *Education*, 212–49. For the three stages of Roman education, see Marrou, *History of Education*, 265. The omnipresence of Homer at all levels of education in the Roman world is particularly borne out by the mounds of homework and exercises preserved on Egyptian papyri (Pack, *Literary Texts*; for discussion, see Cribiore, *Gymnastics*, 178–80, 192–97, 226).

69. The thrust of Bowie, "Greeks"; but cf. the concluding remarks at 37–41. Collusion between local elites and the Romans is more effectively articulated by J. Perkins, *Roman Imperial Identities*, 22–28.

70. Plut. *Def. orac.* 413f–414b; see further Swain, *Hellenism and Empire*, 157–61; Aalders, *Plutarch's Political Thought*, 54–58.

71. Ael. Arist. *Or.* 26.51f; Stertz, "Aristides' Political Ideas," esp. 1268–70.

72. Dio Chrys. *Borysth.* 36.39–61; idem, *Conc. Apam.* 40.35. Generally, see also C. Jones, *Roman World of Dio*, 124–30; Swain, *Hellenism and Empire*, 203–5.

73. See Swain, *Hellenism and Empire*, 348–56, 368–79, with sources and literature ad loc.

74. For Vespasian, see Suet. *Vesp.* 13; Dio Cass. 65.13.2; Philostr. *Vit. Apoll.* 5.27–38, 41. For Domitian, see Dio Chrys. *Exil.* 1 ; idem, *Def.* 1 (cf. Swain, *Hellenism and Empire*, 189, noting that Philostr. *Vit. soph.* 488 relates Dio's exile as voluntary; generally, see D. A. Russell in Dio Chrysostom, *Orations*, 3–5); cf. Philostr. *Vit. Apoll.* 7.4, for Apollonius's encounter with Domitian, on which see Swain, *Hellenism and Empire*, 388–89. For philosophers confronting other rulers, see Herodot. *Hist.* 1.29–33 (Solon); Diog. Laer. 3.18–20 (Plato); Philostr. *Vit. Apoll.* offers a catalogue (7.1–3); see also 4.35–39; idem, *Vit. soph.* 488. More generally, see Bowersock, *Greek Sophists*, 110–11; Hahn, *Philosoph*, 182–91; Rawson, "Roman Rulers"; Flinterman, "Sophists and Emperors"; Swain, *Hellenism and Empire*, 390; Lane Fox, "Movers and Shakers," 20–21.

75. Luc. *Nigr.* 29–33; idem, *Demon.* 40; cf. Swain, *Hellenism and Empire*, 316–17. For Rome's ἀρετή, see Dio. Chrys. *Rhod.* 68 (cf. *Plut. Fort. Rom.* 316c); cf. exhortations to παιδεία in Dio Chrys. *Exil.* 31; for Romans interested in παιδεία in Plutarch, see Blois, "Perception of Politics," 4613–14; Swain, *Hellenism and Empire*, 141–45.

76. Blois, "Perception of Politics," 4578–83, 4590–92; Swain, "Plutarch, Plato, Athens, and Rome," 172–74; idem, *Hellenism and Empire*, 143, 182–86.

77. Porphyry "longed to see Rome, the mistress of the world, so that he might enchain the city by his wisdom" (Eunap. *VS* 4.1.6).

78. For sophists enjoying wealth, positions of high political authority, and the company of emperors, see Dio Chrys. *Cont.* 18; idem, *Grat.* 12; Philostr. *Vit. Apoll.* 6.30; idem, *Vit. soph.* 530, 545–47, 567, 568, 597, 607, 612; Eunap. *VS* 4.1.1, 6.1.1, 7.1.4; Bowersock, *Greek Sophists*, 22ff; Swain, "Plutarch, Hadrian, and Delphi"; Watts, *City and School*, 5–12, 32–33; cf. Anderson, "*Pepaideumenos* in Action," 150–52.

79. Philostr. *Vit. soph.* 488, 520, 530, 548, 601; Bowersock, *Greek Sophists*, 44–47, 76; Swain, *Hellenism and Empire*, 397–400, 406–8.

80. Philostr. *Vit. soph.* 533, 562, 589; Bowersock, *Greek Sophists*, 48.

81. Philostr. *Vit. soph.* 516, 518, 577, 606, 619, 613; Eunap. *VS* 6.6.2.

82. Philostr. *Vit. soph.* 568, 571. I hope to address the abundance of similar accounts in Eunapius in a future article.

83. Bowersock. *Greek Sophists*, 31.

84. Swain, *Hellenism and Empire*, 227–28, on Dio. Chrys. *Rhod.* and *Conc. Apam.*, among others; see further Bowersock, *Greek Sophists*, 23–27; Anderson, "*Pepaideumenos* in Action," 170–71.

85. Philostr. *Vit. soph.* 531–32; idem, *Vit. Apoll.* 1.36–37, 2.39, 4.8–9, 4.33.

86. Philostr. *Vit. soph.* 493, 515, 566, 587, 597, 600, 612.

87. Plut. *Quaest. conv.* 720c–d (on his teacher, Ammonius), 736d; Swain, "Plutarch, Plato, Athens, and Rome," 181. For Dio Chrysostom, see C. Jones, *Roman World*, 95–103; Swain, *Hellenism and Empire*, 231–33. Further, see Philostr. *Vit. soph.* 526, 600.

88. Dio Chrys. *Conc. Apam.* 8; idem, *Def.* 12; idem, *Cont.* 18 (on which see C. Jones, *Roman World*, 104–6); Philostr. *Vit. soph.* 551–52, 568, 582, 613.

89. Hahn, *Philosoph*, 159; Fowden, "Pagan Holy Man," esp. 48–51; André, "Écoles philosophiques," 35; Swain, *Hellenism and Empire*, 413; cf. Dawson, *Allegorical Readers*, 37–38, on the Stoics.

90. Dio. Chrys. *Cont.* 2–3; idem, *Rec. Mag.* 3–15.

91. For a survey of inscriptions about "popular" philosophy, see Nock, "Prolegomena," xxvii; André, "Écoles philosophiques," 54–56.

92. For sources and discussion, see Hahn, *Philosoph*, 159–64.

93. Space does not a permit an analysis of the beliefs of their Stoic rivals about politics, but even a glance shows that the Stoa agreed on the importance of political life for a philosopher, and of civic duty as a metaphor for proper living (Cic. *Nat. d.* 1.7; Senec. *Ot.* 3.2–3; idem, *Tranq.* 1.10; Marc.

Aur. 3.5, 4.24, 6.14, 6.44, 9.23). In addition to the following primary sources on the philosophers' involvement with politics in late antiquity, see the survey of Watts, *City and School*, particularly 17: for philosophers, "a truly virtuous life depended upon the possession and exercise of a set of personal, social, and religious excellences."

94. Porph. *Vit. Plot.* 7. Cf. Edwards's comments ad loc., *Neoplatonic Saints*.

95. For Plotinus's civic involvement, see Porph. *Vit. Plot.* 9; Hahn, *Philosoph*, 165–71; Armstrong, "Plotinus," 201–4. For Gordian, see Porph. *Vit. Plot.* 2; for Gallienus and Platonopolis, see Porph. *Vit. Plot.*, 12. On Platonopolis, see D. O'Meara, *Platonopolis*, 15–16; and Edwards's commentary on the passage ad loc., *Neoplatonic Saints*. This evidence should not be forgotten, even in light of Plotinus's exhortation to the mystic to withdraw from political life (Plot. *Enn.* 1.2 [19] 7; Porph. *Vit. Plot.* 7; cf. Johnson, "Philosophy, Hellenicity, Law," 64).

96. Porph. *Vit. Plot.* 17; Eunap. *VS* 4.1.4; Millar, "Porphyry: Ethnicity," 248–49; Edwards, *Neoplatonic Saints*, 30 nn. 171–73.

97. D. O'Meara, *Platonopolis*, 40–49; Schott, "'Living like a Christian'," 263. Cf. Edwards, *Neoplatonic Saints*, 15 n. 3, and Johnson, "Philosophy, Hellenicity, Law," 63–64, on Porph. *Sent.* 32 (Lamberz), regarding Plot. *Enn.* 1.2 [19]; Brisson, "Doctrine of the Degrees of Virtues," esp. 92–101. See also Alc. *Epit.* 3.3; Macrob. *Comm. somn. Scip.* 1.8.5 (Stahl); Iamb. *Vit. Pyth.* 8.44, tr. Clarke: "again, some things cannot be got by human effort, but we can all be educated by our own choice, and can then be seen to take up our country's business (προσιόντα φανῆναι πρὸς τὰς τῆς πατρίδος πράξεις) not out of self-conceit, but because of our education (ἐκ παιδείας)."

98. Porph. *Vit. Plot.* 7.

99. Eunap. *VS* 5.1.1; Dillon, "Iamblichus," 862 (cf. 864 n. 7). See also Fowden, "Pagan Holy Man," 49 n. 128; Struck, "Speech Acts," 396; Clarke, Dillon, and Hershbell, introduction, xix–xx.

100. Eunap. *VS* 6.1.1–6.2.13; Fowden, "Pagan Holy Man," 41–42.

101. On the survival of the endowment past Justinian's proscription of teaching Neoplatonism in Athens, see Olymp. *Comm. Alc.* 141 (Westerink), and discussion in Cameron, "Last Days," 11; for benefaction more widely, see Watts, *City and School*, 131–41.

102. Mar. *Vit. Procl.* 15–7, 28–31 and Edwards's commentary ad loc., in *Neoplatonic Saints*; Watts, *City and School*, 103–5. For the continuing importance of the public life for the philosopher in the early fifth century, see also Macrob. *Comm. somn. Scip.* 2.17.4–9.

103. Dam. *Vit. Is.* frg. 324 (Athanassiadi); see also frg. 124. See Athanassiadi's commentary ad loc.; D. O'Meara, *Platonopolis*, 48; Lane Fox, "Movers and Shakers," 24.

104. Rawson, "Roman Rulers," 253; Flinterman, "Sophists and Emperors," 376.

105. E.g., Acts 17:17.

106. Philostr. *Vit. soph.* 490, 536, 577, 594–95, 617, 601, 613; see further Bowersock, *Greek Sophists*, 89–91, 100; Anderson, *Philostratus*, 64f; idem, "*Pepaideumenos* in Action," 129–30.

107. Lane Fox, "Movers and Shakers," 21; van den Berg, "Live Unnoticed!" 107–8.

108. Swain, *Hellenism and Empire*, and various articles cited in the following notes; also J. Perkins, *Roman Imperial Identities*, 18.

109. Nock, "Prolegomena," xlvii, with ample citations.

110. Dillon, "'A Kind of Warmth,'" 326; van den Berg, "Live Unnoticed!" 112; O'Donnell, "Late Antiquity," 206–7.

111. Bowersock, *Greek Sophists*, 18–21.

112. Philostr. *Vit. Apoll.* 1.33, tr. Wright (LCL, occasionally modified). For similar sentiments, see Pliny the Younger, *Ep.* 10.40.3; Max. Tyr. *Or.* 1.4, 1.6, 1.10; Whitmarsh, "Greece Is the World," esp. 273; Buell, *Why This New Race?* 40–41. On the historical Apollonius, see Bowie, "Apollonius of Tyre"; Anderson, *Second Sophistic*, 175–97; Swain, *Hellenism and Empire*, 382.

113. Philostr. *Vit. Apoll.* 1.4, 5.4; Apollonius is "Hellenic and wise" (1.28–29) or "Hellenic and divine" (2.17).

114. Idem, *Vit. soph.* 536.

115. Ibid., 571.

116. Ibid., 587; cf. ibid., 591, 609, 617–18, 628.

117. Dio. Chrys. *Borysth.* 10–11, 16–17, 26.

118. Sext. Emp. *Adv. math.* 1.176–240; a survey includes Blank's commentary ad loc., *Against the Grammarians*; Reardon, *Courants littéraires grecs*, 80; Anderson, *Second Sophistic*, 86–100; Swain, *Hellenism and Empire*, 17–64; J. Perkins, *Roman Imperial Identities*, 21–22.

119. Philostr. *Vit. soph.* 491; see also ibid., 589, 600.

120. Philostr. *Vit. Apoll.* 1.7, 1.19, 1.21, 1.32, 2.27, 3.12, 3.16, 4.5; Ps.-Apollonius, *Ep.* 71 (for pseudonymous authorship of the letters, see Anderson, *Philostratus*, 189–89; Swain, *Hellenism and Empire*, 395). On the Greek language in Philostratus, see Anderson, *Philostratus*, 43–48; Swain, *Hellenism and Empire*, 41 n. 62, 386–87.

121. Generally, see Swain, *Hellenism and Empire*, 33, esp. n. 39; Nock, "Prolegomena," lxxvii n. 167; C. Jones, *Culture and Society in Lucian*, 149 ; Anderson, *Second Sophistic*, 15–17; Flinterman, *Power, Paideia, and Pythagoreanism*, 45–51; Swain, "Biography and the Biographic," 7; Cameron, "Poetry and Literary Culture," 344; Watts, *City and School*, esp. 1–23; Schott, *Christianity, Empire*, 6; idem, "'Living like a Christian'," 263. For the practical side of παιδεία, see Anderson, "*Pepaideumenos* in Action," 104.

122. Bowersock, *Greek Sophists*, 66–70.

123. Dio. Chrys. *Exil.* 27; idem, *Consult.* 7–8; idem, *De phil.* 5, 8.

124. Plut. *[Lib. ed.]* 3e–4a; Aalders, *Plutarch's Political Thought*, 22, adding *Quaest. conv.* 649e; *Sera* 558a–b; Luc. *Nigr.* 13, 33; idem, *[Philopatr.]* 6–7; idem, *Somn.* 9–13; Jones, *Lucian*, 22–23; Anderson, "*Pepaideumenos* in Action," 180–81.

125. References collected in von Staden, "Galen and the Second Sophistic," 37 n. 17, 46, esp. Gal. *Praen.* 2.25 (Nutton) and commentary (pp. 145–46, ad loc.); Swain, *Hellenism and Empire*, 359ff.

126. Anderson, "*Pepaideumenos* in Action," 123–26; Reardon, *Courants littéraires grecs*, 254–308, 409; for archaeological evidence, see Galli, "'Creating Religious Identities'," esp. 348.

127. Philostr. *Vit. Apoll.* 1.16 (on which, see Fowden, "Sages, Cities, and Temples," 149–50), 3.53, 4.19, 4.21, 4.24, 4.40.

128. Philostr. *Vit. Apoll.*, 1.31, 3.14, 5.25.

129. On Plutarch as a priest, see Plut. *Quaest. conv.* 700e; C. Jones, *Plutarch*, 1–64; Brenk, "Imperial Heritage," 254–55, 330–36; Lamberton, *Plutarch*, 52–59; esp. Feldmeier, "Philosoph und Priester." On the beauty of religious festivals, see Plut. *Sera* 558a. For his criticisms of superstition, see *Superst.* or *Is. Os.* 353e–f, 355d, 377e, 379e. Scholars such as J. G. Griffiths (in his translation of Plut. *Is. Os.*, p. 25; see also Froidefond, "Plutarque," 228) see Plutarch as a young rationalist advancing toward a mature mysticism. Brenk argues instead for a holistic reading of Plutarch's religious views (*In Mist*, esp. 9, 16–48, 65–82; idem, "Imperial Heritage," esp. 255–62). On superstition in Plutarch in general, see Moellering, *Plutarch on Superstition*; for bibliography, see Brenk, "Imperial Heritage," 260 n. 16. Regardless, Plutarch is sure to emphasize that a philosophical reading of ritual does not excuse one from performing it (*Is. Os.* 355c–d); rather, the goal is to understand its true meaning (*ibid.*, 378a–b; idem, *Def. orac.* 437a).

130. Dio Chrys. *Exil.* 8–11 (naturally, he delivered this discourse in Athens); idem, *Dei cogn.*; D. A. Russell in Dio Chrysostom, *Orations*, 5–7, 14–19, 158–211.

131. Luc. *[Philopatr.]* 4–6; his remarks about the social importance of civic ritual read against a universalist notion of the divine is not incommensurate with his critiques of superstition in *Sacr.* and *Luct.* For religion in Lucian, see Caster, *Lucien et la pensée religieuse*; Robert, "Lucien et son temps."

132. Millar, *Study of Cassius Dio*, 179–81.

133. Porph. *Marc.* 9.

134. Sallust. *Deis* 10 (tr. Nock).

135. Plut. *[Lib. ed.]* 7d.

136. Plot. *Enn.* 4.3 [27] 32.9; 3.2 [47] 8.16–19.

137. Ibid., 2.9 [33] 6.54.

138. Iamb. *Prot.* 15–16, p. 82.4–14 (des Places); see also Iamb. *Vit. Pyth.* 8.43–45.

139. Fowden, "Pagan Holy Man," 51; cf. idem, "Sages, Cities, and Temples," 146.

140. Orig. *Cels.* 5.25, also 3.14, 7.68, 8.12, 8.68. See Benko, "Pagan Criticism," 1106; J. Cook, *Interpretation of the New Testament*, 94.

141. Porph. *Vit. Plot.* 10.

142. A sensitive reading is Clark, "Translate into Greek," 117, 128–29, suggesting that it was written during Porphyry's depression in Sicily in the later 260s.

143. Porph. *Aneb.*; idem, *Marc.* 23; Aug. *Civ. Dei* 10.9–10. For the mind as God's true temple, see Porph. *Marc.* 11. On Porphyry and religion, see

Edwards, *Culture and Philosophy*, 76–93; Speyer, "Porphyrios," esp. 67; on theurgy, see A. Smith, *Porphyry's Place*, 81–150.

144. Porph. *Abst.* 2.33.1; idem, *Antr. nymph.* 39.9–11 (Westerink). Bidez attempts to reconcile these two sides of Porphyry's thought by positing a change in it over time (*Vie de Porphyre*, regarding Eunap. *VS* 4.1.10, an argument widely followed, as by Waszink, "Porphyrios und Numenios," 45, 71; Zambon, *Porphyre*, 270). Edwards, *Culture and Philosophy*, 37, reverses Bidez. A third perspective holds that the sources in toto show a complexity of thought that rejects vulgar superstition but assigns worth to circumspect ritual activity (thus A. Smith, "Porphyrian Studies," 722, 730–37 [cf. Clarke, Dillon, and Hershbell, introduction, xxxi n. 59]). Cf. Johnson, "Philosophy, Hellenicity, Law," 63, for whom Porphyry's philosophy is mutually exclusive with the civic cult; some sort of continuity seems to me to be implied (despite his reading of Porph. *Marc.* 27), given Porphyry's prizing of Hellenic tradition (discussed in the following section).

145. Porph. *Marc.* 18–19, tr. Wicker, slightly modified; see also Clark, "Translate into Greek," 128; Schott, *Christianity, Empire*, 65–66; *pace* Hirschle, *Sprachphilosophie*, 43–44. Fowden ("Pagan Holy Man," 53 n. 163) adds Porph. *Marc.* 16 (μόνος οὖν ἱερεὺς ὁ σοφός), idem, *Abst.* 2.49.1 (Bouffartigue and Patillon) (ὁ φιλόσοφος καὶ θεοῦ τοῦ ἐπὶ πᾶσιν ἱερεύς).

146. (Ps.)-Jul. *Ep.* 77 419a, tr. Wright (LCL); cf. idem, *Ep.* 78 419b; Athanassiadi, *Julian and Hellenism*, 8. For Julian's reforms, see Jul. *Or.* 4; idem, *Ep.* 84; Athanassiadi, *Julian and Hellenism*; Fowden, "Pagan Holy Man," 58–59; D. O'Meara, *Platonopolis*, 120–23.

147. Iamb. *Vit. Pyth.* 8.37–40, 18.82, 28.138; idem, *Myst.* 5.6; generally, see Witt, "Iamblichus," esp. 40, 57; Shaw, *Theurgy*, esp. 3–4; more recently, see Edwards, *Culture and Philosophy*, 111–45; Fowden, "Sages, Cities, and Temples," 149.

148. Eunap. *VS* 5.1.12–15. The tale is probably derivative of Plut. *Gen. Socr.* 580d–e (Dillon, "Iamblichus," 874–75). For defense of animal sacrifice, see Iamb. *Myst.* 5.10 (Clarke, Dillon, and Hershbell); see also Shaw, *Theurgy*, 148. Pythagorean vegetarianism became popular among ancient Platonists, and did lead some to prefer the bloodless verbal sacrifice of speech to the killing of animals (Plut. *E Delph.* 384e; *Corp. herm.* 1.31, 13.18–19, 21; *Ascl.* 41; *Disc.* 8–9 NHC VI,6.57.18–23). However, this did not lead to a wholesale rejection of animal sacrifice, thus informing Iamblichus's own traditionalism on the matter (Porph. *Vit. Pyth.* 34–36; Plut. *Quaest. conv.* 635e–638a, 728d–730d [on which, see Brenk, "Imperial Heritage," 256–57]; Gal. *Usu* 3.10; Iamb. *Vit. Pyth.* 28.147).

149. Macrob. *Comm. somn. Scip.* 1.2.20–21.

150. C. Jones, "Multiple Identities," 20.

151. The birthdays of Socrates and Plato were celebrated in Plotinus's school with a feast and symposium (Porph. *Vit. Plot.* chs. 2, 15).

152. Puech, "Numénius"; Festugière, *Révélation*, 1:19–44; Dörrie, "Religiosität des Platonismus," 270–71; Whittaker, "Platonic Philosophy," 120–21; Clark, "Translate into Greek," 121–24; Hopfner (*Orient*) had collected many of the relevant sources, but has been replaced by Baltes, "Der

Platonismus." Surprisingly, the rhetorical framing of these texts is hardly addressed in Jeck, *Platonica Orientalia*.

153. Num. frg. 8 (des Places) = Clem. Al. *Strom.* 1.22.150.4; cf. Euseb. *Praep. ev.* 11.10.14 (Mras). See also Frede, "Numenius," 1036–37; Edwards, *Culture and Philosophy*, 20. Cf. Dodds, "Numenius," 6: "we might urge that instead of describing Plato as 'Moses talking Attic' Numenius *ought* to have described Moses as 'Plato talking Hebrew'" (italics in original).

154. Num. frg. 1a (des Places), tr. mine. For commentary, see Bidez and Cumont, *Mages hellénisés*, 2:232–33; Puech, "Numénius"; Cumont, *Lux Perpetua*, 344; Waszink, "Porphyrios und Numenios," 45ff; Verniere, *Symboles et mythes*, 334–35; Hadot, "Théologie, exégèse, révélation," 24–25; Droge, *Homer*, 2; Lefkowitz, "Some Ancient Advocates," 247–48; Baltes, "Platonismus," 1–3; Pleše, *Poetics*, 70–71; for a review, see Frede, "Numenius," 1045, 1047.

155. Puech ("Numénius," 777–78) argues that the Gnostics of Porph. *Vit. Plot.* ch. 16 and Plat. *Enn.* 2.9 were the intellectual heirs of Numenius. For similar arguments, see C. Schmidt, *Plotinus Stellung*, 34; Elsas, *Neuplatonische und gnostische Weltablehnung*, 238; Baltes, "Platonismus," 24; H. Jackson, "Seer Nikotheos," 257; Alexander, "Jewish Elements in Gnosticism," 1066; Pleše, *Poetics*, 70–71; cf. Turner, *Sethian Gnosticism and the Platonic Tradition*, 40–41.

156. Puech, "Numénius," 774; Dodds, "Numenius," 11; Dillon, *Middle Platonists*, 378, 384–96; Frede, "Numenius," 1039; Majercik, *Chaldean Oracles*, pp. 3–4. For comparison in the generation of the world from the third member of a triad (Num. frg. 11 [des Places]), allegory of the four rivers of Hades (idem, frg. 36), and belief in unifying cosmic stubstance (idem, frg. 30), see Edwards, "Atticizing Moses?" 70–71. For the possible basis of the doctrine of two Souls in Gnosticism, see Dodds, "Numenius," 7. For criticisms, see Festugière, *Révélation*, 3:42–47, 4:123–32.

157. See also Schott, *Christianity, Empire*, 27–28.

158. Dodds, "Appendix II: Theurgy," esp. 288; idem, *Pagans and Christians in an Age of Anxiety*, 14; Cumont, *Oriental Religions*, 28–38, 162–78, 202–7; Harnack, *Mission and Expansion*, 1:31–39, 239.

159. Lane Fox, *Pagans and Christians*, 35, on Dodds, *Pagans and Christians in an Age of Anxiety*, 133; Hanson, "Christian Attitude," 959.

160. Lane Fox, *Pagans and Christians*, 36, 82–83, 94–100; Nock, "Prolegomena," l–lv, ci–ciii; idem, "Milieu of Gnosticism," 449.

161. Dörrie and Baltes, *Platonismus in der Antike*, 2:76–84, 323–33; also Puech, "Numénius," 749–50; Andresen, *Logos und Nomos*, 248–50; Dörrie, "Schultradition," 21–24; Waszink, "Porphyrios und Numenios," 47; Boys-Stones, *Post-Hellenistic Philosophy*; Schott, *Christianity, Empire*, 18–20.

162. Plut. *Is. Os.* 369d–370d, tr. Babbitt (LCL); cf. 354b; idem, *Def. orac.* 415a; Puech, "Numénius," 764; Andresen, *Logos und Nomos*, 256; Verniere, *Symboles et mythes*, 40–44; Baltes, "Platonismus," 5; cf. Johnson, "Porphyry's Hellenism," 174. See also Plut. *Def. orac.* 415a–b; idem, *An proc.* 1026 b.

163. Baltes, "Platonismus," 4; generally, see Lovejoy and Boas, *Primitivism.*

164. See esp. *Is. Os.* 377f–378a; Andresen, *Logos und Nomos,* 246–51; Brenk, "Imperial Heritage," 271–72; Pleše, "Platonist Orienatlism," 373–74.

165. Cf. Dawson, *Allegorical Readers,* 82.

166. Diog. Laer. 1.27.

167. Alex. Poly. ap. Clem. Al. *Strom.* 1.15.70.1; Plut. *An. proc.* 1012d–e; Hipp. *Haer.* 1.2.12–13; Porph. *Vit. Pyth.* 6, 11–12; Iamb. *Vit. Pyth.* 12.18–19; Ps.-Iamb. [Nic. Ger.] *Theo. Arithm.* 56.10–57.6 (de Falco). For commentary, see Dörrie and Baltes, *Platonismus in der Antike,* 2:178–84, 453–66.

168. Luc. *Vit. auct.* 3; cf. idem, *Gall.* 18.

169. Apul. *Flor.* 15; Hijmans, "Apuleius," 435.

170. Porph. *Vit. Pyth.* 20.2, 21, 22.22, *pace* Edwards's remark that they are "two races whom it was not then the custom of intellectual history to name" ("Two Images," 160).

171. For Persia, see Diog. Laer. 3.6; see also Philostr. *Vit. Apoll.* 1.2. Successful trips are reported in Paus. *Descr.* 4.32.4; Pliny the Elder, *Nat. hist.* 30.8–9. For Egypt alone, see Plut. *Is. Os.* 354e. For a review, see Jeck, *Platonica Orientalia,* 23–25; for a survey of Plato's own discussions of Egypt, see Jeck, *Platonica Orientalia,* 26–34. On seeing India, see Apul. *Dogm. Plat.* 1.3.186 (Siniscalco); for commentary, see Dörrie and Baltes, *Platonismus in der Antike,* 2:166–76, 425–52, 475–78.

172. *Philostr. Apoll.* 2.9; idem, *Vit. soph.* 494.

173. *Philostr. Apoll.* 1.39–40, 2.27–3.52, 5.25, 6.10–11, 8.7.vi, clearly favoring the Indian sages. See also Edwards, *Neoplatonic Saints,* 6 n. 35; Swain, *Hellenism and Empire,* 386–87.

174. Edwards, *Culture and Philosophy,* 92–93. The discussion of hieroglyphs in Plot. *Enn.* 5.8 [31] 6 simply reveals ignorance of traditional Egyptian religion, and his school's reading list (Porph. *Vit. Plot.* 14) is Greek only. The majority opinion in modern scholarship has been to deny Indian influence on Plotinus, Bréhier and Cumont notwithstanding (Wolters, "Survey"; see also Cumont, *Lux Perpetua,* 346). For the journey to Persia, see Porph. *Vit. Plot.* 3.13–17.

175. See also Plut. *Def. orac.* 410a–b; Dio Chrys. *Dei cogn.* 10–12; Philostr. *Vit. Apoll.* 1.18.

176. See T101, 102, in Posidonius, *Fragments* (Kidd) and Kidd's commentary ad loc. (first expressed in Xen. *Mem.* 4.4.19); see further Festugière, *Révélation,* 2:176–95; Boys-Stones, *Post-Hellenistic Philosophy,* esp. 45ff; Pleše, "Platonist Orienatlism," 356; Schott, *Christianity, Empire,* 16ff.

177. Dio. Chrys. *Dei cogn.* 27, 35–40, tr. Russell; see also D. A. Russell in Dio Chrysostom, *Orations,* 176–88, with more sources and discussion.

178. Luc. *Syr. d.* 1.

179. Ps.-Apollonius, *Ep.* 34, 45; see also Swain, *Hellenism and Empire,* 387–88, on Philostr. *Vit. Apoll.* 3.25.

180. "In fact, quite possibly I may appear absurd when, in contrast with Greek lays of grace and charm, I chant a song that is barbarian; but still I dare to do so" (Dio. Chrys. *Borysth.* 43, tr. Russell). See further ibid., 39–60.

Bidez and Cumont, *Mages hellénisés,* 1:81–87, 2:142–53, considered the myth to be Mithraic in origin; modern scholarship has not borne out the claim. Nock ("Sarcophagi," 607) expressed doubts, but cf. idem, "Greeks and Magi," 524–25; Momigliano, *Alien Wisdom,* 146; D. A. Russell in Dio Chrysostom, *Orations,* 22..

181. D. A. Russell in Dio Chrysostom, *Orations,* 22–23, 235–47; Swain, *Hellenism and Empire,* 197–99. Other important passages include Dio Chrys. *Dei cogn.* 9 and idem, *Hom. Socr.* 8 (regarding Plat. *Apol.* 21). T. Schmidt, "Sophistes, barbares, et identité grecque," esp. 106–7, 113–14, emphasizes Dio's genuine occasional sympathy with barbarian cultures.

182. Diog. Laer. 1.1, see also ibid., 1.3 "these (other Orientomaniac) authors forget that the achievements which they attribute to the barbarians belong to the Greeks, with whom not merely philosophy but the human race itself began" (tr. Hicks [LCL]).

183. Ibid., 1.4–6, 1.13.

184. Orig. *Cels.* 1.15.

185. Raised and rejected by Puech, "Numénius," 745; Dodds, "Numenius," 6; Lamberton, *Homer;* 60–61, 75; Edwards, "Porphyry's 'Cave of the Nymphs.'"

186. Orig. *Cels.* 4.51. On his knowledge of Philo, see Winden, *Calcidius on Matter,* 106, 123 (regarding Calc. *Comm. Tim.* 300); Waszink, "Die sogenannte Fünfteilung der Träume," regarding Calc. *Comm. Tim.* 250–56. Dillon is less sure (*Middle Platonists,* 378).

187. Num. frg. 13.4; Puech, "Numénius," 751, 773; Dodds, "Numenius," 15; idem, *Pagans and Christians in an Age of Anxiety,* 130; Waszink, "Porphyrios und Numenios," 49–52; Dillon, *Middle Platonists,* 366; Baltes, "Platonismus," 2 n. 9. For discussion of the textual problem, see Whittaker, "Moses Atticizing" (an approach followed by des Places in his edition); Edwards, "Numenius frg. 13 (des Places)"; idem, "Atticizing Moses?" 65–67; idem, "Numenius of Apamea," 1:117. The line is probably best emended to ὁ μὲν χέων ("he who pours"), as by Tarrant, "Must Commentators Know," 188–89; see Plat. *Tim.* 41c8–d6, for the demiurge that sows, hands over, *pours,* and mixes.

188. Num. frg. 9 = Euseb. *Praep. ev.* 9.8.1–2; Bidez and Cumont, *Mages hellénisés,* 1:41; Edwards, "Atticizing Moses?" 68–69. On the common confusion of Moses and Museus, see Brisson, "Orphée et l'orphisme," 2920–23, 2927, and Mussies, "Interpretario Judaica," 94–97. The theme goes back to Artapanus in the third century BCE (Euseb. *Praep. ev.* 9.27.1–6; Pépin, *Mythe et Allégorie,* 227; Lefkowitz, "Some Ancient Advocates," 245).

189. Thus also Pleše, "Platonist Orientalism," 360–61; Schott, *Christianity, Empire,* 27; Edwards, "Numenius of Apamea," 116.

190. Frede, "Numenius," 1048, on frgs. 31, 33–34, 36, 55; Waszink, "Porphyrios und Numenios," 45–46, 78; Lamberton, *Homer,* 60–61 n. 53, 69; Dawson, *Allegorical Readers,* 199. *Pace* Dörrie and Baltes, *Platonismus in der Antike,* 2:472; Zambon, *Porphyre,* 175; Pleše, *Poetics,* 72.

191. Orig. *Cels.* 1.14–15, 6.80 and Chadwick's notes ad loc.; Frede, "Numenius," 1048; Baltes, "Platonismus," 5–8; J. Cook, *Interpretation of the New Testament*, 81.

192. Orig. *Cels.* 1.9 (cf. Plut. *Pyth. orac.* 407c), 4.14 (on Plat. *Resp.* 381b–c; idem, *Phaedrus* 246d).

193. Philostr. *Vit. Apoll.* 1.40, 2.11, 3.16, 4.40, 6.18, 6.20.

194. Ibid., 3.19.

195. Ibid., 8.7.12.

196. Ibid., 5.27

197. Ibid., 6.41.

198. Ibid., *Vit. Apoll.* 1.2; Dörrie and Baltes, *Platonismus in der Antike*, 2:473–75.

199. D. O'Meara, *Pythagoras*, 101–2; Clark, "Augustine's Porphyry"; Mazur, "Platonizing Sethian Gnostic Background," 324; esp. Johnson, "Porphyry's Hellenism," 168–73. To take one example from Johnson, Porph. *Philos. orac.* p. 141 compares the Greeks unfavorably to the more ancient nations of the Egyptians, Jews, et al. (thus Johnson, "Porphyry's Hellenism," 171–73; idem, "Philosophy, Hellenicity, Law," 65), in a classic expression of what below I term Platonic Orientalism. Even so, it is expressed in a treatise that is a commentary on a series of Apollonic (i.e., Greek) oracles defending traditional religious practices and attacking Christianity (Schott, *Christianity, Empire*, 74–75). More generally, see also Millar, "Porphyry: Ethnicity," 252;.

200. Porph. *Antr. nymph.* 6.10, 10.11–12 (Westerink); Andresen, *Logos und Nomos*, 258 n. 40.

201. Euseb. *Dem. ev.* 3.6.39–7.1 (Heikel); Aug. *Civ. dei* 10.32, 19.23; Porph. *Abst.* book 4, esp. chs. 14–16 (see further J. O'Meara, "Indian Wisdom," 21–22; Schott, *Christianity, Empire*, 58); Porph. *Philos. orac.* p. 141 (Wolff); Waszink, "Porphyrios und Numenios," 52–59.

202. Aug. *Civ. dei* 10.32; see also A. Smith, *Porphyry's Place*, 136–42; Schott, *Christianity, Empire*, 57; Johnson, "Porphyry's Hellenism," 174; cf. Clark, "Augustine's Porphyry," esp. 135–39.

203. Porph. *Marc.* 18, discussed above. It is true that for Porphyry in *Abst.*, "the true ancestral tradition is bloodless sacrifice" (Clark, "Augustine's Porphyry," 140, regarding Porph. *Abst.* 2.5–32, 2.34, 2.59; similarly, "ΠΑΡΑΝΟΜΩΣ ΖΗΝ," 560). And this is true; but when Porphyry redefines traditional sacrifice as bloodless, he jettisons animal sacrifice, not the importance of tradition itself.

204. "Ὅρα δὲ τὴν τῶν Ἑλλήνων σοφίαν!" (Porph. *Agalm.* frg. 3.1 [Bidez]); see also Porph. *Antr. nymph.* 6.18, 36; 34.9.

205. Porph. *Vit. Plot.* 7, tr. Edwards (*Neoplatonic Saints*).

206. Iamb. *Vit. Pyth.* 158 (Egypt, Chaldea), 147, 151 (Orpheus); see also the comments of Dillon and Hershbell and of Clarke, in their respective editions ad loc.; cf. Iamb. *Comm. Tim.* frg. 74 (Dillon) = Procl. *Comm. Tim.* 3.168.5 (Diehl). See also Larsen, *Jamblique*, 1:88–89; Edwards, *Culture and Philosophy*, 91.

207. Iamb. *Vit. Pyth.* 8.44, tr. Clark: "It is upbringing which distinguishes humans from beasts, Greeks from foreigners, free men from household slaves, and philosophers from ordinary people."

208. Iamb. *Comm. Tim.* frg. 70 = Procl. *Comm. Tim.* 3.65.7 (cf. the criticism of Porphyry at ibid, 1.307.4); Iamb. *Comm. Tim.* frg. 16 = Procl. *Comm. Tim.* 1.152.28, on which see Dillon, "Iamblichus," 879.

209. Iamb. *An.* 6.23–27 (Finamore and Dillon); frg. 44.5–9; the division is maintained through the rest of the surviving fragments.

210. Iamb., *Myst.* 1.2.

211. Ibid., 9.4.1–14; cf. also the treatise's opening (1.1).

212. Saffrey, "Refléxions sur la pseudonymie Abammôn-Jamblique."

213. Larsen, *Jamblique* 1:197; D. O'Meara, *Pythagoras*, 93–103, esp. 101. Finamore and Dillon, *Iamblichus De anima*, simply observe Iamblichus's self-identification with "the ancients"—as does Festugière (*Révélation*, 3:236 n. 3, 240–48).

214. On this, see Dillon, "Iamblichus," 870–75.

215. Clark, in her tr. of Iamb. *Vit. Pyth.*, pp. ix–xiii; Dillon and Hershbell in their tr. of Iamb. *Vit. Pyth.*, pp. 26–29; cf. Festugière, *Révélation*, 2:33–34.

216. Dillon in Iamb. *Plat. Dial.* 363.

217. D. O'Meara, *Pythagoras*, esp. 10–44, 86–105. See also Fowden, "Pagan Holy Man," 36; Whittaker, "Platonic Philosophy," 117–20. For a review of the relationship between Porphyry and Pythagoreanism, see Smith, "Porphyrian Studies." 760–63; for Iamblichus, see Dillon, "Iamblichus," 878.

218. Dörrie and Baltes, *Platonismus in der Antike*, 2:247ff; cf. further Macrob. *Comm. somn. Scip.* 2.2.1.

219. Num. frgs. 24, 57, 62, 70; Frede, "Numenius," 1044–47.

220. *Pace* Waszink, "Porphyrios und Numenios," 48.

221. Dörrie, "Religiosität des Platonismus," 270–76. Cf. Sint, *Pseudonymität*, 53.

222. Baltes, "Platonismus," 3–6, on Plutarch (*Pyth. orac.* 402e; *Def. orac.* 415a); and Celsus (ap. Orig. *Cels.* 1.16). On the Thracians as barbarians, see Luc. *Demon.* 34.

223. Plot. *Enn.* 5.8 [29] 10–13.

224. Procl. *Plat. Theo.* 1.5 pp. 25.24–26.4 (Saffrey and Westerink). Cf. idem, *Comm. Tim.* 3.168.10–15; Brisson, "Orphée et l'orphisme," 2925–26.

225. *Pace* Lewy, *Chaldean Oracles and Theurgy*, 399. On the Julianii, see *Suda* 1.433–34 (Adler); cf. Procl. *Comm. Tim.* 3.27.10; Majercik, *Chaldean Oracles*.

226. See most recently Athanassiadi, "Apamea and the *Chaldean Oracles*."

227. Bidez and Cumont, *Mages hellénisés*, 2:251ff; Burns, "The *Chaldean Oracles*."

228. For a survey of the collections, see Copenhaver, *Hermetica*, xxxii–xlvii; see also van Bladel, *Arabic Hermes*. For a survey of the long-standing debate over provenance (Egyptian, Greek, or Jewish?), see Copenhaver,

Hermetica, li–lix; Fowden, *Egyptian Hermes*, 32ff, 187ff; for the dogmatic inconsistency of *Corp. herm.*, see Festugière, *Révélation*, 2:45; cf. Fowden, *Egyptian Hermes*, 97–104.

229. *Corp. herm.* 12.13; 4.3.

230. Ibid., 16.1–2.

231. Porph. *Vit. Plot.* 16; Iamb. *Myst.* 1.1.1–2, 2.5–6, 8.1.260–61, 8.2.262, 8.3.265–4.267; Fowden, *Egyptian Hermes*, 201–5; Copenhaver, *Hermetica*, xliii. Among Christians, see Lact. *Inst.* 1.6, 4.6; idem, *Ir.* 11; Aug. *Civ. dei* 8.22–24, 8.29; Cyr. Al. *Jul.* 548b–c (all cit. Yates, *Giordano Bruno*, 6–8). Further, see Athenag. *Leg.* 28.6 (Schoedel); Clem. Al. *Strom.* 6.4.35–38.

232. Puech, "Numénius," 771–73; Dillon, *Middle Platonists*, 384–96; Majercik, *Chaldean Oracles*, 3–5; Copenhaver, *Hermetica*, xxiv–xxvi.

233. Nor did this approach die out after Plutarch; see *Anon. pro.* 4.8–12 (Westerink).

234. Cf. Momigliano, *Alien Wisdom*, 146–47.

235. As he argues, "the romantic Orientalism is likewise authentic, but it is secondhand, like that of the Greeks. He is a champion of the ancient Persians, not because he is an Iranian himself, or even knows much about them, but because this kind of Orientalism is an integral feature of Pythagoreanizing Neoplatonism" (Walbridge, *Wisdom*, 13, 83; see also Burns, "The *Chaldean Oracles*"). Independently and without reference to Said or Walbridge, Pleše refers to *The Apocryphon of John* as "a Christianized version of Platonist 'Orientalism,' best exemplified in the work of the philosopher Numenius" (*Poetics*, 275).

236. Said, *Orientalism*, 5: "the phenomenon of Orientalism as I study it here deals principally, not with a correspondence between Orientalism and Orient, but with the internal consistency of Orientalism and its ideas about the Orient . . . despite or beyond any correspondence, or lack thereof, with a 'real' Orient." See ibid., 1–9, 12, 15, 56.

237. Several known theological works written in Greek and associated with this figure have been suggested to be the *Apocalypse of Zoroaster*: Puech considered the second-century Middle Platonic hexameter poetry of the *Chaldean Oracles* ("Plotin et les gnostiques," 166). The *Oracles* are traditionally assigned to a late second-century CE provenance; see Majercik, *Chaldean Oracles*, 1–2. They were not assigned to Zoroaster until the edition of the Byzantine Hellene Gemistos Plethon in the fourteenth century CE (Bidez and Cumont, *Mages hellénisés*, 158–63; Burns, "The *Chaldean Oracles*"). Proclus knew a treatise *On Nature* (περὶ φύσεως) assigned to Zoroaster (Procl. *Comm. Remp.* 1.109.7–18 [Kroll]; the passage is echoed by Arnobius's reference to Zostrianos [see below]). A third candidate for the "apocalypse of Zoroaster" is the "book of Zoroaster" preserved in the long recension of the *Apocryphon of John* (NHC II,1; IV,1), but there is little in this text that corresponds to Plotinus and Porphyry's anti-Gnostic polemic, although many have implied otherwise (e.g., Tardieu, "Les gnostiques," 543; Brakke, *The Gnostics*, 40; Edwards, "Atticizing Moses," 72; idem, "How Many Zoroasters?" 285. Cf. Waldstein and Wisse, *Apocryphon*, 7; King, *Secret Revelation of John*, 329 n. 50).

238. For sources, see Bousset, *Hauptprobleme,* 369–82; Bidez and Cumont, *Mages hellénisés,* 1:42–50; Tardieu, "Les livres mis sous le nom de Seth," 204 n. 1.

239. This critique probably proceeded along the same lines as his criticism of the book of Daniel (Tardieu, "Les gnostiques," 541–43).

240. Arn. *Adv. nat.* 1.52; see further Bidez and Cumont, *Mages hellénisés,* 1:46, 155; Puech, "Nouveaux écrits," 132–34; Sieber, "Introduction to the Tractate *Zostrianus,*" 235–36; H. Jackson, "Seer Nikotheos," 259; Turner, "Commentary: *Zostrianos,*" 483–84, followed by P. Perkins, "Christian Books," 724.

241. This difficult tangle of evidence I have summarized and presented in detail elsewhere (Burns, "*Apocalypse of Zostrianos* and Iolaos," esp. 33–36). We are in good company regarding our confusion about the hoary provenance of these ancients—see the remarks of Procl. *Comm. Remp.* 2:110.14 –18 (Kroll), tr. Edwards, "How Many Zoroasters?" 284.

Amelius's refutation of *Zostrianos* is lost to us. Brisson has argued further that Eusebius's quotation of a tract of Amelius arguing against a docetic reading of the prologue to the Fourth Gospel is in fact a reference to the refutation mentioned by Porphyry ("Amélius," 824, 840–43, on Euseb. *Praep. ev.* 11.19). I bracket the evidence, following the critiques of Abramowski, "Nicänismus und Gnosis," 513–20.

242. See below, Chapter 7 n. 63.

243. *Unt.* 232.3–23; for full discussion of the passage, see below, Chapter 6, "Angels Alien to Humanity."

244. M299a 5, in Henning, "Ein manichäisches Henochbuch," 27–28; see also S. Lieu, *Manichaeism in the Later Roman Empire,* 51; Reeves, *Heralds,* 14. On Nicotheus and Marsanes, see C. Schmidt, *Plotins Stellung,* 59–60; Pearson, "Introduction: *Marsanes,*" 230–35; H. Jackson, "Seer Nikotheos," 260.

245. Zos. *Pan. Omega,* chs. 1, 10, respectively. See also Festugière, *Révélation,* 1:263–73; Stroumsa, *Another Seed,* 217–26; H. Jackson, "Seer Nikotheos," 270–71, and commentary in Zos. *Pan. On the Letter Omega* pp. 40, 49.

246. Epiph. *Pan.* 40.7.6, tr. Layton, *Gnostic Scriptures,* 198: "and these (Archontics) say there are also other prophets, a certain Martiades and a Marsianos, who were caught up into the heavens and came back down after three days."

247. Its first syllable means "lord," "master," in Aramaic. H. Jackson ("Seer Nikotheos," 265–66) agrees with Pearson ("Introduction: *Marsanes,*" 233) in rejecting the etymology of Elsas (*Neuplatonische und gnostische,* 36–37).

248. H. Jackson, "Seer Nikotheos," 272.

249. For the epithet expressing "alien" nature, see Chapter 4; as a reference to Seth, see Puech, "Nouveaux écrits," 126–30; Robinson, "Three Steles," 133; H. Jackson, "Seer Nikotheos," 259. A classic passage is Epiph. *Pan.* 40.7.1–3, tr. Layton, *Gnostic Scriptures,* 197–98: "And in turn, they (the Archontics) say, Adam united with Eve his wife and begot Seth, his own

physical son. And next, they say, the higher power descended, accompanied by the ministering angels of the good god, and caught up Seth himself, whom they also call 'the foreigner'; carried him somewhere above and cared for him for a while, lest he be slain, and after a long time brought him back down into this world and rendered spiritual and bodily." See also Tardieu, "Les livres mis sous le nom de Seth," 206.

250. Epiph. *Pan.* 40.7.4–5 (tr. Layton, *Gnostic Scriptures*, 197–98).

251. The eighth-century Syrian philosopher and heresiographer Theodore bar Konai also knew a "Book of the Foreigners" and an "Apocalypse of the Foreigners"—see *Librum Scholiorum*, ch. 63, pp. 319.29–320.26 (text), *Livre des scolies*, ch. 63, pp. 238–39 (tr.), cit. Puech, "Fragments retrouvés"; see also C. Schmidt, *Plotins Stellung*, 51, 57–58. The contents of these books do not match those in Allogenes (NHC XI,3) nor the "Book of Allogenes" of the Tchacos codex, but rather seem to refer to traditions known from the Ophite literature. For a summary of evidence, see Burns, "Apophatic Strategies," 178–79 n. 86.

252. NHC XI.3.68.27–35, 69.14–20. Puech, "Nouveaux écrits," 132; H. Jackson, "Seer Nikotheos," 259.

253. *Pace* Bousset, *Hauptprobleme*, 187, reading the valence of the names as pagan.

254. Cf. Ménard, "Littérature apocalyptique juive," 300, 302.

255. See King, *Secret Revelation of John*, 160.

256. An example from the Gnostic context is the revelation-monologue *Thunder: Perfect Mind*, where the female revealer toys with and subverts this discourse, asking, "Why did you hate me, Hellenes, because I am a barbarian amongst barbarians? For I am the wisdom of the Hellenes and the knowledge of the barbarians; I am the judgment of the Hellenes and the barbarians. It is I, whose image in Egypt is manifold, and who has no image amongst the barbarians. It is I who am hated in every place, and loved in every place" (*Thund.* NHC VI,2.16.1–11).

CHAPTER 2

1. The former title is given in Porph. *Vit. Plot.* chs. 16, 24; the latter, in ch. 5. Igal asserts that the latter title is Porphyry's invention ("The Gnostics and 'The Ancient Philosophy,'" 140); Cilento, that it is Plotinus's (*Plotino: Paideia*, 221). For the chronology and titling of the Plotinian tracts, see Porph. *Vit. Plot.* chs. 4–6, 24–26.

2. Treatises 30–33 = *Enn.* 3.8, 5.8, 5.5, and 2.9, as proposed by Harder, "Eine neue Schrift Plotins." The thesis is still commonly followed (thus Kalligas, "Plotinus Against the Gnostics," 121). For criticism, see Wolters, "Notes on the Structure," esp. 85–87; see also Narbonne's proposal of a *Großzyklus* beginning in the earliest treatises and engaging Gnostic ideas through treatise 51 (*Plotinus in Dialogue*, 2ff); more widely, see Poirier and Schmidt, "Chrétiens, hérétiques et gnostiques," 914–16.

3. Most recently, see Mazur, "Platonizing Sethian Gnostic Background"; Narbonne, *Plotinus in Dialogue*; for a more traditional view (seeing 2.9 [33]

as Plotinus's ultimate break with Gnosticism), see Dörrie, in Puech, "Plotin et les gnostiques," 190.

4. My presentation of the structure of the treatise largely agrees with that proposed by Wolters, "Notes on the Structure," 88–90.

5. Extant in NHC II,1; III,1; IV,1; BG 8502,2. A version of its opening, theogonic section appears to have been known to to Irenaeus as a myth of the "(Barbelo)-Gnostics" (*Haer.* 1.29).

6. The name "Barbelo" is of uncertain origin; recent discussions include Logan, *Gnostic Truth and Christian Heresy*, 98–100; Pearson, *Ancient Gnosticism*, 57.

7. See Burns, "Aeons."

8. Num. frgs. 15, 22 (des Places). See also Armstrong's remarks in Plot. *Enn.* 2 p. 226 nn. 1, 2, 244 n. 2; Wallis, "Soul and Nous," 466–67; Pasquier, "La réflexion démiurgique," 655–56.

9. As described at Plot. *Enn.* 5.1 [10].

10. Ibid., 2.9 [33] 2.3–5. The unnecessary intelligibles include the Sojourn, Repentance, and Aeonic Copies (*Enn.* 2.9 [33] 5–6) mentioned in the *Untitled Treatise* and *Zostrianos*, discussed below in Chapter 5, "The Strange and the Dead." Furthermore, by subdividing intelligible reality and naming its partitions, "they (the Gnostics) think they will appear to have discovered the exact truth, though by this very multiplicity they bring the intelligible nature into the likeness of the sense-world" (*Enn.*, 2.9 [33] 6.29–31; also 10.28–29).

11. Plot. *Enn.* 2.9 [33] 3.7–21. In this book, I employ Armstrong's translation of Plotinus (LCL), modifying it occasionally, as noted.

12. O'Brien, *Théodicée*, 64–65, regarding *Enn.* 1.8 [51] 14; see further Narbonne, *Plotinus in Dialogue*, 88, adducing more evidence.

13. For the definition of the Soul by its demiurgic activity, see Plot. *Enn.* 5.4 [7] 2.20–21; 4.3 [27] 10.13–15; 3.8 [30] 3.13–18, 4.1–14. For background, see D. O'Meara, "Gnosticism and the Making of the World," 371–74; Schroeder, "Aseity," 305.

14. Plot. *Enn.* 3.6 [26] 6–7, 13–14; 4.3 [27] 9.37–40; vis-a-vis the ascent of the soul, 1.6 [1] 5.26–59. See Zandee, *Terminology of Plotinus*, 18; cf. Armstrong, "Man in the Cosmos," 7–8, 11. More generally, see O'Brien, *Théodicée*; idem, "Plotinus and the Gnostics"; Corrigan, "Positive and Negative Matter."

15. Plot. *Enn.* 3.8 [30] 3 (on which see C. Schmidt, *Plotins Stellung*, 76), 4, 8; cf. Matter as "ultimate form" (Plot. *Enn.* 5.8 [31] 7.21–23). For matter as evil, see Plot. *Enn.* 2.4 [12]; 1.8 [51]; 2.3 [52] 17. For the plight of the soul embodied in matter, see 4.3 [27] 4.26–33; 6.7 [38] 28.12, 31.21–27. For the necessity of matter for creation (certainly a good activity), see 3.8 [30] 2.2–3.

16. The creator is good, Zeus qua World-Soul (Plot. *Enn.* 5.8 [31], esp. ch. 8), the third principle in the One-Intellect-Soul triad (3.9 [13]).

17. Ibid., 2.9 [33] 4.4–5.

18. Ibid., 4.7.

19. Ibid., 4.4–7.

20. Plat. *Tim.* 28a–b.

21. Plot. *Enn.* 2.9 [33] 4.9–13.

22. Ibid., 4.14–16.

23. The key passages for the Platonic account are *Tim.* 28c, 29e, 40c; for summary of the Hellenistic critique, see D. O'Meara, "Gnosticism and the Making of the World," 377; Wallis, *Neoplatonism*, 26–27, 63; idem, "Soul and Nous," 464, 471. Cf. Plot. *Enn.* 5.8 [31] 7, 6.7 [38] 1.28, 3.1.

24. The tradition goes back to Speusippus and Xenocrates (Dillon, *Middle Platonists*, 7, 33); see further D. O'Meara, "Gnosticism and the Making of the World," 368; Dillon, *Middle Platonists*, 206–8, 286–87, 368–71, on Phil. *Opif.* 5; Alc. *Epit.* 14.3 (Whittaker and Louis); Num. frgs. 12, 13, 16, 17 (des Places); *Chald. Or.* frgs. 5, 33. Important exceptions include Plut. *An. proc.* 1026f–1027a; idem, *E Delph.* 392e–393b; Att. Frgs. 4, 10, 23 (des Places); Froidefond, "Plutarque," 194–97.

25. This is the substance of Plot. *Enn.* 3.8 [30] and the objection at 2.9 [33] 4.15–17; see also 4.3 [27] 10.15–16; 5.8 [31] 7; 6.7 [38] 1–3; Hadot, "Ouranos," 124–25; Schroeder, "Aseity," 315; Narbonne, *Plotinus in Dialogue*, 119–21.

26. Plot. *Enn.* 2.9 [33] 6.58–60 (condemnation of needless γενέσεις καὶ φθοράς); see also 2.1 [40] 4.29–33.

27. Ibid., 5.8 [31] 7; 6.7 [38] 1.38; 3.2 [47] 2.16–21.

28. Ibid., 2.9 [33] 6.26. D. O'Meara ("Gnosticism and the Making of the World," 375) recalls here another jibe from the Großschrift, probably also against the Gnostics: "what the manner is of the making of the world (τρόπος ποιήσεως) they do not want to understand (συνιέναι), nor do they know that as long as the intelligible shines, the rest will never lack, but exists as its source exists, which 'always was and always will be'" (Plot. *Enn.* 5.8 [31] 12.22–26).

29. As Wallis ("Soul and Nous," 467) notes, later Platonists criticized Plotinus for the same thing! (See Procl. *Comm. Tim.* 1.306.32.) See also Edwards, "Porphyry's 'Cave,'" 96; for the general reception history of the *Timaeus* passage, see Festugière, *Révélation*, 2:275–96.

30. Plot. *Enn.* 2.9 [33] 6.50–65; the critique is fleshed out in chs. 7, 18.25–30. But cf. 4.8 [6] 2.20–46; D. O'Meara, "Gnosticism and the Making of the World," 369.

31. Plot. *Enn.* 2.9 [33] 8.1–2.

32. Ibid., 8.2–5: "first, (this confusion comes from) the people who assume a beginning for what is eternal; then, they think that the cause of the creating was a being who turned from one thing to the next and thus changed."

33. Ibid., 2.9 [33] 10.19–23. C. Schmidt recalls Irenaeus's account of Valentinian myths of the decline of Wisdom (*Plotins Stellung*, 40–41; *Haer.* 1.4.2, 1.5.3, 1.7.1).

34. *Zost.* NHC VIII,1.9.9–22: "when they came upon it (i.e., the aetherial earth) and gazed through it at the things of the world, they condemned its archon to death, because he was a model (τύπος) of the world he was a [. . .], and source of matter (ὕλη), [begotten] of lost darkness. When Sophia looked [at them], she produced the darkness, being [. . .] is beside the [. . .] is a model (τύπος) [. . .] of the essence (οὐσία) of [. . .] form (μορφή), un-[. . .],

an image (εἶδος)" Cf. ibid., 27.12. See also Tardieu, "Les gnostiques," 528; Turner, "Commentary: *Zostrianos*," 519–20.

35. Plot. *Enn.* 2.9 [33] 10.24–34.

36. Ibid., 11.1–9, 12.30–44.

37. Ibid., 4.8 [6] 1, 4; 4.3 [27] 7.16–20. See Sinnige, *Six Lectures*, 68–74; Dillon, "Descent," 364. For Iamblichus's response, see *An.* 6–7 (Finamore and Dillon).

38. Plot. *Enn.* 4.8 [6] 5.26; 2.9 [33] 4.27–32; see also ibid., 4.8 [6] 6.7–9; 3.8 [30] 5.10–14; 1.8 [51] 14.34–59; Dillon, "Descent," 357; Sinnige, *Six Lectures*, 53. Edwards reminds the reader that this view of "necessitated free choice" is perfectly in line with Stoicism (" . . . And Neoscholastica," 177), but it is still difficult to resolve this with other statements that Soul was drawn by desire to its own inferior image in illuminated matter, per *Enn.* 1.6 [1] 8; 4.3 [27] 12.1–3. Thus also Porph. *Antr. nymph.* 59.18–21 (Westerink); *Corp. herm.* 1.14; see also Jonas, *Gnostic Religion*, 146–73; Rist, *Plotinus: The Road to Reality*, 120; O'Brien, *Théodicée*, 74–75; Edwards, "Porphyry's 'Cave,'" 93.

39. Plot. *Enn.* 4.8 [6] 2.52; if anything, the Soul desires ἐπιστροφή to the One (ibid., 4.2, 7.26). Sinnige ("Gnostic Influence," 84; idem, *Six Lectures*, 5–13) sees "corrections" to the Gnostic view of descent at 6.9 [9] 9.11; 5.1 [10] 10.26; 2.9 [33] 4.6. Classic passages on Soul's "daring" include 4.8 [6] 5.16–27; 6.9 [9] 5.29; 5.1 [10] 1.1–5; 3.8 [30] 8; 2.9 [33] 11.22; 3.7 [45] 11; see also Festugière, *Révélation*, 3:83; Mazur, "Plotinus' Philosophical Opposition," 101; Katz, "Plotinus and the Gnostics," 291; Sinnige, "Gnostic Influence," 86; Zandee, *Terminology of Plotinus*, 26–27 n. 38. For usage of αὐτεξούσιος that is similar to τόλμα, see 4.8 [6] 5.26. Cf. Armstrong, "Dualism," 44 (recalling Num. frg. 11; *Tri. Tract.* NHC I,5.77).

40. Plot. *Enn.* 6.4 [22] 16.45, 4.3 [27] 6.26–28, 9.24, 12.4–6, 12.19–26; 1.8 [51] 14.41–44. For Soul gazing into matter, see 1.8 [51] 4.17–32, 9.18–26; 1.1 [53] 8.15–17, 12.22–28. Cf. Corrigan, "Positive and Negative Matter," 38–39, regarding *Zost.*, NHC VIII,1.45.12–46.15.

41. "If it did not come down, but illumined the darkness, how can it rightly be said to have declined?" (Plot. *Enn.* 2.9 [33] 11.1–3)

42. Ibid., 10.27.

43. Ibid., 2.9 [33] 11.27–12.4.

44. Armstrong, "Plotinus," 264–68; Wallis, *Neoplatonism*, 94–95, 112–18; idem, "Soul and Nous," 471–73; Edwards, " . . . And Neoscholastica," 177; *pace* D. O'Meara, *Plotinus*, 39.

45. Arist. *Metaph.* 1.2 982b12 (regarding Plat. *Theaet.* 155d). Cf. Plut. *E Delph.* 385c; Plot. *Enn.* 3.8 [30] 11.33: "as certainly, one who looks up to the sky and sees the light of the stars thinks of their maker and seeks him, so the man who has contemplated the intelligible world and observed it closely and wondered at it must seek its maker, too." After this comes a remarkable description of contemplation of Intellect: "but we must not remain always in that manifold beauty but go on still darting upwards, leaving even this behind, not out of this sky here below, but out of that, in our wondering about who generated it and how" (Plot. *Enn.*, 6.7 [38] 16.1–4).

46. Arist. *Metaph.* E 1.1025b25.

47. His later treatise *On Providence* probably refers to Gnostics when it opens with a remark on individuals who think the "universe is the product of an evil demiurge" (Plot. *Enn.* 3.2 [47] 1.8–9; cf. 3.9–14).

48. Plot. *Enn.* 2.9 [33] 4.25. Cf. 3.3 [48] 3.

49. Armstrong, "Dualism," 39; see also esp. Plot. *Enn.* 4.8 [6] 6; 4.4 [28] 32; 6.8 [39] 16.

50. "What other fairer image of the intelligible world could there be?" (Plot. *Enn.* 2.9 [33] 4.28)

51. "If you are wronged," he asks, "what is there dreadful in that to an immortal . . . and even if you are murdered, you have what you want. But if you have come by now to dislike the world, are you not compelled to remain a citizen of it [πολιτεύεσθαι]?" (ibid., 9.15–18; on these passages see M. A. Williams, *Immovable Race*, 133–34). One is reminded of Tertullian's report of Arrius Antoninus's complaint (*Scap.* 5): "you wretches, if you want to die, you have cliffs or ropes." Further, see Plot. *Enn.* 3.2 [47] 4.44–48, 5–7, 8.16–21, 13.1–17, 15.21, 15.43–47, 15.62; for discussion, see Ferweda, "Pity"; C. Schmidt, *Plotins Stellung*, 78–79.

52. Plot. *Enn.*, 2.9 [33] 15.4, 16.1; for emphasis on the greater good, see 13.18; 4.4 [28] 32.32–47, 39.29–30.

53. Ibid., 2.9 [33] 16.1–5; Armstrong, "Dualism," 45, 48–50.

54. Plot. *Enn.* 2.9 [33] 13.3–4.

55. See, for example, ibid.4.3 [27] 16. Armstrong ("Man in the Cosmos," 10, on Plot. *Enn.* 1, p. xxvi) thinks Plotinus is not too concerned with "a clearly distinguished hierarchy of intra-cosmic and extra-cosmic divinities." Mazur sees Plotinus rejecting a Gnostic hierarchy "which entails a disjunction between ethical status on the one hand and ontological or causal priority on the other" ("Plotinus' Philosophical Opposition," 104, and also 107–9; P. Perkins, *Gnostic Dialogue*, 172; Narbonne, *Plotinus in Dialogue*, 66–67).

56. Plot. *Enn.* 2.9 [33] 3.11–12; 2.3 [52] 18.1–5; cf. 3.2 [47] 9.31–40; 3.3 [48] 1.1–3, 7.1–7.

57. Ibid., 2.9 [33] 8.38; see also 18.17–21, 18.31–32 (cf. 2.3 [52] 1–6, 18), for the charge that the Gnostics wrongly call men, but not stars, their "brothers." Cf. Zandee, *Terminology of Plotinus*, 16; see also Festugière, *Révélation*, 3:60–61; Igal, "The Gnostics and 'The Ancient Philosophy,'" 142; Mazur, "Plotinus' Philosophical Opposition," 98–101. On the beauty of the divine hierarchy, see Plot. *Enn.* 2.9 [33] 5.8–14, 8.32–33; cf. the starry heavens as a place full of beautiful images of gods (3.2 [47] 14.20–30).

58. Plot. *Enn.* 2.9 [33] 13.17–19; see also Armstrong's note ad loc.

59. Ibid., 4.4 [28] 31.41, 38.8–14; 2.3 [52] 7–8, 10–15.

60. Ibid., 2.9 [33] 16.9–15.

61. The operations of the σύνταξις are discussed most explicitly in ibid., 2.3 [52], esp. 7.12, 8.5–11. See also 3.2 [47] 3.26; 3.3 [48] 6.33–39.

62. Ibid., 2.9 [33] 16.14–17.

63. Cf. Celsus's critiques of would-be messiahs (Orig. *Cels.* 7.9).

64. Plot. *Enn.* 2.9 [33] 16.30–38; for the "sons of God," see ibid., 9.56–59; M. A. Williams, *Immovable Race*, 194; Narbonne, *Plotinus in Dialogue*, 105–13.

65. Plot. *Enn.* 2.9 [33] 9.51–58; cf. Edwards, "Porphyry's 'Cave,'" 100, who thinks the Gnostics rejected the life of philosophical advancement. Rather, the passage could be understood as indignation at a lack of respect for Hellenic oracles and the funerary cult (supported at *Enn.* 4.7 [2] 15).

66. Plot. *Enn.* 2.9 [33] 9.27, per Armstrong, "Plotinus and Christianity," 84.

67. *Pace* Edwards, "Pagan and Christian Monotheism," 214 (on Porph. *Vit. Plot.* 10.35); see also Dodds, "Appendix II: Theurgy"; Fowden, "Pagan Holy Man," 52. As Porphyry himself acknowledges, it is hard to understand exactly what Plotinus meant by the statement that "the gods should come to me, not I to them" but as is clear here, Plotinus fully supported the traditional civic cult, and elsewhere in the *Enneads* has no objection to idolatry, although he might interpret it philosophically. See Cumont, *Lux Perpetua*, 351, regarding Plot. *Enn.* 4.8 [6] 1; more generally, see Turcan, "Une allusion de Plotin aux idoles cultuelles," esp. 310, regarding *Enn.* 2.2 [47] 14; Fowden, *Egyptian Hermes*, 129–30. The objection in *Vit. Plot.* 10 is probably, as Edwards (*Neoplatonic Saints*, 21 n. 113) intuits, along the lines of vegetarianism.

68. Plot. *Enn.* 2.9 [33] 12.4–5.

69. "Every soul is a child (of the Father)" (ibid., 16.10); see Harder, "Plotins Abhandlung," 301–2.

70. Armstrong, "Plotinus and Christianity," 84; idem, "Man in the Cosmos," 6, 10.

71. Plot. *Enn.* 2.9 [33] 15.1–4.

72. See, for example, the descriptions of the Carpocratians (Ir. *Haer.* 1.25.4; Clem. Al. *Strom.* 3.2.10) or Borborites (Epiph. *Pan.* 26.4–5); Grant, "Early Christians and Gnostics," 178–80. Less skeptical of the descriptions are Gero, "With Walter Bauer on the Tigris"; van den Broek, "Sexuality and Sexual Symbolism." On the Greco-Roman background of such charges, see Grant's survey of the evidence ("Charges of Immorality"). Scholars occasionally interpret the philosophical libertines attacked by Porphyry at *Abst.* 1.42 to be Gnostics (e.g., Clark, "Translate into Greek," 129), but the passage contains no hint of Gnostic thought.

73. Like Epicurus, they posit ἡδονή as a τέλος; even more "childishly" than him, they assault providence and, particularly, "self-control" (τὸ σωφρονεῖν—Plot. *Enn.* 2.9 [33] 15.5–18). See further C. Schmidt, *Plotins Stellung*, 72–73.

74. Plot. *Enn.* 2.9 [33] 15.28–40.

75. C. Schmidt, *Plotins Stellung*, 34, and H. Jackson, "Seer Nikotheos," 253, respectively; see also Dörrie, "Schultradition," 4; Turner, "Introduction: *Zostrianos*," 211, 224–25; idem, *Sethian Gnosticism and the Platonic Tradition*, 295. Cf. Katz, "Plotinus and the Gnostics," 293.

76. See below, Chapter 5, "The Strange and the Dead."

77. Plot. *Enn.* 2.9 [33] 6.1–10.

78. Cf. ibid., 4.3 [27] 16.1–3, 24.9–12.

79. Ibid.., 2.9 [33] 6.10–43.

80. Ibid., 4.1–3 (regarding Plat. *Phaedr.* 246c), 17.1.

81. Plot. *Enn.* 2.9 [33] 6.28, 6.44–53 (see also Roloff, *Plotin, Die Gross-schrift*, 174, *pace* H. Jackson, "Seer Nikotheos," 254 n. 4). 6.52; see also Plot. *Enn.*, 10.13–14; C. Schmidt, *Plotins Stellung*, 14–15.

82. Plot. *Enn.* 2.9 [33] 6.54.

83. Ibid., 6.48, 6.37, 8.6. Plotinus never explicitly spells out what a proper approach to philosophical problems and "ancient authorities" looks like, but we can imagine it probably resembled something like his remarks at the beginning of *On Time and Eternity* (3.7 [45] 1.13–17): "Now we must consider that some of the blessed philosophers of ancient times have found out the truth (i.e., about time and eternity); but it is proper to investigate (ἐπισκέψασθαι) which of them have attained it most completely, and how we could reach an understanding (σύνεσις) about these things."

84. Ibid., 2.9 [33] 13.10–11, 18.36, 13.13–14.

85. Ibid., 9.47, 27, 47.

86. Ibid., 9.56, 10.11–12.

87. Ibid., 10.12–13; see also the closing of ch. 14, and the personal tone he adopts to his reader there (C. Schmidt, *Plotins Stellung*, 33).

88. Recently, see Dunderberg, "Valentinian Teachers"; Kalligas, "Plotinus Against the Gnostics," 116. For Plotinus as targeting Ptolemaean Valentinianism, see Igal, "The Gnostics and 'The Ancient Philosophy,'" 142–44; for a writing of Valentinus instead, see Sinnige, *Six Lectures*, 71.

89. On the other hand, a group of Valentinians reading Sethian literature could still be possible (Evangeliou, "Plotinus's Anti-Gnostic Polemic," 126 n. 15; Pépin, "Theories of Procession," 297; Tardieu, "Les gnostiques," 538).

90. For Barbelo-Gnostics, see C. Schmidt, *Plotins Stellung*, 52–57, 63. Puech, "Plotin et les gnostiques," 161, 173–74, suggests Archontics, but considers the possibility of Valentinian influence on the group Plotinus dealt with (174). See also Turner, *Sethian Gnosticism and the Platonic Tradition*, 40.

91. See discussion in the Appendix; further, see Bousset, *Hauptprobleme*, 186–87; Schoeps, *Urgemeinde*, 39. Elsas, meanwhile, considers that some of the (Christian) Elchasaites became the pagan Hermetic (non-Christian) *viri novi* attacked by Arnobius; influenced by Numenius, they also encountered Plotinus (*Neuplatonische und gnostische Weltablehnung*, 242). Majercik also invokes Arnobius's evidence, suggesting instead that the *viri novi* were non-Christian Gnostics dependent on Porphyry (Majercik, "Porphyry and Gnosticism," 289–90). The parallels adduced here are interesting, but hardly definitive proof.

92. Hipp. *Haer.* 9.13.1 (Markovich); see H. Jackson, "Seer Nikotheos," 257; Quispel, "Plotinus and the Jewish Gnōstikoi."

93. C. Schmidt, *Plotins Stellung*, 11; Katz, "Plotinus and the Gnostics," 293 n. 31. Gnostics may have even been among his teachers (Narbonne, *Plotinus in Dialogue*, 2 n. 3).

94. C. Schmidt, *Plotins Stellung*, 14, 84.

95. Bos, "World-views in Collision," 22; Armstrong, "Plotinus," 210; Dillon, "Self-Definition," 71 (on Plot. *Enn.* 2.9 itself).

96. Plot. *Enn.* 2.9 [33] 10.3–13.

97. Puech, "Plotin et les gnostiques," 182; Narbonne, *Plotinus in Dialogue*, 69. See also Bos, "World-views in Collision," 23; Roloff, *Plotin, Die Gross-schrift*, 189; D. O'Meara, "Gnosticism and the Making of the World," 376; Attridge, "Gnostic Platonism," 3–4; H. Jackson, "Seer Nikotheos," 252; Corrigan, "Positive and Negative Matter," 25. Igal disagrees, arguing that Plotinus is being ironic, recalling Plato's critique of his poet "friends" in *Resp.* X 595b9–10 by way of Arist. *Eth. Nic.* 1.6.1096a12–17 ("The Gnostics and 'The Ancient Philosophy,'" 140, an argument followed by Edwards, "*Aidōs*," 231–32). Cilento distinguishes the "friends" from the "intimate pupils" of the same passage, and proposes a rupture between them in the school (*Plotino: Paideia*, 244; similarly, see Corrigan, "Positive and Negative Matter," 43–44 n. 77; Rasimus, "Porphyry and the Gnostics," 104). Roloff (*Gross-schrift*, 189) and D. O'Meara ("Gnosticism and the Making of the World," 376 n. 39) doubt this; they do, however, agree that the "friends" and "pupils" are different.

98. See Sinnige, *Six Lectures*, 62, regarding Porph. *Vit. Plot.* 13.10–17, 18.7–23. Thus, treatises 27–29 (Plot. *Enn.* 4.3–5), those immediately prior to the Großschrift, deal with the Soul, while 22–23 (6.4–5) and esp. 32 (5.5) deal with the "omnipresence of Intelligible Being." While Plotinus's prior acquaintance with the Gnostics is probable, it is impossible to say whether the Roman group was already working with Plotinus before Porphyry's arrival. Puech has suggested that Gnostics were part of Plotinus's Roman circle from its inception in 244 ("Plotin et les gnostiques," 182–83, followed by Narbonne, *Plotinus in Dialogue*, 5 n. 16). However, it is also possible that the Roman Gnostics only came to the seminar and circulated their texts after Porphyry became involved (Tardieu, "Recherches," 112).

99. *Pace* Rasimus, "Porphyry and the Gnostics," 105.

100. Plot. *Enn.* 2.9 [33] 9.57–59. The significance of Christian withdrawal from civic religious life is highlighted by J. Perkins, *Roman Imperial Identities*, 34–38.

101. Plot. *Enn.* 2.9 [33] 9.47.

102. His defense of παιδεία coupled with argumentative method is paralleled in Alexander of Lycopolis's criticism of Manichaeism (Alex. Lyc. ch. 10.12–13, p. 17, ch. 16.13, p. 23, ch. 12.2 p. 18 [Brinkmann]; notes ad loc. in the edition of van der Horst and Mansfeld (58 n. 212). See also Turner, *Sethian Gnosticism and the Platonic Tradition*, 295.

103. Plot. *Enn.* 2.9 [33] 10.11–12; J. Cook, *Interpretation of the New Testament*, 88, 156.

104. E.g., Just. Mart. *Dial. Tryph.* 2.

CHAPTER 3

1. Plot. *Enn.* 2.9 [33] 10.12–13; Porphyry calls the *Apocalypse of Zoroaster* νέον τὸ βιβλίον παραδεικνὺς πεπλασμένον (*Vit. Plot.* 16).

2. Per Mazur, "Platonizing Sethian Gnostic Background," 178 n. 8 (the Sethian texts have "very little conceptually in common" with contemporary apocalyptic literature).

3. The lion's share are overviews: Fallon, "Gnostic Apocalypses"; Krause, "Die literarischen Gattungen der Apokalypsen"; Kippenberg, "Vergleich jüdischer, christlicher, und gnostischer Apokalyptik"; Peel, "Gnostic Eschatology"; Frankfurter, "Legacy of Jewish Apocalypses"; Pearson, "Jewish Sources," 458ff; idem, "From Jewish Apocalypticism to Gnosis." More provisionary are Helmbold, "Gnostic Elements in the 'Ascension of Isaiah'"; Janssens, "Apocalypses de Nag Hammadi"; Rowland, "Apocalyptic: The Disclosure," 790–97; Scopello, "Contes apocalyptiques et apocalypses philosophiques"; Turner, *Sethian Gnosticism and the Platonic Tradition*, 87–91; Markschies, *Gnosis*, 52–55 (omitting the Platonizing apocalypses); Logan, *The Gnostics*, 68–71 (omitting *Allogenes* and *Marsanes*). Attridge, "Valentinian and Sethian Apocalyptic Traditions," largely recapitulates the conclusions of Turner while updating Frankfurter and Fallon. Stroumsa does not address the problem of genre (*Another Seed*, esp. 19). Most in depth is Kaler, *Flora Tells a Story*.

4. Schenke, "Das sethianische System"; idem, "Phenomenon." The Sethian texts apud Schenke are: *Apocryphon of John* (NHC II,1; III,1; IV,1; BG,2), *Hypostasis of the Archons* (NHC II,4), *Egyptian Gospel* (NHC III,2; IV,2), *Apocalypse of Adam* (NHC V,5), *Three Steles of Seth* (NHC VII,5), *Zostrianos* (NHC VIII,1), *Melchizedek* (NHC IX,1), *Thought of Norea* (NHC IX,2), *Marsanes* (NHC X), *Allogenes* (NHC XI,3), *Trimorphic Protennoia* (NHC XIII,1), the *Untitled Treatise* in the Bruce Codex, and the individuals mentioned in Ir. *Haer.* 1.29 and Epiph. *Pan.* chapters 26, 39, and 40 (on the Borborites-Gnostics, Sethians, and Archontics, respectively). The Sethians known to Hippolytus (*Haer.* 5.19–22 [Markovich]) seem to have nothing in common with this tradition (thus Pearson, *Ancient Gnosticism*, 52).

5. MacRae, "Seth," 21; Pearson, "Figure of Seth," 489; Stroumsa, *Another Seed*, 125; Rasimus, *Paradise Reconsidered*, 36. Other features are: identification with the pneumatic seed of Seth, the savior; appearance of the divine trinity of Father, Mother, and Son (Adamas); division of the aeon of Barbelo (the Mother) into the triad of Kalyptos, Protophanes, and Autogenes; appearance of the "Four Luminaries"—Harmozel, Oroiaele, Davithai, and Eleleth—who serve as dwelling places for Adam, Seth, and Seth's seed; the presences of the demiurge, Yaldabaoth, who tries to destroy the seed of Seth; the division of history into three ages with corresponding saviors; the presence of the ministers of the Four Luminaries: Gamaliel, Gabriel, Samblo, and Abrasax; and use of the name "Pigeradamas" for Adam. Turner adds mention of the mysterious "rite of the Five Seals" (*Sethian Gnosticism and the Platonic Tradition*, 64).

6. Brakke, *The Gnostics*, 41–42.

7. Wisse, "Stalking," 575, is wary of systematizing a chaotic set of mythologoumena (cf. Stroumsa, *Another Seed*, 5). Luttikhuizen, "Sethianer?" 80–84, argues that *Ap. John* contains fewer Sethian features than a reader of Schenke would expect, but this is hardly surprising given the

composite nature of the text, woven together from Ophite and Barbeloite traditions that were later Sethianized, as proposed by Logan and Rasimus (discussed below).

8. Layton, *Gnostic Scriptures*, xv, 5; idem, "Prolegomena," 341–44.

9. M. A. Williams, *Rethinking "Gnosticism"*, 90–93, 186–209; idem, "Was There a Gnostic Religion?" 77; King, *What Is Gnosticism?* 154–62.

10. Here I synthesize the (overlapping) discussions of Turner, "Sethian Gnosticism: A Literary History"; idem, *Sethian Gnosticism and the Platonic Tradition*, 255–301, 747–59; idem, "Typologies"; idem, "The Gnostic Sethians and Middle Platonism." For skepticism about the attempt to draw up a history of a social group based on such opaque texts, see Couliano, *Tree of Gnosis*, 68 n. 8; M. A. Williams, "Sethianism," 54–55; Pearson, *Ancient Gnosticism*, 99.

11. For the Barbelo-Gnostics, see Ir. *Haer.* 1.29. Turner rightly observed that Barbelo-Gnosticism must be a strain distinct from Sethianism, because Irenaeus's account (ca. 180 CE) describes the generation of the Mother Barbelo but nothing about Seth himself. Veneration of Seth must have a different origin, swallowing the Barbeloite tradition, so that our extant Sethian literature usually contains Barbeloite features (Sevrin, *Dossier baptismal séthien*, 275; Logan, *Gnostic Truth and Christian Heresy*, 29; Turner, *Sethian Gnosticism and the Platonic Tradition*, 266; Rasimus, *Paradise Reconsidered*, 34).

12. On *Zostrianos*, see Stroumsa, *Another Seed*, 102; Turner, *Sethian Gnosticism and the Platonic Tradition*, 182, 293; idem, "Introduction: Zostrianos," 210. Sieber's stance is not clear ("Introduction to *Zostrianos*," 28: it is "non-Christian, non-Jewish, philosophical Gnosticism" and its "author wrote for an audience that interpreted its cultic experience in terms of traditional Greek philosophy"). For *Marsanes* as a "pagan Greek revelation discourse," see Turner, "Introduction: *Marsanes*," 230. A similarly pagan designation for *Allogenes* and *Marsanes* is presumed by Turner's view of the treatises as a further movement away from traditional Sethian mythologoumena (Turner, *Sethian Gnosticism and the Platonic Tradition*, 179–82, 293; idem, "Introduction: *Marsanes*," 1, 163, 168; idem, "Introduction: Zostrianos," 138–39; idem, "Introduction: *Allogenes*," 115–17; idem, "Sethian Gnosticism: A Revised Literary History," 908). *Steles Seth* is problematic here because its metaphysics seems to be equally advanced as those of the other three treatises but it is also extremely focused on Sethian mythologoumena and salvation history, as Turner acknowledges ("Introduction: *Marsanes*," 173–74).

13. For the Sethian apocalypses as pagan, see Doresse, "Les apocalypses de Zoroatre"; Tardieu, "Les livres mis sous le nom de Seth," 209–10; Frankfurter, "Legacy of Jewish Apocalypses," 151; Pearson, "Gnosticism as Platonism," 60; idem, "From Jewish Apocalypticism to Gnosis," 150; idem, *Ancient Gnosticism*, 99–100; Abramowski, "Nicänismus und Gnosis," 561; Kaler, *Flora Tells a Story*, 146. For *Zostrianos*'s ostensible attempt to appeal to Plotinus, see Sieber, "Introduction to the Tractate *Zostrianus*," 239; Koschorke, "Paulus," 204 n. 69. For Turner, genre is a matter of "mutual legitimation of one authoritative tradition by another—and of both traditions as

divine revelation . . . making Sethian tradition appealing to philosophically-inclined non-Sethians, and making the Platonic tradition appealing to Sethians" ("Introduction: *Zostrianos*," 53; see also idem, "Sethian Gnosticism: A Literary History," esp. 56, 85; idem, *Sethian Gnosticism and the Platonic Tradition*, 292; idem, "Introduction: *Marsanes*," 30–31; idem, "Introduction: *Allogenes*," 33–34). See also Sieber, "Introduction to *Zostrianos*," 12; Pearson, "Introduction: *Marsanes*," 248; Frankfurter, "Legacy of Jewish Apocalypses," 160–61; idem, "Apocalypses Real and Alleged," 66; M. A. Williams, *Rethinking "Gnosticism"* 107; Attridge, "Gnostic Platonism," 23; idem, "Apocalyptic Traditions," 197, 205; Mazur, "Platonizing Sethian Gnostic Background," 177, 309 n. 61. Meanwhile, P. Perkins ("Christian Books and Sethian Revelations," 723) is skeptical, followed by Brankaer, "Concept of νοῦς," 79–80; eadem, "*Marsanes*." Brakke, *The Gnostics*, 87, refers to Turner's model as "very plausible," but hesitates to endorse it.

14. Rasimus, *Paradise Reconsidered*, 54–62. The "Ophite" texts include: *Eugnostos the Blessed* (NHC III,3), *The Sophia of Jesus Christ* (NHC III,4), *On the Origin of the World* (NHC II,5), *The Hypostasis of the Archons* (NHC II,4), sections of *The Apocryphon of John*, Irenaeus's testimony about "others [*alii*]" transmitting a Gnostic myth slightly different from that of the Barbelo-Gnostics (*Haer.* 1.30), and the "Ophite" Gnostics mentioned by the second-century Platonic critic of Christianity Celsus (Orig. *Cels.* 6.24–38). Borderline cases include *Test. Truth* NHC IX,3 and "Ophites" (Ps.-Ter. *Haer.* 2.1–4), the Peratae (Hipp. *Haer.* 4.2.1–3; 5.2; 5.12–18; 10.10), and the Naasseni (Hipp. *Haer.*, 5.6.3–4, 5.9.11–12). Rasimus uses Layton's term to refer to Ophite and Sethian traditions together as "Classic Gnosticism" (*Paradise Reconsidered*, 59), since they are worth distinguishing as a whole separate from Valentinian Gnosticism.

15. Following Logan's analysis of *Ap. John* as a third-century "Sethianization" of a text compiled from Barbeloite (theogony, cosmogony, Pronoia hymn) Ophite (anthropology), and Sethian (salvation history) sources (*Gnostic Truth and Christian Heresy*, 16–17; cf. Rasimus, *Paradise Reconsidered*, 279).

16. Thus excising *Hypostasis of the Archons*, *Thought of Norea*, and much of *Apocryphon of John* from analysis of Sethianism, following the argument of Rasimus. The reasons for considering these texts Sethian would be a concern with Sethian salvation history, the presence of Seth's sister Norea, and the appearance of Sethian or Barbeloite mythologoumena. First, the story of *Hyp. Arch.* (and much of *Ap. John*) deals with the "Ophite" Paradise narrative, not Sethian salvation history. Seth is mentioned but is not an actor (*Hyp. Arch.* NHC II,4.91.31–34). Second, Norea was popular enough in Gnostic literature in general that her presence in a text hardly indicates Sethian influence (Pearson, "Introduction: *The Thought of Norea*," 92). Finally, Barbeloite and Sethian mythologoumena are absent. An exception is the appearance in *Hyp. Arch.* of Eleleth, one of the Four Luminaries. In what is probably a later gloss on the manuscript, Eleleth does once claim to be one of the four "luminaries" (φωστήρ) (*Hyp. Arch.* NHC II,4.93.20). The text prefers to call this character a "great angel" (ⲛⲟϭ ⲛ̄ⲁⲅⲅⲉⲗⲟⲥ) (ibid., 93.2,

9, 13, 19; 94.3). Eleleth and the luminary Davithe were known to Egyptian magicians, since they are invoked in Coptic spells (Kropp, *Ausgewählte koptische Zaubertexte*, 2:xxxii, xliii [London MS Or. 5987, 6794], on which see Markschies, *Gnosis*, 96). Eleleth's appearance thus does not indicate robust Sethianism in *Hyp. Arch.* Meanwhile, *Thought of Norea* mentions the Autogenes aeon, a paternal principle called Adamas, and a feminine principle called ἔννοια, alongside four unnamed "helpers" (βοηθός); some have identified these as the Sethian luminaries (Schenke, "Phenomenon," 595; Pearson, *Ancient Gnosticism*, 78). Yet the text also shows Valentinian features (Pearson, "Introduction: *The Thought of Norea*," 91–93), and so is a hybrid work, not "pure" Sethianism.

17. Thus Logan, *Gnostic Truth and Christian Heresy*, 16–17, expanded on in Rasimus, *Paradise Reconsidered*.

18. Both the beginning and end of the text have the alternative title, "*Apocalypse* (ογωнε̄) *of Dositheos*" (Fallon, "Gnostic Apocalypses," 146; Pearson, "From Jewish Apocalypticism to Gnosis," 151; *pace* Janssens, "Apocalypses de Nag Hammadi," 72)—probably secondary scribal glosses (Goehring, "Introduction: *The Three Steles of Seth*," 371–72, following the argument of Robinson, "Three Steles," 133).

The reference to Dositheos has led some to suggest Samaritan influence on Sethianism, but what this would look like remains unclear (*pace* Schubert, "Problem und Wesen der jüdischen Gnosis," 3; Schenke, "Das sethianische System," 171–72, as well as Pearson, "Figure of Seth," 494; H. Jackson, "Seer Nikotheos," 259–60, 274).

19. Pearson, "Introduction: *Melchizedek*"; see also Lahe, *Gnosis und Judentum*, 315–24.

20. A propaedeutic Coptic text recently published by Gesine Schenke [Robinson] mentions "Sethians," Yaldabaoth, and angelic beings whose names resemble those known from Ophite tradition (*Koptische Buch*, plate 128; see also Pearson, *Ancient Gnosticism*, 53). The account is too brief and MS too lacunose to be of much use here. Meanwhile, the proximity of *Gos. Jud.* to Sethian tradition remains under debate and is beholden to how one restores key passages in the text; those who consider it "classic Sethianism" include DeConick, *Thirteenth Apostle*, 22–42; Rasimus, *Paradise Reconsidered*, 40 n. 109; Jennott, "*Gospel of Judas*," 72–73, but cf. G. Schenke [Robinson], "The *Gospel of Judas*"; Turner, "The Place of *The Gospel of Judas* in Sethian Tradition." In any case, a revelatory section in the middle of the text (*Gos. Jud.* TC 47.1–54.12) does discuss the Autogenes aeon, Barbelo, and the birth of the angels of chaos, a scene either derived from or indebted to a source shared with the *Egyptian Gospel*; see Turner, "The Place of *The Gospel of Judas* in Sethian Tradition," 199–201; further, see Jennott, "*Gospel of Judas*", 71, 95–97. Another treatise in TC is totally fragmentary, but does mention a character named "Allogenes" who is clearly identified with Jesus of Nazareth. It is thus probably Sethian (Pearson, *Ancient Gnosticism*, 97; cf. Rasimus, *Paradise Reconsidered*, 58). Jennott suggests "The Wilderness" as an alternate title, restoring πϫ[ⲁⲉⲓⲉ] instead of πϫ[ⲱⲱⲙⲉ | ⲛ̄ⲁⲗⲗⲟⲅⲉⲛⲏⲥ] ("*Gospel of Judas*", 106–7).

21. M. Smith, "On the History of ΑΠΟΚΑΛΥΠΤΩ," 19.

22. Collins, "Morphology," 9. For a summary of criticisms and defense of the definition, see idem, "Genre, Ideology, and Social Movements," 17; idem, *Apocalyptic Imagination*, 1–42; Sanders, "Genre," 454–55; Aune, *Prophecy*, 108–9; Yarbro Collins, "Introduction: Early Christian," 3–5; Kaler, *Flora Tells a Story*, 143. On the problem of genre with respect to apocalypse, see Hartman, "Survey," esp. 336–41; Sanders, "Genre"; Hellholm, *Das Visionenbuch des Hermas als Apokalypse*. Fletcher-Louis seeks to emphasize the importance of experience instead of literary convention in apocalyptic literature ("Religious Experience," 132–33); this problem will be revisited in Chapter 6.

23. E.g., Koch, *Rediscovery of Apocalyptic*, esp. 28–33; Vielhauer and Strecker, "Apocalypses and Related Subjects," esp. 549. Cf. the approach of Sacchi, which focuses on the problem of evil (*L'apocalittica guidaica*); see further Boccaccini, "Jewish Apocalyptic Tradition."

24. Rowland, *Open Heaven*; Carmignac, "Qu'est-ce que l'Apocalyptique?" 20; Hengel, *Judaism and Hellenism*, 1:210; Fletcher-Louis, *Luke-Acts: Angels*, 11; Kaler, *Flora Tells a Story*, 134–37.

25. Collins, *Apocalyptic Imagination*, 41–42; see also Hellholm, "Problem of the Apocalyptic Genre," 28; Aune, "Apocalypse," 87–91; idem, *Prophecy*, 109; Yarbro Collins, "Introduction: Early Christian," 7; eadem, *Cosmology and Eschatology*, 1–20.

26. Yarbro Collins, *Crisis*, 105; Rowland, *Open Heaven*, 26; Aune, *Prophecy*, 121; Stone, "Apocalyptic Literature," 434; Davies, "Social World," 269.

27. Exceptions are Rev and *Hermas*. See Collins, "Morphology," 11–12; Yarbro Collins, "Early Christian Apocalypses," 71. Surveys of pseudepigraphy in the ancient world include K. Aland, "Problem of Anonymity"; Brox, *Pseudepigraphie*; Collins, "Pseudonymity"; Speyer, *Literarische Fälschung*; Metzger, "Literary Forgeries"; Meade, *Pseudonymity*.

28. Sint, *Pseudonymität*, 71; Vielhauer and Strecker, "Apocalypses and Related Subjects," 515; Aune, *Prophecy*, 110; Collins, *Apocalyptic Imagination*, 40.

29. Aune, "Apocalypse," 84–86; McGinn, "Revelation," 526–27.

30. Speyer, *Literarische Fälschung*, 247.

31. Epiph. *Pan.* 40.7.6; *Unt.* 232.3–23.

32. *Mars.* NHC X,1.8.19.

33. Ibid., 10.13–18. As Poirier notes, the use of [ⲡⲁ]ϫⲉϥ indicates a change of speaker, probably a supernatural authority (e.g., an agent of the Barbelo), who addresses Marsanes in the first-person masculine singular. Pearson sees Marsanes as talking to his audience, with the use of the singular instead of the plural as a textual corruption. Turner mentions the problem but does not suggest a solution (Poirier, "Commentaire: *Marsanès*," 400; Pearson, "Notes: *Marsanes*," 278; Turner, "Introduction: *Marsanes*," 5).

34. *Mars.* NHC X,1.4.27–28, tr. Pearson (CGL); noted also by Turner, "Introduction: *Marsanes*," 4, 32–34.

35. *Mars.* NHC X,1.26.12–17, tr. Pearson; also 27.21–23, 39.18–41.7. Turner ("Introduction: *Marsanes*," 6–7) adds 10.12–27, 29.6–17. Pearson,

"Introduction: *Marsanes*," 234, recognizes the background of the paraenetic passages in apocalyptic literature as well as the nature of the distribution.

36. As noted by Turner, "Introduction: *Marsanes*," 8–9 (*pace* Mazur, "Platonizing Sethian Gnostic Background," 178 n. 8), on *Zost.* NHC VIII,1.4.14–7, 130.14–25; *Mars.* NHC X,1.29.7–13, 41.14–17; *Allogenes* NHC XI,3.68.16–20; *Steles Seth* NHC VII,5.121.12–14. The latter hardly constitutes, however, a missionary context.

37. *2 En.* 39; *4 Ezra* 14:13–18, 27–36; *2 Bar.* 31, 44–45, 76:4–77:1. For all three texts I have used the tr. in *OTP*. Each work is probably at least as early as the third century CE, and is thus admissible for comparison to the Sethian texts. For a first-century dating of *2 En.* and complete bibliography, see Orlov, "Origin of the Name 'Metatron,'" esp. 19–20. I follow Andersen (*OTP*, with Böttrich, "Recent Studies," 40; generally, see Charlesworth, "SNTS Pseudepigrapha Seminar," 316–18) in treating the "long" recension as prior to the "short" used by Vaillant (*Le livre des Secrets*, a treatment followed by Milik, *Books of Enoch*, 107–8). Both *4 Ezra* and *2 Bar.* probably date from the second century CE; see Klijn, "Introduction," 616–17; Metzger, "Introduction."

38. Turner, "Introduction: *Allogenes*," 30–31. While "there is nothing to suggest that the author was intended to be an identifiable ancient figure like Zostrianos" (31) and thus an "everyman" member of the elect seed of Seth, other apocalyptic motifs, such as book burial for posterity or superhuman life span (at least two hundred years in addition to the seer's age at the beginning of the text) imply a primeval setting for the narrative.

39. See below, Chapter 4, "Seth and His Avatars."

40. Contrasted with Zostrianos's pre-ascent sorrows by Turner, "Commentary: *Zostrianos*," 49; Frankfurter, "Legacy of Jewish Apocalypses," 159, recalls *Allogenes* NHC XI, 3.59.1–29; cf. *Apoc. Ab.* 17. The latter text can be dated to the first or second centuries CE, given its knowledge of the destruction of the second temple (ch. 27), possible citation in Ps.-Clem. *Recogn.* 1.33, and knowledge of Epiphanius of Salamis (*Pan.* 39.5.1); this argument follows Rubinkiewicz, "Introduction: Apocalypse," 683, in *OTP*.

41. Turner (CGL) translates as "has become"; Scopello (BCNH) as "allé au-delà de."

42. *Allogenes* NHC XI,3.50.8–36.

43. *1 En.* 60:3–5; *2 En.* 21:2–4; *Apoc. Zeph.* 6; *Apoc. Ab.* 13–14 ; *2 Apoc. Jas.* NHC V,4.57.17–29; *Apoc. Peter* NHC VII,3.72.22. The seer's fear is also implied in descriptions of frightening angels: *2 En.* 37; *Seph. raz.* pp. 43–44 (Morgan); *3 En.* 1:7; Schultz, "Angelic Opposition," 285; Himmelfarb, "Heavenly Ascent and the Relationship," 84. For soothing words, see *2 En.* 1:8, 21:3, *4 Ezra* 10:28–37, *Apoc. Ab.* 10:6; Himmelfarb, *Ascent to Heaven*, 102–14; cf. Aune, *Prophecy*, 117. The text *1 En.* is a composite work, most of which has fragments attested at Qumran, but whose *Similitudes* probably go back to the first century CE; *3 En.* is later (fifth- to eighth-century CE at the earliest), but it is worth citing as possibly containing earlier source material (Greenfield and Stone, "Books of Enoch," esp. 99). *2 Apoc. Jas.* and *Apoc. Peter* are both undatable on internal criteria, but are probably

contemporaneous to the Sethian material (Hedrick, "(Second) Apocalypse of James," 108; Desjardins, "Introduction," 214).

44. "A work that can be accomplished in obedience to that reason which we share with the Gods is attended with no fear (ἐκεῖ οὐδὲν δεινόν)" (Marc. Aur. 7.53).

45. Sir 3:20. For the perils of esoteric lore in rabbinic texts, see m. Hag. 2:1; t. Hag. 2:1; y. Hag. 2:1 77a–b; b. Hag. 13a–14b; further, see Maier, "Gefährdungsmotiv," esp. 26–28. For the Hekhalot literature, see *Hekh. Rab.* (Schäfer, *Synopse*, ch. 259), *Hekh. Zut.* (Schäfer, *Synopse*, chs. 405–9). See also *ShirShabb* (4Q405) 23:12–13; Alexander, *Mystical Texts*, 20; Fletcher-Louis, *Luke-Acts: Angels*, 135 n. 156; *pace* Himmelfarb, *Ascent to Heaven*, 135 n. 23; Rowland, "Apocalypse: The Disclosure," 788.

46. *Allogenes* NHC XI,3.52.7–28.

47. 2 *Bar.* 22:1, 43:1; *Apoc. Ab.* 16:4; see also CMC 13.5–9. An exception is Plotinus, per Mazur, "Platonizing Sethian Gnostic Background,"43 n. 35, 201, 284, regarding Plot. *Enn.* 5.5 [32] 8.9–13; 6.7 [38] 22.15. Yet for Plotinus, "empowerment" is not channeled from a heavenly revelator but appears to be a spontaneous product of ecstatic experience.

48. *Allogenes* NHC XI,3.57.24–39.

49. Frankfurter, "Legacy of Jewish Apocalypses," 159 recalls 4 *Ezra* 5:20–22; additionally, see 4 *Ezra* 5:13, 6:29–34; 2 *Bar.* 9, 2.5–6. Cf. also Ezra's consumption of flowers at 4 *Ezra* 9:24–25, 13:50–51; cf. Turner, *Sethian Gnosticism and the Platonic Tradition*, 674–75.

50. As in Turner, "Introduction: *Allogenes*," 30–31.

51. *Mars.* NHC X,1.18.14–17.

52. As suggested by M. A. Williams, *Rethinking "Gnosticism"*, 146, and Valantasis, "Nag Hammadi and Asceticism," 185–87.

53. *Allogenes* NHC XI,3.68.16–31.

54. 2 *En.* 33:8. See also 1 *En.* 68:1–2; 2 *En.* 9–12, 48:6–7, 23, 33, 47:1–2, 54; 4 *Ezra* 12:35–39; *Asc. Is.* 9.22 (thus reading *Asc. Is.* as a unified text—see further R. Hall, "Isaiah's Ascent"; Bauckham, *The Fate of the Dead*, 368–80; *pace* Himmelfarb, *Ascent to Heaven*, 55, 135 n. 30); *Ap. John* NHC II,1.31.28–34; *Disc. 8–9* NHC VI,6.61–63. The theme is popular in Sethianism: *Gos. Eg.* NHC III,2.68.1–69.5; *Apoc. Adam* NHC V,5.85; *Zost.* NHC VIII,1.130.1. Stroumsa suggests that the three "steles of Seth" are meant to recall the three *eschata* of Sethian salvation history in *Gos. Eg.* and *Apoc. Adam* (*Another Seed*, 112). See also Fallon, "Gnostic Apocalypses," 125; Meade, *Pseudonymity*, 78 (an exhaustive list); on the specific motif of twin steles out of stone and clay (the first to survive a flood, the second fire, thus preserving antediluvian wisdom), see Stroumsa, *Another Seed*, 106, discussing *Jub.* 8:17–19 (Enoch as scribe); *L.A.E.* 49–50; Jos. *Ant.* 1.71; Rasimus, *Paradise Reconsidered*, 192–93.

55. Adler, introduction, 13; Collins, "Pseudonymity," 340.

56. Cf. Meade, *Pseudonymity*, 83; Gruenwald, "Knowledge and Vision," 72; idem, *Apocalyptic*, 12.

57. A virgin birth?

58. *Zos.* NHC VIII,1.1.5–31.

59. Ibid., 2.1–3.13–28. The rest of the pericope, identifying Heracles' nephew Iolaos as the father of Zostrianos, shows that the seer's community is probably Hellenic, and their "customs" consist of the traditional Hellenic cult. Like the *Apocalypse of Abraham*, Zostrianos appears to show the conversion of a sage born in a polytheistic community to a type of Jewish Christianity (Burns, *"Apocalypse of Zostrianos* and Iolaos," 36–37, 39).

60. Turner ("Commentary: *Zostrianos,*" 493) recalls 2 *En.* 1:3; see also 4 *Ezra* 3:2–11, 4:12; 2 *Bar.* 5:1–4; *Apoc. Ab.* 3, 6; *Apoc. Enosh. ap.* CMC 58.8–16.

61. On transmogrifying clouds, see Pleše, *Poetics,* 161–71.

62. *Zost.* NHC VIII,1.4.20–31.

63. *1 En.* 14:8–9; *2 En.* 3:2–3; *T. Ab.* 9:8; *Apoc. Peter* (*Eth.*) 1, 6; cf. *Apoc. Adam* NHC V,5.69.19–21, 71.8–10, 75.17–21; *Gos. Jud.* TC 57.22–27; (*Allogenes*) TC 62.9–15. Cf. 2 Kgs 2:2–12; Jos. *Ant.* 9.28.

64. LS: "as knowledge"; BFP: "pour instruire."

65. *Zost.* NHC VIII,1.129.22–130.13.

66. Turner, "Introduction: *Zostrianos,*" 55, 58 recalling *Steles Seth* NHC VII,5; *1 En.* 81; 4 *Ezra* 14:42–15:1.

67. *1 En.* 12:4, 37:4, 92:1; *Jub.* 4:17–19; B. Ḥag. 15a.

68. A difficulty for this reading is the odd choice of the wooden tablets (P. Perkins, "Christian Books," 718–19, as well as Brankaer, "The Concept of νοῦς," 79–80). Usually the texts are made of grander or sterner stuff (*Apoc. Adam ap.* CMC 49; *Apoc. Enosh ap.* CMC 54.12–19; *Seph. Raz.* p. 17). However, Zostrianos's academic musings are interwoven with extensive doxologies, and it was not unusual to inscribe prayers on wooden boards (Jenkins, "The Prayer of the Emanations").

69. *Asc. Is.* 10.24; Helmbold, "Gnostic Elements in the 'Ascension of Isaiah,'" 224–25.

70. *Ap. John* NHC II,1.30.12.; *Trin. Prot.* NHC XIII,1.47.

71. Ir. *Haer.* 1.30.12. See also *Asc. Is.* (used by the Archontic Gnostics—Epiph. *Pan.* 40.2.2), esp. ch. 10.

72. *Asc. Is.* 3.13, 9.15, 10.8;

73. *Pist. Soph.*; *1* and 2 *Jeu*; Basilides (*ap.* Ir. *Haer.* 1.24.5–6); *Apoc. Paul* (NHC V,1.3.23); the classic invocation is Ir. *Haer.* 1.21.5 (Valentinian?) = Epiph. *Pan.* 36.2.1–6 (Heracleonites) = *1 Apoc. Jas.* NHC V,3.33.11–35.25.

74. *Man. Ps.-Bk.*51.24 (Alberry).

75. Bousset, *Himmelsreise,* 5–23; Couliano, *Psychanodia,* 7–14.

76. "I evaded a myriad of torments which almost killed me" (*Zost.* NHC VIII,1.123.2–10).

77. *Zost.* NHC VIII,1.130.13–132.5.

78. Pearson, "Jewish Sources," 445; cf. Speyer, *Literarische Fälschung,* 262–63.

79. Epiph. *Pan.* 26.1.2–1.3 (tr. Layton, *Gnostic Scriptures,* modified). See also ibid., 11.12–12.1: "They blaspheme not only Abraham, Moses, Elijah and the whole choir of prophets, but the God who chose them as well. And they have ventured countless other forgeries (πλασθέντα γραφεῖα)."

80. Epiph. *Pan.* 39.5.1. Pearson suggests ("Jewish Sources," 446–47) that the Mosaic books could be the *Testament of Moses* and *Apocalypse of Moses*. The *Apocalypse Attributed to Abraham* is probably not the *Apocalypse of Abraham* extant in Slavonic, since Theodore bar Konai reports (as discussed in Puech, "Fragments retrouvés," 273) that the Audians (also making use of Sethian literature) possessed a book by the same title, but with Gnostic doctrines (pertaining to the creation of the world by "darkness" and other powers) not present in the Slavonic text.

81. Epiph. *Pan.* 40.2.2.

82. Ibid., 40.7.6–7: "they produced many forgeries in telling their stories and fabricating blasphemies against the true God Almighty (πολλά ἐστιν ἃ μυθοποιοῦντες πλαστῶς ἐκτυποῦσι, βλάσφημά τε πλάττοντες)." Cf. Origen's dismissal of Gnostic accounts of cosmogenesis as "absurdas fabulas" (*Princ.* 1.8.2).

83. *Pist. Soph.* 3.134 (Schmidt and MacDermot); Milik, *Books of Enoch*, 99; Pearson, "Jewish Sources," 449. Together with *Melch.* NHC IX,1.12.8, this is the only explicit reference to Enoch in Gnostic literature (cf. Turner, *Sethian Gnosticism and the Platonic Tradition*, 237–38).

84. *Melch.* NHC IX,1.12.8.

85. S. Lieu, *Manichaeism*, 33; Reeves, *Heralds*; Himmelfarb, "Revelation and Rapture," 79–82; Pearson, "Jewish Sources," 450–51; Attridge, "Valentinian and Sethian Apocalyptic Traditions," 199–202; Tigchelaar, "Baraies on Mani's Rapture." There is no need to assume that these texts originated in Jewish scribal circles; rather, they are probably Manichaean appeals to the authoritative tradition of Jewish scribal culture, although it remains quite possible that such texts actually existed (cf. Frankfurter, "Apocalypses Real and Alleged").

86. CMC 48.16–50.7, 52.1–60.13.

87. Thus Tigchelaar, "Baraies on Mani's Rapture."

88. Such appeals to Jewish and Christian traditions and authorities are thus hardly "not conceived as part of a consistent, organized, and acknowledged tradition," nor constitute a "rebellion" against "historical process" (*pace* Kalligas, "Plotinus Against the Gnostics," 125).

89. See above, Chapter 1, "Conclusion."

90. See also King, *Secret Revelation*, 53, on *Allogenes*: "while the heavenly revelation itself is Gnostic, the stages of ascent were evidently meant to evoke the readers' or audiences' respect for traditional Jewish apocalyptic ascent narratives."

91. For discussion of the archetypes underlying the mythical figures of the apocalypses, see Aune, *Prophecy*, 122–26; Collins, "Sage"; idem, "Cosmos and Salvation," 135.

92. J. Z. Smith, "Wisdom and Apocalyptic," 86 (italics mine).

93. Dan 1:4, 1:17, 1:20, 2:23, 5:11, 5:12, 5:14; *1 En.* 12:4, 37:4, 92:1; *Jub.* 4:17; *4 Ezra* 14:50; also 4:22, 5:22, 14:40; *2 Bar.* 38:4, 50:1. More occasionally, Enoch is described as a prophet: *1 En.* 81; *4 Ezra* 1:4–11; further, see Kvanvig, *Roots of Apocalyptic*, 147, 157.

94. Collins, "Cosmos and Salvation," 121–23; idem, *Apocalyptic Imagination*, 39; J. Z. Smith, "Wisdom and Apocalyptic," 74; Aune, *Prophecy*, 110–11; Müller, "Mantische Weisheit"; VanderKam, *Enoch*; Kvanvig, *Roots of Apocalyptic*; Davies, "Social World," 260–62.

95. Collins, "Sage," 349–50.

96. Couliano, *Psychanodia*, 6–7; idem, *Out of This World*, 156–57; cf. Aune, *Prophecy*, 118.

97. 2 *En.* 64:5.

98. CMC 64.8–65.22, tr. R. Cameron and Dewey, modified.

99. On authority, see Stone, "Apocalyptic Literature," 427; Collins, *Apocalyptic Imagination*, 42–43; Adler, introduction, 13. On higher knowledge, see Festugière, *Révélation*, 1:309–54; Hengel, *Judaism and Hellenism*, 1:210–18; Hadot, "Théologie, exégèse, révélation," 23–34; Adler, introduction, 13–19.

100. Stone, "Apocalyptic Literature," 428, offers a catalogue, but see esp. 4 *Ezra* 14.

101. "(Solomon's) knowledge follows from the use of his natural reasoning. . . . While sapiential revelation is immanent, channeled through the natural human processes of thought, apocalyptic revelation is ecstatic, and conferred from outside" (Collins, "Cosmos and Salvation," 139).

102. Idem, *Apocalyptic Imagination*, 41; cf. idem, "Morphology," 9, 12.

103. Rowland, *Open Heaven*, 21; for critique, see Yarbro Collins, "Review: Rowland, *The Open Heaven*"; cf. Rowland's later discussion of "a revelation direct from God through vision or through divine emissary" ("Apocalyptic: The Disclosure," 780); cf. Fletcher-Louis, "Religious Experience," 131–32, 142.

104. Lincoln, *Theorizing Myth*, 3–28; see also Morgan, *Myth and Philosophy*, 17–19.

105. Emp. frgs. b3.1–5, b114 (DK); Parm. frgs. b2.1, b8.1–2 (DK), cit. in Lincoln, *Theorizing Myth*, 31–32. On unverifiability, see Brisson, *How Philosophers Saved Myths*, 23. Morgan, *Myth and Philosophy*, 87, stresses that for Parmenides, even myth is, like all discourse, subject to the deficiencies of language.

106. Democ. Frg. b297 (DK), my tr. See also Lincoln, *Theorizing Myth*, 30; Kobusch, "Wiederkehr des Mythos," 45.

107. For innocuous use of the term and its cognates in Plato's works, see, e.g., *Men.* 13i; *Theaet.* 197d, 200c; *Resp.* VI 485 d, 9 588 b–d; *Soph.* 239 d–e; *Leg.* II 668e, XI 933b; *Tim.* 26e. For exhaustive data and analysis on the occurrence of μῦθος in Plato, see Brisson, *Plato the Myth Maker*, 141–52.

108. Willms, *EIKΩN*, 2; S. Saïd, "Deux noms," 311–13, 319–23.

109. For complete survey, see Brisson, *Plato the Myth Maker*, 145–52; Janka, "MYTHOS," 22–42, describes context more fully.

110. E.g., Plat. *Symp.* 205b8–c10; idem, *Phaedo* 60b–61b; see further Brisson, *Plato the Myth Maker*, 40–48, 147–48.

111. For a survey, see Willms, *EIKΩN*, 2ff (esp. n. 7); S. Saïd, "Deux noms," 313; Pender, "Plato on Metaphors and Models," 55ff.

112. Plat. *Resp.* X 598b. For the association of εἴδωλα with μίμησις and φαντάσματα, see *Resp.* X 596b–e and elsewhere in Plato's works: *Alcib.* 133a; *Phaedr.* 255d; *Resp.* VII 509e–510a, 515a; X 598 e; *Soph.* 239d–240a, 264c (Willms, *EIKΩN*, 14–21; S. Saïd, "Deux noms," 315–18; Pépin, "L'épisode du portrait de Plotin," 302, to which I am indebted for these citations; see also Struck, *Birth of the Symbol*, 54; Pasquier, "La réflexion démiurgique," 649–50).

113. *Soph.* 235d–236c.

114. *Pace* S. Saïd, "Deux noms," 323.

115. Plat. *Pol.* 277d–279a. 277d, tr. Rowe (in Cooper and Hutchinson, eds., *Plato*). Cf. Plat. *Tim.* 52c.

116. Pender, "Plato on Metaphors and Models," 70, on Plat. *Pol.* 278a–e; Willms (*EIKΩN*, 3) also recalls Plat. *Men.* 80 a–c; idem, *Tim.* 28 c–29 d; Dörrie and Baltes, *Platonismus in der Antike*, 4:258, recall the metaphor of the divided line, esp. Plat. *Resp.* 510b. This distinction is a Platonic innovation (and not always observed: *Tim.* 92c).

117. For εἰκών as shadow or reflection, see Plat. *Phaedo* 99e; *Resp.* III 402b–c, VI 509d–510e; as a copy, see idem, *Tim.* 29b–c, 37d, 92c; *Resp.* 402c6. For the necessary deficiency between image and referent, see idem, *Crat.* 432d, 439a–b; *Resp.* VII 533a. For the problematic ontological status of likeness, see idem, *Soph.* 240b.

118. Plat. *Resp.* VI 506d–e; idem, *Leg.* X 897d–e and *Crit.* 107b, cit. Pender, "Plato on Metaphors and Models."

119. Pender, "Plato on Metaphors and Models," 62; see also Plat. *Symp.* 215a ff (Alcibiades' speech); cf. Plat. *Leg.* VI 773c–d, X 903 a–b.

120. Plat. *Resp.* III 395b8–d3, X 605a–b; idem, *Tim.* 70d7–e5; Brisson, *How Philosophers Saved Myths*, 18. Cf. Tarrant, speculating that myth's effectiveness derives from an ability to stir recollection of the soul's preincarnate contemplation of the forms ("Myth as a Tool of Persuasion," 27; similarly, see Morgan, *Myth and Philosophy*, 233).

121. Plat. *Resp.* II 376e–377c; see also III 386b–c, X 603b; idem, *Leg.* II 664a, cit. Lincoln, *Theorizing Myth*, 229 (Plat. *Pol.* 304d, on state control of rhetoric, is a stretch). Morgan rightfully calls these "educational" myths, as opposed to "philosophical" myths that deal with eschatology and cosmogony (*Myth and Philosophy*, 162–64). However, the former are not entirely distinct from "philosophical" myths, since they operate with similar tools for similar purposes, i.e., using images to provoke good behavior.

122. Plat. *Resp.* III 392a, following Brisson, *Plato the Myth Maker*, 91–115, 96–98; more specifically, see 386b, 387c–389b, 389d, 393c–d; *Resp.* II 382d. Cf. Plat. *Crit.* 110a. On Plato's use of myth to discuss eschatology, see Aune, "Apocalypse of John," 75–76; Morgan, *Myth and Philosophy*, 185–241.

123. Plat. *Gorg.* 523a, tr. Zeyl (in Cooper and Hutchinson, eds., *Plato*).

124. Ibid., 524a–b, 527a. For confidence in verifying myths, see also Plat. *Resp.* II 377a8, 377d2–e3; idem, *Crat.* 408b6–d4.

125. Morgan is thus right to emphasize the philosophical context and intended audience of each Platonic myth (*Myth and Philosophy*, 158–61),

and the following analysis agrees with hers as regards their purpose and function.

126. Plat. *Resp.* II 377d–e, tr. Reeve (in Cooper and Hutchinson, eds., *Plato*).

127. Thus Plat. *Resp.* X 614a, "and these things must also be heard, if both are to receive in full what they are owed by the argument"; see idem, *Gorg.* 523a. See also Morgan, *Myth and Philosophy*, 187, 190–91, 197–99, 209–10, 240–41; Kobusch, "Wiederkehr des Mythos," esp. 46–48.

128. Thus also Willms, *EIKΩN*, 5–10.

129. Esp. Plat. *Tim.* 29b–d; also 30b, 48d, 53d, 55d, 56a, 57d, 90e; see Tarrant, "Myth as a Tool of Persuasion," 24–25; Morgan, *Myth and Philosophy*, 271–77; Brisson, *Plato the Myth Maker*, 129ff; cf. Burnyeat, "*Eikōs Muthos.*"

130. Plat. *Phaedo* 108d, 114c–d; idem, *Gorg.* 493a–c; this argument is in general agreement with Coulter, *Literary Microcosm*, 35; Tarrant, "Myth as a Tool of Persuasion," esp. 21.

131. An exception is Plat. *Tim.* 26e, where Critias assures Socrates that the story of Atlantis will not be "a made-up myth, but a true account (πλασθέντα μῦθον ἀλλ᾽ ἀληθινὸν λόγον)."

132. Colotes' (fourth or third century BCE) attack on the *Myth of Er*; see Macrob. *Comm. somn. Scip.*1.1.5–1.9, 1.4.1 (Stahl); Procl. *Comm. Remp.* 2.96.2ff (Kroll).

133. His immediate predecessor, Philo, wrote so much about allegory that space does not permit a discussion of him here. Suffice to say that his approach is grounded in a Platonic epistemology similar to that here assigned to Plutarch (see, e.g., Dawson, *Allegorical Readers*, 73–126). Philo also agrees with Plutarch et al. in using the term πλάσμα to refer to mythological "fiction" (e.g., *Prov.* 2.66).

134. The word ἀλληγορία means "to say something other than what one means to say" (Dawson, *Allegorical Readers*, 3). Dawson (ibid., 5) significantly distinguishes allegory from metaphor, etymology, and personification by emphasizing its drawn-out, narrative aspect. Thus also Quint. *Inst.* 8.6.44, 9.24.46, cit. Coulter, *Literary Microcosm*, 69. On ancient allegory, see Tate, "History of Allegorism"; Pépin, *Mythe et Allégorie*; Coulter, *Literary Microcosm*, 19–31; Simonetti, *Lettera E/O Allegoria*; Lamberton, *Homer*; Dawson, *Allegorical Readers*; Brisson, *How Philosophers Saved Myths*; Morgan, *Myth and Philosophy*, 62–67, 98; Struck, *Birth of the Symbol*, esp. 1–20; idem, "Allegory, Aenigma, and Anti-Mimesis."

135. Plut. *Adol. poet. aud.* 19e, tr. Babbitt (LCL); see Pépin, *Mythe et allégorie*, 181–82; Brisson, *How Philosophers Saved Myths*, 58–59, 64. Plutarch also of course employs allegory, although he does not call it such (*Is. Os.* 376f–377b).

136. For discussion of allegory in the first Stoics, Ps.-Heraclitus (first century CE?), and Cornutus (second century CE), see Pépin, *Mythe et Allégorie*, 159–67; Most, "Cornutus and Stoic Allegoresis," 2018, 2027; Dawson, *Allegorical Readers*, 23–72; Struck, *Birth of the Symbol*, 111–56; Brisson, *How Philosophers Saved Myths*, 44–55, 71–74.

137. Plut. *Is. Os.* 363d–364e, 365b–368f, 37e–f, 373d–f; Euseb. *Praep. ev.* 3.1–2 (Mras). For a defense of allegory, see Plut. *Is. Os.* 355b–d, 358e–359a. On Plutarch's discussion of the various types of allegory, see Verniere, *Symboles et mythes*, 11–38; Hardie, "Plutarch and the Interpretation of Myth," esp. 4761; Froidefond, "Plutarque," 212; Brisson, *How Philosophers Saved Myths*, 67–71; Hirsch-Luipold, *Plutarchs Denken*, 129–33.

138. Plut. *Is. Os.* 358e–359a, tr. Babbitt (LCL); Brisson, *How Philosophers Saved Myths*, 67.

139. Plut. *Adol. poet. aud.* 20b–c; idem, *E Delph.* 386a; idem, *Sera* 557f. On the latter, see Hirsch-Luipold, *Plutarchs Denken*, 140–41.

140. Hirsch-Luipold, *Plutarchs Denken*, esp. 6, 283–88.

141. Plut. *Is. Os.* 373a, on εἶδος; idem, *Pyth. orac.* 409d, on ἀνάκλασις.

142. Plut. *Pyth. orac.* 398d, 402, idem, *Def. orac.* 421a, 436d. Similarly, see idem, *Pyth. orac.*406c–e, on which see Pépin, *Mythe et Allégorie*, 179; Struck, *Birth of the Symbol*, 180–81. Finally, cf. Plut. *Cor.* 37.4.

143. It also shields the *hoi polloi* from reality, who are not ethically prepared for it (Plut. *Is. Os.* 360f; idem, *Amat.* 763c).

144. Plut. *Glor. Ath.* 348a–b; cf. Ael. Theon. *Progymn.* 72.28 (Patillon) for myth as "a false discourse that expresses images of truth (λόγος ψευδὴς εἰκονίζων ἀλήθειαν)." This definition became a cliché in the Athenian School: see Olymp. *Comm. Gorg.* 46.3 (Westerink), Dam. *Comm. Phaedo* 198.29–30, 237.27–8 (Westerink), cit. R. Jackson, "Olympiodorus," 278.

145. Plut. *Is. Os.* 382a–b, tr. Babbitt (LCL); also 358b, 359a, 365b, 366e; idem, *E Delph.* 393d–e. For the allegorical interpretation of myth explicitly in the service of interpreting ritual, see *Is. Os.* 378a–b; 380f; Hardie, "Plutarch and the Interpretation of Myth," 4752–57; Hirsch-Luipold, *Plutarchs Denken*, 173–224; Graf, "Plutarch und die Götterbilder,"260–62. For a similar defense of idolatry, see Max. Tyr. *Or.* 2.2.

146. Phil. *Opif.* 1.1–3.

147. An exception is Plut. *Is. Os.* 374c, regarding Plat. *Symp.* 203b.

148. Zambon, *Porphyre*, 63. For the order of composition of the myths (post-95 CE), see Verniere, *Symboles et mythes*, 57–59.

149. For a similar reading of Plutarch, see Pleše, "Platonist Orientalism," esp. 369; cf. Verniere, *Symboles et mythes*, esp. 298–305, who reads Plutarch as more generous to the truth value of myth.

150. Plut. *Sera* 561b, tr. Babbitt (LCL), modified. See also ibid., 549f; Hirsch-Luipold, *Plutarchs Denken*, 142.

151. Plut. *Gen. Socr.* 580c, tr. Babbitt (LCL).

152. Ibid., 589f–590a.

153. Ibid., 581a, tr. slightly modified.

154. Verniere, *Symboles et mythes*, 305; Hirsch-Luipold, *Plutarchs Denken*, 284. Others who agree with Plato and Plutarch on the usefulness of myth in encouraging virtue among the young and uneducated include Max. Tyr. *Or.* 4.4; Strab. *Geogr.* 1.2.3, 1.2.8; Ps.-Plut. *Vit. et Poes. Hom.* 92 (cit. *Philosophical*, Trapp. ad loc. in Max. Tyr. *Or.*)

155. Verniere, *Symboles et mythes*, 310; Hirsch-Luipold, *Plutarchs Denken*, 288.

156. Space here does not permit analysis of Numenius (who is closely followed by Porphyry), whose allegorizations also do not deviate from the Platonic framework; representative examples include Num. frgs. 30–35 (des Places), on Hom. *Od.* 13.102–12 and Plat. *Resp.* X (see Lamberton, *Homer,* 64 n. 66; Tarrant, "Introduction to Book 1," 71–72; Cumont, *Lux Perpetua,* 345); frg. 37 = Proc. *Comm. Tim.* I.76.30–77.23 (Diehl), on Plat. *Tim.* 20d–25e. Note that Numenius and Porphyry both allegorize Plato's myths. On Porphyry and allegory in general, see Waszink, "Porphyrios und Numenios," 62; A. Smith, "Porphyrian Studies," 742, 752–53; Lamberton, *Homer,* 108–33. A representative passage showcasing his dependence on Numenius as well as his valorization of storytelling as a philosophical tool is *Antr. nymph.* 36.3–6 (Westerink), tr. mine: "It must not, however, be thought that interpretations of this kind are forced, the merely credible arguments of the adroit; but when we consider the great wisdom of antiquity and how much Homer excelled in practical knowledge and had a sure grasp of every virtue, it must not be denied that he has hinted at images of things of a more divine nature with the fabrication of fable (μὴ ἀπογινώσκειν ὡς ἐν μυθαρίου πλάσματι εἰκόνας τῶν θειοτέρων ἠνίσσετο). For it would not have been possible to mould (πλάσσειν) the hypothesis as a unit unless the fabrication was simply a remodeling (μεταποιοῦντα τὸ πλάσμα) of certain established truths."

157. In fact, as Lamberton points out, Plotinus mixes Platonic and Homeric myth in the same allegory—*Enn.* 6.7 [38] 30.23–29 (*Homer,* 98). For an allegorical treatment of the myth of Eros's birth in Plato's *Symposium,* see *Enn.* 3.5 [50] 9; Pépin, *Mythe et allégorie,* 192; Brisson, *How Philosophers Saved Myths,* 79; Charrue, "Plotin, le stoïcisme," 44–45; Edwards, *Culture and Philosophy,* 105–6. Narbonne rightly distinguishes Plotinus's approach to myth from Sethian revelations (*Plotinus in Dialogue,* 74).

158. Plot. *Enn.* 3.6 [26] 19 (the ithyphallic Hermes), *Enn.* 4.3 [27] 32 (Hercules' shade, regarding Hom. *Od.* 11.601–4, on which, see Pépin, "Héraclès et son reflet").

159. Plot. *Enn.* 4.3 [27] 14; 3.5 [50] 9.24–29; see Pépin, *Mythe et allégorie,* 191; Brisson, *How Philosophers Saved Myths,* 74–75 (recalling also *Enn.* 4.3 [27] 9.15–20); Sinnige, "Gnostic Influence," 90. Later Platonists agreed: Sallust. *Deis* 3 (Nock); Procl. *Comm. Remp.* 1.140.1; Olymp. *Comm. Gorg.* 48.2–3; see Sheppard, *Studies,* 73; R. Jackson, "Olympiodorus," 287; Kobusch, "Wiederkehr des Mythos," 51.

160. Plot. *Enn.* 5.8 [31] 11.4; cf. S. Saïd, "Deux noms," 318.

161. Hes. *Theog.* 154–210, 453–506, criticized by Plat. *Resp.* II 377e–378a; Cic. *Nat. d.* 2.63–64, 3.24.

162. E.g., Plot. *Enn.* 4.3 [27] 14; also, 1.6 [1] 8.16, regarding Hom. *Od.* 9.29, 10.483–84, *Il.* 2.140; Lamberton, *Homer,* 106–7; Edwards, *Culture and Philosophy,* 104.

163. Plot. *Enn.* 5.8 [31] 10–13.

164. Ibid., 5.8 [31] 12.12–27; cf. 5.1 [10] 7.28. On his inconsistency in portraying mythical characters, see Pépin, *Mythe et allégorie,* 203–9.

165. Hadot, "Ouranos," 134.

166. Plot. *Enn.* 2.9 [33] 10.26–27; see Wallis, "Soul and Nous," 464.

167. Plot. *Enn.* 2.9 [33] 11.10–28 (tr. slightly modified).

168. Pasquier, "La réflexion démiurgique," 660–61; S. Saïd, "Deux noms," 318, 327; Fattal, "Bild und Weltproduktion," 45–46. The parallel passage in *Zost.* preserves repetitive use of the word εἴδωλον from the Greek *Vorlage*. However, the demiurge is not identified with the "reflection of a reflection" but simply employs it (NHC VIII,1.10.1–7): "he looked at the reflection (εἴδωλον), and by means of the reflection (εἴδωλον) that he saw in it, he created the world (κόσμος). And in a reflection of a reflection (εἴδωλον), he worked on the world. And (then) (even) the reflection of the manifestation was taken from him."

169. Thus Plot. *Enn.* 4.3 [27] 12–13, cit. Zandee, *Terminology of Plotinus*, 21. On matter as an εἴδωλον, see *Enn.* 2.5 [25] 5.19; cf. the material world as an inferior reflection of the intelligible (6.2 [43] 22.33–47). For "reflection" as associated with φαντασία, see 2.9 [33] 11.24 (cf. 12.30); Wallis, "Soul and Nous" 470; idem, *Neoplatonism*, 26.

170. For Plutarch, see *Is. Os.* 372f; for discussion and many more citations, see Hirsch-Luipold, *Plutarchs Denken*, 159–65, 171–73, 284–85; for Plotinus, see Fattal, "Bild und Weltproduktion," 52–55.

171. On Pandora, see Plot. *Enn.* 4.3 [27] 14.11). For πλάσμα as matter simply obtaining form, see 4.9 [8] 3.15; 6.8 [39] 2.24; 3.3 [48] 4.33; for a negative sense of the term, see 2.4 [12] 8.19, 4.3 [27] 18.23.

172. Edwards, *"Aidōs,"* 230 (suggesting a recollection of Plat. *Resp.* 599a) see also idem, "Porphyry's 'Cave,'" 92. Both studies were inspirational for this discussion.

173. Dio Chrys. *Borysth.*, discussed above, Chapter 1, "Barbarian Wisdom, Alien Wisdom."

174. E.g., *Chald. Or.* or the apophatic inscription discovered at Oenoanda (Robert, "Un oracle gravé à Oenoanda").

175. The use of the terminology of imagery employed in these passages does not seem to be systematic; any attempt to discern such would be complicated by their use of Coptic words for image (ⲉⲓⲛⲉ, ⲧⲟⲩⲱⲧ) and form (ⲥⲙⲟⲧ) in addition to the Greek extant from the Vorlagen of the texts. *Zostrianos* tends to focus on the terms of type/copy, impression/stamp, and reflection (τύπος, ἀντίτυπος, εἴδωλον), mostly in the context of the material world and its border with the intelligible world or of the shared nature between the elect and the intelligible world that permits salvation. See also Mazur, "Platonizing Sethian Gnostic Background," 192–95, 202–5. Meanwhile, the language of forms (μορφή, ἰδέα) is restricted to the Barbelo aeon and the Thrice Powered. There is no such tendency in *Allogenes*, in part, of course, because its topic is chiefly what lies beyond the Barbelo.

176. Helpful discussions of the triads include Turner, *Sethian Gnosticism and the Platonic Tradition*, 407, 697–704; Brankaer, "Concept of νοῦς," 68–73; Rasimus, "Porphyry and the Gnostics," 96–101.

177. As discussed in Turner, *Sethian Gnosticism and the Platonic Tradition*, 532–53, 696–97. The latter is an assimilation of the Son from the triad of Father-Mother-Son in the descent treatises, such as the *Apocryphon of John*.

178. *Allogenes* NHC XI,3.51.12–17.

179. *Zost.* NHC VIII,1.79.16–25; cf. also 2.28–29, on the "three ungenerated likenesses" (ⲉⲓⲛⲉ) of the Spirit. The "triplicity" of the Barbelo represents her status as reflective thought that freezes the diffusion of Being and prevents it (per the function of "Vitality") from streaming into infinite diffusion (Turner, "Commentary: *Zostrianos*," 524, 621).

180. *Zost.* NHC VIII,1.74.25, 67.13 (in the source shared with Victorinus), 68.14; cf. 74.9.

181. E.g., Plot. *Enn.* V.1 [10] 7.

182. *Zost.* NHC VIII,1.78.19–22 ("she stood there, looking at it, and [rejoicing], filled by [its (i.e., the Invisible Spirit's)] kindness"), 118.9–119.3.

183. See also ibid., 5.16, 6.17, 7.4–5.

184. The moon; see below, Chapter 5, "The Strange and the Dead."

185. *Zost.* NHC VIII,1.5.10–22.

186. Reviewed in detail below, Chapter 6.

187. *Zost.* VIII,1.129.25–26; 130.6–9. LS: "[I] put on my image. Because it was ignorant, I strengthened it." BFP: "Je . . . réinvestis ma statue qui était ignorante." Cf. 4.24, where Zostrianos simply leaves his πλάσμα on earth as he begins the ascent.

188. Turner (CGL) takes the ⲛ̄ as gentivial: "Indivisble One of the divisible likenesses," a sense followed by Scopello (BCNH) : "l'indivis parmi les ressemblances divisibles."

189. *Allogenes* NHC XI,3.53.23–31.

190. Turner (CGL) translates: "after the likeness." Similarly, Layton (*Gnostic Scriptures*, 145): "after the resemblance." Scopello (BCNH) : "à la ressemblance de."

191. *Allogenes* NHC XI,3.59.19–26.

192. Ibid., 59.32–60.2

193. Turner (CGL): "limited by limitation"; Layton (*Gnostic Scriptures*): "limited by bestowal of limit"; Scopello (BCNH): "sans limite qui puisse le limiter."

194. Turner (CGL): "what was put on me"; Layton (*Gnostic Scriptures*): "of that (image) which I was wearing"; Scopello (BCNH) : "ressemblance de celui dont j'étais revêtu."

195. *Allogenes* NHC XI,3.60.24–37.

196. Cf. the fine account of Mazur, "Platonizing Sethian Gnostic Background," 197–201, 278–79, stressing parallels in Plotinus. On the ensuing apophasis, see Burns, "Apophatic Strategies,"166.

197. The source of this language is unclear; Platonic and biblical antecedents both present themselves, while also being problematic. The Platonic tradition of course stresses the attainment of "likeness to God" (Plat. *Theaet.* 176b; see further Dillon, *Middle Platonists*, 122–23, 192–93, 299–300, 335), but the context is ethical and not explicitly linked to physical transformation. On the other hand, the period is rife with speculation among philosophically trained Jews and Christians about attaining or regaining Adam's status as εἰκὼν θεοῦ (Gen 1:27); see Bousset, *Hauptprobleme*, 160; Quispel, "Gnostische Anthropos," 188–95; Attridge, *Epistle to the Hebrews*, 270 n.

31 (for Philo); Jervell, *Imago Dei*; F. Williams, *Mental Perception*, 67–70. Mazur suggests that the idea of assimilation to the image of the One is a Gnostic "innovation" that goes back to the myth of Epinoia's awakening of Adam's latent spiritual faculty ("Platonizing Sethian Gnostic Background," 280–81). Yet the figure of Adam is relatively distant in *Zostrianos*, and the seer is changed into an angel, not a primal man. I hope to revisit this problem in a later study.

198. See Attridge, *Epistle to the Hebrews*, 267–77, regarding Heb 2:5, 6:5, 9:10–11, 10:1, 13:14.

199. Meijering, "God Cosmos History," 254.

200. Pépin, *Mythe et allégorie*; Simonetti, *Lettera E/O Allegoria*. A thorough survey of Gnostic allegory remains to be written (see thus far Simonetti, *Lettera E/O Allegoria*, 9–37), but an overview would include *Ex. Soul* (NHC II,6), *Pistis Sophia*, Ptolemy's *Epistle to Flora*, the Ptolemaic descent of Sophia *ap*. Ir. *Haer*. 1.7.3, the Ophite account according to Irenaeus (*Haer*. 1.30.11; cf. *Ap. John* NHC II,1.13 = BG 45), the Naasene Psalm *ap*. Hipp. *Haer*. 5.7.35–36 (regarding Hom. *Od*. 24.5–8; also Hipp. *Haer* 5.8.6 [regarding Is. 44.2], 6.14.7–8), and the fragments of Heracleon preserved by Origen.

201. On Alexander's evidence, see Villey's edition of Alexander; Stroumsa, "Titus of Bostra and Alexander of Lycopolis."

202. Alex. Lyc. ch. 5 pp. 8.8–14 (Brinkmann), tr. van der Horst and Mansfeld, slightly modified. On Manichaean literalism, see also Simpl. *Comm. ench.* 71.13–16 (Brittain and Brennan): "having fashioned monstrous things (τέρατα γὰρ πλάττοντές τινα) which it's not right even to call mythical, they do not use them as myths or believe that they point to something else, but take what they say to be the truth itself (ὡς ἀληθέσιν αὐτοῖς τοῖς λεγομένοις πιστεύουσι)"; S. Lieu, *Manichaeism in the Later Roman Empire*, 22–24; Stroumsa, *Another Seed*, 162.

203. Alex. Lyc., "Actually, though having taken up the decision to show up this mumbo-jumbo for what it is, I am at a loss how to proceed. For their assumptions (αἱ ὑποθέσεις) are not expressed in a generally acceptable ratiocinative form; hence a scrutiny of these assumptions is out of the question. Nor are there any proofs to be found which would be based on postulates (οὔτε τινὲς ἀρχαὶ ἀποδείξεων), which renders it impossible to consider what these postulates would entail" (ch. 5 p. 8.20–22 [Brinkmann]). On Manichaeans' literalist approach to scripture, see Tardieu, "Principes de l'exégèse manichéenne," esp. 128.

204. Alex. Lyc. ch. 5 p. 8.25–32 (Brinkmann); ch. 10.6–9 p. 16.

205. Orig. *Cels.* 1.17, 1.20, 1.28, 2.13, 2.15, 2.55, 3.16, 3.43, 4.49–50, 5.57, 7.11; Mac. Mag. *Apocrit.* 3.4 (many discussed in J. Cook, *Interpretation of the New Testament*, 26, 45, 70–71, 97, 99, 176–77). Cf. the "hostile Jewish mythologizing (διαβεβλημένων Ἰουδαϊκῶν μυθολογημάτων)," disparaged by the anonymous source (Porphyry?) of Euseb. *Praep. ev.* 9.8–10 (Mras), cit. J. Cook, "Porphyry's Attempted Demolition," 7.

206. Collins, *Apocalyptic Imagination*, 39; see also idem, "Pseudonymity," 341; P. Perkins, *Gnostic Dialogue*, 59; Stone, "Apocalyptic Literature,"

431–33; Adler, "Introduction," 13. On esoteric language and secrecy as important for creating sectarian self-definition, see Adler, "Introduction," 17. For the general importance of esotericism and secrecy in apocalyptic, see Bornkamm, "μυστήριον," 815. Cf. Rasimus, "Porphyry and the Gnostics," 109.

207. Edwards, "Gnostic Aculinus," 378–81; Turner, "Introduction: *Zostrianos*," 50, 53, 59; idem, *Sethian Gnosticism and the Platonic Tradition*, 295; "Introduction: *Marsanes*," 172; idem, "Introduction: *Allogenes*," 27, 29–30; idem, "Platonizing Sethian Treatises," 141; Moore and Turner, "Gnosticism," 194–95; Emmel, "Gnostic Tradition in Relation to Greek Philosophy," 127; Mazur, "Platonizing Sethian Gnostic Background," 178 n. 9, 205 n. 7.

208. Famously, in Plat. *Symp.* 201d.

209. Turner recognizes the disruptive nature of revelatory epistemology in a Platonic context (*Sethian Gnosticism and the Platonic Tradition*, 295, 300; idem, "Introduction: *Marsanes*," 50–51; idem, "Introduction: *Zostrianos*," 126). See also Zandee, *Terminology of Plotinus*, 41; Edwards, "Porphyry's 'Cave,'" 97.

210. See also Pleše, "Gnostic Literature," 190.

211. *Pace* Turner, "Coptic Renditions," 524 n. 1; Corrigan, "The *Symposium* and *Republic*."

212. For the crowns, see Burns, "Sethian Crowns, Sethian Martyrs?"

CHAPTER 4

1. Coined by Turner and ubiquitous in his scholarship, e.g., *Sethian Gnosticism and the Platonic Tradition*, 80–85, 214–20; idem, "Typologies," 181; as well as Pleše, "Gnostic Literature," 191.

2. See particularly MacRae, "Jewish Background"; Turner, "Introduction NHC XIII,1*," 375.

3. Turner, *Sethian Gnosticism and the Platonic Tradition*, 755; idem, "Introduction: *Marsanes*," 239.

4. Idem, "Gnostic Threefold Path," 331; "Typologies," 181, 188–89. Indeed, in the ascent texts, the Barbelo aeon remains a second principle, produced by the Invisible Spirit, but is not identified with a descending savior but with Intellect (νοῦς). For a survey, see Brankaer, "The Concept of νοῦς," 65–68, 78–79.

5. Turner, "Typologies," 190 n. 23.

6. Ibid., 193.

7. Thus Turner, "Introduction: *Marsanes*," 161–68; "Introduction: *Zostrianos*," 137–44; "Introduction: *Allogenes*," 109–13.

8. Pearson, "Figure of Seth," 489, quoting MacRae, "Seth," 21; also Stroumsa, *Another Seed*, 125; Lahe, *Gnosis und Judentum*, 283–90; all regarding Gen 5:3 LXX, on which, see Klijn, *Seth*, 2.

9. Klijn, *Seth*, 39 n. 36; see also a Coptic spell invoking "Seth, Seth, the living Christ!" (Kropp, *Zaubertexte*, 3:76; Stroumsa, *Another Seed*, 76 n.

21 [*sic*]); *Man. Keph.* 12.9–13 (Polotsky and Böhlig); *Man. Ps.-Bk.* 142.3–9 (Alberry); *Man. Hom.* 68.15–19; Aug. *Faust.* 19.3.

10. *Pace* Wisse, "Stalking," 571; see *L.A.E.* 25, 49–50, 51:3; cf. *1 En.* 93:1–10, 91:11–17; Nickelsburg, "Some Related Adam Traditions," 529; Lahe, *Gnosis und Judentum*, 289–300.

11. Syncell. *Ek. chron.* 9.22–26 (Mosshammer); Seth also raptured in the *Apocalypse of Sethel* from the CMC (Reeves, *Heralds*, 111, 122).

12. For Seth the astronomer, see Jos. *Ant.* 1.68; Bidez and Cumont, *Mages hellénisés*, 45–56; Klijn, *Seth*, 49; as a scribe, see *L.A.E.* 49.1–3, 50–51; Jos. *Ant.* 1.69–71; Klijn, *Seth*, 17–18. This does not "imply" a "synthesis with Thoth-Hermes" (*pace* Frankfurter, "Apocalypses Real and Alleged," 72–73 n. 31), but perhaps recalls the "Books of Seth" possessed by the Archontics (Epiph. *Pan.* 40.7.4–5). In any case, this role of Seth recalls the apocalyptic tradition of book burial.

13. On ethnic terminology in Gnosticism, see Fallon, "Undominated Race"; Stroumsa, *Another Seed*, 100; M. A. Williams, *Immovable Race*. On translating γενεά as "race" and not "generation" in Gnostic texts, see Fallon, "Undominated Race," 280. For the background of the term "seed" in Jewish apocalyptic, see Frankfurter, "Legacy of Jewish Apocalypses," 149.

14. Gen. 6:2 refers to "sons of God" (υἱοὶ θεοῦ), the "watchers" who were tempted by women and begat with them giants on the earth. Beginning with Julius Africanus (ca. 225 CE), many Christian writers identified these sons of God not with evil angels but with the offspring of Seth. These Sethites inhabited a mountain below Paradise but above the evil Cainites, whose alluring women drew them down into corruption with tools reminiscent of the teaching of the watchers (metallurgy, makeup, etc.—Syncell. *Ek. chron.* 9.26–10.2; Klijn, *Seth*, 61–62; also Ephr. *Comm. Gen. et Exod* 5.1 p. 43 [Tonneau], cit. Klijn, *Seth*, 74; 4QInstruction [4Q417] frg. 2 1:14–15; Stroumsa, *Another Seed*, 125). The Sethites living on the mountain after Adam and Seth were called "gods" on account of their purity, and so were confused with angels (*Cav. Tr.* 7:1–3 [Ri], cit. Klijn, *Seth*, 68 n. 99).

15. Stroumsa, *Another Seed*, 134.

16. Some sources considered this lineage biological (Klijn, *Seth*, 83–86; Pearson, "Figure of Seth," 473–74; M. A. Williams, *Immovable Race*, 180); others, metaphorical (Phil. *Post.* 10, 40–48; further, see Kraft, "Philo on Seth." On Valentinians, see Ir. *Haer.* 1.7.5; Theodotus *ap.* Clem. Al. *Exc.* 54.1; Ter. *Val.* 29, cit. Pearson, "Figure of Seth," 475). See also *Tri. Trac.* NHC I,5.118.14 (no Seth). For Hippolytus's Sethians, see *Haer.* 5.20.2 (Marcovich); cf. also the probably unrelated tradition of allelophagy in *Paraph. Shem* NHC VII,1.44.25–26.

17. *Apoc. Adam* NHC V,5.85. On the "three men" from heaven, see e.g. *2 En.* 1:4; Stone, "Report on Seth Traditions," 469. On the genre of Adam apocrypha, see Pearson, "Figure of Seth," 492–93; Nickelsburg, "Some Related Adam Traditions."

18. *Apoc. Adam* NHC V,5.65.3–9, tr. MacRae (CGL): "it (knowledge) entered into the seed (σπορά) of great aeons. For this reason I have called you

by the name of that man who is the seed of the great generation (γενεά) or from whom (it comes)." See also Pearson, "Figure of Seth," 489.

19. *Apoc. Adam* NHC V,5.66.4–8.

20. Ibid., 69.12–18.

21. Stroumsa, *Another Seed*, 101; Brakke, *The Gnostics*, 73; cf. Schottroff, "*Animae naturaliter salvandae*," 73, 80.

22. *Apoc. Adam* NHC V,5.82.25–28; for the Illuminator as Seth, see Schottroff, "*Animae naturaliter salvandae*," 79; MacRae, "Apocalypse of Adam," 575, followed by Pearson, "Figure of Seth," 497.

23. Pearson, "Figure of Seth,"484–85.

24. *Gos. Eg.* NHC III,2.55.16–56.1. Seth's exact location in the heavenly world is not clear; sometimes he is in the second luminary (III,2.65.16–17), sometimes in the third (IV,2.68.3–5 = III,2.56.20).

25. Ibid., IV,2.65.17–30 = III,2.54.6–11: the Autogenes and other beings praise the Four Luminaries, the Thrice-Male Child, Youel, Esephech, and other beings "in order that they may name [the Father the fourth] with the [immoveable, incorruptible] race (γενεά), of the [Father, and that they] may call [it the] seed (σπορά) of the Father the seed of the great [Seth]" (tr. Böhlig and Wisse [CGL]).

26. Ibid., III,2.68.1–22; thus Böhlig and Wisse, "Introduction: *The Gospel of the Egyptians*," 22, 32–33.

27. Noted by Pearson, "Figure of Seth," 498; Reeves, *Heralds*, 126–27.

28. *Gos. Eg.* NHC IV,2.73.27–74.9 = III,2.62.13–24. See also Klijn, *Seth*, 104.

29. *Gos. Eg.* NHC IV,2.74.17–23, 75.15–24 = III,2.63.5–8, 64.1–9.

30. Ibid., III,2.56.7–22, tr. Böhlig and Wisse, slightly modified.

31. Ibid., IV,2.71.11–18 = III,2.60.2–8; Hormos is also associated with the seed of Seth at *Zost.* NHC VIII,1.47.9. See also M. A. Williams, *Immovable Race*, 145–46.

32. *Gos. Eg.* NHC IV,2.71.30–72.10 = III,2.60.20–61.1 tr. Böhlig and Wisse.

33. With M. A. Williams, *Immovable Race*, 164; Klijn, *Seth*, 104.

34. *Gos. Eg.* NHC IV,2.78.2–10 = III,2.66.2–8, tr. Böhlig and Wisse.

35. Ibid., IV,2.75.24 = III,2.64.9, IV,2.78.10 = III,2.66.8. On the title as a corruption of the name Ἰησοῦς Ναζωραῖος δίκαιος, see Turner, *Sethian Gnosticism and the Platonic Tradition*, 165, 278; cf. Böhlig and Wisse, "Commentary: *The Gospel of the Egyptians*," 194–95. "Yesseus . . . " is also preserved (in the accusative!) at *Apoc. Adam* NHC V,5.85.30, and *Zost.* NHC VIII,1.47.5–7, in both cases with a baptismal context. Rasimus, *Paradise Reconsidered*, 276–79, opines that the title draws from Johannine appellations for the Christ: Jesus as living water (John 4:10–14), Jesus the righteous (John 7:18, 1 John 2:29), and Jesus the Nazarene (John 1:14, 18:5.7, 19:19).

36. *Zost.* NHC VIII,1.54.23, 126.16; see also Abramowski, "Nag Hammadi 8,1 'Zostrianos,'" 5.

37. *Zost.* NHC VIII,1.30.4–14; also ibid., 6.17–31, 51.12–18.

38. *Zost.* NHC VIII,1.47.5–8; see also Turner, "Commentary: *Zostrianos*," 562–63.

39. Also suggested by Pearson, "Figure of Seth," 490, 498, recalling *Zost.* NHC VIII,1.131.10–16; *Melch.* NHC IX,1.5.20, 6.17, concluding that Seth has here "put on" Zostrianos in an effort to awaken "his Seed." See also Pearson, "Gnosticism as Platonism," 59; idem, *Ancient Gnosticism*, 89; H. Jackson, "Seer Nikotheos," 259; Reeves, *Heralds*, 125, 127. Turner asserts that "Zostrianos is clearly a savior figure, presumably in the type of Seth, the 'spiritual' son of Adam," but does not consider whether he is an incarnation of Seth or a descending redeemer (Turner, "Commentary: *Zostrianos*," 484).

40. *Zost.* NHC VIII,1.7.8–9. This "living seed" is associated with Hormos (47.9–14), who presides over its incarnation in *Gos. Eg.*, as noted above.

41. *Zost.* NHC VIII,1.5–7.

42. Ibid.,1.4.14–17.

43. Ibid., 130.4.

44. Turner, "Commentary: *Zostrianos*," 484; Brakke, *The Gnostics*, 73. Cf. Just. Mart.*1 Apol.* 28, *2 Apol.* 8, on which, see Buell, *Why This New Race?* 79.

45. On the doxological parallels, see Turner, "Commentary: *Zostrianos*," 217–22; idem, "Sethian Baptismal Rite," 971.

46. *Allogenes* NHC XI,3.52.26–27.

47. Ibid., 64.14–25.

48. Scopello (BCNH) translates ⲉⲥⲕⲟⲧⲉ ⲙ̄ⲙⲟϥ ⲉⲣ[ⲟⲥ] as "elle (sc. l'étendue) le tourne vers [elle]." Turner (p. 178 in the same volume) suggests instead: "it (i.e., the boundlessness) turns him (i.e., the traverser) to [it] (i.e., the Invisible Spirit)."

49. Funk and Scopello (BCNH) restore and translate as follows : ⲛ̄[ⲧ]ⲉⲛⲁⲓ̈ ϣⲱⲡⲉ ("et [de sorte] que celui-ci devienne salut"). Turner (p. 178 in the same volume) suggests instead: ⲛ̄[ⲉⲣ]ⲉⲁⲓ̈ ϣⲱⲡⲉ ("he was becoming salvation").

50. *Allogenes* NHC XI,3.49.7–18.

51. Ibid., 50.34–36.

52. Ibid., 3.51.28–35; see also ibid., 58.7–19; on the thrice male as "the thought of those who exist together, the Perfect Child," see ibid., 46.17–22; 51.32.37, 56.13–14; 58.12–15. In his editio princeps, Turner considers that a dissociation of the Triple Powered with Geradamas and Autogenes signifies a "de-mythologization" of the text from *Zost.* and *Steles Seth*, which ties the figures together; yet the significance of the Thrice-Male Child is magnified in *Allogenes*, as he notes in a later edition (Turner, "*Allogenes*: Notes," 246–47, on *Steles Seth* NHC VII,5.120.29, 121.8–9; *Zost.* NHC VIII,1.13.7–9, 30.4–14; "Introduction: *Allogenes*," 85–86).

53. Pearson, "Gnosticism as Platonism," 59; Stroumsa, *Another Seed*, 173; Rasimus, "Porphyry and the Gnostics," 106 n. 98. More hesitant are Reeves, *Heralds*, 122; Brakke, *The Gnostics*, 80.

54. As opposed to the character Allogenes in TC 60:13–19, who either is Jesus or quotes him when he says to Satan, "get behind me, Satan!" (regarding Matt 4:10, Luke 4:13).

55. *Steles Seth* NHC VII,5.118.12–13; 119.6–10. All translations of *Steles Seth* are those of Robinson and Goehring (CGL), modified. On Adam as light, Goehring recalls *Gos. Eg.* NHC IV,2.61.11 = III,2.49.8 ("Notes: *The*

Three Steles of Seth," 389; see further Böhlig and Wisse, "Commentary: *The Gospel of the Egyptians*," 177; *Unt.* 230.23–24).

56. *Steles Seth* NHC VII,5.120.1–15.

57. Ibid. NHC VII,5.119.32–34: "the perceptible world too knows you, thanks to you and your seed (σπορά)."

58. Ibid., NHC VII,5.120.18–36.

59. Seth praises the Barbelo thus: "salvation has come to us; from you comes salvation. You are wisdom, you are knowledge, you are truthfulness. Life exists on account of you; from you is life" (*Steles Seth* NHC VII,5.123.15–19). He says that "you are he who will not be saved, nor have been saved, by them" (ibid., NHC VII,5.125.19–21; cf. *Allogenes* NHC XI,3.50.34–36). See also *Steles Seth* NHC VII,5.121.12–14; 127; M. A. Williams, *Immovable Race*, 63.

60. *Steles Seth* NHC VII,5.118.16–18.

61. On the *Steles* as a liturgical text, see Schenke, "Phenomenon," 601–2; Goehring, "Introduction: *The Three Steles of Seth*," 380–82; Turner, *Sethian Gnosticism and the Platonic Tradition*, 122. On the identification with Adam, see M. A. Williams, *Immovable Race*, 62–67, 175.

62. Thus Layton, *Gnostic Scriptures*, 153–54; Turner, "Introduction: *Allogenes*," 83 n. 61.

63. *Marsanes* and *Melchizedek* are too fragmentary to draw any firm conclusions, but certainly compatible with this model. *Marsanes* does not mention Adam or Seth in the extant text. Pearson speculates that the prophet Marsanes is an incarnation of Seth (Pearson, "Introduction: *Marsanes*," 242–43; idem, "Gnosticism as Platonism," 59, *pace* Turner, "Introduction: *Marsanes*," 48, 243–44). It is not clear whether the line "he saved a multitude" refers to Marsanes himself (favored by Pearson) or the Autogenes (*Mars.* X,1.6.16; Pearson, "Notes: *Marsanes*," 266; Poirier, "Commentaire: *Marsanès*," 390). *Melchizedek*, however, does presume an ethnically circumscribed model of salvation (NHC IX,1.5.19–20, 6.17; see Pearson, "Notes: *Melchizedek*," 53), and it is possible that the high priest is an incarnation of Seth (cf. Pearson, noting the tradition in the long recension of 2 *En.* ch. 72, of a series of miraculously born Melchizedeks). However, Vaillant sees this as a Christian interpolation (*Le livre des Secrets*, xi–xiii, *pace* Pearson, "Figure of Seth," 500; idem, "Introduction: *Melchizedek*," 30). The figure of the "Setheus" in *Unt.*, if related to Seth, is unrecognizable (230, 233–35, 238–39, 340.23, 341); Brakke, "Body as/ at the Boundary," esp. 206, seems to favor Bayne's suggestion that the figure expresses celestial movement (but cf. LSJ, s.v. 1592a, "σήθω," "to sift, bolt").

64. Similarly Epiphanius's Sethians, who trace their ancestry to Seth (who reincarnates in history as a savior) and read books titled "Foreigners" (*Pan.* 39.1.3, 39.3.1, 39.3.5, 39.5.1).

65. Hipp. *Haer.* 10.29.1–2, tr. Klijn and Reinink, *Patristic Evidence*, 123; see also Klijn and Reinink, *Patristic Evidence*, 64–65; Stroumsa, Another Seed, 76, 88.

66. Epiph. *Pan.* 30.3.4–5, 53.1.8 (Williams); Ps.-Clem. *Recogn.* 2.22.4. For a survey of this and more material with analysis, see Burns, "Jesus' Reincarnations Revisited"; cf. H. Jackson, "See Nikotheos," 267–68.

67. See below, Chapter 7, n. 17.

68. Studies of ethnic language in Gnosticism in general, not just Sethianism, are sorely lacking (thus Buell, "Rethinking the Relevance of Race," 474, recalling M. A. Williams, *Immovable Race*; see also Fallon, "Undominated Race").

69. J. Hall, *Ethnic Identity*, 35; cf. Buell, "Rethinking the Relevance of Race," 450 n. 3 (but acknowledging Hall at 456 n. 20; Buell, "Race and Universalism," 433).

70. Per J. Hall, *Ethnic Identity*, 2, 36: "An ethnic group should be defined as a social collectivity whose members are united by their subscription to a putative belief in shared descent and to an association with a primordial homeland." See also ibid., 19–32; Buell, "Race and Universalism," 441–44. Cf. Buell's caution that this definition implies an identity too "fixed," centered on biological descent (*Making Christians*, 105; eadem, "Race and Universalism," 441 n. 32).

71. Eadem, *Why This New Race?* 9.

72. *Diogn.* 1.1: the author will explain "why this new race or practice has come to life at this time." See also Aristid. Ath. *Apol.* 17 (Syr.) 17; Clem. Al. *Strom.* 6.13.106.4–107.1; Orig. *Cels.* 8.43. Other epithets include 1 Pet 2:9–10 (ὑμεῖς δὲ γένος ἐκλεκτόν); Athenag. *Leg.* 1.1–3; *Acts Andr.* ch. 18 (Cod. Vat. 808); Just. Mart. *1 Apol.* 14 (on which, see Buell, "Rethinking the Relevance of Race," 464–65; cf. J. Lieu, "Race of the God-Fearers," 490 n. 23). For discussion, see Harnack, *Mission and Expansion*, 1:305–22, 340–51; M. A. Williams, *Immovable Race*, 183; J. Lieu, "Race of the God-Fearers," 488–89; eadem, *Christian Identity*, 259–63; Buell, "Rethinking the Relevance of Race," 456; eadem, "Race and Universalism," 450; eadem, *Why This New Race?*; J. Perkins, *Roman Imperial Identities*, 28–31.

73. Aristid. Ath. *Apol.* 2.1 (Greek); *Pre. Pet. ap.* Clem. Al. *Strom.* 6.5.41.4–7, 42.2, 6.13.106.4–107.1. The source of inspiration is likely 1 Cor 10:32. On these passages, see Harnack, *Mission and Expansion*, 1:336–52; J. Lieu, "Race of the God-Fearers," 489; eadem, *Christian Identity*, 260–64; Buell, "Rethinking the Relevance of Race," 461; eadem, *Why This New Race?* 66. See also *Gos. Phil.* NHC II,3.75.31. In still other texts, Christians are a "fourth race"; see Aristid. Ath. *Apol.* 2.1 (Syriac); Clem. Al. *Exc.* 28, pp. 118–20 (Sagnard) and commentary ad loc. Cf. the four races in *Orig. World* NHC II,5.125.3, on which see Fallon, "Undominated Race," 285; Stroumsa, *Another Seed*, 104.

74. *Mart. Pol.* 3.2; also 14.1, 17.1; see J. Lieu, "Race of the God-Fearers," 485, followed by Buell, *Why This New Race?* 52. See also Ter. *Scorp.* 10.10; idem, *Nat.* 1.8; J. Lieu, "Race of the God-Fearers," 491; Buell, *Why This New Race?* 155–57.

75. Aristid. Ath. *Apol.* ch. 15.1 (Greek), 2.4 (Syriac).

76. See Buell, "Race and Universalism," 448, on Clem. Al. *Protr.* 1.6.4–
6.5 (Mondésert); thus also Justin on Christians produced by the λόγος even
before Christ (2 *Apol.* 8, 13).

77. *Tri. Tract.* NHC I,5.109.24; See Attridge and Pagels, "Notes: The
Tripartite Tractate," 421; Buell, *Why This New Race?* 118. Interestingly,
the *Tri. Tract.*'s quotation of Gal 3:28 (NHC I,5.132.23–24) omits "neither
Greek nor Jew" and does not incorporate the earlier discussion of the earthly
races into its exegesis.

78. J. Lieu, "Race of the God-Fearers," 491; M. A. Williams, *Immovable
Race*, 183 n. 31; Buell, "Rethinking the Relevance of Race," 459;

79. Buell, "Rethinking the Relevance of Race," 461.

80. Similarly, see Schott, "'Living like a Christian'," 263.

81. See further Burns, "Sethian Crowns, Sethian Martyrs?"

82. Buell, *Why This New Race?* 139; see also ibid, 84.

83. Ir. *Haer.* 1.6.1–4; Clem. Al. *Strom.* 2.3.10.2, 2.20.115, 4.13.89.4 (Valentinus and Basilides); Orig. *Princ.* 3.4; for discussion, see Schottroff, "*Animae naturaliter salvandae*," esp. 86; Buell, *Why This New Race?* 121; Kalligas, "Plotinus Against the Gnostics," 126–27; Pleše, "Gnostic Literature,"
190 (on Valentinians); Narbonne, *Plotinus in Dialogue*, 56–59 (despite n. 6).

84. For fate vs. providence, see Plot. *Enn.*3.3 [48] 5.

85. Ibid., 2.9 [33] 16.9–15.

86. "Then, another point, what piety is there in denying that providence
extends to this world and to anything and everything? And how are they
consistent with themselves in this denial? For they say that God does care
providentially for them, and them alone (λέγουσι γὰρ αὐτῶν προνοεῖν αὖ
μόνων)" (ibid., 16.15–17).

87. "Providential care is much more of wholes than of parts (πολὺ γὰρ
μᾶλλον τῶν ὅλων ἢ τῶν μερῶν ἡ πρόνοια), and the participation in God of that
universal Soul, too, is much greater" (ibid., 16.30–31; see also 3.2 [47] 3).

88. Ibid., 2.9 [33] 9.44, 51–58.

89. Similarly, see Mazur, "Plotinus' Philosophical Opposition," 103; King,
Secret Revelation of John, 202–3.

90. Elsas, *Neuplatonische und gnostische Weltablehnung*, 244–45. Cf.
Zandee, who suggests that Plotinus's concern is temporal: rather than being
planned before the world's creation (as in Christianity), providence manifests for him as the eternal creative activity of God (*Terminology of Plotinus*,
30–31). Plotinus certainly would have objected to Christian thought about
creatio providentiae, and temporality *was* an issue, but Zandee is afield from
the evidence.

91. M. A. Williams, *Immovable Race*, 165, 172; idem, "Sethianism,"
58–59. For similar dynamics in the primitive church, see Buell, "Rethinking the Relevance of Race," 466–73; eadem, "Race and Universalism," 445.

92. For a detailed review of this passage, see above, Chapters 1 ("Against
the Gnostic Cosmos") and 3 ("How to Read a Story").

93. *Ap. John* NHC II,1.4.31–32 = BG 27.10; NHC II,1.5.4 = BG 27.18; BG
28.4; NHC II,1.5.16 = BG 28.10; NHC II,1.6.5; [NHC II,1.6.22] = BG 30.14;
NHC II,1.6.31 = BG 31.3; NHC II,1.14.20 (not in short version). Various

Coptic expressions are used to express the terminology of "first thought"; for a thorough survey, see Onuki, "Dreifache Pronoia." Mention of providence controlling the sublunary realm at the behest of the archons later in the treatise certainly refers to a "secondary" πρόνοια roughly equivalent to Middle Platonic Fate, whose activity is not always benign (NHC II,1.12.17 = BG 43.12; NHC II,1.15.15 = BG 49.16; NHC II,1.28.11–32 = BG 72.2–12; see M. A. Williams, "Higher Providence").

94. *Zost.* NHC VIII,1.20.4–18, 58.20, 58.20, 82.7, 91.14, 124.3; *Allogenes* NHC XI,3.48.9–13, 53.26, 64.35. See further Brankaer, "Terminologie et représentations philosophiques," esp. 813; Mazur, "Self-Manifestation and 'Primary Revelation'"; idem, "Platonizing Sethian Gnostic Background," 259–68; Turner, "Commentary: *Zostrianos*," 533–34. On first thought as the hypernoetic mystical faculty of God (and the contemplative seeker), see Mazur, "Self-Manifestation and 'Primary Revelation,'" 4; idem, "Platonizing Sethian Gnostic Background," 221–22; Burns, "Apophatic Strategies," 166–75.

95. *Zost.* NHC VIII,1.11.12, 12.5, 27.5–9.

96. *Zost.* NHC VIII,1.25.6–16, following the syntax of BFP by starting a new sentence; LS continues the sentence here.

97. Turner, "Commentary: *Zostrianos*," 537. See also idem, "Introduction: *Marsanes*," 229; idem, *Sethian Gnosticism and the Platonic Tradition*, 534; *Zost.* NHC VIII,1.19.10, 19.16, 22.14, 48.2. For species and genus, see also *Zost.* NHC VIII,1.19.1–3: "perfect, those things which exist with respect to species (εἶδος) and genus (γένος), and universal (πτηρϥ) and [individual] difference (διαφορὰ μερικόν)." See also *Zost.* NHC VIII,1.2.16. Use of this terminology hardly proves *Zostrianos*'s dependence on Porphyry, *pace* Majercik, "Porphyry and Gnosticism," 283–84. Plot. *Enn.* 6.1–3 [42–44] is evidence enough that these terms circulated in later Platonic circles before Porphyry.

98. E.g., Plat. *Soph.* 267d; for discussion, see Philip, "Platonic Diairesis." Galen's discussion of sorting out the types of diseases also employs this terminology; his handbooks may have influenced Clement's discussion of logic in *Strom.* VIII (Havdra, "Galenus Christianus?" esp. 356). On this point I am indebted to discussion with Riccardo Chiaradonna.

99. Porph. *Isag.* 7.16–19, tr. Sorabji, *Philosophy of the Commentators*, 3:165–69.

100. Follows BFP: τελιο[ϲ ⲛ]ⲕⲁⲧⲁⲟⲩ[ⲁ] ⲛ̅ⲧⲉ ⲛⲓⲡⲁⲛⲧⲉⲗⲓⲟ̣ⲥ [ⲉⲧϣⲟ]ⲟⲡ [ϩⲁ̣ⲑⲏ ⲛ̅], "individualités parfaits, issues des totalement parfaits [qui sont antérieurs aux]." Cf. LS: τελιο[ϲ ⲛⲓ]ⲕⲁⲧⲁ ⲟⲩ[ⲁ] ⲛ̣̅ⲧⲉ ⲛⲓⲡⲁⲛⲧⲉⲗⲓⲟ̣ⲥ [. . ϣⲟ]ⲟⲡ, "[the] individuals of the all-perfect ones [exist]." Turner (BCNH) translates the passage as "the Self-generated aeons are four perfect instances of the all-perfect ones [that exist before] the [perfect individuals]."

101. *Zost.* NHC VIII,1.18.11–17.

102. *Zost.* NHC VIII,1.22.4–9; see Turner, "Commentary: *Zostrianos*," 531–32.

103. *Zost.* NHC VIII,1.23.6–17. See also the discussion of Turner, "Introduction: *Marsanes*," 51–53.

104. "It is there (the Kalyptos) that all the living beings that exist individually (are) all joined together (ϩⲟⲧⲛ̄ ϩⲓⲟⲩⲙⲁ)" (*Zost.* NHC VIII,1.117.1–4; see also 20.10, 116.1–5, 117.21, 119.1).

105. Ibid., 127.3–14.

106. *Steles Seth* NHC VII,5.121.1–5; also ibid., 124.7–13.

107. *Allogenes* NHC XI,3.45.36–37, 48.9–13.

108. In CGL, Turner fills the lacuna with [ⲡⲁⲛⲧⲉⲗⲉⲓⲟⲥ ⲉ]ⲧⲣ̄ϩⲁⲑⲏ, "[all-perfect ones who] are before the perfect ones." In his 2004 translation (BCNH), he offers instead [ϩⲟⲩⲉⲡϫⲱⲕ ⲉ]ⲧⲣ̄ϩⲁⲑⲏ, "the [supra-perfect who] are before" so that Allogenes "would have praised the contents of all three levels of the Barbelo Aeon in ascending order, the 'perfect individuals' in Autogenes, the 'all-perfect ones' who are united in Protophanes, and (perhaps) the 'supra-perfect ones' in Kalyptos" ("Introduction: *Allogenes*," 19). Funk leaves the lacuna blank in the BCNH edition, but Scopello (BCNH) gives the translation, "les [Touts qui] précèdent les par[faits]," presumably working from the text of Funk and Poirier, *Concordance*: ⲛⲓ[ⲡⲧⲏⲣϥ̄ ⲟⲛ ⲉ]ⲧⲣ̄ϩⲁⲑⲏ.

109. *Allogenes* NHC XI, 3.55.12–16.

110. Ibid., 51.28–35; Procl. *El. Theo.* prop. 170 (*Elements*, Dodds) and *Mars.* NHC X, 1.3.21–22 are recalled by Turner, "*Allogenes:* Notes," 254.

111. *Allogenes* NHC XI,3.56.13–14, 46.17–22; Turner, "Introduction: *Allogenes*," 85; *Zost.* NHC VIII,1.41.9–19: "divine Autogenes [. . .] And the divine [Autogenes] [is] [. . .] of the [perfect] Thrice-Male Child. [And] this male (being) is [. . .] and species (εἶδος), perfect [. . .], since it does not have [. . .] through [unique] knowledge (γνῶσις), like that one. [And] it is a [measure] of the individuals; it is [a] unique knowledge of the individuals." Here I follow some, but not all, of the restorations of BFP.

112. On Kalyptos as the final unifier of particulars, see Turner, "Introduction: *Allogenes*," 75, 78; idem, "Platonizing Sethian Treatises," 143 n. 36; idem, "Commentary: *Zostrianos*," 632, recalling Plot. *Enn.* 5.9 [5] 6. (One could add *Enn.* 5.5 [32] 9.29; 6.7 [38] 2.9–11; 6.7 [38] 13; 3.2 [47] 1.27.) For souls distinct but not separate in the Protophanes, see *Allogenes* NHC XI,3.51.19–24; Plot. *Enn.* 6.4 [22] 14.1–4. On the unifying activity of the Numenian "second Intellect," see frgs. 16, 20–22 (des Places); *Chald. Or.* frg. 8 (Majercik); Turner, "Introduction: *Allogenes*," 80.

113. Cf. Plotinus's notion of providence operating in the intelligible realm—e.g., *Enn.* 6.8 [39] 17.9; 5.1 [10] 6.28, 5.3 [49] 12.39–44. Providence is not reasoned out (*Enn.* 2.2 [14] 2.28; 3.2 [47] 3.4–5) or planned (ibid., 6.7 [38] 1.28–35; see Schroeder, "Aseity," 309). Rather, Intellect and the One are beyond providence and determinism (*Enn.* 6.8 [39] 17.7–10).

114. See below, Chapter 5, "Left Behind."

115. Platonists placed individual action under the limited governance of fate as distinct from providence, attempting to leave more room for human freedom (Plut. *Fac.* 927a; Plot. *Enn.* 4.8 [6] 2.27; 3.3 [48] 4; Sallust. *Deis* 9 [Nock]).

116. Cf. Logan, *The Gnostics*, 49.

117. Thus Senec. *Prov.* 5.7–8; idem, *Ep.* 95.50 (on which, see Sharples, "Nemesius of Emesa," 114–15). Even if evils sometimes befall individuals, it is for the benefit of the whole: Chrysippus, ap. Diog. Laer. 7.138–39 = SVF 2.634 = Long and Sedley, *Hellenistic Philosophers*, 47O; Cic. *Nat. d.* 2.115 = SVF 2.1021 = Long and Sedley, *Hellenistic Philosophers*, 54A; Senec. *Prov.* 1.5–6; Marc. Aur. 2.3, 5.8, 6.43–44, 10.6. For discussion, see Sharples, "Alexander of Aphrodisias, *De Fato*," 243; idem, "Nemesius of Emesa," 110; Dragona-Monachou, "Divine Providence," 4424–36. This view was hardly ubiquitous among Stoics (cf. Cic. *Nat. d.* 2.165–67, 3.86; Plut. *Stoic. Rep.* 1051b = SVF 2.1178). Many early Christian thinkers, meanwhile, asserted God's direct, providential supervision over human affairs and especially salvation (*1 Clem.* 24.5; Min. Fel. *Oct.* 10.5; Clem. Alex. *Strom.* 1.11.52.3, 1.17.85.5; Orig. *Princ.* 1.2.9, 1.6.2, 2.1.1; idem, *Cels.* 6.71, 8.70).

118. See Denzey Lewis, *Cosmology and Fate.*

119. Hipp. *Haer.* 10.29.3. This point will be revisited below, in Chapter 7, "Rethinking Sethian Tradition."

120. Plat. *Tim.* 41a; *Pol.* 272e; esp. *Leg.* X 903b–904b. For further references (and reception in Middle Platonism), see Pease's commentary ad loc. in Cic. *Nat d.* p. 973.

121. Porph. *Christ.* frgs. 106, 112 (Berchman) = frgs. 82, 81 (Harnack); Meredith, "Porphyry and Julian," 1134–35; Hargis, *Against the Christians*, 75. See also Arn. *Adv. nat.* 2.63–65, cit. Courcelle, "Anti-Christian Arguments," 155; Jul. *Gal.* 106d–e; Hargis, *Against the Christians*, 124; Frede, "Celsus' Attack," 237.

122. Armstrong, "Plotinus and Christianity," 84; idem, "Man in the Cosmos," 6, 10; cf. Osborn, *Irenaeus*, 61–63; Narbonne, *Plotinus in Dialogue*, 76, both reading Plotinus's criticism as only applying to Gnostic Christianity.

123. E.g., Rom 9–11; 2 Cor 5:15.

CHAPTER 5

1. Alc. *Epit.* 3.1, 3.4 (Whittaker); further, see Dillon, "Commentary: *The Handbook of Platonism*," 57–58.

2. On "eschatology," see Nickelsburg, "Eschatology (Early Jewish)"; S. Cook, "Eschatology of the Old Testament"; Aune, "Early Christian Eschatology." For a *Forschungsbericht*, see Collins, "Apocalyptic Eschatology," 75–84.

3. Stone, "Apocalyptic Literature," 393; Collins, "Apocalyptic Eschatology," esp. 91; *1 En.* 10:9–21, 22; *2 En.* 10; *4 Ezra* 7:32–44, 7:75–87; *2 Bar.* 23, 30, 50.2–4; *Apoc. Peter (Eth.)* 3; *Apoc. Zeph.* 2.1–10; *Apoc. Ab.* 21; *T. Ab.* 13–14; *Apoc. Peter* NHC VII,3.75.21–22, 76.18–23, 38.23–24, 19.17. For "cosmic" vs. "personal" eschatology, see Collins, "Morphology," 17–18; Allison, "Eschatology of the New Testament," 298–99; S. Cook, "Eschatology of the Old Testament," 300, 306. Cf. Aune, who is reluctant to use the term for individuals ("Early Christian Eschatology," 594), and Rowland, who sees the term's use as so diverse as to preclude usefulness (*Open Heaven*; esp. 14, 70–72; idem, "Apocalyptic: The Disclosure," 780).

4. For Gnostic eschatology, see Peel, "Gnostic Eschatology," 156ff; see also Kippenberg, "Vergleich jüdischer, christlicher, und gnostischer Apokalyptik," 751; Logan, *Gnostic Truth and Christian Heresy*, 301; Attridge, "Valentinian and Sethian Apocalyptic Traditions."

5. Plot. *Enn.* 2.9 and *Unt.* are discussed in the following; *Marsanes* mentions the Sojourn and Repentance aeons in passing (*Mars.* NHC X,1.3.17; Turner, "Introduction: *Marsanes*," 11–14). The *Egyptian Gospel* hypostatizes Sophia's personal Repentance into a single aeon that catalyzes Sethian salvation history (NHC III,2.59.9–23, discussed below). This terminology is absent from *Apoc. Adam*, *Steles Seth*, and *Allogenes*, but one would not expect to find it in these treatises, since they do not address the postmortem fate of the soul.

6. Plot. *Enn.* 2.9 [33] 6.1–3.

7. *Unt.* 263.16–23; see C. Schmidt, *Plotins Stellung*, 61–62; Tardieu, "Les gnostiques," 527–28 n. 60 ; Edwards, "Porphyry's 'Cave,'" 98; Turner, *Sethian Gnosticism and the Platonic Tradition,* 570.

8. Zost. NHC VIII,1.8–9.

9. As in BFP; LS leaves the lacuna blank.

10. Zost. NHC VIII,1.12.2–17.

11. Macrob. *Comm. somn. Scip.* 1.11.7. Also see Procl., *Comm. Tim.* 1.147.6–9, 2.48.17–21 (Diehl), Simpl. *Comm. cael.* 7.379.29, 512.18 (Heiberg). Cf. Turner, *Sethian Gnosticism and the Platonic Tradition*, 572 (identifying the "aetherial earth" as the atmosphere). An "aetherial earth" is also mentioned at *Gos. Eg.* NHC III,2.50.10. Plotinus says that the Gnostics identify a "new earth" as the "rational form of the world" (λόγον κόσμου—*Enn.* 2.9 [33] 5.26–27; *Unt.* 249 [Schmidt and MacDermot]); cf. *Enn.* 2.9 [33] 11.11–12; 6.7 [38] 11. References to the "aetherial earth" were mistakenly confused with Plotinus's "new earth" (aetherial, material vs. eschatological, intelligible) by Pépin, "Theories of Procession," 314; Wallis, "Soul and Nous," 462; Stroumsa, *Another Seed*, 126; cf. also C. Schmidt, *Plotins Stellung*, 61–62; Bousset, *Hauptprobleme*, 189–92; Puech, "Plotin et les gnostiques," 168; Tardieu, "Les gnostiques," 527–28 n. 60; Turner, "Introduction: *Zostrianos*," 146. See further below, "Left Behind."

12. *Zost.* NHC VIII,1.11.2–9: "And the impressions (ἀντίτυπος) of the aeons exist as follows: While they did not obtain a form (εἰδέα) of (even) a single power, they did, however, possess eternal glories. And places of judgment of each and every one of the powers exist."

13. See Sieber's note ad loc. (LS) at Zos. NHC VIII,1.5.24–25; LSJ 1342a.

14. Abramowski, "Nag Hammadi 8,1 'Zostrianos,'" 3.

15. Plut. *Gen. Socr.* 591b; idem, *Fac.* 943d (on which, see Stettner, *Seelenwanderung*, 57; Dieterich, *Nekyia*, 145); Porph. frg. 383 (Smith) = Stob. 1.49.61 (Wachsmuth and Hense; see also 6:2.330–34); Iamb. *Vit. Pyth.* 18.82; Lyd. *Mens.* 167.21 (Wuensch), cit. Finamore and Dillon, "*De anima* Commentary," 202. Further in general, see Dörrie and Baltes, 6:2.333. For Numenius (and Proclus's rejoinder), see Iamb. *An.* 26 (Finamore and Dillon); Procl. *Comm. Remp.* 2:128.3–140.25 (Kroll); Dillon, *Middle Platonists*, 97

n. 2, 178, 375; Lamberton, *Homer*, 68; Finamore and Dillon, "*De anima*
Commentary," 191.

16. Cf. Clement's description of punishment as education: σωτήριοι καὶ
παιδευτικαὶ αἱ κολάσεις τοῦ θεοῦ (*Strom.* 6.6.46.3 [Stählin], per Solmsen,
"Providence and the Souls," 366 n. 55).

17. LS reconstructs this as ⲕ[. . .]ⲁ ⲛ̄ⲧⲉ ⲛⲓⲁⲓⲱⲛ ⲟ̣[. . .] ⲛ̄ϭⲓ ⲟⲩⲭⲱⲕⲙ̄ [. . .]
ⲉ. BFP reconstructs it as ⲕ[. . .]ⲁ ⲛ̄ⲧⲉ ⲛⲓⲁⲓⲱⲛ ϥ[ϣⲟⲟⲡ ⲙ̄ⲙⲁⲩ] ⲛ̄ϭⲓ ⲟⲩⲭⲱⲕⲙ̄
[ⲙ̄ⲡⲉⲓ̈ⲣⲏⲧ]ⲉ.

18. BFP reconstructs this as [ⲛ̄ϯⲫⲩⲥ]ⲓⲥ. LS reconstructs it as [ⲛ̄ϯⲅⲛⲱⲥ]ⲓⲥ.

19. *Zost.* NHC VIII,1.24.21–25.8

20. *Zost.* NHC VIII,1.27.13–19. As in BFP. The phrase at the end, "those
who follow the ways of others," could also be, "because they follow the ways
of others."

21. *Zost.* NHC VIII,1.27.21–28.10: "Second (δέ), as for those who [stand
upon] the Repentance, namely, that one who did not [doubt] sin, knowledge is enough [for them], being new. [. . .] And he has [. . .] difference(s)
(διαφορά). While some have sinned with others [. . .], they repented with
others, [. . .], on their own. For [. . .] species (εἶδος) which exist [. . .]. As
for those who have committed all sins and repented, either they are parts
(μέρος), or they desired, on their own, (to repent?). Therefore, their aeons are
six, According to the place that has come to each of them." See also Turner,
"Commentary: *Zostrianos*," 542–43.

22. *Zost.* NHC VIII,1.28.10–22.

23. Ibid., 27.2–14: "while those who are totally [perished (ⲧⲁⲕⲏⲟⲩⲧ)]
possess four [species (εἶδος)], those who [are in] time (χρόνος) are nine
in number. Each one has its own species, custom (ⲧⲱⲡ); their likenesses
(ⲉⲓⲛⲉ) differ, being separate, and they stand upright. Other souls, immortal, join together in dwelling with all the(se) souls, because of [Sophia]
who gazed below; for the species of souls immortal souls are three in
number."

24. Cf. Sieber, "Notes: *Zostrianos*," 106, recalling *Apoc. Peter* NHC
VII,3.83.31—yet the latter passage does not refer to reincarnation. Turner
identifies this type as "materialistic persons with dead souls" who will
undergo reincarnation ("Commentary: *Zostrianos*," 554).

25. LS reconstructs this as ϣⲟⲣⲡ ⲁⲗⲗⲁ ⲉⲩ[ⲟⲩ]ⲟ̣ⲣ̣ⲙ̄ ⲛ̄ⲣ̣[ⲟⲩ]ⲟ [ⲇ]ⲉ ⲉⲩϣⲟⲟⲡ
ⲉⲩⲑⲉⲃⲓⲏⲟ[ⲉ], "first, but they are safe and exist very humbly." BFP reconstructs
as ϣⲟⲣⲡ̄ ⲁⲗⲗⲁ ⲁⲩ[ⲟⲩ]ⲟ̣ⲣ̣ⲙ̄ ⲛ̄[ⲟⲩ]ⲟ ⲡⲉ ⲉⲩϣⲟⲟⲡ ⲉⲩⲑⲉⲃⲓⲏⲟ[ⲩⲧ], "initialement, mais
le [salut] est [plus grand] lorsqu'on est de condition inférieure."

26. *Zost.* NHC VIII,1.42.10–26, leaving the end of the passage unrestored (with LS). BFP restores it as ⲣⲉⲛϫⲓⲙ̄ⲕⲁ<ⲣ̄> ⲛ[ⲉ ⲉⲩⲧⲁⲕ]ⲏⲟ[ⲩⲧ] ⲣⲉⲛ ⲉⲓⲟⲧ[ⲉ]
ⲛ̄ⲧⲉ[ⲣⲉⲛⲛ̄ⲕⲁ ⲛ̄ⲣⲩ]ⲗⲓⲕⲟⲛ. ⲣⲉⲛⲇ̣[ⲉⲙⲱⲛ ⲛⲉ ⲉⲣⲉ]ⲡⲓⲕⲱⲣ̣ⲧ̄ ⲟⲩ[ⲱⲙ ⲙ̄ⲙⲟⲩ . . .], "[Ce
sont] des souffrances [de perdition], des père[s] des [choses hy]liques, [ce
sont] ses d[émons que] le feu [consume.]"

27. *Zost.* NHC VIII,1.43.1–12· In regard to "daimones," LS (pp. 106–7)
mentions that "some Middle Platonic writers" consider that there are three
kinds of daimones: incarnate souls, disincarnate souls, and souls of the dead.
Cf. *Zost.* NHC VIII,1.27.9–20.

28. These individuals seem to commit no great sin, despite 27.14–21, and they are still able to seek (Turner, "Commentary: *Zostrianos*," 555).

29. *Zost.* NHC VIII,1.43.13–19. For "(being) obstacles," BFP has ϫ[ρο]π. LS has ϫ[ωρ]π; the translation "those who stumble" is equally likely.

30. *Zost.* NHC VIII,1.43.19–27.

31. BFP translates as "realités."

32. BFP translates as "mais (lui les a) plutôt (connues) par [la] parole."

33. BFP reconstructs this as ⲁϥϫⲓ ⲙ̄ⲡⲟⲩⲉⲓ[ⲛⲉ].

34. BFP reconstructs this as ϣⲁϥϣⲱⲡⲉ ⲉⲛⲧ[ⲟϥ ⲡⲉ] ⲛⲁⲓ̈ ⲧⲏⲣⲟⲩ.

35. *Zost.* NHC VIII,1.44.1–22. The context of the passage—the soteriological grades of the various types of souls—is certainly different than the Porphyrian passages about saving the self through Intellect adduced by Majercik as evidence of *Zostrianos*'s dependence on Porphyry ("Porphyry and Gnosticism," 282).

36. *Zost.* NHC VIII,1.45.1–9.

37. Cf. Turner, who recalls the four kinds of souls in Plato's *Phaedo* 113d–114c, the nine kinds of mortal life in *Phaedrus* 248c–e, and the curable and incurable sins of *Gorgias* 252a–b, which would refer to sinners who "repent" and those who "perish," respectively (Turner, *Sethian Gnosticism and the Platonic Tradition*, 602–3; "Commentary: *Zostrianos*," 540–41, also on Procl. *Comm. Tim.* 1.147.27–148.16). Yet none of the souls in *Phaedo* 113d–114c perish forever. One kind winds up in Tartaros for good, but it is not destroyed; the other three kinds are reincarnated. Similarly, the nine lives in the *Phaedrus* include the philosopher-king who, like the fourth, philosophical soul in the *Phaedo*, will transcend reincarnation and bodily existence; however, *Zostrianos*'s nine types of temporal existence (27.2–7) are all subcategories of destructible, not "immortal," souls.

38. Turner rightly identifies the fifth type of humanity with the self-generated souls from 28.10–30 ("Commentary: *Zostrianos*," 555–56). The phrase "finds itself" means, as he argues, that they live like philosophers. Like Zostrianos, they are divinized by a fifth baptism in the Autogenes (*Zost.* NHC VIII,1.53.15–24).

39. Turner, "Commentary: *Zostrianos*," 554. *Ap. John* is occasionally cited as universalist, but it also mentions people who undergo eternal punishment (*pace* Couliano, *Tree of Gnosis*, 103, regarding *Ap. John* NHC II,1.26.13–27.30). It is worth adding here that the text also refers to metensomatosis (Couliano, *Tree of Gnosis*; Logan, *Gnostic Truth and Christian Heresy*, 259, 264–55, regarding NHC II,1.26.22–32 = BG 67.19–68.13).

40. *Zost.* NHC VIII,1.128.13–14, 130.21–132.5; *Allogenes* NHC XI,3.64.14–25; *Mars.* NHC X,1.1.14–25, 10.13–18, 40.2–23, discussed below, in this chapter.

41. Perhaps the place of rest "given to Sophia, in exchange for her repentance (μετάνοια)" (*Zost.* NHC VIII,1.10.9), as suggested by Turner (*Sethian Gnosticism and the Platonic Tradition*, 565; "Introduction: *Marsanes*," 114–15). See also *Pistis Sophia*, where Jesus reports how the fallen wisdom has committed twelve "transgressions" against the twelve aeons and so recited

twelve "repentances" that are of a hymnic character (chs. 32–57). Finally (57), she recites a thirteenth repentance for the thirteenth aeon (Barbelo).

42. The topos is "the designation of the Christian self as a stranger, sojourner, foreigner, and/or resident alien in order to communicate varying forms of Christian alterity" (Dunning, *Aliens and Sojourners*, 1).

43. As Scopello notes, "Titres au'fémin," 133; for a survey, see Feldman, "Concept of Exile in Josephus," 145; Gaertner, "Discourse of Displacement" (in the Greek texts he cites, παροίκησις is never used; "exile" is φυγή).

44. Marc. Aur. 4.29; generally, see Dunning, *Aliens and Sojourners*, 25–40.

45. Marc. Aur. 4.3 (the proper frame for Plotinus's and Porphyry's remarks); for Philo, see *Conf.* ch. 77–81, regarding Gen 23:4, 47:9; *Congr.* 20–24; *Agr.* 64–65; see Kidd, *Alterity and Identity*, 123–24; Feldmeier, "The 'Nation' of Strangers," 250–51; Dunning, *Aliens and Sojourners*, 44–46. For Plotinus and Porphyry, see Plot. *Enn.* 1.6 [1] 8 (notably early and exceptional in his corpus); Porph. *Abst.* 1.30.2–4, 1.33.5 (Bouffartigue and Patillon), *Marc.* 6 (Wicker); cf. Clark, "Translate into Greek," 130; Johnson, "Philosophy, Hellenicity, Law," 64, 66.

46. Philo *Abr.* 62; Clem. Al. *Strom.* 1.5.31; Jos. *Ant.* 1.154–157; cit. Dunning, *Aliens and Sojourners*, 48–49. See further Feldmeier, "The 'Nation' of Strangers," 247–49.

47. Van Houten, *Stranger in Israelite Law*; Cohen, *Beginnings of Jewishness*, 121; Rendtorff, "The *Gēr* in the Priestly Laws," 77. For exile in the apocalypses, see VanderKam, "Exile," 109 (on 4 *Ezra*); Halpern-Amaru, "Exile and Return," 140, 140 n. 31 (on *Jubilees*).

48. Most famously, Gen 23:4. See also Gen 15:3; Exod 2:22, 18:3; Jer 14:8; Deut 14:21, 23:8; 2 Sam 1:13; Ps 39:13; 1 Chr 19:15; Ps 119:19; and see Kidd, *Alterity and Identity*, 125; Feldmeier, "The 'Nation' of Strangers," 242; Dunning, *Aliens and Sojourners*, 42. Other discussions of patriarchs and Israel as exile include Gen 17:18, 19:9, 20:1, 21:23, 26:3, 32:5, 35:27, 37:1, 47:4; Exod 6:4; Ps. 105:12; Wis 19:10. The verb παροικεῖν also commonly refers to sojourning in the LXX: Gen 12:10, 28:4, 36:7; Judg 17:8–9; Ruth 1:1; Ps. 5:4, 15:1, 61:4; Is. 16:4, 52:4; Jer 28:20; Sir 21:28, 29:24, 38:32. For the theme of exile as an indication of the elect status of the Qumran community in the *Damascus Document*, see Feldmeier, "The ‹Nation› of Strangers," 249–50.

49. Exod 22:20, but esp. 23:9; Lev 19:33–34; Deut 23:8. For the גר as legally associated with outsiders such as widows and orphans, see Exod 22:21, 22:24; Deut 16:11, 16:14, 24:14–21, 26:13, 27:19. For discussion, see Levenson, "Universal Horizon," 157–60, Rendtroff, "The *Gēr* in the Priestly Laws," 84–86; Cohen, *Beginnings of Jewishness*, 120–25. Cf. Wis 19:14. On Israel's dependence on God during exile, see Kidd, *Alterity and Identity*, 117. Also in early Christian interpretation, see Acts 7:4–6, 7:29, 13:17; Clem. Al. *Strom.* 2.18.88.

50. Exod 12:49; Jer 51:51; 1 Esd 44:7–9, 56:34; *Jos. Asen.* 8:5–8. For the line of Aaron as "*allogeneis*," see Exod 29:33; Num 16:40; Lev 22:10. Foreigners and sojourners are expelled in *Ps. Sol.* 17:31; thus also Phil. *Somn.* 1.

161; *Virt.* 147; *Spec.* 1.124 (re: Lev 22:10), 4.16; *Jos. et. Asen.* 4.12 (cit. Scopello, "Titres au'fémin," 133). See also Sir 29:23–28 (identifying the πάροικος as ξένος). The negative evaluation of exile as associated with foreign idolators may be why some second-temple Jewish writers dissociated Abraham from the theme.

51. Eph 2:19.

52. Heb 11:8–16, esp. 9 (πίστει παρῴκησεν εἰς γῆν τῆς ἐπαγγελίας ὡς ἀλλοτρίαν); see Attridge, *Epistle to the Hebrews*, 323–31; Dunning, *Aliens and Sojourners*, 47–48.

53. 1 Pet 1:1, 2:11; Kidd, *Alterity and Identity*, 123; Feldmeier, "The 'Nation' of Strangers," 256; Buell, *Why This New Race?* 46. On the πάροικος *qua* ἐκλεκτός, see Kidd, *Alterity and Identity*, 127.

54. 2 *Clem.* 5:5.

55. See also Ter. *Cor.* 13 ("you are a foreigner in this world, a citizen of Jerusalem, the city above"); *1 Clem.* 54:4; *Diogn.* 5.4–5.9, 6.8; Greer, "Alien Citizens," 39; Buell, *Why This New Race?* 31; Feldmeier, "The 'Nation' of Strangers," 265; Dunning, *Aliens and Sojourners*, 64; J. Perkins, *Roman Imperial Identities*, 31–34.

56. Clem. Al. *Strom.* 4.26.165.3, responding to Basilides (see below), 3.11.75; idem, *Paed.* 3.12 (Mondésert).

57. "I seemed to them like a foreigner" (*Odes Sol.* 17:6; see also 41:8: "All those who see me will be amazed, because I am from another race"). See also Matt 25:35; Luke 24:18; John 1:10; Scopello, "Titres au'fémin," 134.

58. Orig. *Hom. Jer.* 7.3.4, tr. J. C. Smith.

59. Jonas, *Gnostic Religion*, 49–51.

60. *Apoc. Peter* NHC VII,3.83.17.

61. *1 Apoc. Jas.* NHC V,3.11.17–18; see Dunning, *Aliens and Sojourners*, 99.

62. Clem. Al. *Strom.* 4.26.165.3, tr. Layton, *Gnostic Scriptures*, 437.

63. CMC 44: "I became like a stranger and a solitary in their midst."

64. *ML* p. 223 (Lidzbarski, tr. Rudolph in Foerster, *Gnosis*, 2:243–45), esp.: "By my illumination and my praise have I kept myself a stranger from the world. I have stood among them (the wicked) like a child who has no father."

65. *Apoc. Adam* NHC V,5.69.12–18; these strangers known as the seed of men who receive the "life of Gnosis" are probably the ἕτερον σπέρμα of Gen 4:25 (Pearson, "Figure of Seth," 489). Certainly they are the offspring of Seth (Stroumsa, *Another Seed*, 83). For their identification with the seed of Ham and Japheth later in the text, see NHC V,5.73.16–24: they will "enter into another land and sojourn (ϭⲟⲉⲓⲗⲉ) with those men who came forth from the great eternal knowledge. For the shadow of their power will protect those who have sojourned with them from every evil thing and every unclean desire." See also NHC V,5.74.21–24; Stroumsa, *Another Seed*, 85.

66. *Apoc. Adam* NHC V,5.75.9–76.9.

67. Ibid., 82.25–28.

68. For the inferior seed of Cain and Abel, see Phil. *Post.* 172–77; *Ap. John.* NHC II,1.24.15–31; Klijn, *Seth*, 26, 30–32 (Samaritans), 82–87

("Sethians" known to Ps.-Ter. and Epiph.); Pearson, "Figure of Seth," 481–82; Lahe, *Gnosis und Judentum*, 277–83. For Seth as the father of all, see Theoph. *Autol.* 2.30.18–20; thus also held the Ophites, *ap.* Ir. *Haer.* 1.30.

69. Epiph. *Pan.* 40.7.1–3. See also M. A. Williams, "Sethianism," 49; Brankaer and Bethge, *Codex Tchacos*, 376.

70. Epiph. *Pan.* 26.8.1.

71. [*Allogenes*] TC 60.19–23.

72. *Gos. Eg.* NHC IV,2.50.21 = III,2.41.6–7; *Zost.* NHC VIII,1.128.7.

73. See H. Jackson, "Geradamas," esp. 389–91, followed by Logan, *Gnostic Truth and Christian Heresy*, 102; Pearson, *Ancient Gnosticism*, 65; cf. idem, "Introduction: *Melchizedek*," 37; Turner, "Commentary: *Zostrianos*," 506.

74. (Pi)Geradamas is addressed as "my mind" (*Steles Seth* VII,5.119.1), "eye of Autogenes" (*Zost.* NHC VIII,1.6.23–24), "perfect man, eye of Autogenes" (*Zost.* NHC VIII,1.30.4–7), and "man of light, immortal aeon" (*Melch.* NHC IX,1.6.5–6). "His knowledge comprehends divine Autogenes" as a "mind of truth" (*Zost.* NHC VIII,1.30.4–7).

75. *Steles Seth* NHC VII,5.119.20, 120.20.

76. Abramowski, "Nag Hammadi 8,1 'Zostrianos'," 3, regarding Heb 11:9 and Eph 2:19.

77. H. Jackson, "Geradamas," 389–90.

78. As in *Zost.* VIII,1, "I tried their ways (ⲉⲃⲟⲟⲩⲉ)" (1.22–23); "ways of others" is related to being a stranger (25.4–5). Cf. 2 *Jeu* 101.10; *Ap. John* NHC II,1.26.8, 26.19, 27.3 = BG 69.3.

79. Cf. Turner, "Commentary: *Zostrianos*," 542.

80. Van Houten, *Stranger in Israelite Law*, 180–82, and also J. Lieu, *Christian Identity*, 120–21.

81. Cf. Turner, speculating that these souls "are in a position to make the correct choice for the kind of life they lead in their final incarnation," as do souls in Plato's *Myth of Er* (*Sethian Gnosticism and the Platonic Tradition*, 567; idem, "Commentary: *Zostrianos*," 536).

82. Aug. *Civ. dei* 13.19 = Porph. frg. 300bF, 301aF (A. Smith) = 6:1.180. See further Sorabji, *Time, Creation, and the Continuum*, 188 n. 68; Majercik, *Chaldean Oracles* p. 20; Dörrie and Baltes, 6:2.383ff.

83. For further citations and more detailed discussion of these points, see Burns, "Cosmic Eschatology and Christian Platonism."

84. These are Pearson's restorations, assuming a corrupt text; Poirier translates the original: "et le monde intelligible, il a connu, en distinguant, que, de toute manière, ce monde sensible [est digne] d'être préservé tout entier" (FP).

85. *Mars.* NHC X,1.5.15–28.

86. Ibid., 3.25–4.2. On the demiurgical activity of the Autogenes, see *Allogenes* NHC XI,3.51.25–32; Pearson, "Notes: *Marsanes*," 264; idem, "Gnosticism as Platonism," 71; Turner, *Sethian Gnosticism and the Platonic Tradition*, 577; idem, "Introduction: *Marsanes*," 111–12.

87. Turner, "Introduction: *Marsanes*," 115; idem, "Commentary: *Zostrianos*," 514–15; Poirier, "Commentaire: *Marsanès*," 389. Oddly, Poirier here refers to the BFP text of *Zostrianos*, which does not support Turner's point.

88. *Zost.* NHC VIII,1.130.21–132.5.

89. See above, n. 11, in this chapter; *Unt.* p. 249; Abramowski, "Nag Hammadi 8,1 'Zostrianos,'" 7. On the "new earth," see Rev 21:1–2; 2 Pet 3:13; Is 16:22; 65:17; 4 *Ezra* 7:89–101; 2 *Bar.* 49–52, 72–74.

90. See Plat. *Tim.* 41a ff; more generally, idem, *Leg.* X 900d ff. For the sublunary spheres as corruptible and in need of maintenance, see Arist. *Cael.* 2.3.286a31; idem, *Gen. corr.* 2.10.336a24–32; idem, *Metaph.* L 6.1072a10, cit. Sharples, "Alexander of Aphrodisias on Divine Providence," 200 n. 20; Athenag. *Leg.* 19.3 (Schoedel). For biblical notions of the world's perishability, see Ps 102:25 –27; Is 51:6. For Philo, see *Opif.* 2.10; Runia, *Philo of Alexandria and the 'Timaeus'*, 240–41, 153–54; Winston, "Philo's Theory of Eternal Creation," 599. Among Christians, see Athenag. *Res.* 18.3; Orig. *Princ.* 1.4.3; idem, *Cels.* 5.26.

91. See previous note.

92. *Mars.* NHC X,1.10.13–18, following the syntax of Poirier, "Commentaire: *Marsanès*," 400, *pace* Pearson, "Notes: *Marsanes*," 278. See also *Mars.* NHC X,1.14–25, 40.2–23, 41.3–5; Poirier, "Commentaire: *Marsanès*," 365–66.

93. *Zost.* NHC VIII,1.128.13–14.

94. *Allogenes* NHC XI,3.64.14–23. The passage goes on to say that this individual "has judged himself." Regardless of who is doing the judging, the point is that the text envisages that some individuals are not saved.

95. *Zost.* NHC VIII,1.9.6–15; *Allogenes* NHC XI,3.64.21–25; cf. Turner, "Commentary: *Zostrianos*," 650; idem, *Sethian Gnosticism and the Platonic Tradition*, 565–67.

96. Cf. Turner, "Commentary: *Zostrianos*," 554.

97. *Trim. Prot.* NHC XIII,1.42.1–45.2, 42.19–21. The redactional relationship of this apocalypse to the rest of the text and Sethian tradition is not clear. Turner hypothesizes that it is a secondary "doctrinal" addition, drawing on Hellenistic "Nekyia traditions" and added to the earlier, aretological stratum of the text ("Introduction: NCH XIII.1*," 376–81).

98. *Apoc. Adam* NHC V,5.68–70, 75.9–16, 76.17–20; for background and interpretation, see Stroumsa, *Another Seed*, 83, 106; Brakke, "The Seed of Seth at the Flood," 46–60.

99. *Gos. Eg.* NHC IV,2.72.22–27 = III,2.61.12–15; IV,2.73.27–75.24 = III,2.63.13–64.9; see also Böhlig and Wisse, "Commentary: *The Gospel of the Egyptians*," 189.

100. *Gos. Eg.* NHC IV,2.63.3–8 = III,2.51.10–14, tr. Böhlig and Wisse (CGL), modified.

101. Plot. *Enn.* 2.9 [33] 4.14–23.

102. Ibid., 6.58–60 (condemnation of needless γενέσεις καὶ φθοράς); see also 2.1 [40] 4.29–33. See further above, Chapter 2, "Against the Gnostic Cosmos"; C. Schmidt, *Plotins Stellung*, 68–71; Meijering, "God Cosmos History," esp. 253–54.

103. Plot. *Enn.* 2.9 [33] 8.2–5; see also 5.8 [31] 7; 6.7 [38] 1.38; 3.2 [47] 2.16–21. Plotinus complains further that matter cannot dissolve unless it has

something else (i.e., more matter) to dissolve into (ibid., 2.9 [33] 3.7–21, discussed above, Chapter 2, "Against the Gnostic Cosmos").

104. For the eternity of the cosmos, see Plat. *Tim.* 41b; Plut. *E Delph.* 393; Alc. *Epit.* 15.2; *Corp. herm.* 11.3, 5, 15; *Ascl.* 29, 31; Plot. *Enn.* 4.4 [28] 10.5–7; see also Plot. *Enn.* 3.7 [45] 3.31–34, 6, 12.13–29; 2.1 [40] 1–2, 4–5. As a criticism of Christianity, see Orig. *Cels.* 4.11, 4.79; cf. Min. Fel. *Oct.* 11.1; J. Cook, *Interpretation of the New Testament,* 99.

105. Plat. *Pol.* 269c ; *Tim.* 29a; Arist. *Cael.* 1.10. 280a12–280a23; Macrob. *Comm. somn. Scip.* 2.10.9–16, 12.12–16.

106. Orig. *Cels.* 1.19–20, 4.9, 4.11; Mac. Mag. *Apocrit.* 4.164. J. Cook, *Interpretation of the New Testament,* 98.

107. Sallust. *Deis* 7; also also 13. Mac. Mag. *Apocrit.* 4.158 (Goulet), regarding 1 Cor 7:31; for discussion, see J. Cook, *Interpretation of the New Testament,* 222, 230 n. 383.

108. I thank John D. Turner for drawing my attention to this problem, in conversation and correspondence.

109. For final judgment, see *1 En.* 1:4, 38; *2 En.* 46, 65:5–10; *2 Bar.* 51:1–6, 54:20–22, 83; *Apoc. Ab.* 29–31; *Apoc. Peter (Eth.)* 4; *Apoc. Elij.* 5:30–35; Rev 20:12–15; *1 Clem.* 23–28; Ter. *Marc.* 3.24; idem, *An.* 55; Ps.-Clem. *Hom.* 3.6.3–5. For surveys (to which I am indebted for many of these citations), see May, "Eschatologie 5. Alte Kirche," 300–303; Aune, "Early Christian Eschatology," 2:595; Attridge, "Valentinian and Sethian Apocalyptic Traditions," 184ff; Yarbro Collins, "New Testament Eschatology"; Adams, *The Stars Will Fall from Heaven.* For cosmic eschatology, see Deut 32:22; Matt 5:22, 18:8; Mark 9:43; Rev 20:14, 21:8. For the world's reconstitution, see Is 65:17, 66:22 (see also Zech 14); 2 Pet 3:5–13; Rev 21; *1 En.* 45:4–5, 91:16; *2 Bar.* 32:7, 44; *2 Clem.* 11; *Herm.* 3.4; Euseb. *Hist. Eccl.* 5.16.18–19 (on the Montanists' New Jerusalem). See also D. Russell, *"New Heavens and New Earth,"* 134–210. For Chiliasm, see Rev 20:6; *Apoc. Elij.* 5:36–9; Ir. *Haer.* 5.28.3.

110. Attempts to read Christian eschatology in terms of Greek thought include Just. Mart. *1 Apol.* 20, 28, 60; *2 Apol.* 7, 9; similarly, Clem. Al. *Strom.* 5.1.9. Origen appears to be a trickier case since he affirms the Stoic doctrine of a succession of worlds (*Princ.* 2.3.4–5, 3.5.3), but he elsewhere says there will be an end to this succession (*Comm. Rom.* 6.8.8 [Scheck]; *Cels.* 4.10; *Hom. Jer.* 12.5 [Smith]; *Hom. Lev.* 14.4 [Barkley]). See also May, "Eschatologie 5. Alte Kirche," 301–2; Osborn, *Justin Martyr,* 149–53; Trigg, *Origen,* 213. A surprising majority of Gnostic texts at least mention the end of the world; for a survey, see Peel, "Gnostic Eschatology," 157–58; Attridge, "Valentinian and Sethian Apocalyptic Traditions," 184–85.

111. Adams, *The Stars Will Fall from Heaven,* 34–35, 98–99, 256–57, re: Is 30:26, 60:20, and perhaps 65:17; Zech 14; *1 En.* 45: 4–5; *Jub.* 1:29, 4:26; Rom 8:18–25. More generally, see D. Russell, *"New Heavens and New Earth."*

112. For Basilides, see Clem. *Strom.* 4.165.3 = Layton frg. E (in *Gnostic Scriptures*) = Löhr frg. 12; Orig. *Comm. Rom.* 5.1.27 = Löhr frg. 17; Pearson, "Basilides the Gnostic," 18, *pace* Nautin, "Les fragments de Basilide,"

394–98. See also Orig. *Comm. Rom.* 6.8.8. For Ophites, see Ir. *Haer.*
1.30.14; Epiph. *Pan.* 26.10.8; Orig. *Cels.* 6.33; *Ap. John* NHC II,1.26.36–
27.11. For a survey of the extensive Manichaean sources, see Casadio, "Manichaean Metempsychosis"; see also *Pist. Soph.* 283, 381.17–383.11 (Schmidt
and MacDermot). Generally, see Hoheisel, "Das frühe Christentum und die
Seelenwanderung," 42.

113. See Jennott, *"Gospel of Judas,"* 131–32.

114. As J. Perkins writes, the resident alien motif and ethnic reasoning
helped Christians "hollow out imperial pretensions to power and control.
They were announcing a new space, a new kingdom outside the contemporary configurations of power. . . . Christian spatial discourse contests the
imperial elite's claims to universal control" (*Roman Imperial Identities*, 34).
The readers of the Sethian texts were no exception, and Plotinus reacted
accordingly, as a Hellene.

115. *Pace* Turner, *Sethian Gnosticism and the Platonic Tradition*, 92; see
also idem, "Introduction: *Marsanes*," 39.

116. *Pace* Turner, "Introduction: *Zostrianos*," 50; Idem, "Introduction:
Allogenes," 29; Pleše, "Gnostic Literature," 191; see also Turner, "Introduction: *Marsanes*," 27, 29–30. Cf. Attridge, "Valentinian and Sethian Apocalyptic Traditions," 196: "Texts cast in the form of narratives of 'ascent' experiences have less apocalyptic eschatology, as well as less direct connection
with biblical figures and themes, than the rest of the Sethian tradition."

117. Eschatological change was not always concerned with the resurrection of the dead or creating a new earth but sometimes with "the transition
from one sphere of life to another. Such a transition is vertical rather than
horizontal, spatial rather than temporal" (Collins, "Apocalyptic Eschatology," 91).

118. As noted by Peel, "Gnostic Eschatology." On the following points,
see further Burns, "Apocalypses amongst Gnostics." For Gnostic-apocalyptic dualism, see Schubert, "Problem und Wesen der jüdischen Gnosis," 6; Ménard, "Littérature apocalyptique juive," 301; Vielhauer and
Strecker, "Apocalypses," 550; Scopello, "Contes apocalyptiques et apocalypses philosophiques," 350; Kippenberg, "Vergleich jüdischer, christlicher,
und gnostischer Apokalyptik," 763; Lahe, *Gnosis und Judentum*, 113. For
Gnostic-apocalyptic pessimism, see Schüssler Fiorenza, "Phenomenon,"
303; similarly, see Gruenwald, "Knowledge and Vision," 83, 91; Rowland,
"Apocalyptic: The Disclosure," 790, 796; Lahe, *Gnosis und Judentum*, 141–
42. For Gnostic-apocalyptic interiorization of history, see J. Z. Smith, "Wisdom and Apocalyptic," 86; Rowland, *Open Heaven*, 445.

119. MacRae, "Apocalyptic Eschatology," 324; also ibid., 323; Attridge,
"Valentinian and Sethian Apocalyptic Traditions," 194.

120. Bousset, *Himmelsreise*, 5.

CHAPTER 6

1. *Mars.* NHC X,1.35.1–6. The use of the term "alphabet mysticism,"
employed here to engage Pearson and Turner, should be considered distinct

from any greater implication or discussion about the category "mysticism," instead referring simply to speculation about the anagogic properties of the letters of the alphabet(s).

2. Pearson, "Introduction: *Marsanes*," 249–50; idem, *Ancient Gnosticism*, 93; Turner, *Sethian Gnosticism and the Platonic Tradition*, 614–33; idem, "Introduction: *Marsanes*," 20, 81, 231–34; idem, "Introduction: *Zostrianos*," 72–75; Rasimus, *Paradise Reconsidered*, 278–79; Pleše, "Gnostic Literature," 192; Brakke, *The Gnostics*, 82.

3. On theurgy, see Lewy, *Chaldaean Oracles and Theurgy*; Shaw, *Theurgy and the Soul*; Burns, "Proclus and the Theurgic Liturgy."

4. While the term "glossolalia" is mainly associated with early Christianity, some scholars have used it to describe ecstatic speech in Jewish or Gnostic contexts as well (Scholem, *Jewish Gnosticism*, 33; Turner, "Introduction: *Allogenes*," 46). Sources include Mark 16:17; Rom 8:26; 1 Cor 14:1–25; Is 28:11; Phil. *Her.* 259–66; *T. Job* 47–50; Ir. *Haer.* 5.6; Ter. *Marc.* 5.8; Euseb. *Hist. eccl.* 5.17.3; Allison, "Silence of Angels," 191–92. The term "vowel spell" is also not sufficient for all cases, since much of the unintelligible language recorded in Sethian and Hekhalot literatures appear to be "barbarian" names and words composed of consonants as well as vowels. Thus, the more general term "ecstatic speech" is here employed for the greater phenomenon of unintelligible, wild speech.

5. The ingenious analysis of Turner, "Introduction: *Marsanes*," 19; see also ibid., 75–76.

6. Pearson, "Introduction: *Marsanes*," 236–39, and notes to text ad loc.; Turner, "Introduction: *Marsanes*," 54–76; Poirier, "Commentaire: *Marsanès*," 414–39.

7. This latter point is clear from the author's repeated statements that she or he has instructed the audience about these subjects before.

8. See also Turner, "Introduction: *Marsanes*," 81.

9. *Mars.* NHC X,1.19.18.

10. Pearson, "Notes: *Marsanes*," 286, recalling *Pist. Soph.* chs. 98, 109, 130; *1, 2 Jeu* chs. 37, 40, 43. One could add the *Mithras Liturgy* (see the edition of Betz).

11. *Mars.* NHC X,1.32.1–6, following FP's syntax; Pearson translates this as "from the angels. And there will be some effects."

12. *Mars.* NHC X,1.39.2–24 (Pearson).

13. In this respect, the orientation of Marsanes' alphabet mysticism is distinct from that of the Gnostic Marcus (Ir. *haer.* 1.13–21; cf. Pearson, "Introduction: *Marsanes*," 238; Turner, "Introduction: *Marsanes*," 78).

14. Thus Böhlig and Wisse, "Commentary: *The Gospel of the Egyptians*," 173.

15. *Gos. Eg.* NHC III,2.43.8–44.13 = IV,2.53.4–54.13, tr. Böhlig and Wisse (CGL), modified.

16. *Gos. Eg.* NHC IV,2.51.2 = III,2.41.14; III,2.43.9; for "aeon of the aeons," see III,2.56.1; IV,2.62.4, 65.13. See further Böhlig and Wisse, "Introduction: The Gospel of The Egyptians," 43.

17. For discussion, see Böhlig and Wisse, "Commentary: *The Gospel of the Egyptians*," 41–43; Turner, "Commentary: *Zostrianos*," 647–48. On the Thrice-Male Child, see above, Chapter 4, "Seth and His Avatars."

18. *1 En.* 22:13, 25:3, 27:3–5, 36:4, 40:3, 63:2, 83:8; see also *Apoc. Elij.* 1:3 (passages cit. Wintermute ad loc. in *Apoc. Elij.*, *OTP*).

19. *Man. Keph.* 91.27, 93.9, 113.31, 171.4, 21, 172.16 (Polotsky and Böhlig). See also *Unt.* 260.25.

20. "And the first aeon that is in it, that comes from it, is the first luminary, Solmis; with the god-revealer, he is unlimited with respect to the copy (τύπος) that exists in the Kalyptos aeon together with Doxomedon" (*Zost.* NHC VIII,1.126.1–8). The passage is almost certainly corrupt; see Turner, "Commentary: *Zostrianos*," 647.

21. *Zost.* NHC VIII,1.127.1–11.

22. BFP reconstructs the hymn as follows: ϥⲟⲛϩ ϩⲛ ⲟⲩⲱⲛϩ ϯⲟⲛϩ ⲛ̄ϩⲣⲁⲓ ϩⲛⲟ[ⲩⲱⲛϩ] ⲕⲟⲛϩ ⲡⲓⲟⲩⲁ. ϥⲟⲛϩ ⲛ̄ϭⲓ[ⲓⲡⲏ]ⲉⲧⲉ ⲛ̄[ϣ]ⲟⲙⲧ ⲕⲱ[ⲃ ⲁⲁⲁ] ⲉⲉⲉ.

23. *Zost.* NHC VIII,1.117.14–21.

24. *Allogenes* NHC XI,3.53.32–38. Turner ("*Allogenes*: Notes," 256) and Scopello ("Youel et Barbélo") agree the subject is probably Youel.

25. Thus Turner (CGL, BCNH), a translation followed by FS.

26. *Allogenes* NHC XI,3.54.11–26.

27. As noted by Turner, "*Trimorphic Protennoia*: Notes to Text and Translation," 440, regarding *Gos. Eg.* NHC IV,2.51.2–5 = III,2.41.15.

28. *Trim. Prot.* NHC XIII,1.38.22–30.

29. This interpretation reads the supralinear strokes in ⲙⲁ̄ ⲙⲱ̄ as *nomina sacra* as does Poirier, "Commentaire: *La pensée première*," 245–46. Cf. Turner, "*Trimorphic Protennoia*: Notes to Text and Translation," 440: "Give to the thrice-great One! Thou art last! Thou art first! Thou art (the one who) exists!" Later, he described the doxology as "alphabetic speculation" ("Introduction: *Marsanes*," 78–79). Cf. also Layton, *Gnostic Scriptures*, 92: "Mā! Mō! You are omega, omega, omega! You are alpha! You are being!"

30. BFP reconstructs this as ⲉ[ⲓⲥ]; LS leaves the lacuna blank. See also Turner, "Commentary: *Zostrianos*," 567.

31. LS reconstructs this as ⲛ̄ⲧ[ⲉ ⲡⲛⲟⲩ]ⲧⲉ ⲡⲛⲟⲩⲧⲉ, "O son of [God]." BFP reconstructs ⲛ̄ⲧ[ⲉⲗⲓⲟⲥ ⲛ̄]ⲧⲉ ⲡⲛⲟⲩⲧⲉ, "fils p[arfait de] Dieu."

32. *Zost.* NHC VIII,1.52.15–24; *Gos. Eg.* NHC IV,2.78.1–79.3 = III,2.66.8–22: the vowels here are probably codes and abbreviations, not ecstatic speech (Böhlig and Wisse, "Commentary: *The Gospel of the Egyptians*," 198–205; cf. Turner, "*Trimorphic Protennoia*: Notes to Text and Translation," 440; idem, "Introduction: *Marsanes*," 78–79).

33. *Trim. Prot.* NHC XIII,1.37.27–30; for speculation, see Turner, "*Trimorphic Protennoia*: Notes to Text and Translation," 438–39; Poirier, "Commentaire: *La pensée première*," 224–26.

34. Turner, "Introduction: *Marsanès*," 54 n. 18.

35. *Corp. herm.* 16.1–2, tr. Copenhaver, modified. The closing pun is common in Christian apologetics (Nock and Festugière, *Corpus Hermeticum*, 2:232 n. 6). Cf. *Ascl.* 17; further, see Clark, "Translate into Greek," 125.

36. Iamb. *Myst.* 1.12, tr. Clarke, Dillon, and Hershbell.

37. Nic. Ger. *Exc.* p. 276 (Janus); cit. and tr. Pearson, "Gnosticism as Platonism," 69, a translation followed by Turner, "Introduction: *Marsanes*," 71; see also Dornsieff, *Alphabet*, 52, and for similar texts, 33–34.

38. Plot. *Enn.* 2.9 [33] 14.2–9; see also Hirschle, *Sprachphilosophie*, 39–42.

39. Plut. *Gen. Socr.* 589b–c, tr. Babbitt (LCL): the thought of demons "have no need of verbs or nouns, which men use as symbols in their intercourse, and thereby behold mere counterfeits and likenesses of what is present in thought (ῥημάτων οὐδὲ ὀνομάτων, οἷς χρώμενοι πρὸς ἀλλήλους οἱ ἄνθρωποι συμβόλοις εἴδωλα τῶν νοουμένων καὶ εἰκόνας), but are unaware of the originals except for those persons who are illuminated, as I have said, by some special and daemonic radiance."

40. Porph. *Aneb.* 2.10a–b (Sodano), tr. mine; cit. and discussed in Hirschle, *Sprachphilosophie*, 44; more generally, see Clark, "Translate into Greek," 124–26.

41. Orig. *Cels.* 1.24, 5.45; on the former passage, see Dillon, "Magical Power of Names," 206–7.

42. Porph. *Aneb.* 2.8a. See also ibid., 1.2c: "If the gods are impassive . . . then the invocations of the gods will be in vain . . . for that which is impassive is impossible to adjure, to force, to compel."

43. Iamb. *Myst.* 7.4; for discussion, see Hirschle, *Sprachphilosophie*, 45–48.

44. Iamb. *Myst.* 7.4–5.

45. Ibid., 1.12, 4.2, 6.6.

46. Ibid., 5.10; see Shaw, *Theurgy*, 130–31.

47. Iamb. *Myst.* 9.1; 10.3.

48. Ibid., 1.21; see Shaw, *Theurgy*, 141–42.

49. Orig. *Cels.* 5.45 argued that the proper name yields the proper immaterial presence; see also Fossum, *Name of God*, 84; Dillon, "Magical Power of Names," 211–14.

50. Layton, *Gnostic Scriptures*, 107 n. 53d.

51. Meyer and Smith, *Early Christian Magic*, 285.

52. First attested in a fifth-century CE Milesian inscription (CIG 2:2895).

53. Cf. Dillon, "Magical Power of Names," 204–5.

54. Frankfurter, "Narrating Power," 461.

55. The reading of *Maaseh Merkabah* suggested by Janowitz, *Poetics of Ascent*, esp. 84–92, 101.

56. For Sethian use of magical names, see Thomassen, "Sethian Names."

57. ⲛ̄ ⲉⲟⲟⲩ ⲙⲛ̄ ϩⲉⲛⲉⲟⲟⲩ, tr. by Layton as "along with glories you become the glory" (*Gnostic Scriptures*); "you will become gloriously glorious" (Turner, CGL) ; "vous deviendrez gloire avec des gloires" (Poirier, BCNH).

58. *Trim. Prot.* NHC XIII,1.45.10–20.

59. Tr. "Kinship" (Layton), "fatherhood" (Turner), "paternité" (Poirier).

60. As widely noted (e.g., Scopello, "Un rite idéal d'intronisation," 94; Turner, "*Trimorphic Protennoia*: Notes to Text and Translation," 450; Poirier, "Commentaire: *La pensée première*," 351–52), these are common figures of Sethian mythology who govern baptism, also known from *Gos.*

Eg. NHC IV,2.76.2–10 = III,2.64.14–20; *Ap. Adam* NHC V,5.84.5–22; *Zost.* NHC VIII,1.6.7–17; *Unt.* 263.22–88. There is probably no relation of Michar or Micheu(s) to the archangel Michael, who appears in Jewish ascent texts as guide (*T. Ab.*) and heavenly high priest (*3 Bar.*) (Dean-Otting, *Heavenly Journeys*, 278).

61. As Sevrin (*Dossier baptismal séthien*, 67–68) and Poirier ("Commentaire: *La pensée première*," 352) observe, *Trim. Prot.* is the only Sethian text to feature enthronement.

62. Turner, "*Trimorphic Protennoia*: Notes to Text and Translation," 451, recalls 2 Cor 12:2; see also Poirier, "Commentaire: *La pensée première*," 353. To this should be added *Chald. Or.* frg. 3: "the Father snatched himself away, and did not confine his own fire in his intellectual Power" (tr. Majercik, modified).

63. More common Sethian mythologoumena, servants of the Four Luminaries, known from *Gos. Eg.* NHC IV,2.64.14–20 = III,2.52.20–53.1; *Apoc. Adam* NHC V,5.75.21–31; *Zost.* NHC VIII,1.47.24; *Unt.* 239.24–27 (Schmidt and MacDermot).

64. *Trim. Prot.* NHC XIII,1.48.11–32. Beings are invoked at *Gos. Eg.* NHC III,2.66.2–4; cf. *Trim. Prot.* NHC XIII,1.48.15–30; *Zost.* NHC VIII,1.4.20–26.2, esp. 5.14–22, 6.14–17; *Melch.* NHC IX,1.16.13–16.

65. Protennoia emphasizes that "he who possesses the Five Seals of these names has stripped off the robe of ignorance and put on radiating light" (*Trim. Prot.* NHC XIII,1.49.28–32). The ordering of baptism and investiture differs, with scholars generally regarding the latter as prior (Sevrin, *Dossier baptismal séthien*, 272; Turner, "*Trimorphic Protennoia*: Notes to Text and Translation," 450; followed by Poirier, "Commentaire: *La pensée première*," 322).

66. Schenke (Robinson), *Dreigestaltige Protennoia*, 125–27, 134–35; Turner, "*Trimorphic Protennoia*: Notes to Text and Translation," 453.

67. *Zost.* NHC VIII,1.5.15–18. On the "aetherial earth," see above, Chapter 5, "The Strange and the Dead."

68. Reconstruction following LS. BFP reconstructs ⲉⲟⲟ[ⲩ ⲉⲅⲟⲩ], "gloi[res dépassant] toute mesure."

69. Reconstruction following BFP, ⲁⲩ[ϯⲉⲟ]ⲟⲩ ⲛⲁⲓ; LS reconstructs: ⲁⲩ[ⲟⲩⲟⲛⲅ]ⲟⲩ ⲛⲁⲓ.

70. This reconstructs ⲛⲣⲉϥⲛⲁⲩ ⲉⲛⲟⲩ[ⲧⲉ], as in BFP: "un ange contemplateur de Di[eu]." LS reconstructs ⲛⲟⲩ[ⲛⲉ], "[root]-seeing angel."

71. *Zost.* NHC VIII,1.6.3–21.

72. Reconstruction following BFP: ϯⲙⲁ[ⲁⲩ ⲛ̄ⲧⲉ]ⲛⲓⲁⲅ[ⲅⲉⲗ]ⲟⲥ. LS reconstructs as ⲏ .[. . . . . .]ⲱ ⲁ[. . .]ⲟⲥ.

73. *Zost.* NHC VIII,1.7.1–22. See also the transformations at ibid., 30.29–31.23. The MS here is very fragmentary, and lends little to our analysis. However, it seems that the text, as Turner notes, simply restates the seer's encounter with the Luminaries and concomitant baptisms ("Commentary: *Zostrianos*," 547). See also M. A. Williams, *Immovable Race*, 73–74.

74. *Zost.* NHC VIII,1.4.25, 5.15.

75. Ibid., 46.15–30; see also M. A. Williams, *Immovable Race*, 71–72; cf. Turner, "Commentary: *Zostrianos*," 559.

76. *Zost.* NHC VIII,1.48.23.

77. Ibid., 53.13, 54.17, 62.11, 63.9, 125.13–14; *Allogenes* NHC XI,3.50.19, 52.14, 55.18, 55.34, 57.25.

78. *Zost.* NHC VIII,1.[63.21–22].

79. Ibid., 121.5–12: "But it is the Kalyptos who has divided again, and they (i.e., the luminaries) exist together, and know the things that exist, namely, all the glories. All of them truly are perfect. This is the [one who] knows every act of them all, since it is completely perfect." Ibid., 122.5–17: "and all the glories are these: the Aphredons, unlimited, ineffable, revealers, impassible beings, [. . .] all of them. (Next), revealers of glory, the Marsedons, the twice-manifest, the unlimited Solmises, the revealers of their own selves, being [filled] with glory, those who [wait for] glory; blessers, the Marsedons."

80. See Mazur, "Platonizing Sethian Gnostic Background," 192–95; they are probably not interiorized cultic idols, as in the Plotinian corpus (*pace* ibid., 203–4).

81. *Zost.* NHC VIII,1.17, 4.23–24.

82. Ibid., 129.1–22.

83. Indeed, he has "heard about things that (even) the gods are ignorant of, and which are infinite for the angels" (128.15–18). Cf. P. Perkins, *Gnostic Dialogue*, 86–87.

84. *Zost.* NHC VIII,1.129.22–130.13.

85. *Gos. Eg.* NHC IV,2.59.2–22 (tr. Böhlig and Wisse, modified). See also the description of the heavenly church, whose sole purpose is to hymn God (ibid., IV,2.66.14–67.1 = III,2.55.2–16).

86. "[Having known thee], I have now mixed [with thy] steadfastness, and [I have armed myself]; I have come to be in [an armor of] grace and the [light; I have become light]" (*Gos. Eg.* NHC IV,2.79.14–16 = III,2.67.1–4). See also *Chald. Or.* frg. 2: "Intellect and Soul are armed, clad in a sharp armor of ringing light with thrice-pointed strength. Cast the entire token of the triad into the seat of the Mind, and do not frequent the empyrean streams in a scattered way, but vigorously."

87. *Allogenes* NHC XI,3.58.26–59.3.

88. Most recently, see Scopello, "Portraits d'anges à Nag Hammadi," 886; see also Pearson, *Ancient Gnosticism*, 88–89.

89. *Apoc. Ab.* 11:1–5; on Ioel's appearance, see Gruenwald, *Apocalyptic*, 55; Fossum, *Name of God*, 318; Schäfer, *Origins*, 88–90.

90. Gruenwald, *Apocalyptic*, 54, regarding *Apoc. Ab.* ch. 10:7–8.

91. PG 83:380.1–5.

92. *Allogenes* NHC XI,3.52.15–25, 57.37–39.

93. Barbelo is the "first glory of the Invisible Father" (*Steles Seth* NHC VII,5.121.22); the Invisible Spirit is a "[single glory] before all things" (ibid., 126.4 [Robinson and Goehring]).

94. Ibid., 126.20–28.

95. Ibid., 118.20–23.

96. Ibid., 127.8–11.

97. Porph. *Vit. Plot.* 16.

98. *Unt.* ch. 7, p. 235.4–23 (Schmidt and MacDermot). The vagaries of the Coptic translation force the reader to interpret at times who is speaking, and who is being spoken of, particularly in the final clauses. My tr. here follows that of H. Jackson, "Seer Nikotheos," 261; cf. Brakke, "Body as/at the Boundary," 202–3.

99. As reconstructed in FP: [ⲁⲅⲓⲙⲙⲉ], "[j'ai su]"; Pearson reconstructs ⲙ̄ⲛ̄<ⲡ>ϣⲱϣ, "[and sameness]." Pearson here recalls Plat. *Tim.* 35a; Plut. *An. proc.* 1012d–1013a; Plot. *Enn.* 6.2 [43] 21.

100. *Mars.* NHC X,1.4.24–5.9; see also Turner, "Introduction: *Marsanes*," 139.

101. *Mars.* NHC X,1.7.29–8.29, 10.7–11, 14.15–24, with Turner, "Introduction: *Marsanes*," 142 (although the reference to Plat. *Theaet.* 176a–b is a stretch).

102. Both Turner and Pearson recognize that the positive description of astrological contemplation has an angelological context, but do not raise the question in the context of Marsanes' identity, nor in the context of its relation to contemporary Jewish lore, as explored below (Turner, "Introduction: *Marsanes*," 20–21; Pearson, "Introduction: *Marsanes*," 240).

103. *Apoc. Adam* NHC V,5.64.14, 76.4.

104. For Adam's superiority to angels, see *L.A.E.* 13:1–14:3, 16:1; *Quaest. Barth.* 4.10, 4.52–55; Qur'an 2:34, 7:11–13, 15:29–35, 17:61, 18:50, 20:116, 38:71–78; CMC 48.16–50.7; see also Fletcher-Louis, *Luke-Acts*, 145 n. 209.

105. On the incorporation of Judeo-Christian ideas about divine messengers into Hellenistic culture, see M. Smith, "On the History of Angels," 292–94; see also Sheppard, "Pagan Cults of Angels."

106. Iamblichus asks if souls can change their rank (τάξις) and become angelic (the answer is lost in a lacuna!—*An.* 47); see also Finamore and Dillon, "*De anima* Commentary," 207. A Hermetic treatise features a vision of the ennead during which Hermes and Tat obtain a vision of angels hymning the beyond with silence and proceed to join them, but the seers do not seem to transform (*Disc. 8–9* NHC VI,6.58.17).

107. *2 En* 22:8–10; see Scopello, "Un rite idéal d'intronisation"; Turner, "Ritual," 88 n. 5, also regarding *T. Levi* 8:4; see also Pearson, *Ancient Gnosticism*, 88; Morray-Jones, "Transformational Mysticism," 22–23.

108. *1 En.* 62:15; *3 En.* chs. 3–16; Turner, "Commentary: *Zostrianos*," 504–5; Scopello, "Un rite idéal d'intronisation," 95 n. 15.

109. *1 En.* 62:15; *Apoc. Ab.* 13:14; Rev 7:9–17; *Asc. Is.* 8:14, 9:9; *2 Bar.* ch. 51; *T. Levi* 2:5–5:7, 8:1–19. Cf. Ezek 42:14, 44:17–9. For discussion, see Poirier, "Commentaire: *La pensée première*," 321; see also Bousset, *Himmelsreise*, 8–9; Fletcher-Louis, *Luke-Acts*, 154; Schultz, "Angelic Opposition," 291; Morray-Jones, "Transformational Mysticism," 17; Schäfer, *Origins*, 70–72, 82. In the Dead Sea Scrolls, see *Hodayot* (1QS) XI, 5–8; see also IV, 23, VIII, 5; Schäfer, "Communion with the Angels," 42–43. See also Phil. *Somn.* 1.216–17. The importance of heavenly investiture for angelification is also emphasized by Himmelfarb, *Tours*, 156; Fletcher-Louis, *Luke-Acts*, 134. On angelic priests in general, see ibid., 123 n. 89 (on Philo); idem, *All the Glory of Adam*, 56–87. Himmelfarb rightly cautions against reading

ideological or sectarian elements into descriptions of angelic priests in the heavenly temple, since the motif is so completely widespread in Jewish mystical literature, including texts that do not belong to the secessionist priesthood ("Merkavah Mysticism Since Scholem," 30).

110. Classic references to the glory include Ex 16:10; 3 Kgdms 8:11; Is 6:1, 66; in Merkavah visions: Ezek 1:28; *T. Levi* 3:4; *1 En.* 14:2; *Asc. Is.* 11:32 (regrding *Mark* 14:62), cit. Morray-Jones, "Transformational Mysticism," 2–4. Generally, see Fossum, "Glory"; idem, *Name of God*; Koch, *Rediscovery of Apocalyptic*, 28–33; Stroumsa, "To See or Not to See," 79–80. In early Christianity, see Matt 26:64 and parallels; John 1:14; Heb 1:2–4; Just. Mart. *Dial.* 61.1. Although there are occasional references to "glory" in the singular in Sethian texts, it is not clear if, or if so, how, these might be related to these visions or other Christian and Jewish currents.

111. *Asc. Is.* 9:27; *Odes Sol.* 36:2; *T. Job.* 48:2–3; Phil. *Prob.* 43–44; see also Frank, *ΑΓΓΕΛΙΚΟΣ ΒΙΟΣ*, 189; Fletcher-Louis, *Luke-Acts*, 135. Schäfer, *Origins*, 91–92 emphasizes *Apoc. Ab.* 17:8–21. On the function of this language, see Janowitz, *Poetics of Ascent*, 91.

112. *Apoc. Zeph.* 8:1–5, tr. Wintermute in *OTP*: "(The angels) helped me and set me on that boat. Thousands of thousands and myriads of myriads of angels gave praise before me. I, myself, put on an angelic garment. I saw all of these angels praying. I, myself, prayed together with them, I knew their language, which they spoke with me." See also 2 Cor 12:4; *Sib. Or.* 5:259; *T. Job* 48:2–50:2; *Apoc. Ab.* chs. 15–19; Allison, "Silence of Angels"; Fletcher-Louis, *Luke-Acts*, 135 n. 153; idem, *All the Glory of Adam*, 279.

113. *3 En.* 40:2; *Apoc. Zeph. (Gk.) ap.* Clem. Al. *Strom.* 5.11.77 (Stählin). See also Burns, "Sethian Crowns, Sethian Martyrs?"

114. *1 En.* 104:2–3 (cf. 43:1–4, as discussed by Stone, "Lists," 395–96); Dan 12:3; Matt 13:43; Judg 5:20; Job 38:7; *Sir.* 44:21; Ezek. Trag. *Ex.* l.79–81; cit. and discussed in Collins, "Apocalyptic Eschatology," 87–88. See also idem, "Cosmos and Salvation," esp. 137–42; idem, "Angelic Life," 291–93; Himmelfarb, *Ascent to Heaven*, 50; Fletcher-Louis, *Luke-Acts*, 116, 138; Segal, *Life After Death*, 262. Stone, "Lists," 395–96, adds many more citations.

115. *1QSCommunity Rule* (1QS) IV, 6–8; *1QMWar Scroll* (1QM) XII, 1–7; Mark 12:25; Matt 22:30; Luke 20:35; Frank, *ΑΓΓΕΛΙΚΟΣ ΒΙΟΣ*, 104ff.

116. *Apoc. Zeph.* 8:1–5.

117. *2 Bar.* 51:10–13; *Asc. Is.* 8.13–16, 9:1–6, 9:27–30. Himmelfarb, *Ascent to Heaven*, 56–57, thinks the author of *Asc. Is.* favors this "radical claim" over 8:15's affirmation of equality with angels, without specifying to which source each statement belongs. See also eadem, *Tours*, 156; cf. *Apoc. Paul (Copt.)* NHC 5.2.24.8.

118. For Adam, see *2 En.* 30:8–11. For Enoch, see above passages, as well as *1 En.* 81:1–17. For Abraham, see *T. Ab.* 11 (recension A—see also the glorified Abel in chs. 12–13). For Jacob, see *Pr. Jac.*; *Pr. Jos.* ap. Orig. *Comm. Jo.* 2.188–90 (Heine); idem, *Philoc.* 23.15.31–46 (Junod). For Melchizedek, see Phil. *Leg.* 3.93; Hipp. *Haer.* 7.36.1 (Marcovich). For Moses, see *Mem. Marq.* 5.3 (on which, see Fossum, *Name of God*, 123–24; for many other passages,

see Segal, "Paul and the Beginning of Jewish Mysticism," 102–3; but esp. Meeks, "Moses as God and King"). Generally, see *Asc. Is.* 9:7–10; Morray-Jones, "Transformational Mysticism," 13, 17–20.

119. For ample references, see Stuckenbruck, *Angel Veneration and Christology*, 138–39.

120. Generally, see Collins, "Angelic Life," 309–10; Frank, *ΑΓΓΕΛΙΚΟΣ ΒΙΟΣ*, 190–91. See the sources collected by Frank, 124ff, e.g., Orig. *Cels.* 4.29; Clem. Al. *Strom.* 7.14.84; idem, *Paed.* 2.9.79.2–3 (Mondésert).

121. Schäfer, *Origins*, 152.

122. Ibid., 116.

123. Recent discussions focusing on the *unio liturgica* (as opposed to the individual *unio mystica*) as central to Jewish mysticism include Lesses, *Ritual Practices to Gain Power*, 160; Alexander, *Mystical Texts*; Schäfer, "Communion with the Angels," 66; idem, *Origins*, 213, 281, 341.

124. *Zost.* NHC VIII,1.131.5–9. For more sources and discussion, see Attridge, "On Becoming an Angel," 496; Wisse, "Flee Femininity." As Scholem argues, the sages who undertook the descent to the Merkavah were concerned with purification but not celibacy, and thus were in the mainstream of *halakhah* (*Jewish Gnosticism*, 12). But cf. Josephus's Essenes, some of whom, he says, were celibate (*J.W.* 2.119–21, 160–61). Similarly, Collins explains the absence of children and women from *1QSCommunity Rule* by hypothesizing the practice of celibacy in the community ("Angelic Life," 301–2).

125. As Valantasis observes, there is surprisingly little evidence for asceticism at Nag Hammadi ("Nag Hammadi and Asceticism," esp. 187–90). This analysis thus somewhat expands the range of ascetic discourse within the codices. On living like an angel, see 1 Cor 11:10; Heb 12:22, 13:2; Col 2:18; Clem. Al. *Strom.* 7.14.84; Orig. *Cels.* 4.29; Aune, "Early Christian Eschatology," 596; Attridge, "On Becoming an Angel"; DeConick, "What Is Early Jewish and Christian Mysticism?" 21. Particularly important is Frank's survey of pre-monastic ascetic texts, highlighting the importance of celibacy (*ΑΓΓΕΛΙΚΟΣ ΒΙΟΣ*, 140–97, esp. 146). An important difference between the texts surveyed by Frank and the Sethian literature is the former's interest in "Paradise" as the locus of angelic life, absent in Sethianism.

126. Realized eschatology in Gnostic literature need not come at the expense of cosmic eschatology; indeed, it may be "a metaphor for the transformation that comes with revelation . . . part of the temporal horizon within which salvation takes place" (Attridge, "Valentinian and Sethian Apocalyptic Traditions," 195). Cf. Turner, "Introduction: *Marsanes*," 39; Frankfurter, "Early Christian Apocalypticism," 418–19.

127. See Collins, "Apocalyptic Eschatology," 84–95; Fletcher-Louis, *Luke-Acts*, 184–98; idem, *All the Glory of Adam*; Schäfer, "Communion with the Angels."

128. Fletcher-Louis, *Luke-Acts*, 185; idem, *All the Glory of Adam*, 89–90; Segal, *Life After Death*, 304. Many of these references are simply to angels, without any clear angelomorphic context, as in 4Q511 frgs. 21.8, 8.9, 10.11–12. Other references are to favored humans—certainly the righteous elect, but not obviously an angelic one (much less an elect angelified in this

life): see 1QS XI, 6–8; 1QH VI, 13. For "angelomorphism," see Fletcher-Louis, *Luke-Acts*, 14, regarding Daniélou, *Theology of Jewish Christianity*, 117, which coined the term.

129. Josephus's description of the Essenes highlights asceticism, but certainly these practices are too widespread across ancient religious life to qualify as evidence for Fletcher-Louis's thesis that Josephus's evidence refers to an angelified community (*All the Glory of Adam*, 130). The fantastic angelic race of Rechabites (*Hist. Rech.* 7:10) are too removed from the Essenic community to serve as evidence of angelomorphism there (*pace* Fletcher-Louis, *Luke-Acts*, 199–204; see further Alexander, *Mystical Texts*, 45–47).

130. 1Q*Rules of the Congregation* (1QSa) II, 8–9 says: "these (individuals with physical disabilities) shall not en[ter] to take their place [a] mong the congregation of the men of renown, for the angels of holiness are among their [congre]gation"; see also 1QSb III, 2–6, IV, 24–26; Alexander, *Mystical Texts*, 102, 108. 1Q*War Scroll* (1QM) VII, 6: "and every man who has not cleansed himself of his 'spring' on the day of battle will not go down with them, for the holy angels are together with their armies." See Fitzmyer, "Feature of Qumran Angelology," 55–56, observing that the passages probably derive from the ban on disfigured descendants of Aaron in serving in the priesthood (Lev 21:17–23). See also Schäfer, *Origins*, 120–21.

131. 4Q*Songs of the Sage* (4Q511) frg. 35, *pace* Fletcher-Louis, *All the Glory of Adam*, 189–93.

132. 4Q*Self-glorification Hymn* (4Q491c) I, 6–8 (the speaker sits on the throne in heaven!—an impossibility for angels [b. Hag. 15a; y. Ber. 2c; *Gen. Rab.* 65:1; *3 En.* 16; Gruenwald, *Apocalyptic*, 67; Alexander, *Mystical Texts*, 40, 87]), I, 11, discussed in Schäfer, "Communion with the Angels," 59; idem, *Origins*, 146–51; Alexander, *Mystical Texts*, 86–90, 109–10. Abegg was the first to recognize the *Hymn* as a unit discrete from the *War Scroll* ("4Q471"). On the identity of the speaker, see M. Smith, "Ascent to the Heavens and Deification"; idem, "Two Ascended to Heaven"; Collins, "A Throne in the Heavens," 53–55; idem, "Angelic Life," 305.

133. 1Q*Hodayot a* (1QHa) XI, 20–22; see also ibid, XIX, 10–14; Collins, "Throne in the Heavens," 54; Schäfer, "Communion with the Angels," 38–42.

134. "But [. . .] how shall we be considered [among] them (i.e., the angels)? And how shall our priesthood (be considered) in their dwellings? And [our] holiness their holiness? [What] is the offering of our tongues of dust (compared) with the knowledge of the gods?" (4Q400 II, 5–8)

135. Newsom, *Songs of the Sabbath*, 16–19, 59, 71; eadem, "'He Has Established for Himself Priests'," 115–18; Boustan (Abusch), "Seven-fold Hymns," 236–38; Alexander, *Mystical Texts*, 45–47, 54; Schäfer, "Communion with the Angels," 47, 56–59; idem, *Origins*, 132–46; Collins, "Angelic Life," 299–300.

136. Thus Newsom, *Songs of the Sabbath*, 16–19, 59, 71; eadem, "'He Has Established for Himself Priests'," 115–18; Collins, "Apocalyptic

Eschatology," 90. Cf. Fletcher-Louis, *All the Glory of Adam*, 334; see also 264, 306–10.

137. 4Q500 II, 6–8; Newsom, *Songs of the Sabbath*, 17, 21.

138. On *Trim. Prot.*, see Schenke, "Phenomenon," 602–7; Turner, "To See the Light," 72.

139. J. Z. Smith, "I am a Parrot (Red)," 286.

140. An angelified community is rejected by Lichtenberger, *Studien zum Menschenbild*, 224–37; Davidson, *Angels at Qumran*, 156 n. 1, 200 n. 1; cf. Newsom in *Songs of the Sabbath*, 66; Fletcher-Louis, *All the Glory of Adam*, 185. For "partial" angelification, see Alexander, *Mystical Texts*, 47. For angelification as a proleptic experience of death, see Fletcher-Louis, *Luke-Acts*, 136–37, regarding *Apoc. Zeph.*, *Asc. Is.*, and Himmelfarb, *Ascent to Heaven*, 54. The argument goes back to Bousset, *Himmelsreise*, 136, also followed by Segal, "Paul and the Beginning of Jewish Mysticism," 95–96.

141. For emphasis on the importance of experience behind the production of texts, see Aune, "Apocalypse," 80–81; Segal, "Paul and the Beginning of Jewish Mysticism," 115 n. 2; DeConick, "What Is Early Jewish and Christian Mysticism?" 19; Alexander, *Mystical Texts*, 94; Schäfer, *Origins*, 338–39.

142. Observed by Fletcher-Louis, *Luke-Acts*, 213–14, without reference to Gnostic texts.

143. On Qumran, see Schäfer, *Origins*, 123, 349.

144. Burns, "Sethian Crowns, Sethian Martyrs?"

145. Standard studies of Sethian baptism include Sevrin, *Dossier baptismal séthien*; Turner, "Sethian Gnosticism: A Literary History," 59; idem, "Ritual," esp. 96–97, 128–31; idem, "Introduction: *Zostrianos*," 71–75; idem, "Introduction: *Marsanes*," 49–54, 164–68; idem, *Sethian Gnosticism and the Platonic Tradition*, 64, 80–84, 238–47; other texts will be engaged as well in the following discussion.

146. *Gos. Eg.* NHC IV,2.74.9 = NHC III,2.62.24.

147. *Melch.* NHC IX,1.16.11, on which see Pearson, "Introduction: *Melchizedek*," 26–27.

148. Turner, *Sethian Gnosticism and the Platonic Tradition*, 240, 272; idem, "To See the Light," 67–68.

149. On Zostrianos and his celestial baptism, see Attridge, "On Becoming an Angel"; Turner, "Introduction: *Zostrianos*," 67–72; P. Perkins, "Identification with the Savior," 178–81.

150. *Zost.* NHC VIII,1.131.2–5.

151. *Apoc. Adam* NHC V,5.84.17–23. The passage does not seem to make sense, as it appears to accuse baptismal attendants, clearly positive beings in *Gos. Eg.*, *Trim. Prot.*, and *Zost.*, of having defiled the living water! Turner's suggestion of emending the text so that the attendants accuse others of defiling the water surely is the most sensible of the various proposed readings of the passage (*Sethian Gnosticism and the Platonic Tradition*, 157–58).

152. Epiph. *Pan.* 40.2.6.

153. *Orig. World* NHC II,5.122.6–20; Orig. *Cels.* 6.31; for discussion and a review of scholarship, see Rasimus, *Paradise Reconsidered*, 251.

154. Attridge suggests that *Zost.* rejects baptism of the Pauline mold ("On Becoming an Angel," 486; followed by P. Perkins, "Identification with the Savior," 179). Pearson holds, similarly, that the *Apoc. Adam* rejects only other Christian baptisms (*Ancient Gnosticism*, 74); Morard, that it was a pro-water baptism text emended by a later scribe who opposed the practice ("*L'Apocalypse d'Adam* de Nag Hammadi"); Hedrick, that it rejects Sethians who persist in water baptism with other Christians (*Apocalypse of Adam*, 209–15). Turner suggests a total rejection of water baptism (*Sethian Gnosticism and the Platonic Tradition*, 164–65).

155. It cannot be decisively proven which account of the descent of Pronoia has priority, but Turner observes that the version of the Hymn in *Ap. John* is shorter, and so is perhaps an earlier source expanded by the author(s) of *Trim. Prot* (Turner, "Introduction NHC XIII,*1**,*" 385–86). Similarly, see Logan, "John and the Gnostics," 56–58; Rasimus, *Paradise Reconsidered*, 279.

156. *Ap. John* NHC II,1.30.11–32, 31.22–25; *Trim. Prot.* NHC XIII,1.50.9–15. See also Turner, "*Trimorphic Protennoia*: Notes to Text and Translation," 448.

157. On heavenly beings, see *Gos. Eg.* NHC IV,2.56.25, 58.6, 59.1; IV,2.66.25–26 = III,2.55.12; IV,2.74.6 = III,2.63.3. Received in baptism, see ibid., IV,2.78.4–5 = III,2.66.3.

158. Schenke "Phenomenon," 604, seeing physical and celestial baptisms as cognate.

159. Thus argue Sevrin, *Dossier baptismal séthien*, 37; Turner, "Ritual," 87; King, *Secret Revelation of John*, 152.

160. Schenke, "Phenomenon," 606; Sevrin, *Dossier baptismal séthien*, 256; M. A. Williams, "Sethianism," 42; Pearson, *Ancient Gnosticism*, 68.

161. For the seals as a visionary "baptism," see Turner, *Sethian Gnosticism and the Platonic Tradition*, 242, 258; idem, "Ritual," 89; idem, "To See the Light," esp. 65–66. See also Layton, *Gnostic Scriptures*, 18–19. For the chrism, see Janssens, *La Prôtennoia Trimorphe*, 80; Logan, *Gnostic Truth and Christian Heresy*, 39; idem, *The Gnostics*, 79; more fully, idem, "Mystery of the Five Seals," 190, arguing that: the Barbeloites practiced a three-fold baptism in the name of the Father, Mother, and Son, followed by a five-fold chrismation in the name of the Autogenes and the four illuminators. Bradshaw agrees that the Five Seals is probably a chrism, if one agrees with Logan's reconstruction of the "Gnostic chrism" as original to the first century CE and introduced to Cyril of Jerusalem and the Apostolic Constitutions by Gnostics, perhaps the Archontics (*Reconstructing Early Christian Worship*, 97). Observing that the texts that mention the Five Seals also mention the primordial anointing of the Autogenes and subsequent transformation into the Christ (*Ap. John* NHC II,2.6.23; *Gos. Eg.* NHC III,2.44.22 = IV,2.55.11; *Trim. Prot.* NHC XIII,1.37), Rasimus argues that, together with the Four Luminaries, the Autogenes-Christ formed a "salvific Pentad," and thus "the Five Seals refer to (baptismal) anointing and are performed in imitation of the primordial anointing of the pentadically understood Christ" (*Paradise Reconsidered*, 258).

162. As Brakke describes in *The Gnostics*, 75. On "seals," see Ysaebert, *Greek Baptismal Terminology*, 254–426; Ferguson, "Baptismal Motifs," 212–15.

163. The theogony is itself a comment on Wis 7:25–27; see Sevrin, *Dossier baptismal séthien*, 21; Turner, *Sethian Gnosticism and the Platonic Tradition*, 279; idem, "To See the Light," 65–66; King, *Secret Revelation of John*, 149–50. The pre-Christian origins of Sethianism are still commonly affirmed, e.g., Kalligas, "Plotinus Against the Gnostics," 117; Pleše, "Gnostic Literature," 166–67.

164. Cf. Turner's reading, emphasizing self-performability but only at the expense of communal practice—"*Trimorphic Protennoia*: Notes to Text and Translation," 453; idem, "Introduction: *Zostrianos*," 71–75; idem, "Introduction: *Marsanes*," 49–54, 164–68; idem, *Sethian Gnosticism and the Platonic Tradition*, 64, 80–84, 238–47; idem, "To See the Light," 64–65. This reading is followed by Mazur, "Platonizing Sethian Gnostic Background," 178–79.

165. See Turner citations in previous note; Wisse, "Stalking," 576.

166. Himmelfarb, "Practice of Ascent," 128; see also DeConick, "What Is Early Jewish and Christian Mysticism?"

167. See Burns, "Apophatic Strategies."

168. Noted for the *Steles Seth* by Brankaer, "Is There a Gnostic 'Henological' Speculation?" 174.

169. Plot. *Enn.* 2.9 [33] 8.38.

170. Gruenwald, *Apocalyptic*, 99; Himmelfarb, "Heavenly Ascent," 100; Himmelfarb, "Practice of Ascent," 130, 133.

171. Fowden, *Egyptian Hermes*, 82, 168; Betz, *Mithras Liturgy*, 21.

172. *Corp. herm.* 1.27–29; *Hekh. Rab., Synopse* chs. 84–91, esp. 86, on which see Schäfer, *Origins*, 250–53. Even so, Pearson, *Ancient Gnosticism*, 99, is right to caution against assuming a consistent community spanning the various Sethian texts. At the same time, the paraenetic content of *Zostrianos* and *Marsanes* should not be read as a literary fiction.

173. It seems to me that this is what scholars are getting at when they remark that the Platonizing Sethian literature transposes philosophy onto a Gnostic worldview (thus argues Brankaer, "Terminologie et représentations philosophiques," 819).

174. Certainly some readers of philosophy attained ecstatic states while reading (and writing); thus remarks Phil. *Migr.* 35, in Snyder, *Readers and Texts in the Ancient World*, 130–31.

175. For Gnostic seals, see *Pist. Soph.* or *1* and *2 Jeu*; cf. Basilides (ap. Ir. *Haer.* 1.24.5–6); *Apoc. Paul (Copt.)* NHC V.3.23. On Jewish seals, see Scholem, *Jewish Gnosticism*, 32–33; Alexander, "Comparing Merkavah Mysticism and Gnosticism," 2–3, regarding Orig. *Cels.* 6.27 and *Hekh. Rab., Synopse* chs. 15–23.

176. *Pace* M. A. Williams, "Sethianism," 56.

177. The examples are too numerous to list here; for a survey and discussion, see M. A. Williams, *Immovable Race*, 99–102.

178. One of the most vivid accounts features a sage resting the head between the knees and chanting into the ground, presumably creating a

kind of sensory-deprivation chamber that assists the vision (*Ma'aseh Merkabah, Synopse* ch. 560); most take this as a key account of practice (Scholem, *Major Trends*, 49; Idel, *Kabbalah: New Perspectives*, 90; Segal, "Paul and the Beginning of Jewish Mysticism," 97–98; Himmelfarb, "Practice of Ascent," 128). However, Schäfer is skeptical (*Origins*, 302–3). For wider survey of the practices described in the Hekhalot literature, see Lesses, *Ritual Practices to Gain Power*, esp. 117ff, 158; Davila, "Dead Sea Scrolls and Merkabah Mysticism," 261–62.

179. On the background of the ὄχημα in Greek speculation about the πνεῦμα, see Dodds, "Appendix II: The Astral Body in Neoplatonism"; Shaw, *Theurgy*, 52 n. 12

180. Frg. 120 (Majercik) refers to a "delicate vehicle of the soul" (ψυχῆς λεπτὸν ὄχημα), and frg. 201, quoted by Proclus, says that "particular souls . . . become mundane (ἐγκόσμιαι) through their 'vehicles.'" The vehicle draws "irrational nature" (ἀλόγιστον φύσιν)—frg. 196.

181. See the discussion of Finamore, *Iamblichus and the Theory of the Vehicle*, 59–124; Lewy, *Chaldaean Oracles and Theurgy*, esp. 199, 413; Majercik, *Chaldean Oracles*, 31–45. On the postmortem nature of the ascent, see Lewy, *Chaldaean Oracles and Theurgy*, 419; Couliano, *Psychanodia*, 64 n. 47.

182. Gnosticism is in a sense the ultimate anthropocentrism; for a recent insightful discussion, see Létourneau, "Creation in Christian Gnostic Texts," 432.

183. *Steles Seth* NHC VII,5.124.17.

CHAPTER 7

1. See, e.g., M. A. Williams, *Rethinking "Gnosticism"*, 213–34.

2. See especially Pearson, "Figure of Seth"; Scopello, "Youel et Barbélo." For a survey of the problem in general, see Stroumsa, *Another Seed*, esp. 10 n. 49; Alexander, "Comparing Merkavah Mysticism and Gnosticism"; idem, "Jewish Elements in Gnosticism," 1059–67.

3. A fine recent survey of the materials as well as problems of definition available today is Schäfer, *Origins*.

4. The classic study remains Scholem, *Major Trends*.

5. Scholem, *Jewish Gnosticism*, 10, 34; for discussion, see Lahe, *Gnosis und Judentum*, 122–24, 143.

6. See the oeuvre of Quispel, e.g., "The Jung Codex and Its Significance," 62–78. Similarly, see Fossum, *Name of God*; DeConick, *Seek to See Him*. For criticisms of Scholem, see most recently Schäfer on Scholem's argument that Shi'ur Qomah mysticism pre-dates and influenced Marcus the Gnostic (*Origins*, 311–15, regarding Scholem, *Jewish Gnosticism*, 38).

7. M. A. Williams, "Review: Fossum, *Angel of the Lord*."

8. *Hyp. Arch.* NHC II,4.95.27; *Orig. World* NHC II,5.105.1; see Gruenwald, "Jewish Sources." Cf. Alexander, "Comparing Merkavah Mysticism and Gnosticism," 2 n. 2; generally, see also Rowland, "Apocalyptic: The Disclosure," 794; Alexander, "Jewish Elements in Gnosticism," 1060–62; Pearson, *Ancient Gnosticism*, 77; Lahe, *Gnosis und Judentum*, 118, 124.

9. Scholem, *Jewish Gnosticism*, 34–35, regarding Clem. Al. *Exc.* frgs. 37–39 (Sagnard) and b. Hag. 13b; Morray-Jones, "Transformational Mysticism," 28–29, regarding *Gos. Eg.* NHC IV,2.51.1 = III,2.49.14; see also NHC III,2.43.8–44.13 = IV,2.53.4–54.13.

10. *Hodayot* (1QHa) 14:11:22, 23:6, 19:14; as extended to the angelic elect at Qumran, see ibid, 14:12–13, cit. Schäfer, *Origins*, 125; *ShirShabb* (4Q400) 1.6, (4Q401) 17:4; (4Q403) l 1:30–31, 1:34–37; (4Q403) l 2:19–20; (4Q405) 3 2:9; Newsom, *Songs of the Sabbath*, 239 also recalls 1QS 9:5–8; *Self-Glorification Hymn*, 4Q491c 1:3–4.

11. Newsom, *Songs of the Sabbath*, 239; Alexander, *Mystical Texts*, 16; Lahe, *Gnosis und Judentum*, 129–30, 148–49; see *1 En.* 17–19; *Jub.* 1:27; *4 Ezra* 4. This point was first noted by Scholem, *Jewish Gnosticism*, 3; Alexander agrees that here Qumran "anticipates" Gnosticism (*Mystical Texts*, 107).

12. See Burns, "Sethian Crowns, Sethian Martyrs?"

13. Scopello, "Apocalypse of Zostrianos" (cf. M. A. Williams, *Immovable Race*, 83 n. 26); Turner, "Commentary: *Zostrianos*," 504–5. More generally, see also Frankfurter, "Legacy of Jewish Apocalypses," 160–61; Pearson, "From Jewish Apocalypticism to Gnosis," 153.

14. Fifth to eighth centuries CE; see Greenfield and Stone, "Books of Enoch," 99.

15. For the relationship of *3 En.* to earlier apocalyptic traditions, see Himmelfarb, "Heavenly Ascent"; Schäfer, *Origins*, 343.

16. Thus notes Alexander, *Mystical Texts*, 135.

17. Here I support the broad scholarly consensus that Mani indeed did grow up in a community that was directly related to the Elchasaites or a product of a virtually identical type of Jewish Christianity. For an argument to the contrary, see Luttikhuizen, *Revelation of Elchasai*, esp. 210; idem, "Elchasaites and Their Book"; but cf. F. Jones, "Review of Luttikhuizen, *Revelation of Elchasai*," as well as Rudolph, "The Baptist Sects," 485 n. 36; Gardner and Lieu, *Manichaean Texts in the Roman Empire*, 33–35. On the lifestyle of Mani's community, see *Fihrist*, 327–28, 811 (Dodge); CMC 79, 88.2–9, 106.5–19; Koenen, "From Baptism to the Gnosis." No women are mentioned in the CMC, so it could have been an all-male, encratic community.

18. MacRae, "Apocalypse of Adam," 577, as well as Nickelsburg, "Some Related Adam Traditions," 538; more widely, see Klijn, *Seth*, 109; Pearson, "Figure of Seth," 473. Couliano recognized that the Manichaean myth is an elaborate version of the sort assigned by Hippolytus to Sethians, but this observation must be bracketed since the Sethians known to Hippolytus seem to be unrelated to the traditions preserved at Nag Hammadi dubbed here Sethian (*Tree of Gnosis*, 180).

19. *Apoc Adam* NHC V,5.77.27–83.

20. Ibid., 73.10; *Man. Hom.* 68:18, cit. Böhlig and Labib, *Koptisch-Gnostische Apokalypsen*, 89; Henning, "Book of the Giants," 62; Stroumsa, *Another Seed*, 85.

21. For multiple incarnations of the savior, see above, Chapter 4, "Seth and His Avatars"; on the Elchasaites, see Hipp. *Haer.* 9.14, 10.29 (Marcovich); on the Ebionites, see Epiph. *Pan.* 30.3.3; on the Pseudo-Clementines,

see *Hom.* 3.20.2; Stroumsa, *Another Seed,* 76, 88; Burns, "Jesus' Reincarnations Revisited," 372–80.

22. *Fihrist,* 784–86 (Dodge).

23. In discussion at the 1978 Yale conference (Layton [ed.], *Rediscovery,* 507–8).

24. For sources and bibliography, see S. Lieu, "The Diffusion of Manichaeism in the Roman Empire," 388.

25. Elsas, *Neuplatonische und gnostische Weltablehnung,* 242; H. Jackson, "Seer Nikotheos," 257; Quispel, "Plotinus and the Jewish Gnōstikoi."

26. See for instance Schenke, "Phenomenon," 607; Pearson, "Figure of Seth," 503; M. A. Williams, *Immovable Race,* 199; P. Perkins, *Gnostic Dialogue,* 90; eadem, "Identification with the Savior," 180; Edwards, "Christians and the *Parmenides*," 197. This is of course the central thesis of Turner, *Sethian Gnosticism and the Platonic Tradition* (and many articles), as discussed in Chapter 3.

27. A Christian provenance for the Platonizing treatises has been considered by Logan, *Gnostic Truth and Christian Heresy,* 51; Edwards, "Christians and the *Parmenides*," 2:197.

28. Cf. Mazur, "Platonizing Sethian Gnostic Background," 324–25. Thus the importance of the Plotinus-Gnostic conflict is hardly "exaggerated" (*pace* Rasimus, "Porphyry and the Gnostics," 82, 108), nor are the "doctrinal differences" between Plotinus and the Gnostics merely "subtle" (*pace* Mazur, "Platonizing Sethian Gnostic Background," 20). Rather, as C. Schmidt recognized, "Plotin habe den littarischen Kampf der Neuplatoniker gegen das Christentum inauguriert, und die neuplatonische Schule sei nur den Bahnen ihres Meisters gefolgt" (*Plotins Stellung,* 29).

29. On Prohaeresis and Eunapius, see Eunap. *VS* 10.3.1 (Giangrande). On Gregory and Julian, see Greg. Naz. *Or.* 4.5, 4.103, 5.23.

30. For a summary, see Chuvin, *Chronicle of the Last Pagans,* 86; on Hypatia's death, Watts, *City and School,* 196–200.

31. On Ammonius, see Dam. *Phil. hist.* 118b (Athanassiadi); Sorabji, *Philosophy of the Commentators,* 1:21; Watts, *City and School,* 216–30. On Olympiodorus's caution (and how it saved him from a Christian challenge), see Watts, *City and School,* 235–55, 260–61.

32. Dam. *Phil. hist.* 146b; see Watts, *City and School,* 137.

33. On student emigration to Athens in the fifth century CE and its consequences, see Watts, *City and School,* 201–2.

34. Surveyed in Meredith, "Porphyry and Julian Against the Christians."

35. Eunap. *VS* 6.11.2 (also 6.9.17; cf. 10.8.2); idem, *Hist. univ.* frg. 56 (Blockley).

36. Saffrey, "Allusions antichrétiennes chez Proclus"; Watts, *City and School,* 106; Hoffmann, "Un grief antichrétien."

37. See Watts, *City and School,* 235–55, 260–61, for discussion of Olympiodorus's career.

38. Chuvin, *Chronicle of the Last Pagans,* 45, 104; Shaw, *Theurgy and the Soul,* 14–16; D. O'Meara, *Platonopolis,* esp. 128–31; Burns, "Proclus and the Theurgic Liturgy," 128–31.

39. Iamb. *An.* 6–7 (Finamore and Dillon).

40. Shaw, *Theurgy and the Soul*, 4–5; see also Clarke, Dillon, and Hershbell, introduction, xxviii–xxix.

41. Iamb. *An.* 23.22–23.

42. Brisson also sees Plotinus's rejection of Gnostic ritual as predicated on his assertion of the Soul's undescended nature, implying Gnostic agreement with Iamblichus's position ("Plotinus and the Magical Rites"). Cf. Edwards, "Gnostic Aculinus," 379; cf. also Narbonne, *Plotinus in Dialogue*, 57–77, attributing Plotinus's doctrine of the undescended Soul to his Gnostic conversation partners. He rightfully observes that the Gnostics (*pace* Iamblichus) saw themselves as superior to heavenly beings, but neglects the fact that, like theurgists, they used a variety of rituals to elevate the Soul (Narbonne, *Plotinus in Dialogue*, 108–11). Nor does Narbonne address Iamblichus's remark that the Gnostics *affirmed* Soul's descent.

43. Similarly, see Clark, "Translate into Greek," 129; Mazur, "Platonizing Sethian Gnostic Background," 326 n. 94.

44. For recent *status quaestionis* on the attribution of the fragments of Porph. *Christ.*, see Goulet, "Hypothèses récentes"; Schott, "'Living like a Christian'," 259 n. 2.

45. Porph. *Christ.* frg. 20 (Berchman) = frg. 39 (Harnack) = Euseb. *Eccl. hist.* 6.39.5–8 (tr. Oulton [LCL], slightly modified).

46. See for instance Schott, "'Living like a Christian'," 262; Zambon, "ΠΑΡΑΝΟΜΩΣ ΖΗΝ," esp. 558–59; cf. Clark, "Translate into Greek," 128; Johnson, "Philosophy, Hellenicity, Law," 57–64.

47. *Pace* Johnson, "Philosophy, Hellenicity, Law," 64.

48. On Porphyry's rare but pejorative use of the word ὀθνεῖος, see J. Cook, "Porphyry's Attempted Demolition," 3, 7, regarding Porph. *Abst.* 2.45; further, see *PGL* 936b. Surely Porphyry would not have preferred Origen to value the μῦθος of the Bible on the basis of its extra-Hellenic Jewishness; otherwise he would not refer to it as ὀθνεῖος (*pace* Johnson, "Porphyry's Hellenism," 179).

49. As do Brisson and Goulet, "Origène le platonicien," 806; Digeser, "Origen on the *Limes*," 204. This (invented) problem is one of many issues in the evidence that leads scholars to debate whether or not the philosopher named Origen who studied with Ammonius alongside Plotinus, occasionally mentioned in the Platonic tradition (Porph. *Vit. Plot.* 3, 14, 20; Eunap. *VS* 4.2.1 [Giangrande]; Hierocles, ap. Phot. *Bibl.* 214 173a), was in fact the same as the Christian Origen Porphyry mentions here. While some scholars now regard the two Origens as identical—see Digeser, "Origen on the *Limes*"—others continue to distinguish them (e.g., Goulet, "Porphyre, Ammonius, les deux Origène," esp. 282–85, more recently, Zambon, "Porfirio e Origene," esp. 158–64; Watts, *City and School*, 159–61). For a survey of the (voluminous) older scholarship on the question (and deciding on two Origens), see Schroeder, "Ammonius Saccas."

50. Schott, *Christianity, Empire*, 71; see also Zambon, "ΠΑΡΑΝΟΜΩΣ ΖΗΝ," 557; cf. Johnson, "Porphyry's Hellenism," 179–80.

51. Discussed in Schott, "'Living like a Christian'," 259 n. 2.

52. See also (on Origen and Porphyry), Digeser, "Origen on the *Limes*," esp. 205ff.

53. See Stroumsa, *Another Seed*, 87.

54. The first view is offered by Schenke, "Phenomenon," 607; Pearson, "Figure of Seth," 504; Hedrick, *Apocalypse of Adam*, 214–15. The second view is that of Turner, *Sethian Gnosticism and the Platonic Tradition*, 238–84, esp. 240 n. 17; idem, "To See the Light," 96–98, 111–12; idem, "Sethian Gnosticism: A Revised Literary History," 900. Possible origins in Samaritanism have been suggested (Schenke, "Phenomenon," 592–93, 606–7, and also Fossum, *Name of God*, 50, 122; Lahe, *Gnosis und Judentum*, 128, 178), but this idea has not fared well under criticism (Stroumsa, *Another Seed*, 11; Logan, *Gnostic Truth and Christian Heresy*, 16).

55. Sethian interest in angelification is also evidence that the Sethianism of *Gos. Jud.* is second-hand or an offshoot of other Sethian ideas, since it scorns those who claim to resemble angels (*Gos. Jud.* TC 40.8–16), in contrast to the wide angelomorphism surveyed in Chapter 6. On *Gos. Jud.* as later, "tertiary" Sethianism, see G. Schenke (Robinson), "The *Gospel of Judas*," 88–89; Turner, "The Sethian Myth in the *Gospel of Judas*," 97, 131–33. Others have dated it to the mid-second century: see DeConick, *Thirteenth Apostle*, 169, 174–75; Pearson, *Ancient Gnosticism*, 97; Rasimus, *Paradise Reconsidered*, 40 n. 109; Jennott, '*Gospel of Judas*', 5–6, 131–32. On dating *Ap. John*, see above, Chapter 3, n. 15. Turner assigns *Trim. Prot.* a complex history of redactions, the last of which he dates to the mid-second century ("Introduction: NHC XIII,1*," 375–81; idem, *Sethian Gnosticism and the Platonic Tradition*, 283–84). Poirier suggests instead that a variety of sources were cobbled together at once, working in part with the Greek long recension of *Ap. John*, sometime in the early third century CE ("Introduction: *La pensée première*," 120–23; similarly, see Pearson, *Ancient Gnosticism*, 75).

56. See Logan, *Gnostic Truth and Christian Heresy*, xviii, 26, arguing that a "Sethianization" of the *Apocryphon* and other Barbeloite material took place around 200 CE, when Gnostics who were attacked by other Christians on grounds of novelty turned to the authority of the figure of Seth, who was becoming a popular figure at the time. Rasimus argues instead that the catalyst for Sethianization must have been Jewish, since Christian traditions of authorization (e.g., postresurrection appearances) are not invoked in Sethian literature; rather, accounts of the inscription of antediluvian revelations on steles were used to undercut Mosaic (i.e., Jewish, postdiluvian) authority. The Sethianization of Ophite materials, according to Rasimus, began around 100 CE, drawing from traditions about these revelatory steles as preserved by Josephus and responding to the Johannine community (*Paradise Reconsidered*, 38–39, 197, 287; see also Turner, "Sethian Gnosticism: A Revised Literary History," 900; Luttikhuizen, "Sethianer?" 94). This certainly is possible, but invocations of antediluvian revealers and the pillar-stele tradition were widespread, so the authority of pre-Mosaic texts could have been invoked against Christians as easily as Jews (e.g., CMC 49, 54.12–19). Meanwhile, the dating of Sethianization to the second century

presupposes that the engagement of *Ap. John* with Johannine traditions necessarily indicates engagement with the earliest proponents of these traditions
and fails to explain why Seth would have been the obvious authoritative figure of choice to these Gnostics over a century before he was popular in other
groups.

57. In general agreement with the dating of *Apoc. Adam* by MacRae,
"The Apocalypse of Adam Reconsidered"; Stroumsa, *Another Seed*, 97–103;
Turner, *Sethian Gnosticism and the Platonic Tradition*, 155, 749–50; *pace*
Hedrick, *Apocalypse of Adam*, 214–15, and Pearson, *Ancient Gnosticism*,
74 (both of whom assume first-century traditions); Logan, *Gnostic Truth
and Christian Heresy*, 47–48 (assigning a third-century date, based on presumed dependence on *Ap. John*).

58. Thus argues Pearson, "Introduction: *Melchizedek*," 39–40; idem,
Ancient Gnosticism, 83.

59. Turner, *Sethian Gnosticism and the Platonic Tradition*, 165.

60. Turner, "Introduction: Zostrianos," 142; see also M. A. Williams,
"Sethianism," 45.

61. P. Perkins, "Christian Books and Sethian Revelations," 725. Others see the Greek *Vorlagen* of both *Zostrianos* and *Allogenes* as post-
Plotinian redactions, perhaps under the influence of Porphyry (Majercik,
"Being-Life-Mind Triad," 486–88; eadem, "Porphyry and Gnosticism,"
278; Abramowski, "Marius Victorinus," 123–24; eadem, "Nicänismus
und Gnosis," 559–61; A. Smith, "Porphyrian Studies," 763 n. 282). For
most scholars, meanwhile, Porphyry's evidence functions as a *terminus
ante quem* for these *Vorlagen* (Corrigan, "Positive and Negative Matter,"
44 n. 77; Turner, *Sethian Gnosticism and the Platonic Tradition*, 721, and
in many articles; Layton, *Gnostic Scriptures*, 122, 142; Logan, *Gnostic
Truth and Christian Heresy*, 53; Tardieu, "Recherches sur la Formation,"
113; Zambon, *Porphyre*, 40; Kalligas, "Plotinus Against the Gnostics,"
119; Pearson, *Ancient Gnosticism*, 90; M. A. Williams, "Sethianism," 51;
Rasimus, *Paradise Reconsidered*, 32; idem, "Porphyry and the Gnostics,"
82; Mazur, "Platonizing Sethian Gnostic Background," 31, 179, 309;
Brakke, *The Gnostics*, 40; Narbonne, *Plotinus in Dialogue*, 7 n.23, 71,
104 n. 12; van den Broek, *Gnostic Religion*, 133, 135). With reservations
are Attridge, "Gnostic Platonism," 23; Jennott, *"Gospel of Judas"*, 73 n.
9. Central to the question is dating the anonymous Turin *Commentary on
Plato's "Parmenides"*. Many of its metaphysical ideas are similar to those
in *Zostrianos* and *Allogenes*, and it plays a decisive role in Hadot's system-
atization of the thought of Porphyry ("Métaphysique de Porphyre"), which
is followed by Abramowski, Majercik, and others; if the commentary is
not assigned to Porphyrian authorship but to a pre-Plotinian thinker, then
Abramowski's and Majercik's arguments for a late dating for Platonizing
Sethian texts instead indicate an early dating. However, the authorship
and date of the commentary remain uncertain and debated; the most up-
to-date *Forschungsbericht* is Chase, "Porphyre commentateur."

62. Burns, "Apophatic Strategies."

63. Pearson argued that *Mars.* was written in the early third century CE and circulated in Plotinus's seminar with the other Platonizing treatises, on grounds of the passage in *Unt.* that is ascribed to Nicotheus and cites one "Marsanios" (*Unt.* 232.3–23—"Introduction: *Marsanes*," 250; "*Marsanes* Revisited," 695–96). Turner argued for the early fourth century CE, based on similarities to the philosophy of Iamblichus (the "second One") and his student Theodore of Asine (alphabetic theurgy—"Introduction: *Marsanes*," 1, 229, 246–48), eventually persuading Pearson (*Ancient Gnosticism*, 85, giving an early fourth-century CE date to the text).

64. On reading Nag Hammadi documents as Coptic translations of later or redacted Greek literature instead of simple replications of second- and third-century texts, see Emmel, "Religious Tradition, Textual Transmission, and the Nag Hammadi Codices"; idem, "The Coptic Gnostic Texts as Witnesses."

65. Cf. Turner and Schenke (works above, n. 54, in this chapter); Attridge, "Gnostic Platonism," 6, considers Egypt and Syria.

66. Epiph. *Pan.* 53; Hipp. *Haer.* 9.13–17, 10.29; Origen *ap.* Euseb. *Hist. eccl.* 6.38; *Fihrist*, 327–28, 811 (Dodge).

67. Athanassiadi, "Apamea and the *Chaldaean Oracles.*"

68. Pearson, "Introduction: *Melchizedek*," 40.

69. Hipp. *Haer.* 9.13 alleges that Alcibiades' literature was in the possession of Pope Callistus (ca. 218–23 CE).

70. Hipp. *Haer.* 10.29.3.

71. On the contents of the *Apocalypse*, see Luttikhuizen, "Elchasaites and their Book."

72. I owe this insight to Prof. Jean-Marc Narbonne, in conversation. Cf. Mazur, hypothesizing that Plotinus was influenced by Gnosticism as a youth, but attempted to purge his thought of it when he met a young, Gnosticizing Porphyry ("Platonizing Sethian Gnostic Background," 173, 289–312, esp. 310–12). This model fails to explain why we should suppose Porphyry to have been under the influence of Gnosticism, or why Plotinus would have found it objectionable if he himself was under its influence in the first place.

73. Whether these groups known to Epiphanius were one group broken up by him into different names, as argued by Tardieu, or separate groups that had inherited Sethian traditions, as argued by Turner, cannot be determined (Tardieu, "Les livres mis sous le nom de Seth," an argument followed by Pearson, "Figure of Seth," 474; see also the discussion of Robinson and Wisse, 585; Turner, *Sethian Gnosticism and the Platonic Tradition*, 301). On the *Untitled Treatise*, see Sevrin, *Le dossier baptismal séthien*, 218–20; Turner, *Sethian Gnosticism and the Platonic Tradition*, 195; Brakke, "The Body as/at the Boundary," 201–4.

74. The hypothesis of Abramowski, "Nicänismus und Gnosis," 560–61.

75. On monastic readers of Nag Hammadi, see Wisse, "Gnosticism and Early Monasticism in Egypt"; idem, "Language Mysticism in the Nag Hammadi Texts." Particularly striking are monastic ascetic practices that produce an angelic likeness (Frank, *ΑΓΓΕΛΙΚΟΣ ΒΙΟΣ*, 23) resembling that achieved in Sethian angelification.

APPENDIX

1. LSJ 41b. Classic studies include Staden, "Hairesis and Heresy"; Boulluec, *La notion d'hérésie dans la litterature grecque*; on the *secta* more generally, see André, "Écoles philosophiques," 5–8.

2. Armstrong (LCL); Puech, "Plotin et les gnostiques," 176; Igal, "The Gnostics and 'The Ancient Philosophy,'" 146; Cilento, *Plotino: Paideia*, 10, 26; H. Jackson, "Seer Nikotheos," 255; Evangeliou, "Plotinus's Anti-Gnostic Polemic," 113; Layton, *Gnostic Scriptures*, 184; Brakke, *The Gnostics*, 40; Poirier and Schmidt, "Chrétiens, hérétiques et gnostiques," 925–27; van den Broek, *Gnostic Religion*, 133.

3. As Tardieu argues, "Les gnostiques," 511–15 (acknowledged by Poirier and Schmidt, "Chrétiens, hérétiques et gnostiques," 924–25); see also C. Schmidt, *Plotins Stellung*, 14; idem, *Koptisch-Gnostische Schriften*, 606; Edwards, *Neoplatonic Saints*, 28 n. 155; Mazur, "Platonizing Sethian Gnostic Background," 13, 378.

4. Plot. *Enn.* 2.9 [33] 6.1–10.

5. Thus read Bidez and Cumont, *Mages*, 1:156, 2:249–50; Bousset, *Hauptprobleme*, 186–89; Festugière, *Révélation*, 3:59 n. 3; idem, *Hermétisme et mystique païenne*, 88; Puech, "Plotin et les gnostiques," 163; Doresse, "Les apocalypses de Zoroatre"; H. Jackson, "Seer Nikotheos," 255 n. 6.

6. Cf. Smyth, *Greek Grammar*, §2869, p. 650, for καί as copulative. For minimal contrast between the μέν . . . δέ clauses, especially when the μέν clause expresses time (as here: κατ'αὐτόν), see Denniston, *Greek Particles*, 370. The μὲν καί . . . δέ construction, with the same sense, can be found at Plot. *Enn.* 2.9 [33] 10.1 (πολλὰ μὲν οὖν καὶ ἄλλα, μᾶλλον δὲ πάντα), as discussed in Edwards, "Neglected Texts," 34–35; Majercik, "Porphyry and Gnosticism," 277 n. 6. It is common in Porphyry, as at *Abst.* 1.12.35–13.2 (Bouffartigue and Patillon), 2.38.28–39.3. For the πολλοὶ μὲν καὶ ἄλλοι construction (tr. "[there were] many—and in particular, [some]"), see Poirier and Schmidt, "Chrétiens, hérétiques et gnostiques," 918–23.

7. Thus read Puech, "Plotin et les gnostiques," 163, 176 (with the approval of Dodds); Igal, "The Gnostics and the 'Ancient Philosophy,'" 139 n. 8, 147 n. 10; H. Jackson, "Seer Nikotheos," 255; Janssens, "Apocalypses de Nag Hammadi," 69; Wolters, "Notes on the Structure of *Enneads* II,9," 83; Wallis, "Soul and Nous," 474 n. 10; Layton, *Gnostic Scriptures*, 184; Tardieu, "Les gnostiques"; Corrigan, "Positive and Negative Matter," 24; Edwards, "Neglected Texts," 28; idem, *Culture and Philosophy*, 151, Poirier and Schmidt, "Chrétiens, hérétiques et gnostiques," 918, 923; Mazur, "Platonizing Sethian Gnostic Background," 13, 378; van den Broek, *Gnostic Religion*, 134. Armstrong (LCL) is unclear ("Christians, and others, and sectaries"), a reading followed widely, e.g., by Turner, "Typologies," 203 n. 34; Frankfurter, "Legacy of Jewish Apocalypses," 156; Pearson, "From Jewish Apocalypticism to Gnosis," 149.

8. As argue Tardieu, "Les gnostiques," 516; Poirier and Schmidt, "Chrétiens, hérétiques et gnostiques," 926–27.

9. H. Jackson, "Seer Nikotheos," 253–54, recalling Xen. *Hell.* 1.1.11, 1.6.38.

10. Puech, "Plotin et les gnostiques," 165.

11. Ibid., 112.

For Greco-Roman literature, I have used the LCL (Loeb Classical Library) texts and translations as much as possible, altering them when necessary, as noted; an exception is Plato, where I have used the translations in Cooper and Hutchinson, eds., *Plato*, noting each translator individually. For church fathers, I generally used the translations available in the ANF (*Ante-Nicene Fathers*, ed. Roberts and Donaldson) and NPNF (*Nicene and Post-Nicene Fathers*, ed. Schaff) series, noting critical editions and other translations ad loc. All translations from the Dead Sea Scrolls are Martínez and Tigchelaar, unless otherwise noted; all translations of Jewish apocrypha are those given in the *Old Testament Pseudepigrapha* (ed. Charlesworth), as noted; Christian apocrypha were generally taken from *New Testament Apocrypha* (ed. Hennecke and Schneemelcher, rev. ed. Wilson), except when noted. All translations of Coptic sources are my own, except where noted. Significant differences between the texts and translations of the Nag Hammadi Codices given in CGL and BCNH editions are noted. In general, critical editions are listed by ancient author if known (thus Proclus's works are under "Proclus"), while collected volumes (e.g. "Nag Hammadi Codex") or "authorless" works are listed by editor.

Adler, A., ed. *Suidae lexicon.* 4 vols. Leipzig: Teubner, 1928–35.

Aelius Aristides. *Complete Works.* Ed. and tr. Charles A. Behr. 2 vols. Leiden: E. J. Brill, 1981–86.

Aelius Theon. *Progymnasmata.* Ed. and tr. Michel Patillon, with Giancarlo Bolognesi. Paris: Belles Lettres, 1997.

Alberry, C. R. C., ed. and tr. *A Manichaean Psalm-Book, Part II.* Manichaean Manuscripts of the Chester Beatty Collection vol. 2. Stuttgart: Kohlhammer, 1938.

Alcinous. *Enseignement des doctrines de Platon.* Ed. and tr. John Whittaker and Pierre Louis. Paris: Belles Lettres, 1990.

———. *The Handbook of Platonism.* Tr. John Dillon. Oxford: Clarendon Press, 1993.

Alexander of Lycopolis. *An Alexandrian Platonist Against Dualism: Alexander of Lycopolis' Treatise "Critique of the Doctrines of Manichaeus."* Ed. P. W. van der Horst and Jaap Mansfeld. Leiden: E. J. Brill, 1974.

———. *Alexandri Lycopolitani contra Manichaei opiniones disputatio.* Ed. A. Brinkmann. Leipzig: Teubner, 1895.

———. *Contre la doctrine de Mani: Alexandre de Lycopolis.* Tr. André Villey. Sources Gnostiques et Manichéennes 2. Paris: Cerf, 1985.

Apuleius. *Platon und seine Lehre.* Ed. Paolo Siniscalco, tr. Karl Albert. Texte zur Philosophie 4. Sankt Augustin: Hans Richarz, 1981.

———. *Rhetorical Works.* Tr. Stephen Harrison, John Hilton, and Vincent Hunink; ed. Stephen Harrison. Oxford: Oxford University Press, 2002.

Arnim, Johannes von, ed. *Stoicorum Veterum Fragmenta.* 4 vols. Stuttgart: Teubner, 1924.

Aristotle. *The Complete Works of Aristotle: Revised Oxford Translation.* Ed. Jonathan Barnes. 2 vols. Princeton, NJ: Princeton University Press, 1984.

Athenagoras. *Legatio* and *De Resurrectione.* Ed. and tr. William R. Schoedel. Oxford Early Christian Texts. Oxford: Clarendon Press, 1972.

Atticus. *Fragments.* Ed. and tr. Édouard des Places. Paris: Belles Lettres, 1977.

Augustine. *The City of God Against the Pagans.* Ed. and tr. R.W. Dyson. Cambridge Texts in the History of Political Thought. Cambridge: Cambridge University Press, 2002.

Barry, Catherine, Wolf-Peter Funk, Paul-Hubert Poirier, and John D. Turner, eds. and trs. *Zostrien.* BCNH Section "Textes" 24. Québec: Presses de l'université Laval; Leuven: Peeters, 2000.

Betz, Hans Dieter, ed. and tr. *The "Mithras Liturgy:" Text, Translation, and Commentary.* STAC 18. Tübingen: Mohr Siebeck, 2003.

Blockley, R. C., ed. and tr. *The Fragmentary Classicizing Historians of the Later Roman Empire: Eunapius, Olympiodorus, Priscus and Malchus.* 2 vols. ARCA Classical and Medieval Texts, Papers and Monographs 10. Liverpool: Francis Cairns, 1983.

Böhlig, Alexander, and Pahor Labib, eds. and trs. *Koptisch-Gnostische Apokalypsen aus Codex V von Nag Hammadi, im Koptischen Museum zu*

Alt-Kairo. Halle-Wittenberg: Wissenschaftliche Zeitschrift der Martin-Luther-Universität, 1963.

Böhlig, Alexander, and Frederik Wisse, eds. and trs. *Nag Hammadi Codices III,2 and IV,2: The Gospel of the Egyptians (The Holy Book of the Great Invisible Spirit)*. NHS 4. Leiden: E. J. Brill, 1975.

Brankaer, Johanna, and Hans-Gebhard Bethge, eds. and trs. *Codex Tchacos: Texte und Analysen*. TU 161. Berlin: Walter de Gruyter, 2007.

Cameron, Ron, and Arthur J. Dewey, eds. and trs. *The Cologne Mani Codex (P. Colon. inv. nr. 4780) "Concerning the Origin of His Body."* SBLTT 15. Missoula, MT: Scholars Press, 1979.

Charlesworth, James H., ed. and tr. *The Odes of Solomon: The Syriac Texts Edited with Translation and Notes*. SBLTT 13, Pseudepigrapha Series 7. Missoula, MT: Scholars' Press, 1977.

———, ed. *Old Testament Pseudepigrapha*. 2 vols. Anchor Yale Bible Reference Library. New York: Doubleday, 1983.

Cicero. *De natura deorum: Libri secundus et tertius*. Ed. Arthur Stanley Pease. Cambridge, MA: Harvard University Press, 1958.

Clement of Alexandria. *Extraits de Theodote*. Ed. and tr. Francois Sagnard. SC 23. Paris: Éditions du Cerf, 1948.

———. *Le pédagogue*. Ed. and tr. M. Harl, H.-I. Marrou, C. Matray, and C. Mondésert. 3 vols. SC 70, 108, 158. Paris: Éditions du Cerf, 1960–1970.

———. *Le protreptique*. Ed. and tr. C. Mondésert. SC 2. Paris: Éditions du Cerf, 1949.

———. *Stromateis*, in *Clemens Alexandrinus*. Ed. O. Stählin. 3 vols. Berlin: Akademie, 1960–1970.

Cooper, John M., and D. S. Hutchinson, eds. *Plato: Complete Works*. Indianapolis: Hackett, 1997.

Copenhaver, Brian, tr. *Hermetica*. Cambridge: Cambridge University Press, 1998.

Damascius. *The Greek Commentaries on Plato's Phaedo*. Ed. L. G. Westerink. Amsterdam: North-Holland, 1976–77.

———. *The Philosophical History*. Ed. and tr. Polymnia Athanassiadi. Athens: Apamea Cultural Association, 1999.

Diels, H., and W. Kranz, eds. *Die Fragmente der Vorsokratiker*. Berlin: Weidmann, 1951.

Digesta. Latin Library. http://www.thelatinlibrary.com/justinian.html.

Dio Chrysostom. *Orations VII, XII, and XXXVI*. Ed. Donald A. Russell. Cambridge: Cambridge University Press, 1992.

Dodge, Baynard, tr. *The "Fihrist" of al-Nadīm: A Tenth-Century Survey of Muslim Culture*. 2 vols. New York: Columbia University Press, 1970.

Dörrie, Heinrich, and Matthias Baltes, eds. and trs. *Der Platonismus in der Antike.* 6 vols. Stuttgart: Frommann-Holzboog, 1987–2002.

Edwards, Mark, tr. *Neoplatonic Saints: The Lives of Plotinus and Proclus by Their Students.* Liverpool: Liverpool University Press, 2000.

Ephraem Syrus. *Sancti Ephraem Syri in Genesim et in Exodum Commentarii.* Ed. R. M. Tonneau. 2 vols. CSCO 152–153. Leuven: L Durbecq, 1955.

Epiphanius of Salamis. *Panarion.* Tr. Frank Williams. 2 vols. Leiden: E. J. Brill, 1987–94.

Eunapius of Sardis. *Eunapii vitae sophistarum.* Ed. J. Giangrande. Rome: Polygraphica, 1956.

Eusebius of Caesarea. *Eusebius Werke, Band 6: Die Demonstratio evangelica.* Ed. I. A. Heikel. Die griechischen christlichen Schriftsteller 23. Leipzig: Hinrichs, 1913.

———. *Eusebius Werke, Band 8: Die Praeparatio evangelica.* Ed. K. Mras. Die griechischen christlichen Schriftsteller 43.1, 43.2. Berlin: Akademie, 1954–56.

Foerster, Werner. *Gnosis: A Selection of Gnostic Texts.* 2 vols. Tr. R. McLachlan Wilson. Oxford: Clarendon Press, 1974.

Funk, Wolf-Peter, and Paul-Hubert Poirier. *Concordance des texts de Nag Hammadi les codices XIB, XII, XIII.* BCNH section "Concordances" 7. Québec: Presses de l'université Laval; Leuven: Peeters, 2002.

Funk, Wolf-Peter, Paul-Hubert Poirier, and John D. Turner, eds. and trs. *Marsanès.* BCNH Section "Textes" 27. Québec: Presses de l'université Laval; Leuven: Peeters, 2000.

Funk, Wolf-Peter, Madeleine Scopello, and John D. Turner, eds. and trs. *L'allogène.* BCNH Section "Textes" 30. Québec: Presses de l'université Laval; Leuven: Peeters, 2004.

Galen. *On the Usefulness of the Parts of the Human Body.* Tr. Margaret Tallmadge May. 2 vols. Ithaca, NY: Cornell University Press, 1968.

———. *On Prognosis,* ed. and tr. Vivian Nutton. CMG V.8.1. Berlin: Akademie, 1979.

Gardner, Iain, tr. *The Kephalaia of the Teacher: The Edited Coptic Manichaean Texts in Translation with Commentary.* NHMS 37. Leiden: E. J. Brill, 1995.

Gardner, Iain, and Samuel Lieu, eds. *Manichaean Texts from the Roman Empire.* Cambridge: Cambridge University Press, 2004.

Gregory of Nazianzus. *Grégoire de Nazianze: Discours 4–5 contre Julien; Introduction, texte critique, et notes.* Ed. Jean Bernardi. SC 309. Paris: Les Éditions du Cerf, 1983.

Hedrick, Charles W., ed. *Nag Hammadi Codices XI, XII, and XIII.* NHS 28. Leiden : E. J. Brill, 1990.

Hennecke, Edgar, and Wilhelm Schneemelcher, eds. *New Testament Apocrypha*. Tr. R. McL. Wilson. 2 vols. Louisville: Westminster John Knox Press, 2003.

Hippolytus. *Refutatio Omnium Haeresium*. Ed. Miroslav Marcovich. Berlin: de Gruyter, 1986.

Iamblichus. *Iamblichi Chalcidensis in Platonis Dialogos Commentariorum Fragmenta*. Ed. and tr. John Dillon. Leiden: E. J. Brill, 1973.

——. *Protreptique*. Ed. and tr. Édouard des Places. Paris: Les belles lettres, 1989.

——. *On the Pythagorean Way of Life*. Ed. and tr. John Dillon and Jackson Hershbell. SBLTT 29. Atlanta: Scholars' Press, 1992.

——. *On the Pythagorean Life*. Ed. and tr. Gillian Clark. Liverpool: Liverpool University Press, 1989.

——. *Iamblichus De anima: Text, Translation, and Commentary*. Ed. and tr. John F. Finamore and John Dillon. PA 92. Leiden: E. J. Brill, 2002.

——. *On the Mysteries*. Ed. and tr. Emma C. Clarke, John M. Dillon, and Jackson P. Hershbell. SBLWGRW 4. Atlanta: SBL, 2003.

——. *Pythagoras: Legende—Lehre—Lebensgestaltung*. Ed. and tr. Michael von Albrecht. Sapere 4. Darmstadt: Wissenschaftliche Buchgesellschaft, 2002.

Irenaeus. *Contre les hérésies: denonciation et réfutation de la gnose au nom menteur*. Ed. and tr. L. Doutreleau and A. Rousseau, et al. 10 vols, SC 100, 152–153, 210–211, 263–264, 293–294. Paris: Éditions du Cerf, 1974–2006.

Janssens, Yvonne, ed. and tr. *La Prôtennoia Trimorphe: NH XIII,1*. BCNH Section "Textes" 4. Québec: Presses de l'université Laval, 1978.

Kasser, Rodolphe, Gregor Wurst, Marvin Meyer, and François Gaudard, eds. and trs. *The Gospel of Judas: Critical Edition*. Washington, DC: National Geographic Society, 2007.

Klijn, A. F. J., and G.. J. Reinink, eds. and trs. *Patristic Evidence for Jewish-Christian Sects*. NovTSup. 36. Leiden: E. J. Brill, 1973.

Koenen, Ludwig, and Cornelia Römer, eds. *Der Kölner Mani-Kodex: Abbildungen und Diplomatischer Text*. Papyrologische Texte und Abhandlungen 35. Bonn: Dr. Rudolf Habelt GMBH, 1985.

Konai, Theodore bar. *Librum Scholiorum*. Ed. Addai Scher. Leuven: L. Durbecq, 1954.

——. *Livre des scolies (recension de Séert)*. Tr. Robert Hespel and René Draguet. Leuven: Peeters, 1981–82.

Kropp, Angelicus M., ed. *Ausgewählte koptische Zaubertexte*. 3 vols. Brussels: Édition de la fondation égyptologique, 1930–31.

Layton, Bentley, tr. *The Gnostic Scriptures*. New York: Doubleday, 1987.

Layton, Bentley, and John Sieber. "Zostrianos: Text and Translation." In *Nag Hammadi Codex* VIII, ed. Sieber.

Lidzbarski, Mark. *Ginza. Der Schatz oder das grosse Buch der Mandäer*. Göttingen: van den Hoek & Ruprecht, 1925.

Long, A. A., and David Sedley. *The Hellenistic Philosophers*. 2 vols. Cambridge: Cambridge University Press, 1987.

Lucian. *On the Syrian Goddess*. Ed. and tr. J. L. Lightfoot. Oxford: Oxford University Press, 2003.

Lydus, Ioannes. *De mensibus*. Ed. R. Wuensch. Stuttgart: Teubner, 1967.

Macarius Magnes. *Macarios de Magnésie: Le monogénès*. Ed. and tr. R. Goulet. 2 vols. Paris: J. Vrin, 2003.

MacDonald, John, ed. and tr. *Memar Marqah: The Teaching of Marqah*. 2 vols. Berlin: Alfred Töpelmann, 1963.

Macrobius. *Commentary on the Dream of Scipio*. Tr. William Harris Stahl. New York: Columbia University Press, 1952.

Majercik, Ruth, ed. and tr. *The Chaldean Oracles: Text, Translation, and Commentary*. SGRR 5. Leiden: E. J. Brill, 1989.

Martínez, Florentino García, and Eibert J. C. Tigchelaar, eds. and trs. *The Dead Sea Scrolls: Study Edition*. 2 vols. Leiden: E. J. Brill, 1997.

Maximus of Tyre. *The Philosophical Orations*, tr. Michael B. Trapp. Oxford: Clarendon Press, 1997.

Menander. *Menander Rhetor*. Ed. and tr. Donald A. Russell and Nigel G. Wilson. Oxford: Clarendon Press, 1981.

Meyer, Marvin, and Richard Smith, eds and trs. *Early Christian Magic: Coptic Texts of Ritual Power*. San Francisco: HarperSanFrancisco, 1994.

Migne, J.-P., ed. *Patrologia graeca*. 162 vols. Paris: Migne, 1857–86.

Morgan, Michael A., tr. *Sepher ha-Razim: The Book of the Mysteries*. SBLTT 25. Chico, CA: Scholars' Press, 1983.

Musurillo, H. A. *The Acts of the Christian Martyrs*. Early Christian Texts. Oxford: Oxford University Press, 1972.

Newsom, Carol, ed. and tr. *Songs of the Sabbath Sacrifice: A Critical Edition*. HSS 27. Atlanta: Scholars' Press, 1985.

Nicomachus of Gerasa. *Excerpta ap. Musici scriptores Graeci*. Ed. K. Janus. Leipzig: Teubner, 1895, repr. Hildesheim: Olms, 1962.

———. *[Iamblichi] theologoumena arithmeticae*. Ed. V. de Falco. Leipzig: Teubner, 1922.

Nock, Arthur Darby, and Andre-Jean Festugière, eds. and trs. *Corpus Hermeticum*. 4 vols. Paris: Belles Lettres, 1946–54.

Numenius. *Fragments*. Ed. Edouard des Places. Collection Budé. Paris: Les Belles Lettres, 1973.

Olympiodorus. *Commentary on the First Alcibiades of Plato*. Ed. L. G. Westerink. Amsterdam: Hakkert, 1956.

———. *Olympiodori in Platonis Gorgiam commentaria*. Ed. L. G. Westerink. Leipzig: Teubner, 1970.

Origen. *Origène: Philocalie 21–27: Sur le libre arbitre*. Ed. and tr. E. Junod. SC 226. Paris: Éditions du Cerf, 1976.

———. *Commentary on the Gospel According to John: Books 1–10*. Tr. Ronald E. Heine. FC 80. Washington, DC: Catholic University of America Press, 1989.

———. *Homilies on Leviticus: 1–16*. Tr. Gary Wayne Barkley. FC 83. Washington, DC: Catholic University of America Press, 1990.

———. *Homilies on Jeremiah, Homily on 1 Kings 28*. Tr. John Clark Smith. FC 97. Washington, DC: Catholic University of America Press, 1998.

———. *Commentary on the Epistle to the Romans*. Tr. Thomas P. Scheck. 2 vols. FC 103–4. Washington, DC: Catholic University of America Press, 2001–2.

Parrott, Douglas M., ed. *Nag Hammadi Codices V,2–5 and VI, with Papyrus Berolinensis 8502, "1" and "4"*. NHS 11. Leiden: E. J. Brill, 1979.

Pearson, Birger, ed. *Nag Hammadi Codices IX and X*. NHS 15. Leiden: E. J. Brill, 1981.

———, ed. *Nag Hammadi Codex VII*. NHS 30. Leiden: E. J. Brill, 1996.

Photius. *Bibliothèque*. Ed. R. Henry. 8 vols. Paris: Les Belles Lettres, 1959–77.

Plutarch. *De Iside et Osiride*. Ed. and tr. J. Gwyn Griffiths. Cardiff: University of Wales Press, 1970.

Poirier, Paul-Hubert. Ed. and tr. *La pensée première à la triple forme*. BCNH Section "Textes" 32. Québec: Presses de l'université Laval; Leuven: Peeters, 2006.

Polotsky, Hans J., ed. and tr. *Manichäische Homilien* I. Manichäische Handschriften der Sammlung A. Chester Beatty. Stuttgart: Kohlhammer, 1934.

Polotsky, Hans J., and Alexander Böhlig, eds. and trs. *Kephalaia*. Manichäische Handschriften der Staatlichen Museen Berlin. Vol. 1. Stuttgart: Kohlhammer, 1940.

Porphyry. *Porphyrii de philosophia ex oraculis haurienda*. Ed. G. Wolff. Berlin: Springer, 1856; repr. Hildesheim: Olms, 1962.

———. *"Gegen die Christen", 15 Bucher*. Ed. Adolf von Harnack. Berlin: Königlichen Akademie der Wissenschaften, 1916.

———. Περὶ ἀγαλμάτων. In J. Bidez, *Vie de Porphyre le philosophe néo-platonicien*. Leipzig: Teubner, 1913; repr. Hildesheim: Olms, 1964, 1–23.

———. *Epistula ad Anebonem*. Ed. A. R. Sodano. Naples: L'Arte Tipo-grafica, 1958.

———. *The Cave of the Nymphs in the Odyssey*. Ed. L. G. Westerink. Arethusa Monographs 1. Buffalo: Department of Classics, State University of New York, 1969.

———. *Sententiae*. Ed. E. Lamberz. Teubner: Leipzig, 1975.

———. *De l'abstinence*. Ed. and tr. J. Bouffartique and M. Patillon. 2 vols. Paris: Les belles letters, 1979.

———. *Vie de Pythagore: Lettre à Marcella*. Ed. and tr. Edouard des Places. Paris: Belles Lettres, 1982.

———. *To Marcella*. Ed. and tr. Kathleen O'Brien Wicker. SBLTT 28. Atlanta: Scholars' Press, 1987.

———. *Fragmenta*. Ed. Andrew Smith. Leipzig: Teubner, 1999.

———. *On Abstinence from Killing Animals*. Tr. Gillian Clark. London: Duckworth, 2000.

———. *Porphyry Against the Christians*. Ed. and tr. Robert Berchman. Leiden: E. J. Brill, 2005.

Posidonius. *The Fragments*. Ed. and tr. I. G. Kidd (vol. 1 with L. Edelstein). 4 vols. CCTC 13, 14ab, 36. Cambridge: Cambridge University Press, 1972–99.

Proclus. *Procli Diadochi in Platonis rem publicam commentarii*. Ed. W. Kroll. 2 vols. Leipzig: Teubner, 1899–1901.

———. *In Platonis Timaeum Commentarii*. Ed. E. Diehl. 3 vols. Leipzig: Teubner, 1903–6.

———. *Elements of Theology*. Ed. and tr. Eric R. Dodds. Oxford: Oxford University Press, 1963.

———. *Commentary on Plato's "Timaeus"*. Vol. 1, book 1: *Proclus on the Socratic State and Atlantis*. Tr. Harold Tarrant. Cambridge: Cambridge University Press, 2007.

———. *Théologie Platonicienne*. Ed. and tr. H. D. Saffrey and L. G. Westerink. 6 vols. Paris: Les belles lettres, 1968–97.

Ri, Su-Min, ed. *La Caveme des Tresors: Les deux recensions syriaques*. 2 vols. CSCO 486–487, Syr. 207–8. Leuven: Peeters, 1987.

Sallustius. *Concerning the Gods and the Universe*. Ed. and tr. A. D. Nock. Chicago: Ares, 1996.

Schäfer, Peter, ed. *Synopse zur Hekhalot-Literatur*. Tübingen: JCB Mohr, 1981.

Schenke [Robinson], Gesine, ed. and tr. *Die dreigestaltige Protennoia (Nag-Hammadi-Codex XIII)*. Berlin: Walter de Gruyter, 1984.

——, ed. and tr. *Das Berliner "Koptische Buch" (P20915): Eine wieder hergestellte frühchristlich-theologische Abhandlung*. CSCO 610, CSCO Scriptores Coptici 49. Louvain: Peeters, 2005.

Schmidt, Carl, ed., and Violet MacDermot, rev. and tr. *The Books of Jeu and the Untitled Treatise in the Bruce Codex*. NHS 13. Leiden, E. J. Brill, 1978.

——, *Pistis Sophia*. NHS 9. Leiden: E. J. Brill, 1978.

Sextus Empiricus. *Against the Grammarians (Adversus Mathematicos I)*. Tr. D. L. Blank. Oxford: Clarendon Press, 1998.

Sieber, John, ed. *Nag Hammadi Codex VIII*. NHS 31. Leiden: E. J. Brill, 1991.

Simplicius. *Simplicii in Aristotelis de caelo commentaria*. Ed. J. L. Heiberg. Commentaria in Aristotelem Graeca 7. Berlin: Reimer, 1894.

——. *On Epictetus' "Handbook."* Tr. Charles Brittain and Tad Brennan. 2 vols. Ithaca, NY: Cornell University Press, 2002.

Sorabji, Richard, ed. *The Philosophy of the Commentators, 200–600 AD: A Sourcebook*. 3 vols. London: Duckworth, 2004.

Stobaeus, Ioannes. *Anthologii Libri Duo Priores Qui Inscribi Solent Eclogae Physicae et Ethicae*. Ed. C. Wachsmuth. 2 vols. Berlin: 1884.

Syncellus, Georgius. *Ecloga chronographica*. Ed. A. A. Mosshammer. Leipzig: Teubner, 1984.

Vaillant, André, ed. and tr. *Le livre des secrets d'Hènoch: Texte slave et traduction française*. Textes publiés par l'Institut d'études slaves 4. Paris: Institut d'études slaves, 1952.

Waldstein, Michael, and Frederick Wisse, eds. and trs. *The Apocryphon of John: Synopsis of Nag Hammadi Codices II,1;III,1; and IV,1 with BG 8502,2*. NHMS 33. Leiden: E. J. Brill, 1995.

Westerink, L.G., ed. *Anonymous Prolegomena to Platonic Philosophy*. Amsterdam: North-Holland, 1962.

Zosimus of Panopolis. *On the Letter Omega*. Ed. and tr. Howard Jackson. SBLTT 14. Atlanta: Society of Biblical Literature, 1978.

SECONDARY SOURCES

Abbreviations of titles of journals and standard reference works follow those listed in the *SBL Handbook of Style* (ed. Alexander et al., Peabody, Mass.: Hendrickson, 1999).

Aalders, G. J. D. *Plutarch's Poltical Thought*. Amsterdam: North-Holland, 1982.

Abegg, Martin G. "4Q471: A Case of Mistaken Identity?" In *Pursuing the Text: Studies in Honor of Ben Zion Wacholder on the Occasion of His Seventieth Birthday*, ed. John C. Reeves and John Kamper. JSOTS 184. Sheffield: Sheffield Academic Press, 1994, 135–47.

Abbenes, J. G. J., S. R. Slings, and I. Sluiter, eds. *Greek Literary Theory After Aristotle: A Collection of Papers in Honour of D. M. Schenkeveld*. Amsterdam: Vrij Universiteit Press, 1995.

Abramowski, Luise. "Marius Victorinus, Porphyrius und die römischen Gnostiker." *ZNW* 74 (1983): 108–28.

———. "Nag Hammadi 8,1 'Zostrianos', das Anonymum Brucianum, Plotin Enn. 2,9 (33)." In *Platonismus und Christentum. Festschrift für Heinrich Dörrie*, ed. Horst-Dieter Blume and Friedhelm Mann. JAC Ergänzungsband 10. Münster: Aschendorffsche Verlagsbuchhandlung, 1983, 1–10.

———. "Nicänismus und Gnosis im Rom des Bischofs Liberius: Der Fall des Marius Victorinus." *ZAC* 8 (2005): 513–66.

Adams, Edward. *The Stars Will Fall from Heaven: Cosmic Catastrophe in the New Testament and Its World*. LNTS 347. New York: T&T Clark, 2007.

Adler, William. "Introduction" to *Jewish Apocalyptic Heritage*, ed. VanderKam and Adler, 1–31.

Aland, Barbara, ed. *Gnosis: Festschrift für Hans Jonas*. Göttingen: Vandenhoeck & Ruprecht, 1978.

Aland, Kurt. "The Problem of Anonymity and Pseudonymity in Christian Literature of the First Two Centuries." *JTS* 12:1 (1961): 39–49.

Alexander, Philip S. "Comparing Merkavah Mysticism and Gnosticism: An Essay in Method." *JJS* 35:1 (1984): 1–18.

———. "Jewish Elements in Gnosticism and Magic, c. CE 70–c. CE 270." In *The Cambridge History of Judaism*, ed. Horbury, Davies, and Sturdy, 1052–78.

———. *Mystical Texts: Songs of the Sabbath Sacrifice and Related Manuscripts*. Library of Second Temple Studies 61. London: T&T Clark International, 2006.

Allison, Dale C. "Eschatology of the New Testament." In *The New Interpreter's Dictionary of the Bible*, ed. Sakenfeld et al., 2:294–99.

———. "The Silence of Angels: Reflections on the Songs of the Sabbath Sacrifice." *RQ* 13 (1988): 189–97.

Anderson, Graham. "Aulus Gellius: A Miscellanist and His World." *ANRW* 2.34.2 (1994): 1834–62.

———. "The *Pepaideumenos* in Action: Sophists and Their Outlook in the Early Empire." *ANRW* 2.33.1 (1989): 80–208.

———. *Philostratus: Biography and Belles Lettres in the Third Century* A.D. London: Croon Helm, 1986.

———. *The Second Sophistic: A Cultural Phenomenon in the Roman Empire.* London: Routledge, 1993.

———. "The Second Sophistic: Some Problems of Perspective." In *Antonine Literature*, ed. R.A. Russell. Oxford: Oxford University Press, 1990, 91–110.

André, Jean-Marie. "Les écoles philosophiques aux deux premiers siècles de l'Empire." *ANRW* 2.36.1 (1987): 5–77.

Andresen, Carl. *Logos und Nomos: Die Polemik des Kelsos wider das Christentum.* Arbeiten zur Kirchengeschichte 30. Berlin: de Gruyter, 1955.

Armstrong, Arthur H. "Dualism Platonic, Gnostic, and Christian." In Runia, ed. *Plotinus*, 29–52.

———. "Man in the Cosmos: A Study of Some Differences Between Pagan Neoplatonism and Christianity." In *Romanitas et Christianitas*, ed. W. den Boer et al. Amsterdam: North-Holland, 1973, 5–14.

———. "Plotinus." In *The Cambridge History of Later Greek and Early Medieval Philosophy*, ed. Arthur H. Armstrong. Cambridge: Cambridge University Press, 1967, 193–268.

———. "Plotinus and Christianity with Special Reference to II.9 [33] 9, 26–83 and V.8 [31] 4, 27–36." *StPatr* 20 (1989): 83–86.

Athanassiadi, Polymnia. "Apamea and the *Chaldaean Oracles*: A Holy City and a Holy Book." In *The Philosopher and Society*, ed. A. Smith, 117–43.

———. *Julian and Hellenism: An Intellectual Biography.* Oxford: Clarendon Press, 1981.

Attridge, Harold W. *The Epistle to the Hebrews: A Commentary on the Epistle to the Hebrews.* Philadelphia: Fortress Press, 1989.

———. "Gnostic Platonism." In *Proceedings of the Boston Area Colloquium in Ancient Philosophy.* Vol. 7, ed. John J. Cleary and Daniel Charles. Lanham, MD: University Press of America, 1992, 1–29.

———. "On Becoming an Angel: Rival Baptismal Theologies at Colossae." In *Religious Propaganda and Missionary Competition in the New Testament World*, ed. Lukas Bormann, Kelly dell Tredici, and Angela Standhartinger. Leiden: E. J. Brill, 1994, 481–98.

———. "Valentinian and Sethian Apocalyptic Traditions." *JECS* 8:2 (2000): 173–211.

Attridge, Harold W., and Elaine Pagels. "Notes: The Tripartite Tractate." In *Nag Hammadi Codex I (The Jung Codex)*, ed. Harold W. Attridge. NHS 22. Leiden: E. J. Brill, 1985, 2:217–497.

Aune, David E. "The Apocalypse of John and the Problem of Genre." In *Early Christan Apocalypticism*, ed. Yarbro Collins, 65–96.

———. "Early Christian Eschatology." In *Anchor Bible Dictionary*, ed. Freedman et al., 2:594–609.

———. *Prophecy in Early Christianity and the Ancient Mediterranean World*. Grand Rapids, MI: Eerdmans, 1983.

Baltes, Matthias. "Der Platonismus und die Weisheit der Barbaren." In Matthias Baltes, *EPINOHMATA: Kleine Schriften zur antiken Philosophie und homerischen Dichtung*, ed. Marie-Luise Lakmann. Beiträge zur Altertumskunde. Munich: K.G. Saur, 2005, 1–26.

Barc, Bernard, ed. *Colloque international sur les textes de Nag Hammadi, Québec 22–25 août 1978*. BCNH Section "Études." 1. Québec: Presses de l'université Laval; Leuven: Peeters, 1981.

Barnes, Jonathan, and Miriam Griffin, eds. *Philosophia Togata II: Plato and Aristotle at Rome*. Oxford: Clarendon Press, 1997.

Bauckham, Richard. *The Fate of the Dead: Studies on the Jewish and Christian Apocalypses*. NovTSup 93. Leiden: E. J. Brill, 1998.

Bechtle, Gerald. *The Anonymous Commentary on Plato's "Parmenides"*. Bern: Paul Haupt, 1999.

Benko, Stephen. "Pagan Criticism of Christianity During the First Two Centuries ad." *ANRW* 2.23.2 (1980): 1055–118.

Berg, Robbert van den. "Live Unnoticed! The Invisible Neoplatonic Politician." In *The Philosopher and Society*, ed. A. Smith, 101–16.

Bidez, Joseph. *Vie de Porphyre*. Gand: 1913.

Bidez, Joseph, and Franz Cumont. *Les mages hellénisés: Zoroastre, Ostanès et Hystaspe, d'après la tradition greque*. Paris: Les belles lettres, 1938.

Bladel, Kevin van. *The Arabic Hermes: From Pagan Sage to Prophet of Science*. Oxford Studies in Late Antiquity. Oxford: Oxford University Press, 2009.

Blois, L. de. "The Perception of Politics in Plutarch's Roman 'Lives.'" *ANRW* 2.33.6 (1992): 4568–615.

Blumenthal, Henry J., and Robert A. Markus, eds. *Neoplatonism and Early Christian Thought: Essays in Honour of A. H. Armstrong*. London: Variorum, 1981.

Blumenthal, Henry J., and Gillian Clark, eds. *The Divine Iamblichus*. London: Bristol Classical Press, 1993.

Boccaccini, Gabriele. "Jewish Apocalyptic Tradition: The Contribution of Italian Scholarship." In *Mysteries and Revelations*, ed. Collins and Charlesworth, 33–50.

Böhlig, Alexander. "Die griechische Schule und die Bibliothek von Nag Hammadi." In Alexander Böhlig, *Zum Hellenismus in den Schriften von Nag Hammadi.* Göttinger Orientforschungen 6:2. Wiesbaden: Otto Harrassowitz, 1975, 9–54.

Böhlig, Alexander, and Frederik Wisse. "Commentary: The Gospel of the Egyptians." In *Nag Hammadi Codices III,2 and IV,2,* ed. Böhlig and Wisse, 169–207.

———. "Introduction: The Gospel of The Egyptians." In *Nag Hammadi Codices III,2 and IV, 2,* ed. Böhlig and Wisse, 1–50.

Bonner, Stanley F. *Education in Ancient Rome: From the Elder Cato to the Younger Pliny.* London: Methuen, 1977.

Borg, Barbara E., ed. *Paideia: The World of the Second Sophistic.* Millenium-Studien zu Kultur und Geschichte des erstens Jahrtausends n. Chr. 2. Berlin: de Gruyter, 2004.

Bornkamm, Günther. "μυστήριον, μυέω." Tr. Geoffrey Bromily. *TDNT* 4 (1967): 802–28.

Bos, Abraham P. "World-views in Collision: Plotinus, Gnostics, and Christians." In *Plotinus,* ed. Runia, 11–28.

Bosson, Nathalie, and Anne Boud'hors, eds. *Acts du huitième congrès international d'études coptes: Paris, 28 juin–3 juillet 2004.* 2 vols. OLA 163. Leuven: Peeters, 2007.

Böttrich, Christfriend. "Recent Studies in the Slavonic Book of Enoch." *JSP* 5 (1991): 35–42.

Boulluec, Alain le. *La notion d'hérésie dans la littérature grecque, IIe–IIIe siècles.* Paris: Études augustiniennes, 1985.

Bousset, Wilhelm. *Die Himmelsreise der Seele* Darmstadt: Wissenschaftliche Buchgesellschaft, 1960.

———. *Hauptprobleme der Gnosis.* FRLANT 10. Göttingen: van den Hoeck & Ruprecht, 1973.

Boustan (Abusch), Ra'anan. "Seven-fold Hymns in the *Songs of the Sabbath Sacrifice* and the Hekhalot Literature: Formalism, Hierarchy and the Limits of Human Participation." In *The Dead Sea Scrolls as Background to Postbiblical Judaism and Early Christianity: Papers from an International conference at St. Andrews in 2001,* ed. James R. Davila. STDJ 46. Leiden: E. J. Brill, 2003, 220–47.

Bowersock, Glen Warren, ed. *Approaches to the Second Sophistic: Papers Presented at the 105th Annual Meeting of the American Philological Association in Saint Louis, Mo., Dec. 28–30, 1973.* University Park, PA: American Philological Association, 1974.

———. *Greek Sophists in the Roman Empire.* Oxford: Clarendon Press, 1969.

Bowie, E. L. "Apollonius of Tyana: Legend and Reality." *ANRW* 2.16.2 (1978): 1652–699.

———. "The Geography of the Second Sophistic: Cultural Variations." In *Paideia*, ed. Borg, 65–83.

———. "The Greeks and their Past in the Second Sophistic." *Past and Present* 46 (1970): 3–41.

———. "The Importance of Sophists." *YCS* 27 (1982): 25–59.

Boys-Stones, George. *Post-Hellenistic Philosophy.* Oxford: Oxford University Press, 2001.

Bradshaw, Paul F. *Reconstructing Early Christian Worship.* London: SPCK, 2009.

Brakke, David. "The Body as/at the Boundary of Gnosis." *JECS* 17:2 (2009): 195–214.

———. *The Gnostics: Myth, Ritual, and Diversity in Early Christianity.* Cambridge, MA: Harvard University Press, 2010.

———. "The Seed of Seth at the Flood: Biblical Interpretation and Gnostic Theological Reflection." In *Reading in Christian Communities*, ed. Charles A. Bobertz and David Brakke. Christianity and Judaism in Antiquity Series 14. Notre Dame, IN: University of Notre Dame Press, 2002, 41–62.

Brankaer, Johanna. "The Concept of νοῦς in the 'Sethian Platonizing Treatises' of Nag Hammadi." *ZAC* 12 (2008): 59–80.

———. "Is There a Gnostic 'Henological' Speculation?" In *Plato's "Parmenides" and Its Heritage*, ed. Turner and Corrigan, 1:173–94.

———. "Terminologie et représentations philosophiques dans *Allogène* (NH XI,3)." In *Acts du huitième congrès international d'études coptes*, ed. Bosson and Boud'hors, 2:811–20.

Brenk, Frederick E. "An Imperial Heritage : The Religious Spirit of Plutarch of Chaironeia." *ANRW* 2.36.1 (1987): 248–349.

———. *In Mist Appareled: Religious Themes in Plutarch's Moralia and Lives.* MnemosyneSup 48. Leiden: E. J. Brill, 1977.

Brett, Mark G., ed. *Ethnicity and the Bible.* BIS 19. Leiden: E. J. Brill, 1996.

Brisson, Luc, ed. "Amélius: Sa vie, son oeuvre, son style." *ANRW* 2.36.2 (1987): 793–861.

———. "The Doctrine of the Degrees of Virtues in the Neoplatonists: An Analysis of Porphyry's *Sentence* 32, Its Antecedents, and Its Heritage." Tr. Michael Chase. In *Reading Plato in Antiquity*, ed. Harold Tarrant and Dirk Baltzly. London: Duckworth, 2006, 89–106.

———. "Orphée et l'orphisme à l'époque impériale: Temoignages et interprétations philosophiques de Plutarque à Jamblique." *ANRW* 2.36.4 (1990) : 2867–2931.

———. *How Philosophers Saved Myths: Allegorical Interpretation and Classical Mythology*, tr. Catherine Tihanyi. Chicago: University of Chicago Press, 2004.

———. *La Vie de Plotin.* 2 vols. Paris: J. Vrin, 1982–92.

———. *Plato the Myth Maker.* Tr. Gerard Naddaf. Chicago: University of Chicago Press, 1998.

———. "Plotinus and the Magical Rites Practiced by the Gnostics." In *Gnosticism, Platonism, and the Late Ancient World*, ed. Corrigan et al.

Brisson, Luc, and Richard Goulet. "Origène le platonicien." In *Dictionnaire des philosophes antiques*, ed. Richard Goulet, vol. 1. Paris: CNRS, 1989, 804–7.

Broek, Roelof van den. "The Christian 'School' of Alexandria in the Second and Third Centuries." In *Centres of Learning: Learning and Location in Pre-modern Europe and the Near East*, ed. Jan Willem Drijvers and Alasdair A. MacDonald. Leiden: E. J. Brill, 1995, 39–47.

———. *The Gnostic Religion in Antiquity.* Cambridge: Cambridge University Press, 2013.

———. "Sexuality and Sexual Symbolism in Hermetic and Gnostic Thought and Practice (Second–Fourth Centuries)." In *Hidden Intercourse: Eros and Sexuality in the History of Western Esotericism*, ed. Wouter J. Hanegraaff and Jeffrey J. Kripal. Aries Book Series 7. Leiden: E. J. Brill, 2008, 1–21.

Broek, Roelof van den, and M. J. Vermaseren, eds. *Studies in Gnosticism and Hellenistic Religions: Presented to Gilles Quispel on the Occasion of His 65th birthday.* EPRO 91. Leiden: E. J. Brill, 1981.

Brown, Peter. *The World of Late Antiquity: ad 150–750.* Library of World Civilization. London: W. W. Norbert, 1989.

Brox, Norbert, ed. *Pseudepigraphie in der Heidnischen und jüdisch-christlichen Antike.* Darmstadt: Wissenschaftliche Buchgesellschaft, 1977.

Brunt, P. "The Bubble of the Second Sophistic." *BICS* 38 (1994): 25–52.

Buell, Denise Kimber. *Making Christians: Clement of Alexandria and the Rhetoric of Legitimacy.* Princeton, NJ: Princeton University Press, 1999.

———. "Race and Universalism in Early Christianity." *JECS* 10:4 (2002): 429–68.

———. "Rethinking the Relevance of Race for Early Christian Self-Definition." *HTR* 94:4 (2001): 449–76.

———. *Why This New Race? Ethnic Reasoning in Early Christianity.* New York: Columbia University Press, 2005.

Burns, Dylan. "Aeons." In *The Routledge Dictionary of Ancient Mediterranean Religions*, ed. Eric Orlin, et al. London: Routledge, forthcoming.

———. "The *Apocalypse of Zostrianos* and Iolaos: A Platonic Reminiscence of the Heracleidae at NHC VIII,1.4." *Le muséon* 126:1–2 (2013): 29–44.

———. "Apocalypses Amongst Gnostics and Manichaeans." In *The Oxford Handbook of Apocalyptic Literature*, ed. John J. Collins. New York: Oxford University Press, forthcoming.

———. "Apophatic Strategies in *Allogenes* (NHC XI,3)." *HTR* 103:2 (2010): 161–79.

———. "The *Chaldean Oracles of Zoroaster*, Hekate's Couch, and Platonic Orientalism in Psellos and Plethon." *Aries* 6:2 (2006): 158–79.

———. "Cosmic Eschatology and Christian Platonism in the Coptic Gnostic Apocalypses *Marsanes, Zostrianos,* and *Allogenes.*" In *Symposium of the Patristische Arbeitsgemeinschaft (PAG) "Zugänge zur Gnosis,"* ed. Christoph Markschies and Johannes van Oort. Patristic Studies 12. Leuven: Peeters, 2013, 169–89.

———. "Jesus' Reincarnations Revisited in Jewish Christianity, Sethian Gnosticism, and Mani." In *Portraits of Jesus: Studies in Christology*, ed. Susan Myers, WUNT 321. Tübingen: Mohr Siebeck, 2012, 371–92.

———. "Proclus and the Theurgic Liturgy of Pseudo-Dionysius." *Dionysius* 22 (2004): 111–32.

———. Review of Kevin Corrigan and John D. Turner, eds., *Plato's Parmenides and Its Heritage: Volume 2: Its Reception in Neo-Platonic, Jewish, and Christian Texts. AugStud* 42:2 (2011): 295–301.

———. "Sethian Crowns, Sethian Martyrs? Jewish Apocalyptic and Christian Martyrology in a Gnostic Literary Tradition." *Numen*, forthcoming.

Burnyeat, M. F. "*Eikōs Mythos.*" In *Plato's Myths*, ed. Catalin Partenie. Cambridge: Cambridge University Press, 2009, 167–86.

Cameron, Alan. "The Last Days of the Academy at Athens." *Proceedings of the Cambridge Philological Society* 195 (1969): 1–29.

———. *The Last Pagans of Rome.* Oxford: Oxford University Press, 2010.

———. "Poetry and Literary Culture in Late Antiquity." In *Approaching Late Antiquity*, ed. Swain and Edwards, 327–55.

Carmignac, Jean. "*Qu'est-ce que l'apocalyptique?* Son emploi a Qumran." *Revue de Qumran* 10 (1979): 3–33.

Carrié, Jean-Michel, and Aline Rousselle. *L'Empire romain en mutation des Sévères à Constantin, 192–337.* Nouvelle histoire de l'antiquité 10. Paris: Éditions du seuil, 1999.

Casadio, Giovanni. "The Manichaean Metempsychosis: Typology and Historical Roots." In *Studia Manichaica II: Internationaler Kongreß zum Manichäismus, 6.–10. August 1989, St. Augustin/Bonn*, ed. Gernot Wießner and Hans-Joachim Klimkeit. StOR 23. Wiesbaden: Harrassowitz, 1992, 105–30.

Caster, Marcel. *Lucien et la Pensée religieuse de son Temps*. Paris: Les belles lettres, 1937.

Charlesworth, James H. "The SNTS Pseudepigrapha Seminars at Tübingen and Paris on the Books of Enoch (Seminar Report)." *NTS* 25 (1979): 315–23.

Charrue, Jean-Michel. "Plotin, le stoïcisme et la gnose. Deux formes d'illusion." In *Revue belge de philology et d'histoire* 81:1 (2003): 39–46.

Chase, Michael. "Porphyre commentateur." In *Dictionnaire des Philosophes Antiques*, ed. R. Goulet, vol. 5. Paris: CNRS éditions, forthcoming.

Chuvin, Pierre. *A Chronicle of the Last Pagans*. Tr. B. A. Archer. Revealing Antiquity 4. Cambridge, MA: Harvard University Press, 1990.

Cilento, Vincenzo. *Plotino: Paideia Antignostica*. Florence: Le monnier, 1971.

Clark, Gillian. "Augustine's Porphyry and the Universal Way of Salvation." In *Studies on Porphyry*, ed. George Karamanolis and Anne Sheppard. BICSSuppl. 98. London: Institute of Classical Studies, 2007, 127–40.

———. "Translate into Greek: Porphyry of Tyre on the New Barbarians." In *Constructing Identities in Late Antiquity*, ed. Richard Miles. London: Routledge, 1999, 112–32.

Clarke, Emma C., John Dillon, and Jackson Hershbell. Introduction to Iamblichus, *De mysteriis*, ed. Clarke, Dillon, and Hershbell, xiii–lii.

Cleary, John J., ed. *Traditions of Platonism: Essays in Honour of John Dillon*. Aldershot: Ashgate, 1999.

Cohen, Shaye. *The Beginnings of Jewishness: Boundaries, Varieties, Uncertainties*. Berkeley: University of California Press, 1999.

Collins, John J. "The Angelic Life." In *Metamorphoses: Resurrection, Body, and Transformative Practices in Early Christianity*, ed. Turid Karlsen Seim and Jorunn Økland. Ekstasis 1. Berlin: de Gruyter, 2009, 291–310.

———. "Apocalyptic Eschatology and the Transcendence of Death." In Collins, *Seers*, 75–98.

———. *The Apocalyptic Imagination: An Introduction to Jewish Apocalyptic Literature*. Grand Rapids, MI: Eerdmans, 1998.

———. "Cosmos and Salvation: Jewish Wisdom and Apocalyptic in the Hellenistic Age." *HR* 17:2 (1977): 121–42.

———. "Genre, Ideology, and Social Movements in Jewish Apocalypticism." In *Mysteries and Revelations*, ed. Collins and Charlesworth, 11–32.

———. "Morphology of a Genre." *Semeia* 14 (1979): 1–19.

———. "Pseudonymity: Historical Reviews and the Genre of the Revelation of *John*." *CBQ* 39 (1977): 329–43.

———. "The Sage in the Apocalyptic and Pseudepigraphic Literature." In *The Sage in Israel and the Ancient Near East*, ed. John G. Gammie and Leo G.Perdue. Winona Lake: Eisenbrauns, 1990, 343–54.

———. *Seers, Sybils and Sages in Hellenistic-Roman Judaism*. Leiden: E. J. Brill, 2001.

———. "A Throne in the Heavens: Apotheosis in Pre-Christian Judaism." In *Death, Ecstasy, and Other Worldly Journeys*, ed. Collins and Fishbane, 41–55.

Collins, John J., and James H. Charlesworth, eds. *Mysteries and Revelations: Apocalyptic Studies Since the Uppsala Colloquium*. JSPSup 9. Sheffield: JSOT Press, 1991.

Collins, John J., and Michael Fishbane, eds. *Death, Ecstasy, and Other Worldly Journeys*. Albany: State University of New York Press, 1995.

Cook, John Granger. *The Interpretation of the New Testament in Greco-Roman Paganism*. STAC 3. Peabody, MA: Hendrickson, 2002.

———. "Porphyry's Attempted Demolition of Christian Allegory." *International Journal of the Platonic Tradition* 2 (2008): 1–27.

Cook, Stephen L. "Eschatology of the Old Testament." In *The New Interpreter's Dictionary of the Bible*, ed. Sakenfeld et al., 2:299–308.

Corrigan, Kevin. "Positive and Negative Matter in Later Platonism: The Uncovering of Plotinus's Dialogue with the Gnostics." In *Gnosticism and Later Platonism*, ed. Turner and Majercik, 19–56.

———. "The *Sympoisum* and *Republic* in the Mystical Thought of Plotinus and the Sethian Gnostics." In *Gnosticism, Platonism, and the Late Ancient World*, ed. Corrigan et al., 309–28.

Corrigan, Kevin, et al., eds. *Gnosticism, Platonism, and the Late Ancient World: Essays in Honour of John D. Turner*. NHMS 82. Leiden: E. J. Brill, 2013.

Couliano, Ioan P. *Out of This World: Heavenly Journeys from Gilgamesh to Albert Einstein*. New York: Shambhala, 2001.

———. *Psychanodia: A Survey of the Evidence Concerning the Ascension of the Soul and Its Relevance*. EPARODLR 1. Leiden: E. J. Brill, 1984.

———. *The Tree of Gnosis: Gnostic Mythology from Early Christianity to Modern Nihilism*. Tr. H. S. Wiesner and Ioan P. Couliano. San Francisco: HarperSanFrancisco, 1992.

Coulter, James A. *The Literary Microcosm: Theories of Interpretation of the Later Neoplatonists*, CSCT 2. Leiden: E: J: Brill, 1976.

Courcelle, Pierre. "Anti-Christian Arguments and Christian Platonism: From Arnobius to St. Ambrose." In *The Conflict Between Paganism and Christianity in the Fourth Century*, ed. Momigliano, 151–92.

Cribiore, Rafaella. *Gymnastics of the Mind: Greek Education in Hellenistic and Roman Egypt.* Princeton, NJ: Princeton University Press, 2001.

Cumont, Franz. *Lux Perpetua.* Paris: Paul Geuthner, 1949.

———. *Oriental Religions and Roman Paganism.* New York: Dover Books, 1956.

Danielou, Jean. *Theology of Jewish Christianity: A History of Early Christian Doctrine Before the Council of Nicaea.* Philadelphia: Westminster John Knox Press, 1977.

Davidson, Maxwell J. *Angels at Qumran: A Comparative Study of 1 Enoch 1–36, 72–108 and Sectarian Writings from Qumran.* New York: Continuum, 1992.

Davies, P. R. "The Social World of the Apocalyptic Writings." In *The World of Ancient Israel: Sociological, Anthropological, and Political Perspectives: Essays by Members of the Society for Old Testament Study*, ed. R. E. Clements. Cambridge: Cambridge University Press, 1989, 251–71.

Davila, James R. "The Dead Sea Scrolls and Merkavah Mysticism." In *The Dead Sea Scrolls in Their Historical Context*, ed. Timothy H. Lim et al. Edinburgh: T&T Clark, 2000, 249–64.

Dawson, David. *Allegorical Readers and Cultural Revision in Ancient Alexandria.* Berkeley: University of California Press, 1992.

Dean-Otting, Mary. *Heavenly Journeys: A Study of the Motif in Hellenistic Jewish Literature.* Frankfurt am Main: Peter Lang, 1984.

DeConick, April D., ed. *The Codex Judas Papers: Proceedings of the International Congress on the Tchacos Codex held at Rice University, Houston, Texas, March 13–16, 2008.* Leiden: E. J. Brill, 2009.

———, ed. *Paradise Now: Essays on Early Jewish and Christian Mysticism.* Leiden: E. J. Brill, 2006.

———. *Seek to See Him: Ascent and Vision Mysticism in the Gospel of Thomas.* VCSup 33. Leiden: E. J. Brill; 1996.

———. *The Thirteenth Apostle: What the "Gospel of Judas" Really Says.* London: Continuum Books, 2007.

———. "What Is Early Jewish and Christian Mysticism?" In *Paradise Now*, ed. DeConick, 1–26.

Denniston, John Dewar. *The Greek Particles.* Rev. Kenneth J. Dover. London: Duckworth, 1996.

Denzey Lewis, Nicola. *Cosmology and Fate in Gnosticism and Greco-Roman Antiquity*, NHMS 81. Leiden: E. J. Brill, 2013.

Desjardins, Michel. "Introduction to VII,3: Apocalypse of Peter." In *Nag Hammadi Codex VII*, ed. Pearson, 201–16.

Dieterich, Albrecht. *Nekyia: Beiträge zur Erklärung der neuentdeckten Petrusapokalypse*. Leipzig: Teubner, 1913.

Digeser, Elizabeth DePalma. "Origen on the *Limes*: Rhetoric and the Polarization of Identity in the Late Third Century." In *The Rhetoric of Power in Late Antiquity: Religion and Poltiics in Byzantium, Europe, and the Early Islamic World*, ed. Robert M. Frakes et al. New York: Tauris Academic Studies, 2010, 197–218.

Dillon, John. "The Academy in the Middle Platonic Period." *Dionysius* 3 (1979): 63–77.

———. "Commentary: *The Handbook of Platonism*." In Alcinous, *Handbook*, tr. Dillon, 51–211.

———. "The Descent of the Soul in Middle Platonic and Gnostic Theory." In *Rediscovery*, ed. Layton, 357–64.

———. "Iamblichus of Chalcis (c. 240–325 A.D.)" *ANRW* 2.36.2 (1987): 862–909.

———. "'A Kind of Warmth': Some Reflections on the Concept of 'Grace' in the Neoplatonic Tradition." In *The Passionate Intellect: Essays on the Transformation of Classical Traditions Presented to Professor I. G. Kidd*, ed. L. Ayres. New Brunswick, NJ: 1995, 323–32.

———. "The Magical Power of Names in Origen and Later Platonism." In *Origeniana Tertia*, ed. R. Hanson and H. Crouzel. Rome: Edizioni dell'Ateneo, 1985, 203–16.

———. *The Middle Platonists*. London: Duckworth, 1977.

———. "Philosophy as a Profession in Late Antiquity." In *Approaching Late Antiquity*, ed. Swain and Edwards, 401–18.

———. "Providence." In *The Anchor Bible Dictionary*, ed. Freedman, 520a–521b.

———. "Self-Definition in Later Platonism." In *Self-Definition in the Greco-roman World*, ed. Ben E. Meyer and E. P. Sanders. Jewish and Christian Self-Definitions 3. London: SCM Press; Philadelphia: Fortress Press, 1982, 60–75.

Dillon, John, and Jackson Hershbell. "Introduction: *De vita Pythagorica*." In Iamblichus, *Pythagorean Way of Life*, ed. and tr. Dillon and Hershbell, 1–29.

Dodds, Eric R. "Appendix II: The Astral Body in Neoplatonism." In Proclus, *Elements of Theology*, ed. Dodds, 313–22.

———. "Appendix II: Theurgy." In Eric R. Dodds, *The Greeks and the Irrational*. Berkeley: University of California Press, 1951, 283–311.

———. "Numenius and Ammonius." In *Les Sources des Plotin*. Entretiens sur l'antiqué classique 5 (1960), 1–32.

———. *Pagan and Christian in an Age of Anxiety: Some Aspects of Religious Experience from Marcus Aurelius to Constantine*. New York: W. W. Norton, 1970.

Doresse, Jean. "Les apocalypses de Zoroatre de Zostrien, de Nicothèe." In *Coptic Studies in Honor of Walter Ewing Crum*. Boston: Byzantine Institute, 1950, 255–63.

Dornsieff, Franz. *Das Alphabet in Mystik und Magie*. ΣΤΟΙΧΕΙΑ: Studien zur Geschichte des antiken Weltbildes und der griechischen Wissenschaft 7. Leipzig: Teubner, 1922.

Dörrie, Heinrich, ed. *De Jamblique à Proclus*. Entretiens sur l'antiqué classique 21. Vandœuvres: 1975.

———. "Die Religiosität des Platonismus im 4. Und 5. Jahrhundert nach Christus." In *De Jamblique*, ed. Dörrie, 257–86.

———. "Die Schultradition im Mittelplatonismus und Porphyrios." *Entretiens Hardt* 12 (1966): 3–25.

Dragona-Monachou, M. "Divine Providence in the Philosophy of the Empire." In *ANRW* 2.36.7 (1994): 4417–90.

Droge, Arthur. *Homer or Moses? Early Christian Interpretation of the History of Culture*. HUT 26. Tübingen: Mohr-Siebeck, 1989.

Duncan-Jones, Richard. "Economic Change and the Transition to Late Antiquity." In *Approaching Late Antiquity*, ed. Swain and Edwards, 20–53.

Dunderberg, Ismo. *Beyond Gnosticism: Myth, Lifestyle, and Society in the School of Valentinus*. New York: Columbia University Press, 2007.

———. "The School of Valentinus." In *Companion to Second-Century "Heretics."* ed. Marjanen and Luomanen, 64–99.

———. "Valentinian Teachers in Rome." In *Christians as a Religious Minority in a Multicultural City: Modes of Interaction and Identity Formation in Early Imperial Rome: Studies on the Basis of a Seminar at the Second Conference of the European Association for Biblical Studies (EABS) from July 8–12, 2001, in Rome*, ed. Jürgen Zangenberg and Michael Labahn. JSNTSup 243 (European Studies on Christian Origins). London: T&T Clark International, 2004, 157–74.

Dunning, Benjamin H. *Aliens and Sojourners: Self as Other in Early Christianity*. Divinations. Philadelphia: University of Pennsylvania Press, 2009.

Edwards, Mark J. "*Aidōs* in Plotinus: *Enneads* 2.9.10." *CQ* 39:1 (1989): 228–32.

———. " . . . And Neoscholastica." *JHS* 114 (1994): 175–77.

———. "Atticizing Moses? Numenius, the Fathers, and the Jews." *VC* 44:1 (1990): 64–75.

———. "Christians and the *Parmenides*." In *Plato's 'Parmenides' and Its Heritage*, ed. Turner and Corrigan, 2:189–98.

———. *Culture and Philosophy in the Age of Plotinus*. CLS. London: Duckworth, 2006.

———. "The Gnostic Aculinus: A Study in Platonism." *StPatr* 24 (1993): 377–81.

———. "How Many Zoroasters? Arnobius, 'Adversus Gentes' I 52." *VC* 42:3 (1988): 282–89.

———. "Neglected Texts in the Study of Gnosticism." *JThS* 40:1 (1990): 26–50.

———. "Numenius of Apamea." In *The Cambridge History of Philosophy in Late Antiquity*, ed. Gerson, 1:115–25.

———. "Numenius, Fr. 13 (Des Places): A Note on Interpretation." *Mnemosyne* 42:3–4 (1989): 478–82.

———. "Pagan and Christian Monotheism in the Age of Constantine." In *Approaching Late Antiquity*, ed. Swain and Edwards, 211–35.

———. "Porphyry and the Intelligible Triad." *JHS* 110 (1990): 14–25.

———. "Porphyry's 'Cave of the Nymphs' and the Gnostic Controversy." *Hermes* 124:1 (1996): 88–100.

———. "Two Images of Pythagoras: Iamblichus and Porphyry." In *Divine Iamblichus*, ed. Blumenthal and Clark, 159–72.

Elsas, Christoph. *Neuplatonische und gnostische Weltablehnung in der Schule Plotins*. Religionsgeschichtliche Versuche und Vorarbeiten 34. Berlin: Walter de Gruyter, 1975.

Emmel, Stephen. "The Coptic Gnostic Texts as Witnesses to the Production and Transmission of Gnostic (and Other) Traditions." In *Das Thomasevangelium: Entstehung–Rezeption–Theologie*, ed. Jörg Frey, et al. BZNW 157. Berlin: de Gruyter, 2008, 33–50.

———. "The Gnostic Tradition in Relation to Greek Philosophy." In *The Nag Hammadi Texts in the History of Religions*, ed. Giversen, Petersen, and Sørensen, 125–36.

———. "Religious Tradition, Textual Transmission, and the Nag Hammadi Codices." In *The Nag Hammadi Library After Fifty Years*, ed. Turner and McGuire, 34–43.

Evangeliou, Christos. "Plotinus's Anti-Gnostic Polemic and Porphyry's *Against the Christians*." In *Neoplatonism and Gnosticism*, ed. Wallis with Bregman, 111–28.

Fallon, Francis T. "The Gnostic Apocalypses." *Semeia* 14 (1979): 123–158.

———. "The Undominated Race." *NovTest* 21:3 (1979): 271–88.

Fattal, Michel. "Bild und Weltproduktion bei Plotin. Eine Kritik des gnostischen Bildes." In *Denken mit dem Bild: Philosophische Einsätze des Bildbegriffs von Platon bis Hegel*, ed. Johannes Grave and Arno Schubbach. Eikones. Munich: Wilhelm Fink, 2010, 43–72.

Feldman, Louis H. "The Concept of Exile in Josephus." In *Exile*, ed. Scott, 145–72.

Feldmeier, Reinhard. "The 'Nation' of Strangers: Social Contempt and Its Theological Interpretation in Ancient Judaism and Early Christianity." Tr. David E. Orton and Alan Moss. In *Ethnicity and the Bible*, ed. Brett, 241–70.

———. "Philosoph und Priester: Plutarch als Theologe." In *Mousopolos Stephanos: Festschrift für Herwig Görgemanns*, ed. M. Baumbach et al. Bibliothek der klassischen Altertumswissenschaften: 2. Heidelberg: Reihe, 1998, 412–25.

Ferguson, Everett. "Baptismal Motifs in the Early Church." *Restoration Quarterly* 7 (1963): 202–16.

Ferweda, R. "Pity in the Life and Thought of Plotinus." In *Plotinus*, ed. Runia, 53–72.

Festugière, Andre-Jean. "Cadre de la mystique hellénistique." In *Aux sources de la tradition chrétienne: Mélanges Goguel* (Neuchatel; Paris: Delachaux et Niestlé, 1950), 74–85.

———. *Hermétisme et mystique païenne*. Paris: Aubier-Montaigne, 1966.

———. *La Révélation d'Hermès Trismégiste*. 4 vols. Paris: Les belles lettres, 1944–54.

Finamore, John F. *Iamblichus and the Theory of the Vehicle of the Soul*. Chico, CA: Scholars' Press, 1985.

Finamore, John F., and Robert Berchman, eds. *History of Platonism: Plato Redivivus*. New Orleans: University Press of the South, 2005.

Finamore, John, and John Dillon. "*De anima*: Commentary." In Iamblichus, *De anima*, ed. and tr. Finamore and Dillon, 76–228.

Fitzmyer, Joseph A. "A Feature of Qumran Angelology and the Angels of I Cor. XI. 10." *NTS* 4 (1957–58): 48–58.

Fletcher-Louis, Crispin H. T. *All the Glory of Adam: Liturgical Anthropology in the Dead Sea Scrolls*. STDJ 42. Leiden: E. J. Brill, 2002.

———. *Luke-Acts: Angels, Christology, and Soteriology*. WUANT 2.94. Tübingen: Mohr Siebeck, 1997.

———. "Religious Experience and the Apocalypses." *Experientia* 1 (2008): 125–44.

Flinterman, Jaap-Jan. *Power, Paideia and Pythagoreanism: Greek Identity,*

Conceptions of the Relationship Between Philosophers and Monarchs and Political Ideas in Philostratus' "Life of Apollonius." Amsterdam: J. C. Gieben, 1995.

———. "Sophists and Emperors: A Reconnaissance of Sophistic Attitudes." In *Paideia*, ed. Borg, 359–76.

Fossum, Jarl E. "Glory." In *Dictionary of Deities and Demons in the Bible*, ed. Karel van der Toorn, Bob Becking, and Pieter W. van der Horst. Leiden: E. J. Brill, 1999, 348–52.

———. *The Name of God and the Angel of the Lord: Samaritan and Jewish Concepts of Intermediation and the Origin of Gnosticism.* WUANT 36. Tübingen: Mohr/Siebeck, 1985.

Fowden, Garth. *The Egyptian Hermes: A Historical Approach to the Late Pagan Mind.* Princeton, NJ: Princeton University Press, 1993.

———. "The Pagan Holy Man in Late Antique Society." *JHS* 102 (1982): 33–59.

———. "Sages, Cities, and Temples: Aspects of Late Antique Pythagorism?" In *The Philosopher and Society*, ed. A. Smith, 145–70.

Fowler, Ryan. "The Second Sophistic." In *The Cambridge History of Philosophy in Late Antiquity*, ed. Gerson, 1:100–114.

Frank, P. Suso. *ΑΓΓΕΛΙΚΟΣ ΒΙΟΣ: Begriffsanalytische und Begriffsgeschichtliche Untersuchung zum "engelgleichen Leben" im frühen Mönchtum.* BGAM 26. Münster: Aschendorffsche Verlagsbuchhandlung, 1964.

Frankfurter, David. "Apocalypses Real and Alleged in the Mani Codex." *Numen* 44 (1997): 60–73.

———. "Early Christian Apocalypticism: Literature and Social World." In *The Encyclopedia of Apocalypticism*. Vol. 1: *The Origins of Apocalypticism in Judaism and Christianity*, ed. John J. Collins. New York: Continuum, 1998, 415–56.

———. "The Legacy of Jewish Apocalypses in Early Christianity: Regional Trajectories." In *Jewish Apocalyptic Heritage*, ed. VanderKam and Adler, 129–200.

———. "Narrating Power: The Theory and Practice of the Magical Historiola in Magical Spells." In *Ancient Magic and Ritual Power*, ed. Marvin Meyer and Paul Mirecki. RGRW 129. Leiden: E. J. Brill, 1995, 457–76.

Frede, Michael. "Celsus' Attack on the Christians." In *Philosophia Togata II*, ed. Barnes and Griffin, 218–240.

———. "Numenius." *ANRW* 2.32.2 (1987): 1034–75.

Freedman, David Noel, ed.-in-chief, et al., eds. *The Anchor Bible Dictionary.* 6 vols. New York: Doubleday, 1992.

Froidefond, Christian. "Plutarque et le platonisme." *ANRW* 2.36.1 (1987): 184–233.

Gaertner, Jan Felix. "The Discourse of Displacement in Greco-Roman Antiquity." In *Writing Exile: The Discourse of Displacement in Greco-Roman Antiquity and Beyond*, ed. Jan Felix Gaertner. Mnemosyne Sup 83. Leiden: E. J. Brill, 2007, 1–20.

Galli, Marco. "'Creating Religious Identities': Paideia e religion nella Seconda Sofistica." In *Paideia*, ed. Borg, 315–58.

Geertz, Clifford. "Thick Description: Towards an Interpretative Theory of Culture." In Clifford Geertz, *The Interpretation of Cultures*. New York: Basic Books, 1973, 3–30.

Geiger, Joseph. "Sophists and Rabbis: Jews and Their Past in the Severan Age." In *Severan Culture*, ed. Swain et al., 440–57.

Gero, Stephen. "With Walter Bauer on the Tigris." In *Nag Hammadi, Gnosticism, and Early Christianity*, ed. Hedrick and Hodgson, 287–307.

Gerson, Lloyd, P., ed. *The Cambridge History of Philosophy in Late Antiquity*, 2 vols. Cambridge: Cambridge University Press, 2010.

Gianotto, Claudio. "Pouvoir et salut: Quelques aspects de la 'théologie politique' des Gnostiques et des Manichéens." In *Coptica*, ed. Painchaud and Poirier, 330–56.

Giversen, Søren, Tage Petersen, and Jørgen Podemann Sørensen, eds. *The Nag Hammadi Texts in the History of Religions: Proceedings of the International Conference at the Royal Academy of Science and Letters in Copenhagen, September 19–24, 1995: On the Occasion of the 50th Anniversary of the Nag Hammadi Discovery*. Historisk-filosofiske Skrifter 26. Copenhagen: Royal Danish Academy of Sciences and Letters, 2002.

Goehring, James. "Introduction: *The Three Steles of Seth*." In *Nag Hammadi Codex VII*, ed. Pearson, 371–85.

———. "Notes: *The Three Steles of Seth*." In *Nag Hammadi Codex VII*, ed. Pearson, 386–421.

Gordon, Pamela. "Review of Swain, *Hellenism and Empire*." *BMCR* 97.4.14.

Goulet, Richard. "Hypothèses récentes sur le traité de Porphyre *Contre les chrétiens*." In *Hellénisme et Christianisme*, ed. Michel Narcy and Éric Rebillard. Villeneuve-d'Ascq: Presses Universitaires du Septentrion, 2004, 61–109.

———. "Porphyre, Ammonius, les deux Origène et les autres." In Richard Goulet, *Études sur les vies de philosophes de l'antiquité tardive: Diogène Laërce, Porphyre de Tyr, Eunape de Sardes*. Textes et traditions. Paris: Vrin, 2001, 267–90.

Graf, Fritz. "Plutarch und die Götterbilder." In *Gott und die Götter bei Plutarch*, ed. Hirsch-Luipold, 251–66.

Grant, Robert M. "Charges of Immorality Against Religious Groups in

Antiquity." In *Studies in Gnosticism and Hellenistic Religions*, ed. van den Broek and Vermaseren, 161–89.

———. "Early Christians and Gnostics in Greco-Roman Society." In *The New Testament and Gnosis: Essays in Honor of Robert McLachlan Wilson*, ed. Alistair Logan and Alexander J. M. Wedderburn. Edinburgh: T. & T. Clark, 1983, 176–86.

———. "Theological Education in Alexandria." In *The Roots of Egyptian Christianity*, ed. Birger Pearson and James E. Goehring. SAC. Philadelphia, PA: Fortress Press, 1986, 178–89.

Green, Henry A. *The Economic and Social Origins of Gnosticism*. SBLDS 77. Atlanta: Scholars Press, 1985.

———. "Gnosis and Gnosticism: A Study in Methodology." *Numen* 24:2 (1977): 95–134.

Greenfield, Jonas C., and Michael E. Stone. "The Books of Enoch and the Traditions of Enoch." *Numen* 26:1 (1979): 89–103.

Greer, Rowan. "Alien Citizens: A Marvellous Paradox." In *Civitas: Religious Interpretations of the City*, ed. Peter Hawkins. Atlanta: Scholars' Press, 1986, 39–56.

Griffin, Miriam. "Philosophy, Politics, and Politicians at Rome." In *Philosophia Togata*, ed. Griffin and Barnes, 1–37.

Griffin, Miriam, and Jonathan Barnes, eds. *Philosophia Togata: Essays on Philosophy and Roman Society*. Oxford: Clarendon Press, 1989.

Gruenwald, Ithamar. *Apocalyptic and Merkavah Mysticism*. AGAJU 14. Leiden: E. J. Brill, 1980.

———. "Jewish Sources for the Gnostic Texts from Nag Hammadi?" in *Proceedings of the Sixth World Congress of Jewish Studies: Held at the Hebrew University of Jerusalem, 13–19 August 1973 Under the Auspeices of the Israel Academy of Sciences and Humanities*. Vol. 3. Jerusalem: World Union of Jewish Studies, 1977, 45–56.

———. "Knowledge and Vision: Towards a Clarification of Two 'Gnostic' Concepts in Light of Their Alleged Origins." *ISO* 3 (1973): 63–107.

Hadot, Pierre. "*La métaphysique* de Porphyre." In *Entretiens Hardt 12: Porphyre*. Vandoeuvres: Entretiens de la Fondation Hardt, 1966, 127–63.

———. "Ouranos, Kronos, and Zeus in Plotinus' Treatise Against the Gnostics." In *Neoplatonism and Early Christian Thought*, ed. Blumenthal and Markus, 124–37.

———. *Porphyre et Victorinus*. 2 vols. Paris: Études Augustiniennes, 1968.

———. "Porphyre et Victorinus: Questions et hypothèses." *ResOr* 9 (1996): 117–25.

———. "Théologie, exégèse, révélation." In *Les règles de l'interprétation*, ed. Tardieu, 13–34.

Hahn, Johannes. *Der Philosoph und die Gesellschaft: Selbstverständnis, öffentliches Auftreten und populäre Erwartungen in der hohen Kaiserzeit.* Stuttgart: Franz Steiner, 1989.

Hall, Jonathan M. *Ethnic Identity in Greek Antiquity.* Cambridge: Cambridge University Press, 2000.

Hall, Robert. "Isaiah's Ascent to See the Beloved." *JBL* (1994): 463–84.

Halpern-Amaru, Betsy. "Exile and Return in Jubilees." In *Exile,* ed. Scott, 127–44.

Hanson, R. P. C. "The Christian Attitude to Pagan Religions up to the Time of Constantine the Great." *ANRW* 2.23.2 (1980): 910–73.

Harder, Richard. "Ein neue Schrift Plotins." In Harder, *Kleine Schriften.* Ed. Peter Marg. Munich: C. H. Beck, 1960, 257–74.

———. "Plotins Abhandlung gegen die Gnostiker." In Harder, *Kleine Schriften,* 296–302.

Hardie, Philip R. "Plutarch and the Interpretation of Myth." *ANRW* 2.33.6 (1989): 4743–87.

Hargis, J. W. *Against the Christians: The Rise of Early Anti-Christian Polemic.* New York: Peter Lang, 1999.

Harnack, Adolf von. *The Mission and Expansion of Christianity in the First Three Centuries.* Tr. James Moffett. 2 vols. Gloucester, MA: Peter Smith, 1972.

Harris, R. Baine, ed. *Neoplatonism and Indian Thought.* SNAM 2. Norfolk: ISNS, 1982.

Hartman, Lars. "Survey of the Problem of Apocalyptic Genre." In *Apocalypticism,* ed. Hellholm, 239–43.

Havdra, Matyáš. "Galenus Christianus? The Doctrine of Demonstration in *Stromata* VIII and the Question of its Source." *VC* 65 (2011): 343–375.

Heath, Malcolm. *Menander: A Rhetor in Context.* Oxford: Oxford University Press, 2004.

Hedrick, Charles W. *The Apocalypse of Adam: A Literary and Source Analysis.* ATT. Eugene, OR: Wipf & Stock, 2005.

———. "(Second) Apocalypse of James: Introduction." In *Nag Hammadi Codices V,2–5 and VI,* ed. Parrott, 105–9.

Hedrick, Charles W., and Robert Hodgson Jr., eds. *Nag Hammadi, Gnosticism, and Early Christianity.* Peabody, MA: Hendrickson, 1986.

Hellholm, David, ed. *Apocalypticism in the Ancient Mediterranean World and Near East: Proceedings of the International Colloquium on Apocalypticism, Uppsala, August 12–17, 1979.* Tübingen: Mohr Siebeck, 1983.

———. *Das Visionenbuch des Hermas als Apokalypse: Formgeschichtliche und text-theoretische Studien zu einer literarischen Gattung I: Method-*

ologische Voruberlegungen und makrostrukturelle Textanalyse. CB:NT
13. Lund: Gleerup, 1980.

———. "The Problem of the Apocalyptic Genre and the Apocalypses of
John." In *Early Christian Apocalypticism,* ed. Yarbro Collins, 13–64.

Helmbold, Andrew K. "Gnostic Elements in the 'Ascension of Isaiah'." *NTS*
18 (1972): 222–27.

Hengel, Martin. *Judaism and Hellenism: Studies in Their Encounter in Palestine During the Early Hellenistic Period.* Tr. John Bowden. 2 vols. Philadelphia: Fortress Press, 1974.

Henning, Walter B. "The Book of the Giants." *BSOAS* 9:1 (1943): 52–74.

———."Ein manichäisches Henochbuch." *SPAW* (1934): 27–35.

Hijmans, B. L. "Apuleius, Philosophus Platonicus." *ANRW* 2.36.1 (1987):
395–475.

Himmelfarb, Martha. *Ascent to Heaven in Jewish and Christian Apocalypses.* New York: Oxford University Press, 1993.

———. "Heavenly Ascent and the Relationship of the Apocalypses and the
Hekhalot Literature." *HUCA* 59 (1988): 73–101.

———. *Tours of Hell: An Apocalyptic Form in Jewish and Christian Literature.* Philadelphia: University of Pennsylvania Press, 1983.

———. "Merkavah Mysticism Since Scholem: Rachel Elior's The Three Temples." In *Wege mystischer Gotteserfahrung,* ed. Schäfer and Müller-Luckner, 19–36.

———. "The Practice of Ascent in the Ancient Mediterranean World." In
Death, Ecstasy, and Other Worldly Journeys, ed. Collins and Fishbane,
121–36.

———. "Revelation and Rapture: The Transformation of the Visionary in
the Ascent Apocalypses." In *Mysteries and Revelations,* ed. Collins and
Charlesworth, 79–90.

Hirschle, Maurus. *Sprachphilosophie und Namenmagie im Neuplatonis-
mus: Mit einem Exkurs zu "Demokrit" B 142.* Meisenheim am Glan:
Anton Hain, 1979.

Hirsch-Luipold, Rainer, ed. *Gott und die Götter bei Plutarch: Götterbilder–
Gottesbilder–Weltbilder.* RVV 54. Berlin: Walter de Gruyter, 2006.

———. *Plutarchs Denken in Bildern.* STAC 14. Tübingen: Mohr Siebeck, 2002.

Hoek, Annewies van den. "The 'Catechetical' School of Early Christian
Alexandria and Its Philonic Heritage." *HTR* 90:1 (1997): 59–87.

Hoffmann, Philippe. "Un grief antichrétien chez Proclus: L'ignorance in
théologie." In *Les chrétiens et l'hellénisme: Identités religieuses et culture
grecque dans l'Antiquité tardive,* ed. Arnaud Perrot. Études de littérature
ancienne 20. Paris: Éditions Rue d'Ulm, 2012, 161–97.

Hoheisel, Karl. "Das frühe Christentum und die Seelenwanderung." *JAC* 27–28 (1984–85): 24–46.

Hopfner, Theodor. *Orient und griechische Philosophie*. Beihefte zum Alten Orient 4. Leipzig: Hinrichs, 1925.

Horbury, William, W. D. Davies, and John Sturdy, eds. *The Cambridge History of Judaism*. Vol. 3, *The Early Roman Period*. Cambridge: Cambridge University Press, 1999.

Houten, Christiana van. *The Stranger in Israelite Law*. JSOTSup 107. Sheffield Academic Press, 1991.

Idel, Moshe. *Kabbalah: New Perspectives*. New Haven, CT: Yale University Press, 1988.

Igal, Jesús. "The Gnostics and 'The Ancient Philosophy' in Porphyry and Plotinus." In *Neoplatonism and Early Christian Thought*, ed. Blumenthal and Markus, 137–49.

Jackson, Howard. "Geradamas, the Celestial Stranger." *NTS* 27 (1981): 385–94.

———. "The Seer Nikotheos and His Lost Apocalypse in the Light of Sethian Apocalypses from Nag Hammadi and the Apocalypse of Elchasai." *NovT* 32:3 (1990): 250–77.

Jackson, Robin. "Olympiodorus and the Myth of Plato's *Gorgias*." In *Greek Literary Theory*, ed. Abbenes et al., 275–99.

Jackson-McCabe, Matt. "What's in a Name? The Problem of 'Jewish Christianity.'" In *Jewish-Christianity Reconsidered: Rethinking Ancient Groups and Texts*, ed. Matt Jackson-McCabe. Minneapolis: Fortress Press, 2007, 7–38.

Janka, Markus. "MYTHOS im *Corpus Platonicum*." In *Platon als Mythologe*, ed. Janka and Schäfer, 20–43.

Janka, Markus, and Christian Schäfer, eds. *Platon als Mythologe: Neue Interpretationen zu den Mythen in Platons Dialogen*. Darmstadt: Wissenschaftliche Buchgesellschaft, 2002.

Janssens, Yvonne. "Apocalypses de Nag Hammadi." In *L'apocalypse johannique et l'apocalyptique dans le Nouveau Testament*, ed. Jan Lambrecht. BETL 53. Gemblout: Duculot, 1980, 69–75.

Janowitz, Naomi. *The Poetics of Ascent: Theories of Language in a Rabbinic Ascent Text*. SUNY Series in Judaica: Hermeneutics, Mysticism, and Culture. Albany: State University of New York Press, 1989.

Jeck, Udo Reinhold. *Platonica Orientalia: Aufdeckung einer philosophischen Tradition*. Frankfurt am Main: Vittorio Klostermann, 2004.

Jenkins, R. G. "The Prayer of the Emanations in Greek from Kellis (T. Kellis 22)." *Le Muséon* 108 (1995): 243–63.

Jennott, Lance. *The "Gospel of Judas"*. STAC 64. Tübingen: Mohr Siebeck, 2011.

Jervell, Jacob. *Imago Dei: Gen 1,26 f. im Spätjudentum, in der Gnosis und in den paulinischen Briefen*. Göttingen: van den Hoeck & Ruprecht, 1960.

Johann, Horst-Theodor, ed. *Erziehung und Bildung in der heidnischen und christlichen Antike*. Wege der Forschung 377. Darmstadt: Wissenschaftliche, 1976.

Johnson, Aaron P. "Philosophy, Hellenicity, Law: Porphyry on Origen, Again." *JHS* 132 (2012): 55–69.

———. "Porphyry's Hellenism." In *Le traité de Porphyrye contre les chrétiens*, ed. Morlet, 165–81.

Jonas, Hans. *The Gnostic Religion: The Message of the Alien God and the Beginnings of Christianity*. Boston: Beacon Press, 1963.

Jones, A. H. M. *The Greek City: From Alexander to Justinian*. Oxford: Oxford University Press, 1940.

Jones, Christopher P. *Culture and Society in Lucian*. Cambridge: Harvard University Press, 1986.

———. "Multiple Identities in the Age of the Second Sophistic." In *Paideia*, ed. Borg, 13–22.

———. *Plutarch and Rome*. Oxford: Oxford University Press, 1971.

———. *The Roman World of Dio Chrysostom*. Cambridge, MA: Harvard University Press, 1978.

———. "The Teacher of Plutarch." *HSCP* 71 (1966): 205–13.

Jones, F. Stanley. "Review of Luttikhuizen, *Revelation of Elchasai*." *JAC* 30 (1987): 200–209.

Kaler, Michael. *Flora Tells a Story: The Apocalypse of Paul and Its Contexts*. SCJ 19. Waterloo, ON: Wilfrid Laurier University Press, 2008.

Kalligas, Paul. "Plotinus Against the Gnostics." *Hermathena* 169 (2000): 115–28.

Kappler, Claude-Claire, ed. *Apocalypses et voyages dans l'au-delà*. Paris: Cerf, 1987.

———. "Introduction générale." In *Apocalypses*, ed. Kappler, 15–53.

Katz, Joseph. "Plotinus and the Gnostics." *Journal of the History of Ideas* 15 (1954): 289–98.

Kennedy, George A. *Classical Rhetoric and Its Christian and Secular Tradition: From Ancient to Modern Times*. Chapel Hill: University of North Carolina Press, 1980.

Kidd, José E. Ramirez. *Alterity and Identity in Israel: The 'gr' in the Old Testament*. BZAW 283. Berlin: Walter de Gruyter, 1999.

King, Karen. *The Secret Revelation of John*. Cambridge, MA: Harvard University Press, 2006.

———. *What Is Gnosticism?* Cambridge, MA: Harvard University Press, 2003.

Kippenberg, Hans G.. "Ein vergleich jüdischer, christlicher und gnostischer Apokalyptik." In *Apocalypticism in the Ancient Mediterranean World*, ed. Hellholm, 751–69.

Klijn, A. F. J. "Introduction: 2 Baruch." In *OTP*, ed. Charlesworth, 1:615–20.

———. "A Seminar on Sethian Gnosticism," *NovT* 25:1 (1983): 90–94.

———. *Seth in Jewish, Christian and Gnostic Literature*. NovTSup 46. Leiden: E. J. Brill, 1977.

Kobusch, Theo. "Die Wiederkehr des Mythos." In *Platon als Mythologe*, ed. Janka and Schäfer, 44–57.

Koch, Klaus. *The Rediscovery of Apocalyptic: A Polemical Work on a Neglected Area of Biblical Studies and Its Damaging Effects on Philosophy and Theology*. Tr. Margaret Kohl. London: SCM Press, 1972.

Koenen, Ludwig. "From Baptism to the Gnosis of Manichaeism." In *Rediscovery*, ed. Layton, 734–56.

Koschorke, Klaus. "Paulus in den Nag-Hammadi-Texten." *ZTK* 78 (1981): 177–205.

Kraft, Robert. "Philo on Seth: Was Philo Aware of Traditions Which Exalted Seth and His Progeny?" in *Rediscovery*, ed. Layton, 457–58.

Krause, Martin, ed. *Gnosis and Gnosticism: Papers Read at the Seventh International Conference on Patristic Studies, Oxford 1975*. NHS 8. Leiden, E. J. Brill, 1977.

———. "Die literarschen Gattungen der Apokalypsen von Nag Hammadi." In *Apocalypticism in the Ancient Mediterranean World*, ed. Hellholm, 621–38.

Kvanvig, Helge S. *Roots of Apocalyptic: The Mesopotamian Background of the Enoch Figure and the Son of Man*. WMANT 61. Neukirchen-Vluyn: Neukirchener, 1988.

Lahe, Jaan. *Gnosis und Judentum: Alttestamentliche und jüdische Motive in der gnostischen Literatur und das Ursprungsproblem der Gnosis*. NHMS 75. Leiden: E. J. Brill, 2012.

Lamberton, Robert. *Homer the Theologian: Neoplatonist Allegorical Reading and the Growth of the Epic Tradition*. Transformation of the Classical Heritage 9. Berkeley: University of California Press, 1986.

———. *Plutarch*. New Haven, CT: Yale University Press, 2001.

Lane Fox, Robin. "Movers and Shakers." In *The Philosopher and Society*, ed. A. Smith, 19–50.

———. *Pagans and Christians.* New York: Alfred A. Knopf, 1986.

Larsen, Bent Dalgaard. *Jamblique de Chalcis: Exégète Et Philosophe.* 2 vols. Aarhus: Universitetsforlaget, 1972.

Layton, Bentley, ed. "Prolegomena to the Study of Ancient Gnosticism." In *The Social World of the First Christians: Essays in Honor of Wayne Meeks,* ed. L. Michael White and Larry O. Yarbrough. Minneapolis: Fortress Press, 1995, 334–50.

———. *The Rediscovery of Gnosticism: Proceedings of the International Conference on Gnosticism.* Numen Book Series. Leiden: E. J. Brill, 1981.

Lefkowitz, Mary R. "Some Ancient Advocates of Greek Cultural Dependency." In *Greeks and Barbarians: Essays on the Interactions Between Greeks and Non-Greeks in Antiquity and the Consequences for Eurocentrism,* ed. John E. Coleman and Clark A. Walz. Occasional Publications of the Department of Near Eastern Studies and the Program of Jewish Studies, Cornell University, 4. Bethesda, MD: CDL Press, 1997, 237–53.

Lesses, Rebecca Macy. *Ritual Practices to Gain Power: Angels, Incantations, and Revelation in Early Jewish Mysticism.* HTS 44. Harrisburg, PA: Trinity Press International, 1998.

Létourneau, Pierre. "Creation in Gnostic Christian Texts, or: What Happens to the Cosmos When Its Maker Is Not the Highest God?" In *Theologies of Creation in Early Judaism and Ancient Christianity: In Honour of Hans Klein,* ed. Tobias Nicklas, Korinna Zamfir, and Heike Braun. Deuterocanonical and Cognate Literature Studies 6. Berlin: De Gruyter, 2010, 415–34.

Levenson, Jon D. "The Universal Horizon of Biblical Particularism." In *Ethnicity and the Bible,* ed. Brett, 143–70.

Lewy, Hans. *Chaldaean Oracles and Theurgy: Troisième édition par Michel Tardieu avec un supplément "Les Oracles chaldaïques 1891–2001."* Collection des Études Augustiniennes, Série Antiquité 77. Paris: Institut d'Études Augustiniennes, 2011.

Lichtenberger, Hermann. *Studien zum Menschenbild in Texten der Qumrangemeinde.* Göttingen: Vandenhoek and Ruprecht, 1980.

Liddell, H. G., R. Scott, and H. S. Jones. *A Greek-English Lexicon. 9th ed. with revised supplement.* Oxford: Oxford University Press, 1996.

Lieu, Judith M. *Christian Identity in the Jewish and Graeco-Roman World.* Oxford: Oxford University Press, 2004.

———. "The Race of the God-Fearers." *JTS* 46 (1995): 483–501.

Lieu, Samuel N. C. *Manichaeism in the Later Roman Empire and Medieval China: A Historical Survey.* Manchester: Manchester University Press, 1985.

———. "The Diffusion of Manichaeism in the Roman Empire." In *A Green Leaf: Papers in Honour of Professor Jes P. Asmussen*, ed. Werner Sundermann, J. Duchesne-Guillemin, and F. Vahman. Acta Iranica 28. Leiden: E. J. Brill, 1988, 383–99

Lincoln, Bruce. *Theorizing Myth*. Chicago: University of Chicago Press, 1999.

Logan, Alastair H. B. *The Gnostics: Identifying an Early Christian Cult*. London: T&T Clark, 2006.

———. *Gnostic Truth and Christian Heresy: A Study in the History of Gnosticism*. Edinburgh: T&T Clark, 1996.

———. "John and the Gnostics: The Significance of the Apocryphon of John for the Debate About the Origins of the Johannine Literature." *JSNT* 14 (1991): 41–69.

———. "The Mystery of the Five Seals: Gnostic Initiation Reconsidered." *VC* 51 (1997): 188–206.

Löhr, Winrich A. *Basilides und seine Schule*. WUNT 83. Tübingen, Mohr/Siebeck, 1996.

Lovejoy, Arthur O., and Geroge Boas. *Primitivism and Related Ideas in Antiquity*. New York: Octagon Books, 1973.

Luttikhuizen, Gerard P. "Elchasaites and Their Book." In *Companion to Second-Century Christian "Heretics,"* ed. Marjanen and Luomanen, 335–64.

———. *The Revelation of Elchasai: Investigations into the Evidence for a Mesopotamian Jewish Apocalypse of the Second Century and Its Reception by Judeo-Christian Propagandists*. TSAT 8. Tübingen: Mohr/Siebeck, 1985.

———. "Sethianer?" *ZAC* 13:1 (2009): 76–86.

MacMullen, Ramsay. *Roman Government's Response to Crisis: a.d. 235–337*. New Haven, CT: Yale University Press, 1976.

MacRae, George. "The Apocalypse of Adam Reconsidered." In *Society of Biblical Literature 1972 Proceedings*, ed. L. C. McGaughy (Missoula, MT: Scholars' Press, 1972), 573–79.

———. "Apocalyptic Eschatology in Gnosticism." In *Apocalypticism in the Ancient Mediterranean World*, ed. Hellholm, 317–25.

———. "The Jewish Background of the Gnostic Sophia Myth." *NovT* 12 (1970): 86–101.

———. "Seth in Gnostic Texts and Traditions." In *1977 SBL Seminar Papers*, ed. P. J. Achtemeier. Missoula, MT: Scholars' Press, 1977, 17–24.

Maier, Johann. "Das Gefährdungsmotiv bei der Himmelsreise in der jüdischen Apokalyptik und 'Gnosis.'" In *Kairos: Zeitschrift für Religionswissenschaft und Theologie* 5 (1963): 18–40.

Majercik, Ruth. "The Being-Life-Mind Triad in Gnosticism and Neoplatonism." *CQ* 42 (1992): 475–88.

———. "Porphyry and Gnosticism." *CQ* 55 (2005): 277–92.

Marjanen, Antti, ed. *Was There a Gnostic Religion?* Publications of the Finnish Exegetical Society 87. Finnish Exegetical Society: Helsinki, 2005.

———. "What Is Gnosticism? From the Pastorals to Rudolph." In *Was There a Gnostic Religion?*, ed. Marjanen, 1–53.

Marjanen, Antti, and Petri Luomanen, eds. *A Companion to Second-Century Christian "Heretics."* VCSup. 76. Leiden: E. J. Brill, 2005.

Markschies, Christoph. *Gnosis: An Introduction.* Tr. John Bowden. London: T&T Clark, 2003.

Marrou, Henri-Irénée. *A History of Education in Antiquity.* Tr. George Lamb. Madison: University of Wisconsin Press, 1982.

———. "Synesius of Cyrene and Alexandrian Neoplatonism." In *The Conflict Between Paganism and Christianity*, ed. Momigliano, 126–50.

May, Gerhard. "Eschatologie V. Alte Kirche." In *TRE* 10:299–305.

Mazur, Zeke. "The Platonizing Sethian Gnostic Background of Plotinus' Mysticism." Ph.D. diss., University of Chicago, 2010.

———. "Plotinus' Philosophical Opposition to Gnosticism and the Axiom of Continuous Hierarchy." In *History of Platonism*, ed. Finamore and Berchman, 95–112.

———. "Self-Manifestation and 'Primary Revelation' in the Platonizing Sethian Ascent Treatises and Plotinian Mysticism." Paper presented at the Nag Hammadi and Gnosticism section at the annual meeting of the Society of Biblical Literature in Boston, November 2008.

McGinn, Bernard. "Revelation." In *The Literary Guide to the Bible*, ed. Robert Alter and Frank Kermode. Cambridge, MA: Belknap Press of Harvard University Press, 1987, 523–41.

Meade, David G. *Pseudonymity and Canon: An Investigation into the Relationship of Authorship and Authority in Jewish and Earliest Christian Tradition.* WUNT 39. Tübingen: Mohr Siebeck, 1986.

Meeks, Wayne. "Moses as God and King." In *Religions in Antiquity: Essays in Memory of Erwin Ramsdell Goodenough*, ed. Jacob Neusner. Leiden: E. J. Brill, 1970, 354–71.

Meijering, E. P. "God Cosmos History: Christian and Neo-Platonic Views on Divine Revelation." *VC* 28:4 (1974): 248–76.

Ménard. "Littérature apocalyptique juive et littérature gnostique." *RevSR* 47 (1973): 300–323

Meredith, Anthony. "Porphyry and Julian Against the Christians." *ANRW* 23:2 (1980): 1119–49.

Metzger, Bruce. "Introduction: The Fourth Book of Ezra." In *OTP*, ed. Charlesworth, 1:517–24.

———. "Literary Forgeries and Canonical Pseudepigrapha." *JBL* 91:1 (1972): 3–24.

Milik, Józef T. *The Books of Enoch: Aramaic Fragments of Qumrân Cave 4*. Oxford: Clarendon Press, 1976.

Millar, Fergus. "Porphyry: Ethnicity, Language, and Alien Wisdom." In *Philosophia Togata II*, ed. Barnes and Griffin, 241–62.

———. *A Study of Cassius Dio*. Oxford: Clarendon Press, 1964.

Mirecki, Paul, and Marvin Meyer, eds. *Magic and Ritual in the Ancient World*. Religions of the Greco-Roman World 141. Leiden: E. J. Brill, 2002.

Moellering, H. Armin. *Plutarch on Superstition: Plutarch's "De superstitio", Its Place in the Changing Meaning of Deisidaimonia and in the Context of His Theological Writings*. Boston: Christopher, 1962.

Momigliano, Arnaldo. *Alien Wisdom: The Limits of Hellenization*. Cambridge: Cambridge University Press, 1975.

———, ed. *The Conflict Between Paganism and Christianity in the Fourth Century*. Oxford: Clarendon Press, 1964.

Moore, Edward, and John D. Turner. "Gnosticism." In *The Cambridge History of Philosophy in Late Antiquity*, ed. Gerson, 1:174–96.

Morard, Françoise. "*L'Apocalypse d'Adam* de Nag Hammadi: Un essai d'interprétation." In *Gnosis and Gnosticism*, ed. Krause, 35–42.

Morgan, Kathryn A. *Myth and Philosophy from the Presocratics to Plato*. Cambridge: Cambridge University Press, 2000.

Morlet, Sébastien (ed.) *Le traité de Porphyre contre les Chrétiens: Un siècle de recherches, nouvelles questions: Actes du colloque international organisé les 8 et 9 septembre 2009 à l'Université de Paris IV-Sorbonne*. Collection des Études Augustiniennes, Série Antiquité 190. Paris: Institut d' Études Augustiniennes, 2011.

Morray-Jones, C. R. A. "Transformational Mysticism in the Apocalyptic-Merkabah Tradition." *JJS* 43:2 (1992): 1–31.

Most, Glenn W. "Cornutus and Stoic Allegoresis: A Preliminary Report." *ANRW* 2.35.3 (1989): 2014–65.

Müller, H.-P. "Mantische Weisheit und Apokalyptik." *VTSup* 22 (1972): 268–93.

Mussies, Gerard. "Interpretario Judaica." In *Studies in Egyptian Religion dedicated to Jan Zandee*, ed. Matthieu Sybrand, Huibert Gerard, and Heerma van Voss. Leiden: E. J. Brill, 1982, 89–120.

Narbonne, Jean-Marc. *Plotinus in Dialogue with the Gnostics*. Studies in

Platonism, Neoplatonism, and the Platonic Tradition 11. Leiden: E. J. Brill, 2011.

Nautin, Pierre. "Les fragments de Basilide sur la souffrance et leur interprétation par Clement d'Alexandrie et Origène." In *Mélanges d'histoire des religions offerts à Henri-Charles Puech*. Paris: Presses Universitaires de France, 1974, 393–404.

Newsom, Carol. "'He has Established for Himself Priests': Human and Angelic Priesthood in the Qumran Sabbath Shirot." In *Archaeology and History in the Dead Sea Scrolls*, ed. Schiffman, 101–20.

Nickelsburg, George W. E. "Eschatology (Early Jewish)." In *Anchor Bible Dictionary*, ed. Freedman et al., 2:579–94.

———. "Some Related Adam Traditions in the *Apocalypse of Adam*, the Books of Adam and Eve, and *1 Enoch*." In *Rediscovery*, ed. Layton, 515–39.

Nock, A. D. *Essays on Religion and the Ancient World*, ed. Zeph Stewart. 2 vols. Oxford: Clarendon Press, 1983.

———. "Greeks and Magi." In Nock, *Essays*, 2:516–26.

———. "The Milieu of Gnosticism." In Nock, *Essays*, 1:444–51.

———. "Prolegomena." In Sallustius, *Concerning the Gods and the Universe*, xvii–cxxiii.

———. "Sarcophagi and Symbolism." In Nock, *Essays*, 2:606–42.

O'Brien, Denis. "Plotinus and the Gnostics on the Generation of Matter." In *Neoplatonism and Early Christian Thought*, ed. Blumenthal and Markus, 108–23.

———. *Théodicée plotinienne, théodicée gnostique*. PA 57. Leiden: E. J. Brill, 1993.

O'Donnell, James. "Late Antiquity: Before and After." *TAPA* 134:2 (2004): 203–14.

O'Meara, Dominic J. "Gnosticism and the Making of the World in Plotinus." In *Rediscovery*, ed. Layton, 365–78.

———. *Platonopolis*. Oxford: University Press, 2006.

———. *Plotinus: An Introduction to the "Enneads."* Oxford: Oxford University Press, 1993.

———. *Pythagoras Revived: Mathematics and Philosophy in Late Antiquity*. Oxford: Clarendon Press, 1989.

O'Meara, John J. "Indian Wisdom and Porphyry's Search for a Universal Way." In *Neoplatonism and Indian Thought*, ed. Harris, 5–25.

Onuki, Takashi. "Die dreifache Pronoia: Zur Beziehung zwischen Gnosis, Stoa und Mittelplatonismus." In Takashi Onuki, *Heil und Erlösung*. WUNT 165. Tübingen: Mohr Siebeck, 2004, 240–70.

Orlov, Andrei. "The Origin of the Name 'Metatron' and the Text of 2 (Slavonic Apocalypse of) Enoch." *JSP* 21 (2000): 19–26.

Osborn, Eric Francis. *Irenaeus of Lyons*. Cambridge: Cambridge University Press, 2001.

———. *Justin Martyr*. Beiträge zur historischen Theologie 47. Tübingen: Mohr Siebeck, 1973.

Pack, Robert A. *The Literary Texts from Greco Roman Egypt*. Ann Arbor: University of Michigan Press, 1952.

Paget, James Carleton. "Jewish Christianity." In *The Cambridge History of Judaism*, ed. Horbury, Davies, and Sturdy, 731–75.

Painchaud, Louis, and Anne Pasquier, eds. *Les texts de Nag Hammadi et le problème de leur classification: Actes du colloque tenu à Québec du 15 au 19 Septembre 1993*. BCNH Section "Études" 3. Québec: Presses de l'université Laval; Leuven: Peeters, 1995.

Painchaud, Louis, and P.-H. Poirier, eds. *Coptica - Gnostica - Manichaica: Mélanges offerts à Wolf-Peter Funk*. BCNH Section "Études" 7. Québec: Presses de l'université Laval; Leuven: Peeters, 2006.

Parrott, Douglas M. "Eugnostos and 'All the Philosophers.'" In *Religion im Erbe Ägyptens: Festschrift für Alexander Böhlig*, ed. Manfred Görg. Ägypten und Altes Testament 14. Wiesbaden: Harrassowitz, 1988, 153–67.

Pasquier, Anne. "La réflexion démiurgique ou la 'terre étrangère' chez les gnostiques (*Ennéade* 2.9.10–12)." In *Coptica*, ed. Painchaud and Poirier, 647–61.

Pearson, Birger. *Ancient Gnosticism: Traditions and Literature*. Minneapolis: Fortress Press, 2007.

———. "Basilides the Gnostic." In *Companion to Second-Century "Heretics,"* ed. Marjanen and Luomanen, 1–31.

———. "The Figure of Seth in Gnostic Literature." In *Rediscovery*, ed. Layton, 473–504.

———. "From Jewish Apocalypticism to Gnosis." In *The Nag Hammadi Texts in the History of Religions*, ed. Giversen, Petersen, and Sørensen, 146–64.

———. "Gnosticism as a Religion." In *Was There a Gnostic Religion?* ed. Marjanen, 81–101.

———. "Gnosticism as Platonism: With Special Reference to *Marsanes* (NHC 10,1)." *HTR* 77:1 (1984): 55–72.

———. "Introduction: *Melchizedek*." In *Nag Hammadi Codices IX and X*, ed. Pearson, 19–40.

———. "Introduction: *The Thought of Norea*." In *Nag Hammadi Codices IX and X*, ed. Pearson, 97–93.

———. "Introduction: *Marsanes*." In *Nag Hammadi Codices IX and X*, ed. Pearson, 229–50.

———. "Jewish Elements in Corpus Hermeticum I (*Poimandres*)." In *Studies in Gnosticism and Hellenistic Religions*, ed. van den Broek and Vermaseren, 336–48.

———. "Jewish Sources in Gnostic Literature." In *The Literature of the Jewish People in the Period of the Second Temple*, ed. Michael Stone. CRINT 2.2. Assen: Van Gorcum; Philadelphia: Fortress Press, 1984, 443–81.

———. "*Marsanes* Revisited." In *Coptica*, ed. Painchaud and Poirier, 685–96.

———. "Notes: *Melchizedek*." In *Nag Hammadi Codices IX and X*, ed. Pearson, 42–85.

———. "Notes: *Marsanes*." In *Nag Hammadi Codices IX and X*, ed. Pearson, 252–347.

Peel, Malcolm. "Gnostic Eschatology and the New Testament." *NovT* 12 (1970): 141–65.

Pender, Elizabeth E. "Plato on Metaphor and Models." In *Metaphor, Allegory, and the Classical Tradition: Ancient Thought and Modern Revisions*, ed. G. R. Boys-Stones. Oxford: Oxford University Press, 2003, 55–81.

Pépin, Jean. "Héraclès et son reflet dans le néoplatonisme." In *Le Néoplatonisme: Actes du colloque international sur le néoplatonisme organisé dans le cadre des colloques internationaux du Centre National de la Recherche Scientifique, à Royaumont du 9 au 13 juin 1969*, ed. P. M. Schuhl and Pierre Hadot. Paris: CNRS, 1971, 167–92.

———. "L'épisode du portrait de Plotin." In *La vie de Plotin*, ed. Brisson, 301–30.

———. *Mythe et allégorie: Les origines grecques et les contestations judéochrétiennes*. Aubier: Éditions Montaigne, 1958.

———. "Theories of Procession in Plotinus and the Gnostics." In *Neoplatonism and Gnosticism*, ed. Wallis with Bregman, 297–335.

Perkins, Judith. *Roman Imperial Identities in the Early Christian Era*. Routledge Monographs in Classical Studies. London: Routledge, 2009.

Perkins, Pheme. "Christian Books and Sethian Revelations." In *Coptica.*, ed. Painchaud and Poirier, 697–730.

———. *The Gnostic Dialogue: The Early Church and the Crisis of Gnosticism*. New York: Paulist Press, 1980.

———. "Identification with the Savior in Coptic texts from Nag Hammadi." In *The Jewish Roots of Christological Monotheism: Papers from the St. Andrews Conference on the Historical Origins of the Worship of Jesus,* ed. Carey C. Newman, James R. Davila, and Gladys S. Lewis. JSJSup 63. Leiden: E. J. Brill, 1999, 166–84.

Pétrement, Simone. *A Separate God: the Origins and Teaching of Gnosticism*. San Franscisco: HarperCollins, 1993.

Philip, James A. "Platonic Diairesis." *TAPA* 96 (1966): 335–58.

Pleše, Zlatko. "Gnostic Literature." In *Religiöse Philosophie und philosophische Religion der frühen Kaiserzeit,* ed. Rainer Hirsch-Luipold, Herwig Görgemanns, and Michael von Albrecht, with Tobias Thum. STAC 51. Tübingen: Mohr Siebeck, 2009, 163–98.

———. "Platonist Orientalism." In *Historical and Biographical Values of Plutarch's Works: Studies Devoted to Professor Philip Stadter by the International Plutarch Society,* ed. Aurelio Pérez Jiménez and Frances Titchener. Málaga: Universidad de Málaga; Logan, UT: University of Utah, 2005, 245–71.

———. *Poetics of the Gnostic Universe: Narrative and Cosmology in the Apocryphon of John.* NHMS 52. Leiden: E. J. Brill, 2005.

Poirier, Paul-Hubert. "Commentaire: *Marsanès.*" In *Marsanès,* ed. and tr. Funk, Poirier, and Turner, 363–468.

———. "Commentaire: *La pensée première.*" In *La pensée première à la triple forme,* ed. and tr. Poirier, 171–370.

———. "Introduction: *La pensée première.*" In *La pensée première à la triple forme,* ed. and tr. Poirier, 1–122.

Poirier, Paul-Hubert, and Thomas Schmidt. "Chrétiens, hérétiques et gnostiques chez porphyre: Quelques precisions sur la *Vie de Plotin* 16.1–9." In *Académie des Inscriptions et Belles Lettres: Comptes rendus des séances de l'année 2010. Avril-juin,* ed. P. de Boccard. Paris: CRAI, 2010, 913–42.

Potter, David. *Prophecy and History in the Crisis of the Roman Empire: A Historical Commentary on the Thirteenth "Sibylline Oracle."* Oxford Classical Monographs. Oxford: Clarendon Press, 1990.

Puech, Henri-Charles. *En quête de la Gnose.* Vol. 1 : *La Gnose et le temps et autres essais.* Paris: Gallimard, 1978.

———. "Fragments retrouvés de *l'Apocalypse d'Allogène.*" In Puech, *En quête de la Gnose,* 271–300.

———. "La gnose et le temps." In Puech, *En quête de la Gnose,* 215–70.

———. "Les nouveaux écrits gnostiques découverts en Haute-Égypte." In *Coptic Studies in Honor of Walter Ewing Crum.* Bulletin of the Byzantine Institute 11. Boston: Byzantine Institute, 1950, 91–154.

———. "Numénius d'Apamée et les théologies orientales au second siècle." In *Mélanges Bidez: Annuaire de l'Institut de philologie de d'histoire orientales.* 2 vols. Brussels: Secrétariat dee l'institut, 1934, 745–78.

———. "Plotin et les gnostiques." *In Les sources de Plotin: Dix exposés et discussions. Vandoeuvres-Genève 21-29 août 1959*, ed. E. R. Dodds. Entretiens sur l'antiqué classique 5. Geneva: Foundation Hardt, 1960, 161–90.

Quispel, Gilles. "Die Gnostische Anthropos und die jüdische Tradition." In Gilles Quispel, *Gnostic Studies*. Istanbul: Nederlands Historisch-Archaeologisch Institut, 1974, 173–95.

———. "The Jung Codex and Its Significance." In *The Jung Codex: A Newly Recovered Gnostic Papyrus*, ed. and tr. Frank L. Cross. London: A. R. Mowbray, 1955, 35–78.

———. "Plotinus and the Jewish Gnōstikoi." In *Il Manicheismo: Nuove prospettive della richerca: Quinto Congresso Internazionale di Studi sul Manicheismo, Atti, Dipartimento di Studi Asiatici, Università degli Studi di Napoli "L'Orientale." Napoli, 2–8 Settembre 2001*, ed. Aloïs van Tongerloo in collaboration with Luigi Cirillo. Leuven: Brepols, 2005, 287–329.

Rasimus, Tuomas. *Paradise Reconsidered in Gnostic Mythmaking: Rethinking Sethianism in Light of the Ophite Evidence*. NHMS 68. Leiden: E. J. Brill, 2009.

———. "Porphyry and the Gnostics: Reassessing Pierre Hadot's Thesis in Light of the Second- and Third-Century Sethian Treatises." In *Plato's "Parmenides" and Its Heritage*, ed. Turner and Corrigan, 2:81–110.

Rawson, E. "Roman Rulers and the Philosophic Adviser." In *Philosophia Togata*, ed. Griffin and Barnes, 233–57.

Reardon, B. P. *Courants littéraires grecs des IIe et IIIe siècles après J.-C.* Paris: Les belles lettres, 1971.

Reeves, John C. *Heralds of That Good Realm: Syro-Mesopotamian Gnosis and Jewish Traditions*. NHMS 41. Leiden: E. J. Brill, 1996.

Rendtorff, Rolf. "The *Gēr* in the Priestly Laws of the Pentateuch." In *Ethnicity and the Bible*, ed. Brett, 77–88.

Rist, John M. *Plotinus: The Road to Reality*. Cambridge: Cambridge University Press, 1967.

Robert, Louis. "Lucien et son temps." In Louis Robert, *À travers l'Asie Mineure: Poètes et prosateurs, monnaeis greques, voyageurs et géographie*. Paris: École Française d'Athènes, 1980, 393–436.

———. "Un oracle gravé à Oenoanda." *CRAI* (1971): 597–619.

Robinson, James M. "Nag Hammadi: The First Fifty Years." In *The Nag Hammadi Library After Fifty Years*, ed. Turner and McGuire, 3–34.

———. "The Three Steles of Seth and the Gnostics of Plotinus." In *Proceedings of the International Colloquium on Gnosticism, Stockholm August 20–25, 1973*, ed. Geo Widengren. Stockholm: Almqvist & Wiksell, 1977, 132–42.

Roloff, Dietrich. *Plotin, Die Gross-Schrift III,8–V,8–V,5–II,9*. Berlin: de Gruyter, 1970.

Rowland, Christopher. "Apocalyptic: The Disclosure of Heavenly Knowledge." In *The Cambridge History of Judaism*, ed. Horbury, Davies, and Sturdy, 776–97.

———. *The Open Heaven: A Study of Apocalyptic in Judaism and Early Christianity*. New York: Crossroad, 1982.

Rubinkiewicz, R. "Introduction: Apocalypse of Abraham." *OTP*, ed. Charlesworth, 1:681–88.

Rudolph, Kurt. "The Baptist Sects." In *The Cambridge History of Judaism*, ed. Horbury, Davies, and Sturdy, 471–500.

———. *Gnosis: The Nature and History of Gnosticism*. Tr. Robert McLachlan Wilson. San Francisco: HarperSanFrancisco, 1980.

Runia, David T. *Philo of Alexandria and the 'Timaeus' of Plato*. PA 44. Leiden: E. J. Brill, 1986.

———, ed. *Plotinus amid Gnostics and Christians: Papers Presented at the Plotinus Symposium Held at the Free University, Amsterdam on 25 January 1984*. Amsterdam: VU Uitgeverij, 1984.

Russell, David Michael. *The "New Heavens and New Earth": Hope for the Creation in Jewish Apocalyptic and the New Testament*. Studies in Biblical Apocalyptic Literature 1. Philadelphia: Visionary Press, 1996.

Sacchi, Paolo. *L'apocalittica giudaica e la sua storia*. Brescia: Paideia, 1990.

Saffrey, Henri-Dominique. "Allusions antichrétiennes chez Proclus, le Diadoque Platonicien." In Henri-Dominique Saffrey, *Recherches sur le Néoplatonisme après Plotin*. Librarie Philosophique. Paris: Vrin, 1990, 201–11.

———. "Refléxions sur la pseudonymie Abammôn-Jamblique." In *Traditions of Platonism*, ed. Cleary, 307–19.

Said, Edward. *Orientalism*. New York: Vintage Books, 1979.

Saïd, Suzanne. "Deux noms de l'image en grec ancien: Idole et icône." *Comptes-rendus des séances de l'Académie des inscriptions et belles-lettres* 131:2 (1987): 309–30.

Sakenfeld, Katharine Doob, et al., eds. *The New Interpreter's Dictionary of the Bible. D–H*. Vol. 2. Nashville: Abingdon Press, 2007.

Sanders, E. P. "The Genre of Palestinian Jewish Apocalypses." In *Apocalypticism in the Ancient Mediterranean World*, ed. Hellholm, 447–60.

Säve-Söderbergh, Torgny. "The Pagan Elements in Early Christianity and Gnosticism." In *Colloque international sur les textes de Nag Hammadi*, ed. Barc, 71–85.

Schäfer, Peter. "Communion with the Angels: Qumran and the Origins of

Jewish Mysticism." In *Wege mystischer Gotteserfahrung*, ed. Schäfer and Müller-Luckner, 37–66.

———. *The Origins of Jewish Mysticism*. Tübingen: Mohr Siebeck, 2009.

Schäfer, Peter, and Elisabeth Müller-Luckner, eds. *Wege mystischer Gotteserfahrung: Judentum, Christentum, und Islam*. Schriften des Historischen Kollegs, Kolloquien 65. Munich: R. Oldenbourg, 2006.

Schenke, Hans-Martin. "The Phenomenon and Significance of Gnostic Sethianism." Tr. Bentley Layton. In *Rediscovery*, ed. Layton, 588–616.

———. "Das sethianische System nach Nag-Hammadi-Handschriften." In *Studia Coptica*, ed. P. Nagel. Berlin: Akademie, 1974, 165–73.

Schenke [Robinson], Gesine. "The *Gospel of Judas*: Its Protagonist, Its Composition, and Its Community." In *The Codex Judas Papers*, ed. DeConick, 75–94.

Schiffman, Lawrence H., ed. *Archaeology and History in the Dead Sea Scrolls: The New York University Conference in Memory of Yigael Yadin*. JSPSup 8. Sheffield: Sheffield Academic Press, 1990.

Schmidt, Carl. *Koptisch-Gnostische Schriften*. Leipzig: J. C. Hinrichs, 1905.

———. *Plotins Stellung zum Gnosticismus und kirchlichen Christentum*. Leipzig: J. C. Hinrichs, 1901.

Schmidt, Thomas. "Sophistes, barbares, et identité greque: Le cas de Dion Chryostome." In *Perceptions of the Second Sophistic and Its Times—Regards sur la Seconde Sophistique et son époque*, ed. Thomas Schmidt and Pascale Fleury. Phoenix Suppl. 49. Toronto: University of Toronto Press, 2011, 105–19.

Schoeps, Hans-Joachim. *Urgemeinde, Judenchristentum, Gnosis*. Tübingen: Mohr/Siebeck, 1956.

Scholem, Gershom. *Jewish Gnosticism, Merkabah Mysticism, and Talmudic Tradition*. New York: Jewish Theological Seminary of America, 1960.

———. *Major Trends in Jewish Mysticism*. New York: Schocken Books, 1995.

Schott, Jeremy. M. *Christianity, Empire, and the Making of Religion in Late Antiquity*. Divinations. Philadelphia: University of Pennsylvania Press, 2008.

———. "'Living like a Christian, but Playing the Greek': Accounts of Apostasy and Conversion in Porphyry and Eusebius." *Journal of Late Antiquity* 1:2 (2008): 258–77.

Schottroff, Luise. "*Animae naturaliter salvandae*: Zum Problem der himmlischen Herkunft des Gnostikers." In *Christentum und Gnosis*, ed. Walther Eltester. BZNW 37. Berlin: Alfred Töpelmann, 1969, 65–97.

Schroeder, Frederic M. "Ammonius Saccas." *ANRW* 2.36.1 (1987): 493–526.

———. "Aseity and Connectedness in the Plotinian Philosophy of Providence." *Gnosticism and Later Platonism*, ed. Turner and Majercik, 303–17.

Schubert, Kurt. "Problem und Wesen der jüdischen Gnosis." *Kairos* 3 (1961): 2–15.

Schultz, Joseph P. "Angelic Opposition to the Ascension of Moses and the Revelation of the Law." *JQR* 61:4 (1971): 282–307.

Schüssler Fiorenza, Elizabeth. "The Phenomenon of Early Christian Apocalyptic: Some Reflections on Method." In *Apocalypticism in the Ancient Mediterranean World*, ed. Hellholm, 295–316.

Scopello, Madeline. "The Apocalypse of Zostrianos (Nag Hammadi VIII .1) and the Book of the Secrets of Enoch." *VC* 34 (1980): 376–85.

———. "Contes apocalyptiques et apocalypses philosophiques dans la bibliothèque de Nag Hammadi." In *Apocalypses*, ed. Kappler, 321–50.

———. "Portraits d'anges à Nag Hammadi." In *Acts du huitième congrès international d'études coptes*, ed. Bosson and Boud'hors, 2:879–92.

———. "Titres au'fémin dans la bibliothèque de Nag hammadi." In Madeleine Scopello, *Femme, gnose et manichéisme: De l'espace mythique au territoire au reel*. NHMS 53. Leiden: E. J. Brill, 127–53.

———. "Un rite idéal d'intronisation dans trois textes gnostiques de Nag Hammadi." In *Nag Hammadi and Gnosis: Papers read at the First International Congress of Coptology (Cairo, December 1976)*, ed. Robert McLachlan Wilson. Leiden: E. J. Brill, 1978, 91–95.

———. "Youel et Barbélo dans le Traité de l'Allogène." In *Colloque international sur les Textes de Nag Hammadi*, ed. Barc, 374–82.

Scott, James M., ed. *Exile: Old Testament, Jewish, and Christian Conceptions*. JSJSup 56. Leiden: E. J. Brill, 1997.

Segal, Alan F. *Life After Death: A History of the Afterlife in the Religions of the West*. New York: Doubleday, 2004.

———. "Paul and the Beginning of Jewish Mysticism." In *Death, Ecstasy, and Other Worldly Journeys*, ed. Collins and Fishbane, 93–122.

Sevrin, Jean-Marie. *Le dossier baptismal séthien: Études sur la sacramentaire gnostique*. BCNH Section "Études" 2. Québec: Presses de l'université Laval; Leuven: Peeters, 1986.

Sharples, Robert W. "Alexander of Aphrodisias, De Fato: Some Parallels." *CQ* 28:2 (1978): 243–66.

———. "Alexander of Aphrodisias on Divine Providence: Two Problems." *CQ* 32:1 (1982): 198–211.

———. "Nemesius of Emesa and Threefold Providence: The History and Background of a Doctrine." In *Ancient Approaches to Plato's "Timaeus,"* ed. R. W. Sharples and Anne Sheppard. *BICSSup* 78. London: University of London, 2003, 107– 27.

Shaw, Gregory. *Theurgy and the Soul: The Neoplatonism of Iamblichus.* University Park: Pennsylvania University Press, 1995.

Sheppard, Anne. "Pagan Cults of Angels in Roman Asia Minor." *Talanta* 12–13 (1980–81): 77–101.

———. *Studies on the 5th and 6th Essays of Proclus's Commentary on the Republic.* Hypomnemata 61. Göttingen: van den Hoeck and Ruprecht, 1980.

Sieber, John. "An Introduction to the Tracatate *Zostrianus* from Nag Hammadi." *NovT* 15 (1973): 233–40.

———. "Introduction to *Zostrianos.*" In *Nag Hammadi Codex VIII,* ed. Sieber, 7–28.

———. "Notes: Zostrianos." In *Nag Hammadi Codex VIII,* ed. Sieber, 30–225.

Simonetti, M. *Lettera E/O Allegoria: Un contributo alla studio dell'esegesi patristica.* Studia Ephemeridis Augustinianum 23. Rome: n.p., 1985.

Sinnige, Theo Gerard. "Gnostic Influence in the Early Works of Plotinus and in Augustine." In *Plotinus,* ed. Runia, 73–97.

———. *Six Lectures on Plotinus and Gnosticism.* Dordrecht: Kluwer Academic, 1999.

Sint, Josef A. *Pseudonymität im Altertum: Ihre Formen und ihre Gründe.* Innsbruck: Universitätsverlag Wagner, 1960.

Smith, Andrew, ed. *The Philosopher and Society in Late Antiquity: Essays in Honour of Peter Brown.* Swansea: Cassical Press of Wales, 2005.

———. "Porphyrian Studies Since 1913." *ANRW* 2.36.1 (1987): 717–73.

———. *Porphyry's Place in the Neoplatonic Tradition: A Study in Post-Plotinian Neoplatonism.* The Hague: Nijhoff, 1974.

Smith, Jonathan Z. "I Am a Parrot (Red)." In J. Z. Smith, *Map Is Not Territory,* 265–88.

———. *Map Is Not Territory: Studies in the History of Religions.* Chicago: University of Chicago Press, 1993.

———. "Wisdom and Apocalyptic." In J. Z. Smith, *Map Is Not Territory,* 67–87.

Smith, Morton. "Ascent to the Heavens and Deification in 4QMa." In *Archaeology and History in the Dead Sea Scrolls,* ed. Schiffman, 181–88.

———. "On the History of Angels." In *"Open Thou Mine Eyes": Essays on Aggadah and Judaica Presented to Rabbi William G. Braude on His Eightieth Birthday and Dedicated to His Memory,* ed. Herman J. Blumberg et al. Hoboken, NJ: Ktav, 1992, 285–94.

———. "On the History of ΑΠΟΚΑΛΥΠΤΩ and ΑΠΟΚΑΛΥΨΙΣ." In *Apocalypticism in the Ancient Mediterranean World*, ed. Hellholm, 9–20.

———. "Two Ascended to Heaven—Jesus and the Author of 4Q491." In *Jesus and the Dead Sea Scrolls*, ed. James M. Charlesworth et al. New Haven, CT: Doubleday, 1992, 290–301.

Smyth, Herbert Weir. *Greek Grammar*. Rev. Gordon Messing. Cambridge, MA: Harvard University Press, 1984.

Snyder, H. Gregory. *Readers and Texts in the Ancient World: Philosophers, Jews and Christians*. Religion in the First Christian Centuries. London: Routledge, 2000.

Solmsen, Friedrich. "Providence and the Souls: A Platonic Chapter in Clement of Alexandria." In Friedrich Solmsen, *Kleine Schriften*. 3 vols. Hildesheim: Georg Olms, 1982, 352–74.

Sorabji, Richard. *Time, Creation, and the Continuum: Theories in Antiquity and the Early Middle Ages*. Ithaca, NY: Cornell University Press, 1983.

Speyer, Wolfgang. *Die Literarische Fälschung im Heidnischen und Christlischen Altertum: Ein Versuch ihrer Deutung*. Munich: C. H. Beck, 1971.

———. "Porphyrios als religiöse Persönlichkeit und als religiöser Denker." In *Griechische Mythologie und frühes Christentum*, ed. Raban von Haehling. Darmstadt: Wissenschaftliche, 2005, 65–84.

Staden, Heinrich von. "Galen and the Second Sophistic." In *Aristotle and After*, ed. Richard Sorabji. BICSSup 68. London: Institute of Classical Studies, 1997, 33–54.

———. "Hairesis and Heresy: The Case of the *haireseis iatrikai*." In *Jewish and Christian Self-Definition*, ed. B. F. Meyer and E. P. Sanders. Self-Definition in the Greco-Roman World 3. Philadelphia: Fortress, 1982, 76–100.

Stanton, G. R. "Rhetors and Philosophers: Problems of Classification." *AJP* 94 (1973): 350–64.

Sterling, Gregory E. "'The School of Sacred Laws': The Social Setting of Philo's Treatises." *VC* 53:2 (1999): 148–64.

Stertz, Stephen A. "Aelius Aristides' Political Ideas." *ANRW* 2.34.2 (1994): 1248–70.

Stettner, Walter. *Die Seelenwanderung bei Griechen und Römern*. Tübinger Beiträge zur Altertumswissenschaft 22. Stuttgart: W. Kollhammer, 1934.

Stone, Michael E. "Apocalyptic Literature." In *Jewish Writings*, ed. Stone, 383–442.

———, ed. *Jewish Writings of the Second Temple Period: Apocrypha, Pseudepigrapha, Qumran Sectarian Writings, Philo, Josephus*. Assen: von Gorcum; Philadelphia: Fortress Press, 1984.

———. "Lists of Revealed Things in the Apocalyptic Literature." In Michael

E. Stone, *Selected Studies in Pseudepigrapha and Apocrypha with Special Reference to the Armenian Tradition*. SVTP 9. Leiden: E. J. Brill, 1991, 379–418.

———. "Report on Seth Traditions in the Armenian Adam Books," in *Rediscovery*, ed. Layton, 460–71.

Stroumsa, Gedaliahu G. *Another Seed: Studies in Gnostic Mythology*. NHS 24. Leiden: E. J. Brill, 1984.

———. "Titus of Bostra and Alexander of Lycopolis: A Christian and a Platonic Refutation of Manichaean Dualism." In *Neoplatonism and Gnosticism*, ed. Wallis with Bregman, 337–49.

———. "To See or Not to See: On the Early History of the *Visio Beatifica*." In *Wege mystischer Gotteserfahrung*, ed. Schäfer and Müller-Luckner, 67–80.

Struck, Peter T. "Allegory, Aenigma, and Anti-Mimesis: A Struggle Against Aristotelian Rhetorical Literary Theory." In *Greek Literary Theory*, ed. Abbenes et al., 215–34.

———. *Birth of the Symbol: Ancient Readers at the Limits of Their Texts*. Princeton, NJ: Princeton University Press, 2004.

———. "Speech Acts and the Stakes of Hellenism." In *Magic and Ritual*, ed. Mirecki and Meyer, 387–403.

Stuckenbruck, Loren T. *Angel Veneration and Christology: A Study in Early Judaism and in the Christology of the Apocalypse of John*. WUNT 2/70. Tübingen: Mohr Siebeck, 1995.

Swain, Simon C. R. "Biography and the Biographic in the Literature of the Roman Empire." In *Portraits: Biographical Representation in the Greek and Latin Literature of the Roman Empire*, ed. Mark Edwards and Simon C. R. Swain. Oxford: Oxford University Press, 1997, 1–38.

———. *Hellenism and Empire: Language, Classicism, and Power in the Greek World, ad 50–250*. Oxford: Oxford University Press, 1996.

———. "Introduction," to *Late Antiquity*, ed. Swain and Edwards, 1–20.

———. "Plutarch, Hadrian, and Delphi." *Historia: Zeitschrift für alte Geschichte* 40:3 (1991): 318–30.

———. "Plutarch, Plato, Athens, and Rome." In *Philosophia Togata II*, ed. Barnes and Griffin, 165–87.

———. "Sophists and Emperors: The Case of Libanius." In *Approaching Late Antiquity*, ed. Swain and Edwards, 355–401.

Swain, Simon C. R., and Mark J. Edwards, eds. *Approaching Late Antiquity: The Transformation from Early to Late Empire*. Oxford: Oxford University Press, 2004.

Swain, Simon C. R., et al., eds. *Severan Culture*. Cambridge: Cambridge University Press, 2007.

Tardieu, Michel. "Les gnostiques dans *La vie de Plotin*." In *La vie de Plotin*, ed. Brisson, 503–46.

———. *"Les livres mis sous le nom* de Seth et les Sethiens de l'heresiologie." In *Gnosis and Gnosticism*, ed. Krause, 204–10.

———. "Principes de l'exégèse manichéenne du nouveau testament." In *Les règles de l'interprétation*, ed. Tardieu, 123–46.

———, ed. *Les règles de l'interprétation*. Paris: Les Éditions du Cerf, 1987.

———. "Recherches sur la formation de l'Apocalypse de Zostrien et les sources de Marius Victorinus." *ResOr* 9 (1996): 7–114.

Tarrant, Harold. "Introduction to Book 1." Proclus, *Commentary on Plato's "Timaeus"*, tr. Tarrant, 21–84.

———. "Must Commentators Know Their Sources? Proclus *In Timaeum* and Numenius." In *Philosophy, Science and Exegesis in Greek, Arabic and Latin Commentaries*, ed. P. Adamson et al. BICSSup 83.1. London: University of London Press, 2004, 175–90.

———. "Myth as a Tool of Persuasion in Plato." *Antichthon* 24 (1990): 19–31.

———. "Platonist Educators in a Growing Market: Gaius; Albinus; Taurus; Alcinous." In *Greek and Roman Philosophy, 100 b.c.–200 a.d.*, ed. Robert W. Sharples and Richard Sorabji. 2 vols. BICSSup 94. London: University of London Press, 2007, 449–65.

Tate, J. "On the History of Allegorism." *CQ* 28:2 (1934): 105–14.

Thomassen, Einar. "Sethian Names in Magical Texts: Protophanes and Meirotheos." In *Gnosticism, Platonism, and the Late Ancient World*, ed. Corrigan et al., 63–78.

Tigchelaar, Eibert. "Baraies on Mani's Rapture, Paul, and the Antediluvian Apostles." In *The Wisdom of Egypt: Jewish, Early Christian, and Gnostic Essays in Honour of Gerard P. Luttikhuizen*, ed. Anthony Hilhorst and George H. van Kooten. AGJU 59. Leiden: E. J. Brill, 2005, 429–42.

Trapp, Michael. "Philosophy, Scholarship, and the World of Learning in the Severan Period." In *Severan Culture*, ed. Swain et al., 470–88.

Trigg, Joseph Wilson. *Origen: The Bible and Philosophy in the Third-century Church*. Atlanta: John Knox Press, 1983.

Turcan, Robert. "Une allusion de Plotin aux idoles cultuelles." In *Mélanges d'histoire des religions offerts à Henri-Charles Puech*. Paris: Presses Universitaires de France, 1974, 307–14.

Turner, John D. "*Allogenes*: Notes to Text and Translation." In *Nag Hammadi Codices XI, XII, and XIII*, ed. Hedrick, 243–68.

———. "Commentary: *Zostrianos*." In *Zostrien*, ed. and tr. Barry, Funk, Poirier, and Turner, 483–662.

———. "Coptic Renditions of Greek Metaphysics: the Platonizing Sethian treatises *Zostrianos* and *Allogenes*." In *Christianity in Egypt: Literary Production and Intellectual Trends: Studies in Honor of Tito Orlandi*, ed. Paola Buzi and Alberto Camplani. Studia Ephemeridis Augustiniarum 125. Rome: Institutum Patristicum Augustinianum, 2011, 523–54.

———. "Gnosticism and Platonism: The Platonizing Sethian Texts from Nag Hammadi and Their Relation to Later Platonic Literature." In *Neoplatonism and Gnosticism*, ed. Wallis, 425–59.

———. "The Gnostic Threefold Path to Enlightenment: The Ascent of Mind and the Descent of Wisdom." *NovT* 22 (1980): 324–51.

———. "Introduction: *Allogenes* (BCNH)." In *L'allogène*, ed. and tr. Funk, Scopello, and Turner, 1–175.

———. "Introduction: NHC XIII,1*: Trimorphic Protennoia." In *Nag Hammadi Codices XI, XII, and XIII*, ed. Hedrick, 373–401.

———. "Introduction: *Marsanes*." In *Marsanès*, ed. and tr. Funk, Poirier, and Turner, 1–248.

———. "Introduction: *Zostrianos*." In *Zostrien*, ed. and tr. Barry, Funk, Poirier, and Turner, 1–225.

———. "The Place of the *Gospel of Judas* in Sethian Tradition." In *The Gospel of Judas in Context: Proceedings of the First International Conference on the Gospel of Judas: Paris, Sorbonne, October 27th–28th, 2006*, ed. Madeleine Scopello. NHMS 62. Leiden: E. J. Brill, 2008, 187–238.

———. "The Platonizing Sethian Treatises, Marius Victorinus's Philosophical Sources, and Pre-Plotinian *Parmenides* Commentaries." In *Plato's "Parmenides" and Its Heritage*, ed. Turner and Corrigan, 1:131–72.

———. "Ritual in Gnosticism." In *Gnosticism and Later Platonism*, ed. Turner and Majercik, 83–139.

———. "The Sethian Baptismal Rite." In *Coptica*, ed. Painchaud and Poirier, 941–92.

———. "Sethian Gnosticism: A Literary History." In *Nag Hammadi, Gnosticism, and Early Christianity*, ed. Hedrick and Hodgson, 55–86.

———. *Sethian Gnosticism and the Platonic Tradition*. BCNH Section "Études" 6. Québec: Université Laval; Leuven: Peeters, 2001.

———. "Sethian Gnosticism: A Revised Literary History." In *Acts du huitième congrès international d'études coptes*, ed. Bosson and Boud'hors, 2:899–908.

———. "The Sethian Myth in the Gospel of Judas: Soteriology or Demonology." In *The Codex Judas Papers*, ed. DeConick, 95–133.

———. "*Trimorphic Protennoia*: Notes to Text and Translation." In *Nag Hammadi Codices XI, XII, and XIII*, ed. Hedrick, 435–54.

———. "To See the Light: A Gnostic Appropriation of Jewish Priestly Practice and Sapiential and Apocalyptic Visionary Lore." In *Mediators of the Divine: Horizons of Prophecy, Divination, Dreams and Theurgy in Mediterranean Antiquity*, ed. Robert Berchman. Atlanta: University of South Florida and Scholars' Press, 1998, 63–114.

———. "Typologies of the Sethian Gnostic Treatises from Nag Hammadi." In *Les texts de Nag Hammadi*, ed. Painchaud and Pasquier, 169–217.

———. "The Gnostic Sethians and Middle Platonism: Interpretations of the *Timaeus* and *Parmenides*." VC 60 (2006): 9–64.

———. "Victorinus, *Parmenides* Commentaries, and the Platonizing Sethian Treatises." In *Platonisms: Ancient, Modern, and Postmodern*, ed. Kevin Corrigan and John D. Turner. Studies in Platonism, Neoplatonism, and the Platonic Tradition 4. Leiden: Brill, 2007, 55–96.

Turner, John D., and Kevin Corrigan, eds. *Plato's "Parmenides" and Its Heritage*. 2 vols., SBLWGRWSup 2–3. Atlanta: SBL, 2010.

Turner, John D. and Ruth Majercik, ed. *Gnosticism and Later Platonism: Themes, Figures, and Texts*, SBLSymS 12. Atlanta: Society of Biblical Literature, 2001.

Turner, John D., and Anne McGuire, eds. *The Nag Hammadi Library After Fifty Years: Proceedings of the 1995 Society of Biblical Literature Commemoration*. NHMS 44. Leiden: E. J. Brill, 1997.

VanderKam, James C. *Enoch and the Growth of Apocalyptic Tradition*. CBQMS 16. Washington, DC: Catholic Biblical Association of America, 1984.

———. "Exile in Jewish Apocalyptic Literature." In *Exile*, ed. Scott, 89–111.

VanderKam, James C., and William Adler, ed. *The Jewish Apocalyptic Heritage in Early Christianity*, CRINT 3.4. Minneapolis: Fortress Press, 1996.

Valantasis, Richard. "Nag Hammadi and Asceticism: Theory and Practice." In *StPatr* 35 (2001): 172–90.

Verniere, Yvonne. *Symboles et mythes dans la pensée de Plutarque: Essai d'interprétation philosophique et religieuse des Moralia*. Paris: Belles Lettres, 1977.

Vielhauer, Philipp, and Georg Strecker. "Apocalypses and Related Subjects. Introduction." Tr. R. McL. Wilson. In *New Testament Apocrypha*, ed. Hennecke and Schneemelcher, 2:542–602.

Walbridge, James. *The Wisdom of the Mystic East: Suhrawardī and Platonic Orientalism*. Albany: State University of New York Press, 2001.

Wallis, Richard T. *Neoplatonism*. Indianapolis: Hackett, 1995.

———. "Soul and Nous in Plotinus, Numenius, and Gnosticism." In *Neoplatonism and Gnosticism*, ed. Wallis with Bregman, 461–82.

Wallis, Richard T., with Jay Bregman, eds. *Neoplatonism and Gnosticism*.

Studies in Neoplatonism 6. Albany: State University of New York Press, 1992.

Waszink, Jan H. "Porphyrios und Numenios." *Entretiens Hardt* 12 (1966): 33–78.

———. "Die sogenannte Fünfteilung der Träume bei Calcidius und ihre Quellen." *Mnemosyne* 9 (1940): 65–85.

Watts, Edward J. *City and School in Late Antique Athens and Alexandria*. Transformation of the Classical Heritage 41. Berkeley: University of California Press, 2006.

Whitmarsh, Tim. "Greece Is the World." In *Being Greek Under Rome: Cultural Identity, the Second Sophistic, and the Development of Empire*, ed. Simon Goldhill. Cambridge: Cambridge University Press, 2001, 269–305.

Whittaker, John. "Moses Atticizing." *Phoenix* 21 (1967): 196–201.

———. "Platonic Philosophy in the Early Centuries of the Empire." *ANRW* 2.36.1 (1987): 81–123.

Wilken, Robert L. "Alexandria: A School for Training in Virtue." In *Schools of Thought in the Christian Tradition*, ed. Patrick Henry. Philadelphia: Fortress Press, 1984, 15–30.

Williams, Francis E. *Mental Perception, a Commentary on NHC VI, 4: The Concept of Our Great Power*. NHMS 51. Leiden: E. J. Brill, 2001.

Williams, Michael Allen. "Higher Providence, Lower Providences and Fate in Gnosticism and Middle Platonism." In *Neoplatonism and Gnosticism*, ed. Wallis with Bregman, 483–507.

———. *The Immovable Race: A Gnostic Designation and the Theme of Stability in Late Antiquity*. NHS 29. Leiden: E. J. Brill, 1985.

———. *Rethinking "Gnosticism": Arguments for Dismantling a Dubious Category*. Princeton, NJ: Princeton University Press, 1995.

———. "Review: Fossum, *The Angel of the Lord*." *JBL* 107:1 (1988): 153–56.

———. "Sethianism." In *Companion to Second-Century "Heretics,"* ed. Marjanen and Luomanen, 32–63.

———. "Was There a Gnostic Religion? Strategies for a Clearer Analysis." In *Was There a Gnostic Religion?* ed. Marjanen, 55–79.

Willms, Hans. *EIKΩN: Eine begriffsgeschichtliche Untersuchung zum Platonismus: I. Teil: Philon von Alexandreia: Mit einer Einleitung über Platon und die Zwischenzeit*. Münster, Aschendorff, 1935.

Winden, J. C. M. van. *Calcidius on Matter: His Doctrine and Sources: A Chapter in the History of Platonism*. PA 9. Leiden: E. J. Brill, 1959.

Winston, David. "Philo's Theory of Eternal Creation: 'De Prov.' 1.6–9." *Proceedings of the American Academy for Jewish Research* 46 (1979–80): 593–606.

Winter, Bruce. *Philo and Paul Among the Sophists: Alexandrian and Corinthian Responses to a Julio-Claudian Movement.* SNTS 96. Grand Rapids, MI: Eerdmans, 2001.

Wisse, Frederik. "Flee Femininity: Antifemininity in Gnostic Texts and the Question of Social Milieu." In *Images of the Feminine in Gnosticism*, ed. Karen King. SAC 10. Harrisburg, PA: Trinity Press International, 1988, 297–308.

———. "Gnosticism and Early Monasticism in Egypt." In *Gnosis*, ed. Aland, 431–40.

———. "Language Mysticism in the Nag Hammadi Texts and in Early Coptic Monasticism I: Cryptography." *Enchoria* 9 (1979): 101–20.

———. "Stalking Those Elusive Sethians." In *Rediscovery*, ed. Layton, 563–76.

Witt, Rex E. "Iamblichus as a Forerunner of Julian." In *De Jamblique*, ed. Dörrie, 35–68.

Wolters, Albert M. "Notes on the Structure of *Enneads* II,9." In *Life Is Religion: Essays in Honor of H. Evan Runner*, ed. Henry van der Goot. St. Catharine's, ON: Paideia Press, 1981, 83–96.

———. "A Survey of Modern Scholarly Opinion on Plotinus and Indian Thought." In *Neoplatonism and Indian Thought*, ed. Harris, 293–308.

Yarbro Collins, Adela. *Cosmology and Eschatology in Jewish and Christian Apocalypticism.* Leiden: E. J. Brill, 1996.

———. *Crisis and Catharsis: The Power of the Apocalypse.* Philadelphia: Westminister Press, 1984.

———. "Early Christian Apocalypses." *Semeia* 14 (1986): 61–121.

———, ed. *Early Christian Apocalypticism: Genre and Social Setting. Semeia* 36. Decatur, GA: Scholars' Press, 1986.

———. "Introduction: Early Christian Apocalypticism." In *Semeia* 36, ed. Yarbro Collins, 1–11.

———. "New Testament Eschatology and Apocalypticism." In "Aspects of New Testament Thought." *The New Jerome Biblical Commentary*, ed. Raymond E. Brown, S.S., Joseph Fitzmyer, S.J., and Roland Murphy, O.Carm. Englewood Cliffs, NJ: Prentice-Hall, 1990.

———. "Review: Rowland, *The Open Heaven.*" *JBL* 103:3 (1984): 465–67.

Yates, Frances. *Giordano Bruno and the Hermetic Tradition.* Chicago: University of Chicago Press, 1964.

Ysaebert, Joseph. *Greek Baptismal Terminology: Its Origins and Early Development.* Nijmegen: Dekker & van de Vegt, 1962.

Zambon, Marco. "ΠΑΡΑΝΟΜΩΣ ZHN: La critica di Porfirio ad Origene

(Eus., *HE* VI, 19, 1–9)." In *Origeniana Octava* vol. 1, ed. L. Perrone et al. BEThl. 164. Leuven: Peeters, 2003, 553–63.

———. "Porfirio e Origene, uno status quaestionis." In *Le traité de Porphyre contre les chrétiens*, ed. Morlet, 107–64.

———. *Porphyre et le moyen-platonisme*. Paris: Vrin, 2002.

Zandee, Jan. *The Terminology of Plotinus and of Some Gnostic Writings, Mainly the Fourth Treatise of the Jung Codex*. Istanbul: Nederlands historisch-archaeologisch instituut in het nabije oosten, 1961.

ACKNOWLEDGMENTS

I never do anything right the first time, and this book is no exception. Its thought, structure, and goals have all undergone many revisions, which have benefitted enormously from years of conversation, advice, and criticism, for which I am indebted to the following in particular: Harold W. Attridge, Tilde Bak Halvgaard, David Brakke, Johanna Brankaer, John J. Collins, Ismo Dunderberg, Troels Engberg-Pedersen, René Falkenberg, Lance Jennott, Bentley Layton, Outi Lehtippu, Nicola Denzey Lewis, Hugo Lundhaug, Antti Marjanen, Nicholas Marshall, Zeke Mazur, Nanna Liv Elkjær Olsen, Tuomas Rasimus, Ulla Tervahauta-Helin, Ruth Tsuria, Michael Allen Williams, and Adela Yarbro Collins. Perhaps everything good in this book is nothing other than a synthesis of my encounters with these (and other) extraordinary individuals; in any case, the author of everything bad in it must be yours truly. Finally, I must single out John D. Turner for appreciation as mentor, friend, and sparring partner. This book is an attempt to build on his pioneering work, which introduced me to the "Platonizing" Sethian treatises and inspired me to dedicate my scholarly energies to the study of Gnosticism and Neoplatonism.

Special thanks goes to Virginia Burrus, Jerry Singerman, the editorial team at Divinations, and my anonymous referees, who were generous with criticisms, advice, patience, and common sense in transmuting my arcane drafts into a presentation that I hope is not the dullest of reads. Tim Roberts and his team at UPenn were a delight to work with in preparing the final text. I am grateful for the efforts of Chloe Sugden, who checked references and the bibliography, of Sonja Anderson, Christopher Hutchings, and Matthew Neujahr, who edited copy and saved me from countless infelicities, and of Martin White, who prepared the lovely index. Grisha Bruskin was extremely responsive and generous in granting permission to use his art, to which I was guided by Jonathan Schorsch. I thank them both. The last year of work on the manuscript was vivified in large part by Naida Šehić, who furnished soundtrack, recognized the lyrics to "Flamme," and reminded me that I actually like coffee.

I can only express the utmost appreciation to the University of Copenhagen's Department of Biblical Exegesis at the Faculty of Theology, who granted me a research postdoc from September 2011 to April 2013. Every young scholar knows the desperate hunt for the next library card, and I will always remember Copenhagen as the city that provided that and (much) more. This book was completed during those special northern hours where light and dark do not differ.

Lightning Source UK Ltd.
Milton Keynes UK
UKHW010228070521
383296UK00008B/237/J